GANDHIAN UTOPIA

RICHARD G. FOX

Gandhian Utopia

▴ EXPERIMENTS ▴

▴ WITH CULTURE ▴

BEACON PRESS BOSTON

Beacon Press
25 Beacon Street
Boston, Massachusetts 02108-2800

Beacon Press books
are published under the auspicies of
the Unitarian Universalist Association of Congregations.

96 95 94 93 92 91 90 89   8 7 6 5 4 3 2 1

Text design by Gwen Frankfeldt

Library of Congress Cataloging-in-Publication Data
Fox, Richard Gabriel
   Gandhian Utopia: experiments with culture/Richard G. Fox.
     p. cm.
   Bibliography: p. 293.
   Includes index.
   ISBN 0–8070–4100–9
   1. Social movements—India—History—20th century.   2. Gandhi,
Mahatma, 1869–1948—Political and social views.   3. India—
Civilization.   4. Utopias.   I. Title.
HN683.F69   1989
303.4'84—dc19   88-43315

For Judy

Socialists . . . of this kind . . . want to improve the condition of every member of society, even that of the most favored. . . . they wish to attain their ends by peaceful means, and endeavor, by small experiments, necessarily doomed to failure . . . to pave the way for the new social Gospel.

KARL MARX and FRIEDRICH ENGELS,

The Communist Manifesto

I simply want to tell the story of my numerous experiments with truth. . . . my life consists of nothing but those experiments. . . . I claim for them nothing more than does a scientist who, though he conducts his experiments with the utmost accuracy, forethought and minuteness, never claims any finality about his conclusions. . . .

MOHANDAS K. GANDHI, *An Autobiography*

The complete disappearance of the utopian element from human thought and action would mean that human nature and human development would take on a totally new character . . . after a long, tortuous, but heroic development, just at the highest stage of awareness, when history is ceasing to be blind fate, and is becoming more and more man's own creation, with the relinquishment of utopias, man would lose his will to shape history and therewith his ability to understand it.

KARL MANNHEIM, *Ideology and Utopia*

Contents

Acknowledgments

Many friends helped me write this book. Judith Fox collected the newspaper sources, and she read the manuscript with a special expertise. Nick Dirks and Deborah Johnson helped me see what I had to say and thereby helped clarify how and where I had to say it. Louise Kennedy helped me say it better. Friends at the School of American Research in Santa Fe, where I wrote this book in 1987–88, gave me good help: I thank Jonathan Haas, Winifred Creamer, David Montejano, Barbara King, Peggy Trawick, Glenn Stone, Priscilla Stone, and Jane Kepp. Matt Mines, Stephen Hay and others at the University of California, Santa Barbara, also helped me by their responses, often quite critical, to my presentation of some parts of this book in May 1988. At Duke University, where most of the printed materials were reviewed during 1985–87, Avinash Maheshwary and Elizabeth Bramm as well as other friends on the staff of Perkins Library helped me a great deal. Also at Duke, Carol Smith made me more sensitive to the value loading of some of the words I was using to describe Gandhian utopia, and she gave me other helpful criticism. In India, where I made a brief trip during March and April 1988, I had help from many friends: Bipan Chandra, Aditya Mukherjee, Mridula Mukherjee, Amrit Srinivasen, Mohinder Singh, Andrea Menefee Singh, and Har Kirat Singh. Others at the Gandhi Peace Foundation, the Gandhi Smarak Nidhi, the Deendayal Research Institute, and the Gandhian Institute of Studies, whom I shall not name in the interests of confidentiality, also aided me. Katherine Verdery, Gene Irschick, Amit Mitra, and Sherry Ortner have also helped me clarify my ideas in important ways.

A National Science Foundation grant from 1985 to 1987 allowed me to collect the materials for this book. I held a John Simon Guggenheim Memorial Foundation fellowship in 1987–88, while writing the book. In addition, the School of American Research awarded me a National Endowment for the Humanities Fellowship and provided a friendly and supportive environment for my work.

The Smithsonian Institution provided travel funds for my trip to India.

I thank these people and institutions, and the others I have inadvertently omitted, for their friendship to my work.

ONE
Introduction

"Was he Indira's father?"
Overheard [in Hindi] 16 March 1988, Gandhi shrine at Rajghat, Delhi

Perhaps, Mohandas Gandhi once speculated, it had been divine wisdom that made India fall behind while the West progressed. India could then "fulfill its special mission of resisting the onrush of materialism" and reach "her destiny through Truth and Non-violence" (Gandhi 1965: 10, 4). India would attain a *purna swaraj*, a true and complete independence, not only from the British but also from Western materialism; not only for the society, but also for the human spirit. It would be India's privilege, Gandhi predicted hopefully, "to turn a new leaf" for a world weary of hate, whose railways, telegraphs, hospitals, parliaments, armies, machinery, and modernity still left nations and individuals "thirsting" for peace and satisfaction.

In 1931, Gandhi wrote, "This is the India of my dreams, for which I shall struggle." Fifteen years later, he noted, "But, of course, it is too rich a dream to be realized in a day" (Gandhi 1965: 101). Today, Gandhi might find that many Indian villages continued to be the "dung-heaps" he deplored rather than the "Gardens of Eden" he dreamt of. He would find his rich dream of spiritual government and "organized anarchy," the nonviolent *ramrajya* he wished for India and all the world, unrealized. Not only would he discover the Indian capitalists he wanted to preserve still in existence, but also the capitalism he dreamt of destroying; the welfare for all (*sarvodaya*) he envisioned realized as wealth for a few; and

1

the "oceanic circles" composed of India's villages, which he imagined building up into a great wave of Indian nationhood, now become a whirlpool of ethnic, sectarian, and regional conflicts.

Today, Gandhi might discover that even his patrimony to India was in some doubt. The young woman I overheard at the Gandhi shrine mistook him for the father of Indira Gandhi, who was really Nehru's daughter, instead of recognizing him as the Father of the Nation. Yesterday's risky and defiant actions against colonialism have become today's empty political promotions. So Gandhi might feel about the reenactment of his 1930 Salt March *satyagraha* campaign staged in March 1988 by Prime Minister Rajiv Gandhi, still another Gandhi to whom the Mahatma bears no relationship.

Gandhi would probably not be daunted. Even in 1946, when Indian independence, for which he had struggled so nonviolently, was very close, Gandhi allowed that his dream might never transpire; however, he still took "happiness in living in that dreamland" (Gandhi 1965: 97). The reason, as Maureen Swan perceptively but somewhat critically notes, was that "for Gandhi himself, 'success' lay in the mere fact of opposition" (Swan 1985: 178). Gandhi felt this way because he believed that any opposition based on "soul force," or spiritual commitment, and nonviolence was an experiment in bettering society and the human condition. Such confrontations tested an individual's utopian ideals against the existing state of society. If they succeeded, such experiments could move society forward to greater humanity and spiritual satisfaction; if they failed, the utopian ideals were proved false or the individuals were shown to have lacked the courage of their convictions. Gandhi dissected his own life into a barely connected set of experimental episodes: the volume labeled his "Autobiography" is also titled "My Experiments with Truth." As any scientist who confronts existing knowledge with new ideas would believe, so Gandhi believed: experimentation in pursuit of truth became its own justification. In Gandhi's case, the experimental method was nonviolent resistance; that was the means by which he confronted existing society with new ideals.

Gandhi as saint, as politician, as health faddist, as humanitarian reformer, as child-like humorist, as spokesman for bourgeois interests, as peacenik, as anarchist, and as Luddite — these are familiar portrayals. Strangely, there is no portrayal of him as the scientist or, at least, the utopian experimentalist forever pursuing elusive truth, he thought he was:

I may be taunted with the retort that it is all Utopian . . . If Euclid's point, though incapable of being drawn by human agency, has an imperishable value, my picture has its own for mankind to live. . .

Euclid's line is one without breadth, but no one has so far been able to draw it and never will. All the same it is only by keeping the ideal line in mind that we have made progress in Geometry. What is true here is true of every ideal (Gandhi 1965: 115, 168).

I write in this book about the history of this utopian dream and the experiments with society it inspired and inspires. Too often, these Gandhian experiments do not enlighten us enough, because we picture Gandhi and his legacy only in a halo of saintliness that actually casts shadows over the person and his vision. In this poor light, we often cannot clearly see whether Gandhi and the others who undertook Gandhian experiments failed or succeeded; success or failure in fact become interchangeable images: Gandhi either appears as a token saint, the Mahatma too good for this world and therefore leaving no useful legacy for ordinary people, or he becomes an icon. Especially in India, he is memorialized and invoked in all manner of public representation, yet without much meaning: worshipers who know only that he is enshrined may ask, "Did he father modern India or Indira?"

With no other light than this, only the bare historical outlines of Gandhi are apparent, and the utopian experiments he envisioned and inspired are left in shadow. We see only a small figure clad in country dress, already partially apotheosized in South Africa, returning to India in the early years of World War I to take charge of a faltering Indian nationalist movement. A Westernized elite controls this Indian nationalism, and its members have yet to mobilize mass resistance. The extremists among them toy with revolutionary sabotage, but British repression renders them ineffective. The others, moderate nationalists, are often bought off by the colonial power with small concessions and reforms. These English-speaking and English-thinking nationalists commonly fight more among themselves than against the British. The Indian masses remain inert.

We see further that very quickly Gandhi becomes canonized as the Mahatma, or Great Soul of Indian resistance. His saintliness appeals to the Indian masses, and they follow him religiously as he leads them to protest British colonialism. Gandhi's saintliness also bestows on Indian nationalism an effective method of mass protest, satyagraha or nonviolent resistance, based on spiritual commitment (soul force). Given satyagraha's moral and spiritual foundation, British repression of Gandhi and Gandhians betrays any claim that British colonialism exercises moral authority over Indians — which is a significant revelation for the British (when they eventually acknowledge it), but also for the Indian elite. In the early 1920s, Gandhi's vision of satyagraha spiritually instructs the anti-colonial Noncooperation Movement across India: Indian students leave British-style schools; the elite gives up preferments and titles conferred by British colonial rulers; lawyers abandon the Anglo-Indian courts; and the Indian masses, through strikes, processions, and boycotts, rapidly enlist in the nonviolent protest.

Then we see that a single immoral act, an act of violence against the police in the name of Indian nationalism, is enough to make Gandhi call off the noncooperation campaign. There follow inconclusive discussions with the British and the incarceration of Gandhi. Then in 1930 Gandhi blesses another major act of satyagraha, a civil disobedience campaign that nonviolently flouts British law. Gandhi himself leads the famous Salt March; he trespasses on the British colonial monopoly and taxation of a staple, salt, by marching to the sea and making his own. As thousands of other Indians make illegal salt, transport it, and sell it, the British respond with mass arrests and police brutality. Gandhi is again arrested. In the aftermath, there are still more inconclusive discussions with the British, but they too founder. Now, it is not only British intrasigence that wrecks the talks. There is also an increasingly perilous Hindu-Muslim antagonism to deal with, even though Gandhi insists that this sectarian difference, while real enough and worthy of respect and protection, has no bearing on Indian national unity. Next we see the conclusive satyagraha, the Quit India movement early in World War II, when the British finally understand that India has passed out of their hands. They learn that jailing Gandhi and the other nationalist leaders stops the satyagraha campaign but brings on a wave of popular violence their police and military can barely control. Gandhi's morally disciplined and nonviolent nationalism now, in a real sense, protect British colonialism in India from a greater calamity.

We next see that independence shortly follows, in 1947, but only at substantial cost. British India becomes two nations: the avowedly Islamic state of Pakistan and the ostensibly secular but predominantly Hindu India. Massive Hindu-Muslim rioting and mass killings break out among celebrations of approaching independence

4

and continue after independence is achieved, as large-scale migrations take place across the borders of the new countries.

The final image is therefore tragic: an independent India victorious against the British, but a defeated Gandhi, his utopian vision of a spiritual and humane India shattered by Hindu-Muslim hatred; that vision is even abandoned in the remnant India that claims his inspiration, as Nehru's own vision of an India patterned after the Western industrial countries — that is, a vision of mass production, state centralization, and spiraling productivity — comes to govern the country. Finally, for Gandhi, in 1948 comes a martyrdom that many see as a deus ex machina, saving him and his utopian vision from further embarrassment in a world that no longer had any real place for them — and may never have had, except perhaps momentarily in the struggle against colonialism. Afterward, we see that attempts in India by Vinoba Bhave and others to carry forward Gandhian experiments fail, and by their failure seemingly give further testimony against the Gandhian dream.

Outside these highlights, however, shadows lie over the history of Gandhi and Gandhian experiments, both before and after Indian independence. Many questions remain: did satyagraha and the other elements of Gandhian utopia develop from Gandhi's personal struggle to discipline himself into spirituality? Or did Gandhi construct his utopia over time and modify it to meet ongoing circumstances? Was his saintly image imposed by others or self-proclaimed? We must also ask whether he attracted a mass following because his message of spiritual discipline resonated with widespread Indian cultural meanings, or because his public image as a spiritual guide led others to follow, even many who did not understand his moral philosophy. We must ask whether Gandhi constructed an effective cultural resistance to British domination in India, or was merely a lesser evil the British cultivated. Was his utopian vision truly effective in directing the course of Indian nationalism? Did it make any difference to India at the time of independence, or would Indian nationalism have been much the same without the Gandhian experiments?

Further questions surround the influence of the Gandhian dream in defining cultural and political expectations in India after independence. Did Nehru and others have to reckon with that dream, if only in the interest of controlling or subverting it? Or could it be ignored, and the Gandhian experiments after independence be permitted to fail because they were simply unworkable and otherworldly? Then again, perhaps the outcome of those experiments was not predetermined; what if their failure came about only after confrontations and active struggle? Most puzzling, perhaps, is the present state of Gandhian ideas in India. We must ask how Gandhi's ideas came to be appropriated by Hindu nationalists, as they have been, and used to justify a unitary India, which gives a place to Muslims, Untouchables, and other minorities only if they recognize an essential Hindu-ness in themselves. Was this Hindu chauvinism always implicit in the Gandhian utopian vision, or has Gandhian utopianism been subverted by some historical process into a Hindu apologetic?

I want to throw light on these questions because I come to the study of Gandhi and Gandhian experiments with these concerns: what role do individuals play in cultural change? How do individual utopian projects get transformed into mass action for social change? How does an effective cultural resistance develop in societies subject to colonial domination? How are utopian visions appropriated or controlled, and how are they subverted into justifying ideologies? What, if anything, can liberate them once they are subverted? Therefore I write with no notion of Gandhi as saint or colonial tool or health faddist or Luddite; given my concerns, these are images that cast deep shadows over the Gandhian utopian experiments I hope to understand. Instead, my image of him and other Gandhians (broadly construed) is that they were social experimentalists, struggling with new visions of culture. It is in this light that I try to portray Gandhi and his utopian vision. The Gandhian experiments with truth in society, in turn, provide the context for my own experiments with anthropology and history, as I shall shortly make clear.

My history consists of singularities: namely, Gandhi's revolutionary dream for India and the utopian intentions of many others before and after him. It also consists of structures — the colonialism of India's past and its recent class and caste inequalities, which these intentions confronted and over which they rarely fully prevailed. The ordered anarchy, the spiritual governance that Gandhians have envisioned and experimented with, do not yet exist in India; many Indians, perhaps most, would not want them anyway. Therefore I write about something that has never been and may never be — an India as unreal as all the Orientalized images of the subcontinent spawned by European domination. But the fantasies constituting the Gandhian dream and the Orientalist nightmare are quite different. Orientalism tried to keep India subject by projecting false images: Indian culture was otherworldly, passive, effeminate, and superstitious. The Gandhian vision fantasized about a future India more humane, spiritual, egalitarian, and enlightened than the present. The Orientalist fantasy of India complemented and abetted its current state of foreign domination; the Gandhian condemned it. This book therefore is the history of the experiments with truth that Gandhi and the other authors of what I call "Gandhian utopia" undertook. The Gandhian utopian vision asserted that India, given its traditions, could develop a more humane and rewarding future society than either Western socialism or Western capitalism had accomplished.

My chronicle begins late in the nineteenth century, when Indian nationalists and Western nonconformists developed the cultural assumptions about India and India's destiny that configured Gandhian utopia. I pick Gandhi up in 1893, at the age of 24, when he left India for South Africa. I follow the development of his utopian dream in South Africa and in India after his return in 1915. In South Africa, I show the immediate circumstances behind Gandhi's innovative combination of the three essential elements defining nonviolent resistance. Satyagraha as Gandhi envisioned it required civil disobedience, a morally committed (not simply expedient) nonviolence or *ahimsa*, and mass action. Gandhi's satyagraha was both a political technique to be used against British colonialism and a moral philosophy that clarified his utopian vision. Gandhi the experimentalist, as I shall try to show him to be, did not develop satyagraha single-handedly or in a single piece. After his original synthesis in South Africa, Gandhi experimented with the elements of satyagraha in his initial Indian campaigns from 1916 through 1919. I detail the way these immediate circumstances helped Gandhi fully construct his utopian vision shortly after World War I.

I also show the concurrent sanctification of Gandhi as the saintly Mahatma and the institutionalization of his utopian experiments, from about 1920 until Indian independence in 1947. Gandhi often had to conspire at his own popular sanctification in order to maintain authority over his utopian vision. Therefore, although he remonstrated against the title of Mahatma (after Rabindranath Tagore bestowed it on him), Gandhi also used this apotheosis when he needed it (see Gandhi 1957: xii; Fischer 1950: 128; Erikson 1969: 385) — and in some instances, which I will describe, his public image as the Mahatma dictated to Mohandas.

After Gandhi's assassination in 1948, I note the heirs and would-be heirs to the Gandhian patrimony, the claims they placed against his legacy, and the uses they made of it. My chronicle concludes in the present, when many Gandhian utopian meanings have unexpectedly come to instruct Hindu nationalism and its vision of a future India perfected on the basis of invented Hindu "tradition."

Gandhian utopia was forged by individual experimentalists like Swami Vivekananda or Annie Besant or Gandhi undertaking particular experiments such as spiritual public service, home rule, and civil disobedience. As the experiments accumulated over time, however, this utopia became a complex culture trait. That is, it became a set of cultural meanings — a utopian experiment with future possibilities — constituting social identity and practice in twentieth-century India. Once formed, the Gandhian utopian dream came to compel Indian social experimentation in ways no one of its authors could have predicted, and in ways outside the control of any one of them. It also enabled new experiments unforeseen and therefore unintended by its authors — and among these, some they probably would have forsworn. I chronicle not the history of the individual authors or experimentalists, but the ensemble of experiments themselves, and the new set of cultural meanings they produced. I write about Gandhian utopia, not Gandhi's utopia; about Gandhian experiments, not only Gandhi's experiments. Most important, I detail the development and authority achieved by the Gandhian vision, and I deal with Gandhi's personal development and authority only when it is relevant to that purpose. This volume, then, is a culture history. That is, it is a history of a complex set of cultural meanings in a specific society — Gandhian utopia in twentieth-century India — and how that set of meanings came to compel belief and practice over the last half-century and how it continues to enable social experimentation today.

Experiments with Anthropology

Gandhi's vision of experimenting with truth in society instructs my experimentation with anthropology in this volume. Just as Gandhi's so-called autobiography consisted of a progression of social experiments, so this book consists of a succession of conceptual experiments. Gandhi, as I understand him, took the term "experiment" to mean any confrontation with society or with oneself; an experiment was an effort to overcome resistance, whereby new social arrangements or personal dispositions could be achieved. In scholarship, I take the term "experiment" in a derivative sense to mean a struggle over ideas, a confrontation with existing intellectual positions whereby new knowledge and understanding may be found.

The culture history of Gandhian utopia serves as the test case for the following experiments.

Culture History and Postmodernism

Through this study of Gandhian utopia, I hope to help develop a new approach to culture history in anthropology, one that will encompass human agency, world-systemic power relations, and social inequality better than Boasian culture history did. This, my initial experiment, appears in Chapters 2 and 3.

Under the pioneer anthropologist Franz Boas and his students, during roughly the first thirty years of the twentieth century, culture history treated cultures as historical residues. That is, cultures were distinctive because each was a historical concatenation; each was a composite made up of internal patterns of development plus an accretion of beliefs and practices through diffusion from other cultures (Fox 1985: 189–90). Culture history, the major endeavor of Boasian anthropology, was to be the study of the shredding and patching of culture. Anthropology, that is, was to analyze the historical processes by which cultures made contact, culture traits moved and were adopted, and new cultures came about. Although Boasian culture history studied the way new cultural assemblages developed, it did not deal well with questions of human agency — the constructive role played by individuals — in culture's making (Radin 1933: 42–43ff. criticized his fellow Boasians on this point). It also made too little of the compelling effect of material conditions and power inequalities on culture contact and change (see Wolf 1974: 256).

A reinvigorated culture history, I believe, promises a future authority for anthropology. My field has seen its primary scholarly product or "text," the ethnography, deauthorized by recent trenchant criticism. This criticism impugns anthropology's ability to communicate the "native point of view" — the Otherness of another culture — through ethnography. It uncovers the literary devices by which ethnographies have claimed authoritatively to

represent the Other. It argues that by making such claims in ethnographic texts, anthropologists have constructed fictions not only
about anthropology's capacity to represent the Other but also about
the nature of culture.

The experimental works in what has come to be known as "reflexive," "dialogic," or "polyphonic" anthropology, which hope
to reinvigorate the ethnographic text in more puissant postmodern
form, do not appear to me to promise anthropology any future
authority, however. In fact, they only continue to beat a dead or
dying text, the ethnography, without mercy. I experiment with an
altogether different anthropological genre in this volume — one, I
hope, that does less violence to past work in anthropology. A
culture history dedicated to understanding the historical relationship between material conditions and cultural forms, and focused
on the range from world-system inequality down to individual
human intention, I feel, would authorize new "texts" for
anthropology.

In Chapter 2, I set the anthropological intention of "getting the
native point of view" against the recent criticisms offered by reflexive or postmodern anthropology. I maintain this intention can
best be fulfilled through culture history, and in this chapter I experiment with a reconception of it. I work with the ideas of Karl
Mannheim and Paul Ricoeur about "ideology" and "utopia" — but
ultimately I depend most heavily on the approach of Mohandas
Gandhi to "utopian dreams" and "experiments with truth." I argue
for a contingent culture history, combining the "singular," the
chronicle of personages, with the "structural," the analysis of processes (to use Ricoeur's terms). What combines them, I also argue,
are the confrontations between individual intentions and existing
cultural meanings — in effect, Gandhi's experiments with truth.

Chapter 3 provides one empirical element in such a culture history, a structural presentation of the Gandhian dream as a utopian
vision of India's future perfectibility.

Great Men and Ready Cultures

To incorporate human agency better than the Boasians did, my
culture history must next experiment with this complex question:
how do new sets of cultural meanings arise, and what is the role
of the individual in cultural change? Specifically, I ask in Chapter
4: are utopian visions and the visionaries who create them effective

10

agents of cultural innovation? The following intellectual confrontation defines my major concern:

1. Do the individual's intentions (conscious and goal-directed thought and action), when they are utopian and run counter to the existing culture, play an enabling role in cultural innovation?

Or, conversely,

2. Do existing systems of cultural meaning so coerce or compel individuals into certain behaviors and beliefs that active human authors cannot affect or enable cultural innovation?

In the past, scholars have often expected to answer these questions with an uncomplicated "yes" or "no." Yes, "great man" theorists argued, extraordinary individuals do change their cultures. No, cultural determinists countered, cultures change only through internal, supra-individual forces that constitute what individuals believe and practice; cultures change, then, only when they are ready to.

Underlying these two extreme positions is a real quandary about how to reconcile an enabling role for the individual in cultural change with the formative role of cultural meanings. Phrased more complexly, then: is social experimentation produced by human intention truly effective in altering cultural meanings — even if these experiments do not completely achieve their revolutionary goals — as Gandhi would maintain? Or are human intentions ever truly innovative? Are they only illusions, as cultural determinists would assert, because culture ultimately constitutes what succeeds or fails?

Even the two positions as I have outlined them have further complications. Some cultural determinists devalue human intention because they believe that material conditions — the system of production and the pattern of social inequality — strictly compel cultural meanings and that these meanings, in turn, constitute or determine the innovations that individuals can achieve. Friedrich Engels, one such cultural determinist, insisted that human intentions were only utopian fantasies. Human intentions, such as the hopes of the Utopian Socialists for a new society, attempted a giant leap forward when, Engels in effect asserted, "you can't get there from here." Such a large leap forward was impossible, Engels argued, because material conditions were not ripe, and therefore the culture was not ready. Other cultural determinists do not give material conditions primacy, but they give existing cultural meanings so influential a role that human intentions are minimally ef-

11

fective in changing them. Again, culture changes only when (in this case, cultural) conditions are ripe.

I maintain, as I shall make clear later, that ongoing cultural meanings always encode existing social inequalities, always, in other words, bear the imprint of current material conditions. For my purposes, then, a cultural determinism based on the determinative power of material conditions and one resting on the formative role of cultural meanings are one and the same. Given that, the main question remains: to what extent does cultural innovation occur only when the culture constitutes or enables it?

The concept of the "individual" is also problematic. Do we mean to take the extraordinary individual, the Great Person or so-called genius, as the only important author of cultural innovation? Then we must fall back on a rather flimsy explanation, that greatness depends on superior genetic endowment. We assert human capacity to change culture, but only by reducing effective individual action to inherited biology. Or do we see all individuals in society as potential cultural innovators — all persons possibly great, depending on their luck at being in the right place at the right time? But then the culture or, anyway, the social structure is still ultimately the deciding factor. Just like the genetic argument for greatness, so the "right time, right place" approach deauthorizes individuals as cultural innovators. Again, the major question remains: to what extent do individuals intentionally author cultural innovation — to what extent can individuals make the culture ready for their utopian visions? Furthermore, if such authorship is possible, is it individual capacity or social recognition that makes some persons acknowledged authors, whereas others are not?

Any case of cultural innovation, many anthropologists would assert, involves some mix of individual intentions and cultural constitution (that is, public acceptance of the innovation). Will this intellectual compromise do? Not really, because the problem remains: what weight are we to assign each of these factors, when it would appear that giving importance to one necessarily invalidates the other? If culture constitutes the individual (because it is a response to existing material conditions or because of its necessary symbolic role), then what weight can be given to human intention? If individuals (Great Persons or just little ones, it does not matter which) make their cultures, then culture would seem to weigh only very lightly on them.

12

In the opening segment of Chapter 4, I experiment with a re-definition of the individual and culture to confront this problem. My thinking depends on the ideas of Roy Bhaskar, Anthony Giddens, and Alvin Gouldner — but, again, stems in large part from Gandhi's approach, as discussed in Chapter 2. By arguing that cultural meanings always encode social inequality, I move away from the argument within cultural determinism between the so-called materialists and idealists (see Fox 1985). By arguing that individual authorship is only realized through social networks, I show that Great Persons are always authorized by little people, and so the individual is not simply a genetic given or a culture carrier.

This reorientation allows me to redefine the question of weighing human intentions against cultural constitution. I test this redefinition against the sociological and historical literature on Western scientific innovation in the closing segment of Chapter 4. What better and better-studied example of cultural innovation than Western scientific "progress" can there be? If the culture history of science conforms well to the weighing system I use, so, I believe, should other histories of cultural innovation, even if the experimental process is more obscure and the cultural authorship is moot. My surmise is, again, based on an insight from Gandhi: his perception, noted earlier in this chapter, that experiments with truth in revolutionizing society are akin to scientific investigations and breakthroughs.

Orientalism, Hegemony, and the World System

The next experiment, in Chapter 5, follows from the need to add the dimensions of power to culture history. First, I use the concept of hegemony, as it is understood by Raymond Williams, to measure the degree to which social inequality can be encoded by existing cultural meanings. Then, by employing Immanuel Wallerstein's model of the world system, with some modifications, I measure the spatial spread of such deeply rooted systems of inequality. Merging these two concepts permits me to propose a world system of cultural domination, or hegemony, to which India was subject. I next look for a pejorative set of stereotypes of India that justified European control in the world system. This search leads me to another conceptual experiment, the enlargement of the concept of Orientalism to encompass a world system.

Edward Said's (1978) image of Orientalism aptly portrays a European vision of India that was dominating, or hegemonic: Orientalized India was backward, priest-ridden, superstitious, unenterprising, effeminate, otherwordly, and passive. Orientalism, however, did not stop at Europe's shores. I try to show it as a specific set of meanings dominating India within a world system of cultural domination. Some Indians — many of the early nationalists, for example — came under the hegemony of Orientalism, nearly or just as much as Europeans did. Orientalism swept away existing indigenous images of India *in* India, just as the world economy harnessed indigenous pre-capitalist labor and production systems — but not without struggle and resistance. The problem has been how to allow for effective struggle and resistance and still retain the concepts of an embracing world system and a deeply encoded cultural hegemony.

In Chapter 5, I experiment with this combination of world system, hegemony, and Orientalism on the culture history of Gandhian utopia. Starting with a chronicle of the singular, I show how Gandhi confronted a world system of cultural domination in the specific form of an Orientalized image of India. I then reflect on how resistance to this domination can arise — specifically, the compelling and enabling factors behind Gandhi's denial of modern civilization in 1909. I argue that an effective cultural resistance, such as Gandhian utopia, can arise from confrontations with an existing cultural hegemony, even though the resistance never fully escapes that hegemony.

Culture History and Gandhian Utopia

The remaining chapters apply these experiments to the culture history of the Gandhian utopian vision. In Chapter 6 I show the complex authorship of Gandhian utopia through a network of human agents — whom I call experimentalists, following Gandhi's idea of experiments with truth — linked intellectually and in some cases socially. I indicate how such an intellectual work group precipitates a public figure, such as Gandhi, in the sense that it prefigures many of the themes and elements of the Gandhian utopia later authored by Gandhi. Chapter 7 shows how an individual must labor to define his or her exclusive or predominant authorship: in

14

his South African and early Indian satyagrahas, Gandhi is seen hard at work defining his authority and authorship in the nationalist movement. I also show that Gandhi's labors sometimes did not succeed and that he constantly had to adapt himself and his developing vision to immediate circumstances. My intention in these two chapters is to indicate that the concepts of person, as in the case of Gandhi, and of authorship, as in the case of Gandhian utopia, are culture-historical constructions (that is, they are both historically contingent and culturally defined, but not determined).

Although individuals and authorship are constructions, they are unique ones, and their uniqueness has consequences for history and culture thereafter. In Chapter 8, I address this question: what effect, if any, did Gandhi and his utopian dream have on the course of Indian nationalism and the circumstances of India after independence in 1947?

The following chapters chronicle the ways in which the Gandhian utopian vision, once authored and authorized before independence, has constituted or compelled, but also enabled, cultural experiments in India thereafter. Pressed by ongoing human intentions and situated within existing social inequalities, these experiments progress from true (in the Gandhian sense of revolutionary) utopian visions to ideological legitimations and back again (but never exactly back to their original place).

Chapter 9 shows how Gandhian thinking in the Nehru years lost its confrontational, or experimental, character, and with it its utopian vision. Under Vinoba Bhave's authority, what passed as Gandhian experiments abetted the status quo of India's "intermediate regime." Precisely because their utopian character fell away, "experiments" like Vinoba's voluntary land reform program could be attempted piecemeal up to the early 1970s, and they consequently failed badly. Under the Nehru government's limited and calculated subsidy, Gandhian utopia was also "hijacked" and made to legitimate experiments antithetical to Gandhian intentions.

In Chapter 10, I show that a resurgent utopian vision emerged from these failures, as the movement for "total revolution" led by Jayaprakash Narayan burst out in the mid-1970s. Only severe government repression ended this experiment. Gandhian utopia then progressed into ideology and was appropriated by Hindu nationalism in the 1980s, as Chapter 11 documents.

Hindu nationalism — the movement to make India a Hindu nation — is an ideology that developed in response to cultural dom-

15

ination in the world system, much as Gandhian utopia did. Almost from its beginnings, however, Hindu nationalism ideologically safeguarded the status quo in India, rather than challenging it with a utopian vision. Chapter 12 analyzes Hindu nationalist ideology, the present-day class and caste interests it serves, and its recent incorporation of Gandhian utopia as an ideology. This chapter also speculates about the possibility that a new utopian vision might develop even from the currently unpromising ideological synthesis of Gandhism and Hindu nationalism.

A concluding chapter then reviews the question of the individual and culture in the light of Gandhi and Gandhian utopia. It also discusses the relevance of Gandhi's notion of experiments with truth to current scholarship, beset by the postmodern critique. Gandhi believed that confrontations with culturally entrenched oppression and inequality could revolutionize the future and make for a more humane and progressive society — a society that recognized truths about human happiness and satisfaction more nearly correctly and completely. So too, I argue, confrontations with existing scholarly understandings promise better understanding and progress in knowledge, even if, as Gandhi recognized, the struggle is never easy, the points of attack are ever shifting, and the outcome is always dubious until the next confrontation begins the struggle anew.

Utopian Visions and Cultural Innovations

I believe this culture history shows how new sets of cultural meanings develop as human actors originate ideas about their society out of cultural meanings already constituted and then experiment with these ideas. Such ideas, which, following Mannheim, Ricoeur, and Gandhi, I call utopian visions or utopian dreams or simply utopia, contest the present and conceive a revolutionized future. As individuals labor to implement utopia, existing material conditions and cultural meanings — or, in other words, the social inequalities encoded in the existing culture — define, limit, but do not completely compel the outcome; rather they can enable still more cultural innovations brought about by intentional human action. Utopian visions, such as the Gandhian dream, can fail and turn into ideologies legitimating (or, at least, tolerating) the status quo, like Vinoba Bhave's postindependence program of voluntary

16

land reform. But their utopian vision can be reasserted through human agency, as in the Gandhian-inspired "total revolution" of 1974–75, which struggled against a Gandhism that had lost its revolutionary purpose. Human intention may even transform ideologies like the Hindu nationalism of the 1980s into utopian experiments.

Once forged, a set of cultural meanings like Gandhian utopia limits or compels, but also enables or furthers, future cultural experimentation. It stipulates the form that new utopian experiments, attacking present conditions or the ideologies that defend them, will take. Thus my culture history ends up analytically where it began: with a mixture of constituted cultural meanings, the material conditions they encode (in the form of social inequalities), and the human intentions that play on them. This mixture is weighted not by which constituent is most important in some absolute sense, but by history: the specific historical relationships and contingencies through which this process of individual action and cultural innovation was happening and new cultural meanings were in the making.

Why do I not ask the questions, "which constituent explains the most variance?" or "which constituent best predicts the outcome?" Why, in other words, do I not look for behavioral regularities and predictive generalizations? To ask such questions is to pursue a goal of developing general laws about human behavior and human society outside the context of history, outside the constellations of specific material conditions, human agents, and cultural meanings, and the relationships they create.

I believe these questions cannot be answered in any meaningful way, that is, in any way that is not trite or overgeneralized. In this volume, I follow what has been called a "realist" approach as against this "empiricist" goal (see Isaac 1987: 41–71). Understanding the outcome of historical contingencies and social relationships is central to realism, rather than positing generalized hypotheses and making predictions. I deal with the general attributes of individuals and culture — human intentionality, cultural meanings, social inequalities — and the relationships that create those attributes. I show how these relationships and attributes cause specific processes of cultural change or cultural reproduction over a particular time. I am content to try to answer these general questions: assuming that the culture of twentieth-century India is not entirely compelled (that is, teleologically determined), then it follows that

17

it could have gone several ways. How did it come to go the way it did? What mix of social inequality, cultural meanings, and human intention, as they worked out contingently over time, took it there? How does where it did go affect where it might go? What does where it went tell us about the overall relationship of human intention to social inequality and cultural meanings? What, furthermore, do we learn about the general processes of cultural innovation — particularly, what do we learn about the role of the individual in culture change — from the specific outcome of the Gandhian dream? Finally, I face the question of what this experiment with culture history says about future experiments within anthropology.

The following chapter begins my experiments.

TWO

Experimenting with Gandhi

> The assumption that the sole method of studying mankind
> is to sit on a Melanesian island for a couple of years and
> listen to the gossip of villagers is not our idea of humani-
> tarian study.
>
> G. Elliot Smith (quoted in Langham 1981: 184)

Gandhi's belief in revolutionary social experimentation, as directed by his utopian dream, constitutes my major subject matter. It also constitutes one "native point of view," and, given that, I have used it to constitute this volume's format and theoretical design. I have thereby tried to respect the old anthropological injunction to use the "native point of view," honored formerly too often only in the breach — or so recent criticism from within anthropology would make it seem. In this chapter, I honor the injunction by explaining what Gandhi has taught me about culture, the individual, and culture history (and not only in India). By using his point of view, I also hope to answer the so-called postmodern critique of anthropology.

The Postmodern Critique

Even before Bronislaw Malinowski formally stated it a half-century ago, getting — and communicating — the "native point of view" have been anthropology's major goals. One intention has been to get beyond the biased and exotic portrayal of other life-ways and to construct knowledge carefully about cultural beliefs and practices elsewhere. Another has been to use such knowledge to question the social beliefs and practices of American and Western European societies. Still another intention has been to unmask Western ways of knowing as culturally mediated, as Westerners would assume to be true of knowledge claims in any other culture. Commonly taken to be "natural," "rational," or "scientific," Western ways of knowing, anthropology argues, are simply one culture's version of epistemology. They often owe their prominence to Western cultural domination in the world system rather than any intrinsic superiority. Anthropology's ultimate purpose here, if fully achieved, would be to reform Western epistemologies by "native" viewpoints, meaning ways of knowing or ways of experimenting (to use a Gandhian phrasing), that would move closer to the truth.[1] "Getting the native point of view," as I use this phrase, therefore encompasses all the important goals of anthropology.

Although it has long been anthropology's intention, achieving these goals is still quite distant, in the opinion of many recent critics. Deconstructing anthropology's past and finding it wanting, they hope to reconstruct the field along "reflexive" or postmodernist lines.

Recognizing that all ethnographic accounts are fictions, in the sense that they are constructed, James Clifford argues that what often passes for the "native point of view" is only the assertion and certification of the anthropologist, who actually suppresses the collaboration of his "native" informants in the ethnographic fiction. "Who [in truth] writes . . . an interpretation of custom produced through intense conversations with knowledgeable native collaborators?" Clifford (1986: 118) asks. In a similar way, Vincent Crapanzano attacks the work of a major ethnographer, Clifford Geertz. Crapanzano (1986: 74) accuses Geertz of projecting his sensibilities upon the Javanese in spite of his pretensions to a hermeneutic account of what the natives think; ultimately, Crapanzano finds Geertz's account "unconvincing."

Other critics have uncovered the artifice by which anthropologists convince readers (presumably less astute than Crapanzano) that their accounts are true representations of native viewpoints, at the same time monopolizing all the rights of authorship and suppressing the role of native collaborators. Clifford (1983: 118, 127–30) speaks of the appeal to authority based on a sensitive but objective rapport between ethnographer and informants — the "I was there" claim to authority of Malinowski, Mead, and other early professional anthropologists that put the ethnographer at the center of the ethnographic fiction. By asserting such "authority," anthropologists not only maintained that they were the exclusive authors of valid ethnographic accounts; they also "authorized" a professional identity for themselves. Authorship is always therefore an assertion of power, a claim to "authority" that, when successful, becomes an "authorization." Later ethnographers have claimed authority as interpreters or translators of the cultures they study. Here, culture is treated as a series of texts, and the ethnographer presents an "integrated portrait" of some generalized Other, free of the diversity, contradictions, and ambiguities of the ethnographic situation (Clifford 1983: 132; also see Rosaldo 1986). George Marcus and Dick Cushman (1982: 29–36) note that the stylistic markers, such as the personalized accounts of fieldwork experiences, by which ethnographers validate their rapport with the Native are usually relegated to preface or postscript, whereas the main ethnographic text finds the ethnographer carefully removed from the account, like an omniscient author. Mary Louise Pratt (1986: 50) shows that ethnographies often use the same literary conceits as travel literature, and Clifford (1983: 32) finds the "sudden baptism into native society" (my term) an equally common convention — both mandating the ethnographer as skilled interpreter, both thus deauthorizing indigenous interlocutors.

Getting "the native point of view" in truth, many of these critics suggest, requires recognizing "native informants," now labeled "interlocutors," as "coauthors" (Clifford 1986: 17). Critics propose a "dialogic" model that "attempts to show that the heart of ethnographic analysis must be in the negotiation between ethnographer and subject of shared realities" (Marcus and Cushman 1982: 43). By this model, an ethnography would consist in good measure of extended quotations from a variety of indigenous interlocutors, and the ethnographer would be not only or mainly interpreter but also "scribe and archivist" (Clifford 1986: 17). Still more radical would be the ethnography as "a utopia of plural authorship" based on a "polyphonic authority," with the dominant voice of the anthropologist/single author deleted (Clifford 1983: 140–141). The result would be a "polyphonic text" based on "the mutual, dialogical production of a discourse . . . [a] cooperative story making," in which no one has the final word (Tyler 1986: 126).

Such dialogic or polyphonic anthropologies may neither be easily implemented nor conserve the intentions of anthropology, however. In deauthorizing the anthropologist as skilled interpreter, may not such anthropologies only substitute a babble of numerous interlocutors? If some selectivity is required, how to choose which natives will speak? How to recognize whose indigenous meanings are being inscribed? How to organize the many voices into a coherent understanding and analysis of another culture? Marcus and Cushman (1982: 45) suggest we probably must abandon this intention.

How, finally, are we to use our understanding of another culture not merely to critique various Western institutions (which Marcus and Fischer [1986] take as anthropology's goal), but to reform our ways of gaining knowledge about the world, through understanding other ways? (Rabinow [1986] shows how historically naive about even Western epistemology much of this critical literature is.) Taking cover neither in a preface nor in a postscript, I raise the question of anthropological authority here to explain why I use Gandhi's point of view as both a format and a theory. It is my response to the postmodern critique.

Gandhi: Experimentalist and Interlocutor

The native speaker who informs my understanding throughout this work is Gandhi, and I let his ideas speak out in the following pages to the best of my ability and, obviously, in the way his thoughts persuade me. This is my response to the compelling anthropological injunction to get the native point of view, but also my proof that getting the native point of view is not just the anthropologist's bizarre rite of passage. It also enables better understandings of other life-ways, more substantial critiques of world conditions, and greater recognition of culture-bound Western epistemology — the three intentions of getting the native point of view, as I understand it.

Gandhi does not represent some generalized Other, "always singular and always capitalized" (Geertz 1985: 624), however. Nor is he lost in a dialogic babble of Others, where the provenance of the cultural meanings recorded by the anthropologist is moot. He is a specific "native" (as we all are) with particular "indigenous meanings" (as we all have), situated within an individual historical and cultural environment. Nor will he be heard only through this volume, an otherwise anonymous co-author. He has spoken for himself through 89 volumes (currently) of *Collected Works*. In addition, he spoke out through a long independence struggle and

22

activated cultural meanings like nonviolent resistance that now have a world public.

In this volume, I have tried to make Gandhi my interlocutor, but not only because he is indisputably an important author of the Gandhian utopian vision. Nor do I wish to claim the imprimatur of the Great Soul for what I say herein. The chronicle of Gandhian utopia is mine alone, not the cooperative story urged by Tyler and Clifford. Gandhi is a collaborator in what I take to be a more profound sense, that is, because I have authored this volume along Gandhian principles of understanding. I have taken one "native" point of view, the cultural meanings it contains, and the epistemology it embeds, as best I understand them, and used them to reform the text and theory of my experiment with anthropology. Gandhi's ideas, especially his notion of experiment and his utopian dream, as I perceived them, helped lead me to the other authors who have influenced this work — Paul Ricoeur and Karl Mannheim, for example. His ideas also led me to read familiar authors, like Roy Bhaskar or Alvin Gouldner, in a different way. Without my intellectual discourse with Gandhi, or should I say my experiment in discourse with this single other, I believe I would not have been either compelled or enabled to write this work. Let me give instances.

Discontinuous Personhoods

Gandhi disowned the notion, usually attributed as Western, of the integral individual, of the person, configured in infancy and youth, who then lives out a "life-course" predicated on and compelled by this early socialization. Why do most biographies and autobiographies (Gandhi's own included, it must be said) start from birth, if not from the (Western cultural or perhaps only Western scholarly) belief that the child's living gives proof of the adult life. For Gandhi, it was another matter: a human had lives, not a life-course, and, unlike a cat, there was no predetermined number of lives. An individual over time could be composed of nonconforming identities: as the person experimented with truth and came to understand and live truth more or better, there could be radical breaks, discontinuities in personhood. The individual was precipitated at any moment by his or her intentions and the ongoing experiences that gave rise to them; the individual was not compelled by the traditions of childhood into a life-span.

23

In Gandhi's life, for instance, his nascent Indian nationalism led him to eat meat as a youth in India. His idea, common to many young Indians then, was that India's freedom required British-style strength, which depended on devouring other creatures. Later, in England, during his early adult life, he fell in with British vegetarians like Henry Salt, who disowned feasting on their fellow creatures as well as cannibalizing by capitalist wage labor their fellow humans. In that life, Gandhi embraced vegetarianism by choice, and perhaps with just as strong a nationalism as earlier had led him to carnivorism. Although both were responses to colonialism, Gandhi did not choose to explain them through a presumed continuity of personhood.

Gandhi, not surprisingly, disclaimed any intention of writing a "real" autobiography, although the volume published in 1927 was so called. He had no life-long moral precepts to instill in the reader, no life-course of which he was the product. Today's Gandhi might not prefigure tomorrow's. The order of his life came only from the sequence of his personal experiments. Each experiment made him a somewhat different person. Perhaps the only continuity was in his name, although even in this respect, he experienced essential transformations. Young Mohandas in Gujarat was known in South Africa as Mr. Gandhi the attorney, and then, back in India again, he went by the title of Mahatma. Jailed by the British, it was the Mahatma, not Mohandas or Mr. Gandhi, who used his prison term to write a collective biography of these several Gandhis. He began with his childhood only because his serial experiments with truth began then. "I simply want to tell the story of my numerous experiments with truth," he wrote at that time, and then emphasized that no matter how confident (constituted, anthropologists might say) a person's self-identity might be at one moment in life, there was always the potential for existential discontinuity:

> As my life consists of nothing but those experiments, it is true that the story will take the shape of an autobiography. But I shall not mind if every page of it speaks only of my experiments. . . .
>
> Far be it from me to claim any degree of perfection for these experiments . . . I am far from claiming any finality or infallibility about my conclusions. One claim I do indeed make and it is this. For me they appear to be absolutely correct and seem for the time being to be final. For if they were not, I should base no action on them (Gandhi 1957: xii).

24

Gandhi reasserted this belief even more strongly some twenty years afterward (clearly, at least this one aspect of his personal identity had not changed):

> I never really wrote an autobiography. What I did write was a series of articles narrating my experiments with truth . . . I can give no guarantee that I will do or believe tomorrow what I do or hold to be true today (quoted in Iyer 1986: 39–40).

He noted that an extension of his biography could only be done after he was dead and presumably his experiments were finished. Gandhi phrased this principle perhaps most eloquently in 1933:

> I am not at all concerned with appearing to be consistent. In my search after Truth I have discarded many ideas and learnt many new things. Old as I am in age, I have no feeling that I have ceased to grow . . . What I am concerned with is my readiness to obey the call of Truth, my God, from moment to moment, and therefore, when anybody finds any inconsistency between any two writings of mine, . . . he would do well to choose the later of the two . . . (Gandhi 1957: 4)

In this work, I take Gandhi's belief in the possibility of discontinuous and, uncommonly, revolutionary personhoods as a principle for understanding the individual, human agency, and the authorship of cultural change. Rather than locating an individual's intentions and actions in some individualized self, presumed to be originally constructed in childhood, which thereafter leads him or her to act and think in a relatively consistent fashion, I see the individual and his action as precipitated by ongoing networks of intellectual and social relations, which work on an existing personhood and can sometimes enable radical alterations in it. Only our strong presumption of integral individuals and therefore individualized authorship, which I discuss further in Chapter 4, misleads us. We then mistakenly look for special personality constellations, ostensibly set by childhood experiences, in cultural innovators like Gandhi, rather than the contemporary formative experiences that precipitated Gandhi as he was in South Africa, or Gandhi in the early Indian satyagraha campaigns, or Gandhi, disconsolate after the partition of India and Pakistan. In other words, individual experiments make for constant personal becoming.[2]

I use the term "personhood" rather than "selfhood" to emphasize that I refer to changes in the public actions and ideas of the individual and in the individual's altered social relations with others. Whether such discontinuities in personhood are also ruptures of an internal, psychological selfhood is not a question I entertain. My approach treats the "person" as an empirical manifestation of underlying but nondeterminate relationships in society, not as a psyche with an internal cognitive structure. Gandhi too manifested spiritual experiments through external public and social representations: he tested his internal resolve by following new diets, contravening old relationships, or protesting existing domination.

Such discontinuities in personhood, which many individuals experience and which we often label "personal growth," vary considerably. Most attempts to master ongoing circumstances leave the individual basically "the same old person," as we say. Some struggles, however, produce such a great discontinuity that personal growth gives way to personal revolution: the person "was never the same after that," we assert. These revolutions in personhood do not come easily, if they happen at all. Gandhi often noted that his experiments with society required struggles with himself. That is, individuals must struggle with themselves as they attempt to master surrounding circumstances and ongoing experiences. These struggles can fundamentally alter the intentions of the individual and therefore manifestly change the individual's personhood and social relations; in fact, they can revolutionize them. The individual's altered intentions can in turn redefine existing circumstances, as I make clear in Chapter 7. Most individuals will not risk personal reproduction to accomplish self-revolution; many who have the courage to risk never successfully master ongoing circumstances with their reformed intentions. Commonly, because of the intense personal struggle, sudden behavioral shifts mark these revolutions in personhood. For instance, Gandhi took a vow of celibacy (*bramacharya*) in 1906 as the South African resistance reached a critical stage of nonviolent resistance; he gave up Westernized fashion and reverted to Indian dress in 1913 as he initiated a mass mobilization of Indian indentured laborers in South Africa; he suffered a nervous breakdown in 1918 when his recruiting effort for the British military failed. All these instances, I shall try to show, were symptoms of the personal revolution he experienced from 1906 to 1920.

26

Cultural Experiments

Just as persons change through individual experiments, so Gandhi believed that cultures change through collective experiments. This idea, that cultures are constantly being made, unmade, and remade, is another aspect of Gandhi's thinking I use in this work.[3] Gandhi, to be sure, believed in deeply rooted cultural traditions, as when he contrasted the West's successful materialism with India's antique spirituality, but he saw these traditions as always historically contingent, not as forever historically constitutive. Worthy traditions, like the Indian village community, had to be buttressed against erosion; evil ones, like Untouchability, had to be destroyed. Cultural traditions therefore do not reproduce on their own; active human endeavor is necessary to keep them going. Conversely, cultural traditions do not disappear through inertia; getting rid of them requires positive human action.

Gandhi's position may seem inconsistent: how can traditions require active support (the worthy ones) *and* active opposition (the evil ones)? In this fashion, Gandhi instructs us in the limitations of a definition of "traditions" that assumes an inherent longevity or inertial reproduction for them. That traditions constitute a culture, Gandhi understood, but he also saw that such constitution must be affirmed or denied in each historical context. Culture is then "constantly in the making," as its constituted meanings at any one moment are lived out anew and afresh in the next. Making culture in that next moment includes the possibility of remaking the old cultural meanings so they continue, as well as unmaking them so they disappear and new ones intervene.

I am not able to provide a brief but pithy statement of this principle from Gandhi. The notion of culture unmade and remade was perhaps too close to his quotidian practice for him to articulate. What Gandhi did about Indian cultural forms is perhaps the best measure of his conviction. He worked just as hard at cultural conservation — of the Indian village, home spinning, nonpossession, and other Indian traditions he valued — as he did at cultural revolution — against Untouchability, suppression of women, caste inequality, and other traditions he disowned. Cultural traditions would neither survive nor revolutionize without active husbandry: this conception of culture constantly in the making was Gandhi's underlying practice, and it was my operating principle throughout this volume.

Experimental Struggle and Making History

Gandhi gives me a final idea, a summation of his understanding of the individual and culture. It is his perception of the historical

27

process and the way culture history takes place, which he embodied in the practice of satyagraha and ahimsa. As I have already mentioned, Gandhi's concept of experiment, of the constant pursuit of truth, beginning with the individual and extending to the group, forms the center of history for him:

> Socialism begins with the first convert. If there is one such you can add zeros to the one and the first zero will account for ten and every addition will account for ten times the previous number. If, however, . . . no one makes the first move, multiplicity of zeros will also produce zero value (Gandhi 1984 [1946]: 76).

For Gandhi, Indians conspired at their own servitude in South Africa or British India: "The English have not taken India; we have given it to them" (Gandhi 1982 [1909]: 38). ". . . [W]e hug the chains that bind us," he wrote in 1934 (Gandhi 1965: 30). Freedom for the individual and for the nation could only come from experiments based on novel conceptions of self and society — in a real sense, experimentation was tantamount to freedom. In South Africa, he believed that

> We are the creators of this position of ours, and we alone can change it. We are fearless and free, so long as we have the weapon of Satyagraha in our hands (Gandhi 1972 [1928]: 147).

Satyagraha and ahimsa ("soul force" and "nonviolent resistance"), most importantly for Gandhi, powered the experiments in truth, and they, most significantly for this volume, depended on struggle and confrontation. Gandhi wrote, much before India's independence.

> Real *Swaraj* will come not by the acquisition of authority by a few, but by the acquisition of the capacity by all to resist authority when it is abused . . . by educating the masses to a sense of their capacity to regulate and control authority (Gandhi 1965 [1925]: 87);

and then just before independence he repeated the admonition in terms of class:

> Exploitation of the poor can be extinguished not by effecting the destruction of a few millionaires, but by removing the ignorance of the poor and teaching them to non-cooperate with their exploiters (Gandhi 1965: 87, 43).

Satyagraha was the proper experimental means by which to resist the existing cultural meanings and material conditions under which people lived and suffered. It was the hopeful use of forceful non-violence to test out, and thus to achieve, a better future world. Struggle for Gandhi had to be principled and nonviolent, but it also had to be brave and unyielding till proved wrong. It was not the refuge of the weak, as passive resistance was (see Gandhi 1972 [1928]: 103–106). A failed act of satyagraha, like a failed scientific experiment, indicated that truth resided elsewhere, and the experimenter, the *satyagrahi*, had to be prepared to accept death to gain even this "disconfirmation." The only constancy was experimentation through opposition:

> Nonviolence is a universal principle and its operation is not limited by a hostile environment. Indeed, its efficacy can be tested only when it acts in the midst of and in spite of opposition (Gandhi 1984 [1938]: 80).

I take several ideas from Gandhi's insistence on satyagraha as experiment through (nonviolent) struggle,[4] and I develop them in this work:

Cultural innovation occurs only in the context of people's resistance to and struggle against the cultural meanings and material conditions that rule them. Cultural change is never a matter of negotiated construction, a simple dialectic between the existing cultural meanings and what people make of them in everyday life.[5] Culture, like the inequalities embedded in it, always has a hard and resistant character. Struggle and opposition, based on dreams of perfection (such as Gandhi's utopian vision), motivate culture history.

A Gandhian perspective, furthermore, unlike Scientific Marxism's, does not regard the outcomes of struggle as predetermined by supposed laws of history. Experiments in truth are, as this Marxism would also argue, rooted in human action and conflict; but for Gandhi the process of experimentation itself is "essentially creative and inherently constructive" (Bondurant 1965: 192). Opposition and struggle cultivate indeterminate outcomes precisely because the outcomes result from the experiments.

I trust I have truthfully represented Gandhi's view of individuals under construction, culture in the making, and culture history under production through struggle and experiment. The next section details the way I believe such a culture history can be studied and written.

29

Experimenting with Culture History

Marc Bloch (1953: 26) used a fantastic image to advise historians that their major subject matter should be individuals: "The good historian is like the giant of the fairy tale. He knows that wherever he catches the scent of human flesh, there his quarry lies." Contrast Bloch's view with Leslie White's "demythologizing" of the individual in history:

> To explain culture history psychologically is of course to lean on mystery . . . In the evolutionist process, the individual is . . . relatively insignificant . . . The culturologist [White's term for a practitioner of his kind of anthropology] . . . by working upon the supra-psychological, supra-sociological level of culture, by explaining culture in terms of culture, really makes it [culture history] intelligible (White 1949: 230–32).

Alfred Kroeber had, some thirty years earlier, articulated the same view of history that White later would much more vocally champion:

> The concrete effect of each individual upon civilization is determined by civilization itself . . .
> Social science, if we may take that word as equivalent to history, does not deny individuality any more than it denies the individual. It does refuse to deal with either individuality or individual as such. And it bases this refusal solely on denial of the validity of either factor for the achievement of its proper aims (Kroeber 1952 [1917]: 48).

Bloch's historian in pursuit of individuals and White's and Kroeber's anthropologist in pursuit of systems and forces beyond any individual . . . these two positions represent the antipodes of a long-standing debate about the proper study of culture history. A culture history true to Gandhian principles, as I understand them, would require both. It would have to be a saga of people and their individual experiments in opposition, but it would also have to be an account of the social system within and against which the individual struggled and before whose force the individual might succumb.

Paul Ricoeur proposes such a culture history, and on this subject as well as in his conception of utopia I discuss later, he produces a scholarly agenda in keeping with Gandhi's understandings.[6] Ricoeur (1965: 38) contrasts two sorts of history, the one whose object is to find structure and system in history (White's and Kroeber's history), and the other, which speaks of individuals and the way they individually may remake the world (Bloch's history). He argues that history is history only when it is shown as a combination of the system and the singular. If the presentation moves to the extreme of system, there is "a false objectivity" (Ricoeur 1965: 40); there is system but no history (Ricoeur 1965: 76). An account that deals only with singularities has equivalent problems, because history also must include forces and systems. Historians, and I suppose Ricoeur would include culture historians, have to "tackle an event-filled history and a structural history at the same time . . . [a history] between the great personages who make their appearance and the slowly progressing forces" (Ricoeur 1965: 39).

Ricoeur's distaste for overly systemic approaches to history is critically important for anthropology, which, as White and Kroeber indicate, has always had a predilection for them. Ricoeur finds that the sociology of knowledge followed by Marx, Mannheim, and Lukacs, especially their treatment of ideology, has too much of the structural and too little of the singular. For them, Ricoeur says, "ideology is *anonymous*," which means they treat an ideology as "typical" of a group or class rather than as singular, the production of a particular thinker. They do not acknowledge that before an ideology becomes a generalized "answer" (an "envehicled" cultural meaning, in anthropological terms), it is first of all an individual "problematic" or question, a philosophy — in Gandhi's terms, a dream — posed by an individual thinker. An individual problematic, to be sure, has a relationship to its sociocultural milieu, but it also defines that milieu by being posed. Any philosophy has a "situation," in Ricoeur's terminology. We have to look at it to see the situation that it in some measure reflects, but we must also see the situation defined by the philosophy's very existence and by what it "brought to the surface and exhibited" (Ricoeur 1965: 60–61, 70).

Gandhi precisely understood that any cultural innovation was first of all an individual problematic, an experiment based on a utopian dream of the future, and only afterward, as it gained devotees who struggled against their current world, might it lead to new revolutionary realities. Gandhi's notion of experiment and utopian dream anticipates very closely the way to develop, according to Ricoeur, a history both singular and structural. Ricoeur's conception, in turn, builds on Karl Mannheim's discussion of utopia and ideology.

31

Mannheim distinguished three sorts of ideas or conceptions about the world: first, there are situationally congruous ideas, which correctly describe the social situations in which they arise. According to Mannheim, these are very rare because they depend on full sociological awareness. The other two types are situationally incongruous ideas. They do not correctly describe the current social reality; instead, they distort and transcend it. Mannheim labels one incongruous type "ideology," by which he means a distorted view of the world that never comes to pass. Ideologies are ideas that do not challenge the existing social order and fail to transform the world according to their vision. For example, the idea of Christian brotherly love was incongruous in a society with serfdom, like feudal Europe; furthermore, it never happened, and so it was, for Mannheim, an ideology. In spite of their incongruity, ideologies continue in a society, Mannheim says ([1936]: 193–95), because powerful social institutions generate "false consciousness" among individuals, because the individual wishes to be deluded for emotional reasons, or because the individual wishes to delude others.

Mannheim labels the other kind of incongruous idea "utopia." Utopias are distinguished from ideologies by their success in transforming existing historical reality according to their incongruous vision of the present. Mannheim ([1936]: 204) suggests that hindsight allows the discrimination of ideologies from utopias:

> ideas which later turned out to have been only distorted representations of a past or potential social order were ideological, while those which were adequately realized in the succeeding social order were relative utopias.

Success or failure, ideology or utopia, depends on the outcome of the struggle for dominance in society. Dominant groups will label as utopian anything that seems unrealizable given an existing social order. They will brand such ideas *absolutely* unrealizable, impossible in any social order. Every social order, however, gives rise to utopias that break through existing circumstances and allow society to evolve to the next order of existence. Mannheim therefore believes his approach to be "dialectical," but there is a teleology built into it: utopias appear as the "needs of the age." An individual's idea of utopia only succeeds, Mannheim argues, when it reflects currents of thought from the wider population.

Ricoeur reformulates Mannheim's distinction between utopia and ideology and, although unintentionally, brings it better into line with Gandhi's notion of experiment and utopian dream. He disputes the distinction between congruous ideas and incongruous ones. Congruous ideas would require a "distanced onlooker," impossibly far removed from cultural conditioning (Ricoeur 1986: 173).

Ricoeur also casts doubt on Mannheim's belief that utopian ideas prove not to be ideologies only when they succeed in changing the existing order. Instead, he argues that "utopia is what shatters order and ideology is what preserves order (sometimes by distortion but also sometimes by a legitimate process)." Ricoeur sees utopia as a "view from nowhere" or a "leap outside" whose function is to constitute the rethinking of social life (compare Gusfield 1971: 76). "Does not the fantasy of an alternative society and its exteriorization 'nowhere' work as one of the most formidable contestations of what is?" (Ricoeur 1986: 16). So the important criterion is not that utopias are realized and ideologies are not. Rather, the essential distinction is that utopias unmask ideologies, which are in fact always realized because they confirm the current, whereas utopias can never fully succeed because they show the "distance" between the current and the hoped-for perfected future (Ricoeur 1986: 179).

Ricoeur says that the major asset of utopian thinking is to preserve a distance between the present and the future, to make a gap between a system of authority claiming legitimacy and the population's actual belief in that legitimacy. Utopia's most radical function thus contravenes the most radical function of ideology, which is to legitimate a system of authority.[7] Ricoeur also believes that both ideology and utopia can have a pathological character. Falsehood (in the interests of legitimating a system of authority) constitutes the pathology of ideology. Escapism (out of desire to deny the system of authority) represents a pathological utopia (Ricoeur 1986: 16–17). In such cases, ideology cannot conceive of a nowhere, and utopia does not confront a somewhere.

How does a utopian vision avoid escapism? How does it remain linked to the problems of existing society? On this issue, Ricoeur says little, whereas Gandhi is forthright. Utopian visions, or dreams in Gandhi's language, motivate a continuing human struggle — translated by Gandhi as "experiment" — to achieve them, which in turn requires a confrontation with existing systems of authority and their legitimizing ideologies.

In sum, an understanding of utopian and ideological thinking inspired by Gandhi might be of this sort: both ideology and utopia are experiments in truthful understanding. Ideologies are false or failed experiments because they only confirm the present cultural constitution, whereas utopian dreams succeed as truthful experiments because they challenge that constitution and catalyze experiments that confront it. Utopian visions must always develop in confrontation with ideologies, therefore, and ideologies often carry forward a utopian aspect that has failed in confrontation. Culture history, then, moves along in this manner: new utopian dreams can arise from within the ideology constituting an existing system of domination and authority. The utopia, if it fails in confrontation, can in turn be taken to legitimate the current order as a new ideology. If it succeeds, however, new cultural forms constituting other patterns of domination and authority appear. And so on — with each progression possibly taking humanity closer to a perfected world, or at least to the truth about human possibilities, but with no specific outcome certain or even probable. The human endeavor to build more nearly perfect cultures within existing material conditions and out of existing cultural meanings and ideologies is the agency behind this progression. Experiments, however they progress, are then not anonymous; they are authored by individual dreams, authorized by group struggle, and deauthorized by the opposition they meet — until the next time. This progression in turn authorizes a culture history that is at once structural and singular, with which the rest of this work experiments.

This chapter began with the postmodern critique of ethnography. The doubt it casts on ethnography's claims to represent the "native point of view" is especially troubling. Taking the critique seriously, I named Gandhi himself as my major interlocutor or informant, and I noted the important understandings he helped me reach. His thinking ultimately brought me to the culture history I have just proposed. In turn, this culture history replies to the postmodern critique, as I hope to show by the example of this work — and by the following comments.

Bronislaw Malinowski urged anthropologists in the 1920s to "come down off the verandah . . . and join the people," as Ian Jarvie (1964: 43) aptly phrases it. Malinowski's dictum soon became anthropology's credo. Anthropologists did "fieldwork," which meant they figuratively set up their tents in the midst of a foreign culture. Once home, they produced authoritative "ethnographies." These texts captured the native viewpoint, or claimed to capture it, precisely because the anthropologist "had been there." Even when anthropologists later made "thick descriptions" and said they could expertly translate and interpret other cultures as arcane texts, they claimed the authority to do so from their ethnographic fieldwork.

The postmodern critique warns us that these ethnographies are "fictions," however. Their claims to represent the "native point of view" are buttressed by textual conventions and devices that often dismiss the native coauthors and exaggerate the anthropologist as empathetic, but objective observer. The critique also makes us wary of too tidy ethnographic representations; it requires us to pay heed to the way in which an anthropologist creates the culture in the very act of writing the ethnography. In sum, the critique reminds us that an ethnography, like any knowledge — in fact, like any aspect of culture — is a human construction. We can only perceive "reality," ethnographic or otherwise, after it is mediated by such cultural and personal construction (see Watson 1987: 30–31).

Yet the "reflexive," "polyphonic," or "dialogic" ethnography now urged upon us does not escape fiction (in the sense of construction) any better. That is, it cannot overcome the essential reflexivity, as Graham Watson (1987) terms it, of our knowledge. The long quotations from informants, the emphasis on the dialogue between an ethnographer and an interlocutor, the babel of many native voices — these new devices and conventions of ethnography seem additional burdens on an already overtaxed text form. They are unnecessary because they are ineffectual. Heaping on such new conventions will not cover up the fact that all ethnography takes the native point of view out of context and reconstructs it elsewhere — no matter how extended the quotations from informants, how intensive the dialogue between interlocutors, or how many the voices the ethnography speaks for. Such new devices, perhaps inadvertently and no doubt unfortunately, may revive ethnography artificially (in the original meaning of the word). Similarly, the postmodern critique, by continuing to beat a dead or dying horse, only succeeds in preserving a text form, ethnography, as central to anthropology, or even identical with it.

Perhaps it is time to remount anthropology by proposing new texts, other than ethnography, to carry it forward. New texts, one of which is the culture history I propose in this volume, need not — 35 probably dare not — abandon all the conventions that have characterized the fieldwork done by anthropologists, especially the concern for everyday life, participant-observation, cultural relativism, and, most recently, self-reflection. New texts, however, can augment these conventions of fieldwork with others: concern for historical process, for individual intention, and for the relations from afar that structure inequality in local, everyday life.

The culture history of Gandhian utopia I will present is no less a fiction than an ethnography, but it avoids some of the fictions involved in constructing the old ethnography. It does not, for example, tie up the loose ends of culture into a neatly tied ethnographic package. This culture history is a chronicle of intentions, contingencies, and relationships: among people, in a culture, over time. Such a culture history conserves anthropology's intention of getting the native point of view (in the broad sense I defined it at the beginning of this chapter) because it confronts questions that ethnography, even in postmodern form, often finesses. Ethnography has never questioned that there are Others to be met in the course of fieldwork, among whom the anthropologist figuratively pitches camp. Culture history pursues the question of who these Others are and how they have come to be. Gandhian utopia, which I describe in the next chapter, is a set of cultural meanings that condensed over a century from individual utopian visions and that today helps make India Other and makes Indians Others whom anthropologists study. How well can we possibly know our interlocutors in the field if we do not have this history in mind? Ethnography also finesses the question of where anthropologists should pitch their tents. It too often specifies a physical location . . . an inhabited jungle clearing, a village community, an urban barrio . . . in place of an intellectual position. Ethnography then has to claim authority on the basis of "having been there" and the special empathy it creates. How otherwise could it justify its construction of "fieldwork" as meaning physical, rather than scholarly, placement? Culture history avoids these fictions about empathy; it need not take "fieldwork" to mean space instead of stance. Culture history requires that anthropologists intellectually occupy the middle ground between the individual and culture, between persons and processes. The next chapter moves in this direction.

*T*HREE

Gandhian Utopia

| *And was not Jesus Christ an Asiatic?*
| *Keshub Chandra Sen (quoted in Hay 1970: 21).*

By asserting a separate course of development for India, ostensibly based on a greater humanism and a higher morality, Gandhian utopia represents a revolutionary rejection of what is often referred to as secular economic progress but what the Gandhians[1] see as the insatiable consumption, undisciplined production, and alienated existence of the West. Gandhians label this idea of material progress "Western," although they acknowledge that Western thinkers like Tolstoy, Ruskin, and Carpenter also resisted it. Those thinkers are exceptions, however, to the Western hegemony of materialism, individualism, and possessiveness. Having come to rule advanced industrial nations, this materialist view attempts to extend its empire to the rest of the world, the Gandhians argue. Gandhian utopia resists the domination of this set of ideas. It argues that the social belief and practice of advanced industrial societies, whether capitalist or socialist, are not universal, no matter the hegemony they claim. It prescribes experiments in spiritual modernization, rather than in the economic development engineered by Western socialism or capitalism.

In this chapter, I present Gandhian utopia as a set or structure of cultural meanings, in the well-developed form it had achieved about the time of Indian independence in 1947 and into the early 1950s. I show it as a utopian dream of a future India, perfected on the basis of its presumed ancient culture. I also show the contemporary experiments it authorized, that is, the short-term practices undertaken by Gandhian "experimentalists" as they hopefully struggle toward the future. I use the convention of the present tense, the so-called "ethnographic present," throughout this structural presentation. Later chapters take up the authorship of Gandhian utopia within a particular history of world-system domination.

The vision I label "Gandhian utopia" has many other names and forms. It also goes by the name "Gandhian socialism" (Fisher and Bondurant 1956), "Indian socialism" (Rao 1982; Sampuranand 1961), "*sarvodaya*" ("welfare for all") (Devadoss 1974; Kantowsky 1980; Tandon 1965), "sarvodaya society and economy" (Sethi 1979), "Vedic socialism" (Banerjee n.d.), "Gandhian economics" (Das 1979; Mathur n.d.), "decentralised economic development" (Mehta 1964), and "Indian anarchism" (Ostergaard and Currell 1971; Dalton 1986: 278).

These terms in varying degrees emphasize the following significant characteristics of the utopian vision:

It is a program for reordering society, which, although possessing an economic policy ("decentralised economic development," "sarvodaya economy"), conceives of a revolutionary reconstitution of social life in general ("anarchism," "socialism," "sarvodaya").

This program emphasizes human values that Western capitalism and socialism supposedly downgrade or negate. These characteristics, which I will discuss presently, are said to be deeply rooted in Indian culture; for example, they are considered coterminous with ancient Vedic society or held to develop from the Vedanta philosophy of the Indian middle ages ("Vedic socialism," "Indian socialism," "Indian anarchism").

Gandhi is the major author and practitioner of this program ("Gandhian socialism," "Gandhian economics"), although earlier Indian nationalists contributed to his original vision, just as later nationalists have continued and also extended Gandhi's ideas.

My term, "Gandhian utopia," emphasizes two points. First, it acknowledges Gandhi as the ostensible author of this vision but also recognizes a long and complex process of authorization ("Gandhian"). Gandhi's pre-independence program of sarvodaya publicly articulated the cultural meanings constituting Gandhian utopia most clearly, but it was foreshadowed in images of India held by earlier reformers and nationalists — sometimes Indian by birth, like Swami Vivekananda and Sri Aurobindo, and sometimes Indian by persuasion, like Annie Besant and Margaret Noble (Sister Nivedita). The Gandhian dream continued to inform belief and practice in independent India — as, for example, in Vinoba Bhave's *bhoodan* program of voluntary land reform during the 1950s and 1960s and in the movement for total revolution during 1974–75. Right up to the present, various social welfare, research, and antiwar organizations maintain a Gandhian perspective (see Ostergaard and Currell 1971; Ostergaard 1985). In spite of the exclusive authorship commonly ascribed to Gandhi, the reality, which Chapter 6 will further clarify, is a long genesis within a world system of authorship. This set of cultural meanings began to develop late in the nineteenth century, came to be associated with Gandhi early in the twentieth, started to constitute Indian belief and practice from the 1920s onward, and became an undeniable aspect of Indian social and political consciousness from independence in 1947 up to the present day.

My term "Gandhian utopia" also emphasizes that this dream of a future, perfected India effectively condemns the present — it is a "utopia," and its vision of the "no where" and the "not yet" sponsors current experiments in radical social change. Yet the future of India, according to the Gandhian vision, depends on her past. India can avoid Western failures only if the society develops in line with its ancient cultural traditions, said to be so different from the West's. These cultural traditions are essentials — of India's former glory and for her future perfection — and they underlie the cultural meanings compelling Gandhian experiments with utopia.

Essential India

The Gandhian dream bases its utopian hopes on the cultivation of certain Indian cultural essentials, taken to represent the deep and ancient values of India's civilization. These cultural essentials, according to Gandhian experimentalists, give India the possibility of a more humane, less materialistic, more egalitarian, and less alienated society than Western socialism or capitalism has achieved. Spirituality is one such cultural essential, undoubtedly the most important one (although this avowal is not exclusively Gandhian). India has from ancient times, it is said, cultivated individual self-

39

knowledge and society's regulation through spiritual advancement, rather than the materialist progress advanced in the West.

The excessive materialism of the West and the false development it begets have been weighed against India's cultivation of spiritual development — and found wanting — for well over 150 years. Starting early in the nineteenth century with Rammohun Roy's acceptance of India as a uniquely spiritual civilization (Hay 1970: 21ff., 51), then moving later in the century to Swami Vivekananda's assertion that in matters of the spirit, India must instruct the West (French 1974: 58–59, 91–95; Dalton 1986: 278), this assumption of India's historic primacy in matters of religion became an essential element in a worldwide catechism of Indian national identity. Indians like Rabindranath Tagore (Hay 1970: 4), Bankim Chatterjee (Chatterjee 1986a: 50–51, 1986b: 78), Madan Mohan Malaviya (Dar and Somaskandan 1966: 49), Gandhi (1938 [1909]: 61) and many others intoned it (see Chandra 1969). Europeans like Edward Carpenter (1910: 179), Max Müller (1883: 122, 127; Dar and Somaskandan 1966: 49), and other Orientalist scholars (see Schwab 1984: 76ff.) also numbered among its catechists. "In-Betweens," sometime Europeans who now claimed to be of India, like Annie Besant (see, for example, Besant 1913: 3), were among its most assertive adherents. Gandhi, too, maintained that

> Just as in the West, they have made wonderful discoveries in things material, similarly Hinduism has made still more marvellous discoveries in things of religion, of the spirit, of the soul . . . We are dazzled by the material progress that Western science has made. I am not enamoured of that progress . . . After all, there is something in Hinduism that has kept it alive up till now . . . And the reason why it has survived is that the end which Hinduism set before it was not development along material but spiritual lines (Gandhi 1965 [1921]: 10).

At present, Indian spirituality has the force of a national commandment, as when the head of a Hindu nationalist organization warns:

> India is a nation that has always nurtured religion . . . [it is] something in the soil . . . If India forgets her spiritual heritage it will become one of many nations; it will not even remain a single nation (Singh 1983: 15).

Another presumed Indian cultural essential is the deeply rooted tradition of an organic society, filled with cooperation, in sharp contrast to the excessive individualism and the competition fostered in the West. In ancient Indian culture, it is said, individuals "subordinated" themselves to their families, their villages, their castes. Their subordination, however, was not exploitation; rather, individuals fulfilled themselves only as they fulfilled their duty to others. Duty therefore characterized the individual, literally, and also constructed the society. Society's division of labor came from the fourfold system of *varnas* (mistakenly confused by Westerners with its later, decadent form, the caste system): Brahmans, Kshatriyas, Vaisyas, and Shudras each had their divinely appointed and hereditary duties. Together, they worked for the common good. Society's governance came from the village *panchayat*, a group of elders who spoke by consensus for, and in support of, community values. No class struggle rent the village, no disharmony came between the varnas, and the ugly competition for power, precedence, and possessions that characterizes the West was absent. Society's ethics and morals came from the family, in which statuses ascribed by gender, age, and birth order enrolled individuals into lifetime positions. The family was at once demanding and supportive of its members, just as the varna system and the village community were. Each of these, the family, the varna, and the village, was more than the individuals it comprised, and they, in turn, came together to compose an organic, or corporate, society superior to any of the parts. Social harmony and consensus were natural outcomes of this organic composition, which explains how the individual could put society before himself but thereby create a sustaining social environment, one that permitted maximum individual self-expression (compare Dalton 1986: 288–89).

Gandhi hoped to "resuscitate" the varna system in his Indian ashram. For him, the ancient varnas did not symbolize a hierarchy of castes. Therefore, his ashram could not admit of Untouchability or any other distinction "of high and low." By belonging to a varna, Gandhi believed, an individual found harmony with others. In such a society, the carpenter's labor was as valuable as the priest's. All persons had equal status, and each individual could help the others with his or her special, hereditary endowment (Gandhi 1955 [1932]: 84–90). From the ancient varnas, Gandhi derived this contemporary principle:

Talents of all kinds are a trust and must be utilised for the benefit of society. The individual has no right to live unto himself. Indeed, it is impossible to live unto oneself. We fully live unto ourselves when we live unto society (Gandhi 1955 [1932]: 85).

41

India's essential spirituality and organic structure are the basic cultural meanings proposed by Gandhian experimentalists, which have now become common and public belief in India (and, often, common belief about India in the West). For many, these cultural meanings primarily configure consciousness of the past; for Gandhian experimentalists, they are also propositions about the future. They specify a program for India's future development, whose particulars I list below.

Sarvodaya

India's age-old concern for spirituality means that a revolutionary program must begin with individual change of consciousness, that is, an alteration of human spirit, rather than just a revolution in economic and political institutions. Spiritual advancement and welfare, an "inward improvement" (Shi 1985: 126), not just material development, should be the major goal. Economic development cannot be separated from individual ethical uplift, and whenever the two conflict, spiritual welfare should have priority (compare Rao 1982). Secular progress alone is spurious, sinful, alienating, and ultimately nonegalitarian, as Western development under capitalism or socialism supposedly demonstrates. The first to be revolutionized spiritually must of course be the national leadership, whose personal reconstitution will ensure a proper revolution of national institutions.

Reading John Ruskin's *Unto This Last* on a long train trip during the South African protest, Gandhi (1957 [1927]: 299) recognized the future society India should strive for. Gandhi used the term "sarvodaya" to translate Ruskin's message, and this term came to symbolize the spiritual revolution prescribed by Gandhian utopia. Ruskin repudiated Europe's capitalism, its concern for "money-gain" and "coin-glitter" rather than the "true gain, which is humanity" (1967 [1860]: 86). In words that inspired Gandhi's "deepest convictions," Ruskin defined society's progress in terms of spiritual development. Not by uncontrolled material consumption and the greed it engenders, nor by unlimited production of goods and the debasement of workers it creates, instead, the order of society should be given by the principle:

42

THERE IS NO WEALTH BUT LIFE. Life, including all its powers of love, of joy, of admiration. That country is the richest which nourishes the greatest number of noble and happy human beings . . . The maximum of life can only be reached by the maximum of virtue (Ruskin 1967 [1860]: 88–89).

Gandhi took sarvodaya to mean "welfare for all," with Ruskin's special emphasis on spiritual satisfaction. The priority Gandhi gave to spiritual well-being led him to attack human meanness and personal selfishness with great vigor. Untouchability in the Indian caste system was especially abhorrent, and his first ashram in India almost failed because he welcomed an Untouchable into it. Throughout Gandhi's life, there were abundant instances when he gave of himself for the welfare of others. Never self-consciously grandiloquent, Gandhi took pleasure in small services as well as large ones. He was, for example, happy to iron the scarf of his political mentor G. K. Gokhale, when he visited South Africa (Gandhi 1957: 213). He found inspiration in tending sick family members and prescribing regimens for friends. He dressed a leper's "wounds" (as he called them) and later the injuries of Britons wounded in the Boer War (Gandhi 1957: 202, 214–15). Gandhi took spiritual strength, too, from cleaning latrines at the annual meeting of the Indian National Congress he attended early in his political career (Gandhi 1957: 224). For other nationalists, this was service fit only for Untouchables; for Gandhi, it well befitted a spiritual revolutionary like himself.

Advocating a revolution in spirit rather than simply radical institutional change, Gandhian utopian thinking fell between camps in the early Indian nationalist movement; it alienated one camp, because its emphasis on *spiritual* change was perceived as mystifying, and frightened the other, because the very same emphasis on spiritual *change* was regarded as dangerously revolutionary. Representing the former reaction, the nationalist B. G. Tilak asserted that politics was a "game of worldly people and not of *sadhus* [saints]" (quoted in Wolpert 1961: 291–92). For Tilak, any means was fair in politics; for Gandhi, if politics was revolutionized by spirituality, so too would national development be. The other, frightened reaction came from Bengali nationalists, who believed in what J. H. Broomfield calls "national radicalism" — that is, getting rid of British colonialism — but who feared "social radicalism" — reordering Indian society. Although the Bengalis also disliked Gandhi's appeals to the simple and moral life, they worried more about the social radicalism of the Gandhian program and

43

criticized it severely (Broomfield 1968: 149–51, 225). Broomfield concludes that the portrayal of Gandhian spiritual politics as centrist, between extremists and moderates in the nationalist movement, misses the point that this program was seen as revolutionary (Broomfield 1968: 161). Similarly today, the Gandhian advocacy of spiritual over material revolution impresses some commentators as a true revolutionary program (see Ostergaard 1985: 4–5 on "revolutionary Gandhism") and others as a deferment of revolution (see Chatterjee 1984: 155 for the concept of "passive revolution" derived from Gramsci and applied to Gandhism; also Sarkar 1983: 72 for the concept of "deferred revolution," and Frankel 1978: 11 for a portrayal of Gandhism as backward-looking).

The Simple Life

Disciplined consumption, another proposition of Gandhian utopia, grows out of the presumed subordination of individual desires to the needs of society. Basic needs should be met — the most radical phrasing is that wealth inequalities and income disparities should be limited so that the wealthy do not prosper by impoverishing others; but the unlimited desires generated by Western capitalism and socialism, and a national economy whose goal is to satisfy such desires, represent wrongheaded approaches to development. The main point, again, has to do with a revolution in consciousness, rather than in economic production: in this case, it means doing away with personal greed. Western socialism changes institutions, such as the private ownership of property, but it does not change consciousness. It "destroyed possessions but did not destroy possessiveness" (Rao 1982: 75, adapting a phrase from Gandhi). A true, Gandhian revolution would discipline greed as well as dispel poverty. In the short term, however, Gandhian experimentalists must personally detach themselves from possessiveness.

Gandhi's own commitment to simplification was sometimes sensible and sometimes not (by his own admission), but always passionate. After a royal audience, when reporters chided him for waiting upon the king in his scant Indian garb (loincloth, sandals, and shawl), Gandhi is said to have remarked that the king had worn enough clothing for both of them. He constantly experimented with a simplified diet, finally reducing his intake to nuts and fruit, and only added goat's milk upon a doctor's orders and his wife's pleading and, even then, mainly because he had become

44

seriously ill. At various times in Gandhi's life, simplification meant walking to his office in Bombay, rather than riding a bus; prescribing "quack" cures for his and others' ailments, rather than calling on physicians; reducing what he wore to so little that a hostile Winston Churchill could give him the sobriquet of the "half-naked fakir"; starching and ironing his own collars (when he still wore shirts) instead of employing washermen; and requiring Indian nationalists to hand-spin cotton thread that could be woven into clothing.

Swaraj

The cultural essentials of spirituality and individual subordination come together in the Gandhian notion that spiritual self-discipline by the individual underlies national strength — and true independence. Through self-discipline, individuals build up the spiritual and moral power needed to gain consciousness (gain Truth) of the world as it is and to confront that world. Gandhi's concept of *swaraj* best expressed this necessary conjunction of individual discipline and national strength. Throughout the nationalist movement, the term commonly referred to Indian home rule and, later, to national independence. Gandhi emphasized its relevance to the individual as well as the nation:

> Swaraj really means self-control. Only he is capable of self-control who observes the rules of morality . . . A State enjoys *Swaraj*, if it can boast of a large number of such good citizens (Gandhi 1965: 85).

For Gandhi, the most difficult of his experiments with truth, the one he never resolved to his complete satisfaction and therefore continued to test up to his last years, was the vow of *brahmacharya*. Although commonly associated with celibacy, which is only one of the disciplines it enjoins, the vow of brahmacharya in fact requires control over all the senses (Gandhi 1957 [1927]: 210). It is therefore the ultimate self-control. Even though Gandhi allowed that individuals themselves must work out the appropriate means of discipline, he made clear that for him the self-discipline of brahmacharya was absolutely necessary for truthful service to the nation. He wrote, in explanation of the vow he took in 1906, "I clearly saw that one aspiring to serve humanity . . . could not do without it" (Gandhi 1957 [1927]: 316; see also Gandhi 1982 [1909]: 84). Gandhian utopia does not require chastity of its adherents, but it does

45

stress individual control and selflessness in aid of the nation. It believes that in this way a strong national effort can emerge from the spiritual discipline valued in Indian culture. Self-discipline thus becomes an important short-term experiment for the individual, a self-preparation for the future utopia.

Swadeshi

A disciplined individual should serve his neighbor before he serves a foreigner. Gandhi vowed *swadeshi* in exaltation of the local, the native, and the national over the Western and foreign. Swadeshi means buying Indian clothing and burning Western cloth, by which Indians rejected the economic domination of Lancashire. It means buying home products even when they were inferior to imported goods, such as foreign cloth before independence (Gandhi 1965 [1925]: 76). That superiority is purchased, Gandhi admonished, at the expense of thousands of impoverished spinners and weavers in India. Swadeshi also means rejecting Western styles and habits and emphasizing that Indian customs were superior. Perhaps because Indians wearing the *dhoti* (an untailored male garment wrapped between the legs and covering the knees) were thought unmanly by trousered Europeans, Gandhi made his point by citing Scottish native dress:

> The Scotch Highlanders hold on to their kilts even at the risk of their lives. We humorously call the Highlanders the "Petticoat Brigade." But the whole world testifies to the strength that lies behind that petticoat, and the Highlanders of Scotland will not abandon it even though it is an inconvenient dress and an easy target for the enemy (Gandhi 1965: 74).

Indians should similarly resist foreign cultural domination — but never vindictively or punitively. Swadeshi does not aim to hurt the foreigner; it only hopes to aid the native and the local. Vowing swadeshi means buying from your neighbor, not from afar; it means going to your village barber, even if his skill is less. It means doing without goods that India did not produce. Above all, it means being proud of India and Indian things and resisting the sense of inferiority inculcated by Western domination:

46   If we have no regard for our respective vernaculars, if we dislike our clothes, if our dress repels us, if we are ashamed to wear the sacred [thread], if our food is distasteful to us, our climate is not good enough,

our people uncouth . . . , our civilization faulty . . . in short, if everything native is bad and everything foreign pleasing . . . , I should not
know what *Swaraj* can mean for us (Gandhi 1965: 74).

Before independence, swadeshi became one of the most successful short-term experiments in the Gandhian dream. Indeed,
experiments with swadeshi, primarily the burning of foreign cloth,
predate Gandhi's authorship, as we shall see in Chapter 6. Swadeshi also subsidized the formation of indigenous banks and manufacturing. Following independence, swadeshi experiments do not
involve destruction or condemnation of foreign goods. Rather, they
hinge on images of Indian self-sufficiency, on fears of multinational
entanglements, and on pleas to make do with simple and rustic
crafts or inferior manufactures from India rather than sophisticated
commodities from abroad.

Satyagraha and Ahimsa

Spiritual and spirited resistance against inequality and domination
is the Indian way, not the violent resistance of the West. *Ahimsa*
(respect for life) and *satyagraha* ("soul force" in the sense of nonviolent resistance) are the cultural meanings at the heart of the
Gandhian program. Gandhi was at great pains to distinguish his
satyagraha from the passive resistance and pacifism of the West.
Although he allowed that Tolstoy was the greatest modern expo-
nent of this doctrine and that Jesus had also lived it, Gandhi believed that "In India, the doctrine was commonly understood and
practised long before it came into vogue in Europe" (Gandhi 1984
[1933]: 90).

Passive resistance was a technique of the powerless, whose abject
status disallowed their use of violence. There was then no spiritual
commitment to nonviolence; it was simply a reflection of practical
necessity. Gandhi (1972 [1928]: 103–7) opposed his satyagraha, with
its moral commitment to nonviolence, to the passive resistance of
the English suffragettes. They embraced nonviolence because
"They were weak in numbers as well in physical force." But the
"suffragist movement did not eschew the use of physical force"
(Gandhi 1972 [1928]: 104). Europeans confused satyagraha in South
Africa with passive resistance because Gandhi did not understand
at first that Europeans took passive resistance to imply weakness.
As soon as he came to see this, Gandhi stopped using the English

47

term, "passive resistance," and even offered a prize in his newspaper for a suitable new coinage. Eventually he settled on satyagraha (Gandhi 1972 [1928]: 103–7, 1957 [1927]: 318–19), which,
when translated as "soul force," properly represents Gandhi's emphasis on the moral commitment and courage underlying such
resistance.

Without moral conviction, satyagraha would not bring about true
revolution. Just before his death, Gandhi characterized the nonviolent resistance of the thirty years before India's independence
in 1947 as actually passive resistance, the weapon of the weak,
rather than real nonviolent resistance, the nonviolence of the brave.
He saw what had happened in India as expedient nonviolence —
that is, the Indians could not do anything else, given British power
or their own fears — and therefore concluded that it was not morally persuaded nonviolent resistance (Sharp 1979: 99). The partition
of India and Pakistan, the Hindu-Muslim-Sikh carnage and pillage,
the statism of Nehru's Congress had all deeply unsettled him; he
went into mourning on India's liberty day. This conclusion, that
India had resorted to expedient nonviolence rather than true nonviolent resistance, gave Gandhi an explanation for his great disappointment with independence.

Gandhi also distinguished satyagraha from absolute pacifism, or
meekness under all circumstances, which he associated with the
West. In 1920, he wrote that "[nonviolence] does not mean meek
submission to the will of the evil-doer" (Gandhi 1984: 95). He
believed that under certain circumstances, violence becomes a
valid, even necessary response. For example, sometimes the individual might lack the courage to undertake satyagraha, yet be in
circumstances that demanded some defensive action. Tolstoy
Farm, Gandhi's first real ashram in South Africa, was infested with
poisonous snakes. Because only one person had enough courage
to deal with the snakes nonviolently, Gandhi reluctantly allowed
them to be killed when they became threats to life (Gandhi 1972
[1928]: 230–31).

Cowardice was always worse, for Gandhi, than violence. He
strongly chastised some villagers who had deserted their homes
and let their wives be molested in the name of nonviolence. Best
of all, Gandhi told them, would have been to defend their homes
and families nonviolently; next best would have been to use violence in their defense; the worst was to run away, as they had, to

save their own skins (Gandhi 1984 [1927]: 92). Sometimes violence was not only unavoidable but required:

> To allow crops to be eaten up by animals, in the name of *ahimsa*, while there is a famine in the land, is certainly a sin . . . I will have to use the minimum unavoidable violence, in order to protect my fields . . . I will have to kill monkeys, birds and insects . . . (Gandhi 1982 [1946]: 91).

A spiritual resistance also means a disciplined resistance. So many times in his life, Gandhi was ashamed of the lack of discipline among the poor. He deplored the unsanitary habits of the poor in third-class railway coaches or as boat-deck passengers (Gandhi 1957 [1927]: 384–85, 387). He was dismayed at a "hungry scramble" for sweets by beggars and other poor people (Gandhi 1957 [1927]: 433–34). As Partha Chatterjee shows (1984: 184–87), Gandhi's deep suspicion of mob action led him to emphasize the discipline enforced by the satyagraha leader, which would control the danger posed by the mob.

Gandhi's nonviolence, which became compelling in Gandhian utopia, came not from want of any better form of protest or from a complete disavowal of all violence but as a disciplined response to circumstances. For Gandhians, nonviolence is not a token expression of an individual's moral outrage, although it might start that way. It is a means to transform conditions, with justice and freedom as its ends. Nonviolence, although directed against an opponent, wells up from deep spiritual commitment, and therefore could never mean harm. If through courageous, spiritual self-sacrifice, nonviolent protesters could convince an opponent to recognize their common humanity, then the opponent would be shamed — but never forced — into abandoning his unjust behavior. One of Gandhi's early political lessons was that "pursuit of truth did not admit of violence being inflicted on one's opponent but that he must be weaned from error by patience" (Gandhi 1984 [1919]: 80); nonviolence is "when we love those that hate us" (Gandhi 1984 [1934]: 78).

Joan Bondurant compares Gandhi's satyagraha to various protest techniques found in precolonial India. These include sitting *dharna*, in which Brahmans coerced their opponents by sitting in front of their houses and fasting, thus making the offenders (and their souls) responsible for any ill that might befall them. There were also *hartals*, or strikes, in which shopkeepers, artisans, and other workers ceased their normal employments, or were forced to cease them (Bondurant 1965: 118–20). Gene Irschick (1986: 1281–82) also mentions the pre-British analogue of the present-day *gherao*, or "mobbing," whose victims are surrounded by protesters and denied access to water, food, and other amenities. Bondurant believes that Gandhi's nonviolent resistance, although it might appear to have used these forms of protest, has little in common with them, no matter that Gandhi did call strikes and did use fasts as means of satyagraha. The difference is that the precolonial protests attempted to coerce and harm an opponent into submission, whereas nonviolent resistance avoids any harm and never extracts revenge. Gandhi, for example, refused to renew his South African satyagraha concurrently with a strike by white railway workers. "I declared," Gandhi later recorded (1972 [1928]: 295) "that the Indians could not thus assist the railway strikers, as they [the Indians] were not out to harass the Government." Bondurant (1965: 118–20) suggests that the very use of these old methods by Gandhi but in new ways may have limited his ability to communicate a true sense of satyagraha to his followers. Gandhi would have called these traditional protest methods passive resistance and disowned them.[2]

For Gandhian experimentalists, India's spirited resistance, precisely because it is also spiritual, could never be confused with coercive protest, just as a liberating Gandhian utopia could never be confused with Western, that is, Soviet, communism, "which is imposed on a people" (Gandhi 1965 [1937]: 27).

Whereas so many other aspects of Gandhian utopia could only come true in a distant future, satyagraha can be lived in the present—indeed, it has to be lived immediately, for it is the means to bring about the future utopia. Gandhi's 1930 Salt March exemplified satyagraha as an ongoing utopian experiment contesting the current state of society. Gandhi decided to make his own salt and not pay the tax the British colonial government levied on it. He also chose to break the law publicly and dramatically. Setting out with a small, loyal following of the ashramites he had disciplined to nonviolence, Gandhi marched from his Sabarmati ashram to the Arabian sea, about two hundred miles away. Along the way, he attracted a mass following and much media coverage. When they reached the sea, he and his followers made salt.

The salt tax fell on all Indians, and Gandhi's protest overcame the sectarian, caste, and class differences that often separated Indians politically. Soon, Indians in the thousands were making their own salt, selling or giving it away to others, and marching nonviolently on the British salt mines. Gandhi's symbolic gesture against British colonialism quickly became a mass civil disobedience campaign. At first the authorities did nothing, but the public and dramatic way in which Gandhi flouted their regulations—and the many Indians who then seconded his protest—forced the British into action. Police brutally beat off the demonstrators at the salt works, and they just as violently rounded up and incarcerated thousands of protesters. Gandhi himself was arrested and jailed with no trial and no specified term of imprisonment.

The Salt March skillfully combined the essential elements of satyagraha: civil disobedience, morally committed nonviolence (implying noncoercion), and mass protest. Gandhi broke a British law, which made his civil disobedience against British power a real confrontation, but he could only be accused of threatening British colonial authority in a symbolic sense (in contrast, for example, to sowing mutiny among British Indian troops or blowing up bridges). It was hard to imagine that one Indian, or even many, making salt could coerce the British into leaving India. The colonial power stood to lose prestige and authority, not revenue from the salt the Gandhians made. The British could not ignore the confrontation, however. They had to defend their so-called "rule of law," but at the same time they were shamed by the repressive punishments they meted out to the salt makers, who were criminals only in official eyes. The fact that these "criminals" did violence only to British laws took even further moral authority from their violent enforcement. The satyagraha therefore succeeded in confronting and shaming the opponent without harming or coercing him. Again appropriately, Gandhi and the others who offered satyagraha suffered most. The truth of their experiment and their moral determination to carry it through were sorely tried by British brutality, yet the Gandhians endured; it could then be rightly said that their experiment with truth had succeeded. They had proved that the British had no moral authority in India. Gandhi's satyagraha was a real confrontation for another reason: most Indians perceived it as a true defiance of foreign domination, which meant both that large numbers of them were motivated to join it and that they were more willing to stay within the bounds of nonviolence.

Gandhi called off the satyagraha in 1931, for reasons I discuss in Chapter 8, but it was probably the most successful anticolonial protest British India ever witnessed.

51

Satyagraha after Indian independence became the major short-term experiment in Gandhian utopia. In the event, it became the significant point of struggle among Gandhian experimentalists, as they fought over the way to accomplish their utopian dream. When Vinoba Bhave gave up satyagraha, he took away the possibility of struggle and confrontation, as we shall see later. No longer able to confront the existing society in any forceful way, Vinoba's Gandhian experiments soon became utopian daydreams.

Trusteeship

India, if it follows its ancient ways, will not be divided by class conflict — this possibility, say Gandhian experimentalists, emerges from the strongly corporate Indian social tradition. Gandhi, like many other Indian nationalists, argued that

> class war is foreign to the essential genius of India . . . the Ramarajya of my dream ensures the rights alike of the prince and pauper . . . You may be sure that I shall throw the whole weight of my influence in preventing a class war . . . The socialism and the communism of the West are based on certain conceptions which are fundamentally different from ours. One of such conceptions is their belief in the essential selfishness of human nature (Gandhi speaking in 1935, quoted in Narayan 1980: 36; see also Gandhi 1965 [1946]: 32).

What else could one make of the ancient varna system of four interdependent "castes" than that it was a means of justly regulating society's high and low? There is then no ancient charter or modern necessity to expropriate the wealthy; as Gandhi maintained (1965 [1931]: 41), "we seek not to destroy the capitalist, we seek to destroy capitalism." Differences in innate skills and intelligence would not disappear under utopia; therefore, society would always have — and need to reward — its most enterprising and successful members, among them those capitalists who produced the wealth that could provide welfare for all. The trouble is not the capitalist, but the greed culture taught in capitalism's "gobble gobble school" (John Muir, quoted in Shi 1985: 195).

52   Gandhi steadfastly rejected class confrontation throughout the Indian independence movement. In late 1931, while under arrest, he took strong exception to this aspect of a no-rent campaign (in which Indian tenants held back rents from Indian landlords) that

Jawaharlal Nehru had launched in his home state of Uttar Pradesh (then called the United Provinces). Gandhi authored a resolution that denied class warfare as the motivation behind the no-rent campaign; it was only sympathy for the tenants' impoverishment that motivated it, he wrote (see Frankel 1978: 51–52). Gandhi assured land owners in 1935 that his Congress movement meant no harm to their property rights. Gandhi never dreamt of wholesale liquidation of wealth and forced property redistribution, and as independence drew nearer, Gandhi increasingly tried to discipline followers like Nehru, whose utopian vision included them.

How, then, are the rich to be disabused of their greed but not dispossessed of their wealth? Gandhi's concept of "trusteeship" demands a spiritual regeneration of the rich — in keeping with the ancient organic composition of India's civilization — that would provide for the poor. The rich are not to see their wealth as exclusive private property; rather, they possess it only as trustees of the poor. Should they hoard their wealth, should they use it to exploit the poor even further, should their only concern be self-satisfaction rather than social satisfaction, the poor must nonviolently protest until the wealthy recognize the injustice and accept the responsibilities of trusteeship.

Rather than class warfare, trusteeship in Gandhian utopia hopes to achieve a more nearly egalitarian society (Gandhi never believed absolute equality was possible or healthy) by giving the rich a chance to reform. The Gandhian utopia recognizes private property rights only when they promote social welfare for the many, and it asserts that the state has the obligation to regulate property to that effect. Just as there ought to be a minimum wage or a guaranteed minimum subsistence, there should also be a maximum income (see Rao 1979: 178). Overall, their sense of social responsibility must dictate to the propertied. If that is not sufficiently convincing, then the fear of class war ought to be (compare Gandhi 1965 [1946]: 38).

The trusteeship enjoined on the wealthy is part of a general emphasis on reciprocity as the basis for human relationships. Reciprocity incorporates the society through gift giving (*dan*) rather than impersonal market relations. Gifts may be of various sorts, depending on what persons have to share. Some will give wealth or land, others will donate labor, still others will dedicate their lives to humanitarian service. Therefore, Gandhi insisted, the poor can give gifts just as easily as the rich; his utopian dream can serve for princes and paupers. Generating donations of wealth, land, and

53

lifetime service became an important short-term experiment for Gandhian experimentalists, as they worked toward their ultimate dream.

Bread Labor

For Gandhi, rejecting Western materialism meant rejecting its technology as well as its human relations — indeed, the two cannot be separated. Western technology requires mass production and therefore large-scale mechanization, which Gandhi condemned. Mass production also demands the wage slavery of the masses. Bound to his work station but alienated from his labor product, the Western worker cannot avoid despiritualization. Much else is wrong with mass production. Not only does it produce mass consumption of unnecessary products, oversupply goods, and thus waste resources, it also produces massive economic inequalities. Furthermore, machinery, meaning modern technology, is inherently bad (Gandhi 1982 [1909]: 96); railways, for instance, carry off food grains to far markets leaving famine behind, transfer plague germs from region to region, and bring rogues rather than true devotees to pilgrimage centers. Good, Gandhi believed (1982 [1909]: 44–45), travels by bullock-cart; evil runs the tracks. So it is with all machinery — from trams to planes to electric lights and printed books. For the early twentieth-century Gandhi, modern industrialism and technology were everywhere inhumane. Wage slavery in a Bombay textile mill was no better for being indigenous than wage slavery in Lancashire, just as an Indian Rockefeller would be no more humane than an American one (Gandhi 1982 [1909]: 94).

Gandhi's answer was bread labor, a concept he came upon in reading Tolstoy (Gandhi 1984 [1928]: 161). "Bread labor" means self-provisioning. Individuals would produce what they themselves need — they would thus escape alienation and wage slavery. Bread labor is also a means of discipline; it compels the well-off leadership to concentrate on the basic needs and the plight of the "dumb millions of India" (Gandhi 1965: 186). Hand-spinning is undoubtedly the best-known form of bread labor. Gandhi required Congress workers to spin yarn a few hours a day.

54   Gandhi never tempered his deep suspicion of Western mass production and technology, but he did quiet his condemnation of modern civilization in the 1920s and 1930s and therefore gave dif-

ferent reasons for his distrust of machinery. He no longer based his condemnation on the moral emptiness of modern technology and the corruption it would bring to India's spirituality, or, in any case, he was much less strident on this issue. Instead, he shifted to India's other presumed cultural essential, her organic structure, and argued that mass production and heavy industry would destroy the essential character of Indian society. Gandhian utopia continues the distaste of the early Gandhi for modern technology, but usually justifies that distaste in the terms the later Gandhi embraced.

Machinery, for the later Gandhi, was still dehumanizing, but he had more hope that it sometimes could be made to serve a humanitarian purpose, especially when it was employed on a small scale. Sewing machines, Gandhi thought, saved humanity from drudgery, and Gandhi speculated that Mr. Singer must have wanted to spare his wife hard labor. Technology has to suit the culture, Gandhi came to feel — which in his judgment was not the case for heavy industry in India. In this notion, Gandhi anticipated many of the themes found in recent development literature: the concern for "appropriate technology," the idea of "decentralized economies and systems of production," the proposition that "small is beautiful." In India's case, the massive reserves of labor argued for a labor-intensive program; India's poverty additionally militated against a capital-intensive, heavy-industry scheme. Most persuasive, however, was the need to buttress the basic or essential segment of Indian society, the village. A capital-intensive, heavy-industry approach would condemn the village community; a labor-intensive, bread-labor plan would affirm it.

Gandhian utopia puts its faith in village industries, like *khadi* (hand-loomed cloth), oil-pressing, tailoring, and other artisan and small-scale industrial undertakings. Such village industries are a short-term experiment, a prelude to the full decentralization of production called for in the Gandhian utopian vision. Village industries would give employment to peasants during slack times in agriculture; they would require little machinery; they would provide basic foodstuffs or other subsistence items. Village industries are therefore labor-intensive and minimally mechanized; they also situate production in the village community rather than in an urban factory. Gandhi (1984 [1924]: 115) even admitted that some technology, such as the sewing machine, which was created out of love for humans (Mr. Singer's for his wife), would fit well with village industries — a typically Gandhian construction of what we might now call "user-friendly" technology. Gandhi also downplayed village industries as forms of bread labor and emphasized them as solutions to rural underemployment: production was for market sale, not for self-provision. Shortly before his death he did reaffirm khadi as bread labor. Homespun cloth, he said, should be for home consumption (see Chatterjee 1986a: 117–21), as he increasingly emphasized village self-sufficiency and political autonomy (see the sections on *panchayat raj* and *ramrajya* below). He did not revert, however, to his earlier severe moral condemnation of Western technological civilization; rather, the new emphasis grew out of his concern to preserve India's organic civilization. The Gandhian utopian vision, similarly, discontinued the heavy censure of modern technology and advocated decentralized, village industrial development because it is best fit to India's society.

Panchayat Raj

For Gandhian utopia, India's deeply rooted, organic, and consensual social order did not depend in the past on an all-powerful state and should certainly not depend on it for the future. Unlike much corporatist thinking, which sees the state as a powerful broker enforcing social harmony on antagonistic social classes, the Gandhian dream distrusts the state as a naturally oppressive institution and foresees a future without it. In the interim, Gandhian utopia pursues experiments in restricting and resisting state intrusion.

The seat of India's consensual and organic social order is in the village community. "We are inheritors of a rural civilization," Gandhi said (1965 [1929]: 108). For him, this statement of presumed historical fact was also a prescription for the future: "if the village perishes, India will perish, too" (Gandhi 1965 [1935]: 109). The village is the source of spiritual values, social order, and material production, as it is said to have been throughout Indian history. Cities are colonial implants — perhaps, even, social malignancies — certainly, foreign growths. A future, perfected India must build on her villages and make sure that they do not become subordinate to urban places.

56 Extolling the ancient virtues of Indian villages does not make Gandhian experimentalists blind to their current limitations. They recognize that corruption has gained a foothold, a result of foreign

conquest and colonialism, they maintain. Villages today as well as in Gandhi's day are tragic reminders for them of how much Indian civilization has lost. This corruption, whether it be the unsanitary health conditions that horrified Gandhi, or the social contamination of Untouchability that tried him even more, has to be removed. Village regeneration therefore becomes a major aspect of the Gandhian utopian vision. Whereas the Untouchable leader B. R. Ambedkar trashed India's villages for all time — "What is the village but a sink of localism, a den of ignorance, narrow-mindedness and communalism," he wrote (quoted in Kantowsky 1980: 90) — Gandhian experimentalists, acknowledging the same deplorable qualities, want to clean them up. For only then can India's villages be reinstated as the arteries through which the civilization courses, as they were long ago.

Panchayat raj, or rule by a group of elders, is a plan to reinstate autonomous governance to the Indian village, on what was taken to be an ancient model. Villages are to be remade into the "little republics" they were of old. That model presupposes a self-sustaining village economy and society, which reaches its highest expression in the adjudication of everyday village life by a small group ("panchayat" refers to a council of five, although the actual number is a minor point) of leaders. Panchayat leaders govern, rather than rule, through the admiration and respect of their fellow villagers. They authorize collective action and superintend cooperative effort. Their decisions, not decrees, are empowered by general approbation rather than force. They reach these decisions by consensus, and thus, on the small scale of village governance, they act out the rule of consensus, by which all of Indian civilization is ruled. The panchayats, in this way, at once embody and enforce village opinion — and they also enact the Indian cultural essence.

More myth than history, the image of a cooperative and consensual ancient Indian village community is nevertheless a powerful aspect of the Gandhian vision. Gandhians say that planning for a future perfected India must start in the village and then rise up to the nation. For the short-term experiment, the village panchayat must be restored and entrusted with setting programs of economic and social development; the village must be purged of Untouchability and sanitized. Another short-term experiment is to make education relevant to village life. Gandhi expressed this program in his idea of *nai talim* ("basic education"). For him, the best education was craft training, not Western-style university book-learning. Gandhian experimentalists maintain that village-level and village-relevant education is an important short-term experiment toward their final goal of village regeneration. The ultimate Gandhian dream is a fully decentralized development, which safeguards the political autonomy, economic independence, and social integrity of the village community. Only then will the village again become the seat of India's greatness (see Unnithan 1969: 42–49).

Oceanic Circles and Ramrajya

Gandhi in 1946 conceived of a future organic Indian nation, lacking hierarchy, cohering, rather, like one vast level sea, as discipline, reciprocity, and nonviolence ripple outward from every individual and village and wash over all of India:

> Life will not be a pyramid, with the apex sustained by the bottom. But it will be an oceanic circle whose centre will be the individual always ready to perish for the village, the latter ready to perish for the circle of villages, till at last the whole becomes one life composed of individuals, never aggressive . . . but ever humble, sharing the majesty of the oceanic circle of which they are integral units (Gandhi, quoted in Kantowsky 1980: 19).

In the Gandhian dream, India will be ruled by *ramrajya* — a "divine rule," a Kingdom of God on earth, in which there will be nonviolence, equality, self-imposed discipline or renunciation, self-enforced moral restraint, and therefore "prosperous, happy, and self-contained villages" (Gandhi 1965 [1945]: 96). In sum, it will be an "ordered anarchy" (Gandhi 1965 [1940]: 170) because the state will not need to exert control or exercise authority. In the ultimate dream, ramrajya, the state would exist only to represent the communal will of the many oceanic circles. As for a short-term experiment, Gandhian utopia argues, the less state the better. State centralism, bureaucracy, public-sector economic development, and their necessary concomitants — totalitarian governance, nepotism and general corruption, and waste — certainly should be distrusted and feared and might even have to be resisted.

For Gandhian experimentalists, competition for government office and dependence on state power or funding are inherently 58 dangerous and very possibly corrupting. At independence, Gandhi warned the Congress to become a voluntary welfare association rather than a political party if it wished to preserve its moral goals.

Latter-day Gandhian experimentalists have a similar mistrust of the electoral process and of political power. They are wary of electoral competition and state undertakings, rather than voluntary experiments, toward the goal of welfare for all.

Typifying Gandhian Utopia

Dennis Dalton (1986: 278) categorizes the Gandhian dream as anarchist because the state is distrusted and the society is made primary. Like European anarchists, Dalton (1986: 292–95) says, Indian anarchists, those I have called Gandhian experimentalists, require the individual to put society first. They presume an organic society in which consensus and harmony would be natural. Dalton proposes the anarchist label against W. H. Morris-Jones's belief that there were totalitarian aspects to the Gandhian vision. Morris-Jones specifically refers to the subordination of the individual to group consensus. Geoffrey Ostergaard (1984; Ostergaard and Currell 1971) also categorizes the Gandhian vision as anarchist, although he believes "gradualist" Indian anarchism shows greater acceptance of the state in the short term than "immediatist" Western anarchism does (Ostergaard 1984: 91). Detlef Kantowsky (1980: 198–201) typifies Gandhian utopia as populist because it is, among several other things he mentions, moralistic, loosely organized, ill-disciplined, anti-establishment, class concessional (that is, against class struggle) but nevertheless egalitarian, and fundamentally nostalgic. Margaret Fisher and Joan Bondurant (1956), however, characterize it as socialist.

Does anarchism, socialism, populism, corporatism, totalitarianism, or some other ism typify the foregoing set of cultural meanings? Gandhian utopia is all of these, as I hope to have made clear by my structural description. Perhaps it is closer to Western anarchism and socialism in some aspects, such as its egalitarian thrust and its distrust of the state. Other qualities, such as its emphasis on individual discipline in the national interest, on consensus, and on supposed Indian cultural essentials, link it more closely with corporatism or even totalitarian thought. Still other characteristics, such as its commitment to nonviolence, its strong rural bias, its concern for bread labor and nonpossessiveness may link it to Christian socialisms or perhaps to no Western model. The salient characteristics of Gandhian utopia — the very reasons I term it "utopia" rather than socialism or anarchism or corporatism — are that it was revolutionary and that it experimented with contemporary reform because it dreamt of a world that could be.

What remain to be shown are the "somewhere" and the "some-ones" from which this vision of "nowhere" came. Showing these particulars amounts to experimenting with a history of the singular, whose conception I struggle with in the following chapter.

$\mathcal{F}$OUR

Experiments and Innovations

> The Western conception of the person as a bounded, unique,
> more or less integrated motivational and cognitive uni-
> verse . . . organized into a distinctive whole and set con-
> trastively both against other such wholes and against its
> social and natural background is . . . a rather peculiar idea.
>
> *Clifford Geertz (1983: 59)*

We must now move from the previous chapter's structural approach to history, which portrayed the Gandhian dream as an
"anonymous" utopian vision, an untimed and unauthored set of
cultural meanings. Ricoeur's (real) "history" or Gandhi's "experiment with truth" requires another element besides the structural:
the singular, which I introduce in this chapter. The singular in
history, meaning an "event-filled history" with "great personages," must be chronicled and then combined with the structural
so that history becomes, as Stanley Diamond puts it (1964: 44), "a
thread of contingencies, woven by decisions into cultural forms."
This culture history therefore must take account of the contingencies of authorship and authority that made Gandhian utopia first
the "problematic" or experiment of individuals, and then a "generalized" utopian vision for the culture. Ricoeur calls for such a
history without giving specific lessons in doing it. In particular, he
does not say how to link the "singular" of individual intentions
with the "structural" of cultural meanings and material conditions.
In this chapter, I set out conceptions of the individual and culture,
informed by Gandhi's ideas, by which I believe a culture history,
both singular and structural, can proceed. I then experiment with
these conceptions on the culture history of what has truly been a
continuous experiment in innovation and discovery: Western science. If a Gandhian approach is truthful, it should comprehend

61

the "real" experiments of science and scientists, just as well as it analyzes the utopian experimentation with the Gandhian dream.

Individual and Culture

Among the longest-standing issues in the social sciences and humanities is the role of the individual in cultural change. Scholars who treat individuals as mere carriers of an all-defining culture have long opposed other scholars who approach society as an epiphenomenon produced by the sum of individual actions. Among the earliest examples, William James (1927 [1880]: 229) declared his belief in the "fermentative influence of geniuses" on social life, in opposition to Herbert Spencer's conviction that "Before [the genius] can remake his society, his society must make him" (quoted in James 1927 [1880]: 233). Both sides of this debate, however, assume the existence and separation — and sometimes even the opposition — of the two categories "individual" and "society," and differ only as to the character of their "relationship."

Raymond Williams shows that these categories in their modern sense are the construction of the last three or four hundred years. He suggests they are coincident with the rise of capitalism. In late sixteenth-century England, the definition of "individual" changed from its original meaning, a representative or particular instance of a general class or group, that is, the individual as an exemplar. The term began to refer to the individual "in his own right," an abstracted entity and no longer exemplary of any larger set. The term "society" also changed, from denoting a web of relationships, as in "the society of his fellows," to an abstracted and reified absolute. As early as the Renaissance and Reformation, but only then, the two positions that continue adversarily in late capitalism today were staked out: one stance is that the "individual man is the axiom, and society is the derivative"; the other, which Williams seems to regard as the weaker tradition (but it is the stronger in anthropology), champions an abstracted and reified society or culture over individuals. Concepts like "class" and "community" then developed to mediate the "relationship" between the individual and society — a mediation only necessary once the two concepts had been polarized (Williams 1961: 77–78).

Anthropologists for the past several generations have been willing participants in a scholarly confrontation that has served to reproduce these abstracted and reified categories. Leslie White's (1949: 233–81) fervid denunciation of the "Great Man" theory opposed Robert Redfield's (1957: 130–33) equally strong evocation of an American Indian cultural innovator. A generation of American anthropologists earlier, A. L. Kroeber (1952 [1917]), with his notion of the "superorganic" existing above all individuals, and Paul Radin (1933: 42–43ff), with his concern for individual biography, represented the polar positions in this debate. Outside the United States, too, (proto-)anthropologists have stood on either side. France in the nineteenth century saw Gabriel Tarde (1969) posit cultural change through the ripple effect of individual imitation, whereas Emile Durkheim (1938 [1895]) thought that a collective conscience representing society coerced individuals into identical action. In England, Bronislaw Malinowski championed his "plain" (he also called it "pure") functionalism, which took cognizance of the individual, or so Malinowski asserted. He contrasted it with the "hyphenated" functionalism of Archibald Reginald Radcliffe-Brown, which "neglected the individual" for the sake of overarching social structure (Malinowski 1939: 939n.).

The terms of this debate have not been very illuminating, however. Idealism and individualism suffused the Great Man or Genius theory of cultural innovation. Such notions dissuaded investigations of when and why great persons appeared and how great persons achieved their goals in actual social practice. The other position, that great cultural innovators succeed only when the culture is ready for them, has had equivalent limitations. It smashes all individual intention, all independent action, under a cultural determinism whose postulated durability and tyranny make it more likely to be brittle in actual fact.

The debate could hardly be illuminating, given the reified and polarized categories "individual" and "culture" in the making since the Renaissance. They committed scholarship to one pole or the other — they enforced either a cultural determinism that placed culture over the individual or an individualism that broke culture completely into persons. It was very hard to bridge the reified constructs. Ostensibly linking concepts, like "class," were often put forward in as deterministic a fashion as culture. Or, to take another example, the "self-regulating market" proceeded from much the same individualism as the Great Man theory. Thus, such linking ideas only confirmed the gap between the differentiated concepts.

Anthropologists therefore could not avoid choosing either the singular individual or the cultural structure, and, even when they hoped to encompass both, they found it very difficult to do so. Contrary to the motif Williams regards as dominant in the West, anthropologists gave preference to culture over the individual. The upshot was that anthropology could not easily deal with the relationship of individual consciousness and intention to cultural innovation and change, as I show in the truncated history below.

For anthropology, the cultural determinists, arguing that culture constitutes and compels the individual, have usually prevailed, although never to unanimous acclaim. Anthropologists have spent their energies disputing "materialist" versus "idealist" approaches or "ecological" versus "symbolic" orientations (see Fox 1985: 186–89), and they have strenuously disputed whether culture is a reflex of demographic, environmental, and economic conditions or a more or less autonomous symbolic realm. They have generally agreed, however, that "culture was the axiom and the individual was derivative," to paraphrase Williams.

Unfortunately, cultural determinism created a major problem for anthropology. If a culture constituted individual consciousness, and so human intentions and actions could only reproduce the culture, then individuals could not be agents of cultural innovation. Lacking an individual agency, anthropologists found it difficult to deal with culture change, and even when they tried, they were wont to speak of the "mechanisms" of culture change, like acculturation, rather than the actions of innovating individuals. Culture itself then had to explain culture change, as White insisted (see chapter 2), which only caught anthropology in tighter coils of tautology and teleology.

Some anthropologists, however, did claim the capacity to account for individuals. Malinowski, for instance, believed his plain functionalism to be superior for just this reason. The way these anthropologists brought individuals into their accounts, however, indicates just how little sense of individual agency they made and how much they confirmed "individual" and "culture" as reified constructs. Individuals entered Malinowski's analysis not primarily as conscious persons, with perspectives on their cultures and intentions about its reproduction or change; they came in as physical beings, possessors of certain minimal biological needs, to which any culture had to respond. Human agency came from the sexual, alimentary, environmental, and other requirements of the human organism, and even these, Malinowski (1939: 940–45) believed, were greatly modified by culture. Malinowski thus recognized culture and individual biology, but little individual human consciousness in between. Even though Malinowski asserted that individualism existed in primitive societies (compare Beteille 1988: 12–13) and allowed that individuals might have independent ideas, he believed that such human consciousness was "culturally null and void" until it was manifested "within organized groups" (Malinowski 1944: 45–46). For him, the way in which social groups organized individual intentions had priority over the impact of such intentions on society.

Ruth Benedict's anthropology, like Malinowski's, encompassed the individual, but also in a way that confirmed cultural determinism. Benedict denied any antagonism between individual and culture. The great majority of persons simply "assume . . . the behavior dictated by that society" (Benedict 1948 [1934]: 235). When an individual, congenitally or by upbringing, cannot meet these dictates, he or she is "unsupported by the standards of his time and place and left naked to the winds of ridicule" (Benedict 1948 [1934]: 250). Benedict thus allowed for two configurations: a cultural configuration that most persons obey, so that in the majority of cases, there could be no antagonism between individuals and their culture; and an uncommon personal configuration, which makes some individuals aberrant. Such "aberrancy" seems to have no role in social change; opposition to cultural dictates is as futile as Don Quixote's anachronistic chivalry, to use Benedict's own imagery. At most, Benedict pleaded for more toleration of the deviant individual, precisely because the deviancy, being quixotic, threatens no change to society.

In prescribing for American society, Margaret Mead saw the situation somewhat more complexly but still within the cultural determinist tradition. Unlike Samoa, American culture had room for many individual temperaments and produced them, but operated as if only one was right or normal. The result was high levels of anxiety and instability (Mead 1962 [1928]: 115–45, especially 144–45). Educating children to new ways was not sufficient, because no matter how they were socialized at home or in school, they would come up against the "iron strength of the cultural walls" within which individuals must act (Mead 1953 [1930]: 163). Instead,

65

people constituted by a "rich culture" must transmit it to children, and a satisfied and adjusted individual would then emerge (Mead 1953 [1930]: 161–64).

Even when Mead found the cultural walls to be "ever-yielding, ever-accommodating," as she did for Samoan social structure, individual initiatives proved ineffective. Its very pliancy conserved Samoan culture against the individualism it seemingly fostered. It simply yielded and accommodated, while individuals "with original minds and social ambitions slid, sated with too easy victories, into undistinguished grooves" (Mead 1931 [1928] 560–61).

The only kind of individual consciousness that Mead and Benedict recognized was either deviant or socially ineffective, or both. There the question of the individual's role in cultural change pretty much stayed throughout the 1940s and 1950s and even into the 1960s, as successive forms of cultural determinism, whether materialist or idealist — cultural evolution, cultural ecology, cultural materialism, ethnoscience, symbolic anthropology, and structural anthropology — reproduced the standard anthropological treatment, a compelling culture and a constituted individual. Well into the 1970s, anthropologists otherwise interested in the practice of culture portrayed individual variation as ultimately structured by their class or group affiliations. For example, Pierre Bourdieu, who in other contexts rejected cultural determinism, saw individual behavior as simply a variation on the social practices dictated by class membership (see Bourdieu 1977: 86, Greenblatt 1986: 33, and note 3 below).

A sharp break with this standard treatment began in the 1960s but proved relatively short-lived. At that time, some anthropologists stood cultural determinism on its head. Transactional studies, interactional studies, network analysis, or situational analysis — this orientation went by several names, but there was basic agreement that the individual was the axiom and culture was derivative. Society was the sum of individual actions and transactions. Individuals pursued strategies for gaining certain ends and manipulated social interactions with this intent. These individual strategies, multiplied by the number of individuals manipulating social relations and modified by the transactions that then resulted, added up to society. Social relations were likened to a game and society was seen as a playing field; culture became a set of rules that limited individual "moves" in pursuit of status, wealth, se-

66

curity, or whatever these same cultural rules specified as the symbols of winning (compare Bailey 1969; Cohen 1974).

This approach, a form of what I shall call "voluntarism" later in this chapter, did not link individual and culture any better than cultural determinism. For transactionalists, social life was a construction of individual intentions, and therefore cultural meanings were always negotiable within limits, as people played their status, wealth, or power games. The problem was: what set the limits, what generated the cultural rules? Could the negotiations of individuals give rise to the compelling character of cultural rules? Could individual manipulative strategies lead to group constitutive norms? Transactionalists rarely addressed this problem; they took cultural rules as givens. In the best effort, Fredrik Barth (1966: 18–21) imagined situations where cultural "entrepreneurs," by selecting one of several existing cultural meanings as strategic, cut off the options for social renegotiation by their followers. Although Barth successfully showed how such entrepreneurs institutionalized normative behaviors for their followers, his free-wheeling cultural entrepreneurs seem superior to any cultural conditioning.

Starting with individuals, the transactionalists ended with individuals, just as cultural determinists could only explain culture tautologically in terms of culture itself. The cultural determinists could not easily conceive of individual intention and agency; the transactionalists could not readily explain the constitutive and compelling character of cultural meanings.

The problem is: how can we combine the concepts of individual and culture but at the same time keep them distinct? Keeping them separate emphasizes both that culture has authority over individuals and at the same time that individuals are independent agents in cultural change. Combining them avoids having to choose one over the other or having to posit supposedly universal categories like class or market, outside of history, to mediate them.

Is there a way to conceive of culture that recognizes its constitution of the individual but not so much that individuals are completely compelled by it? Conversely, is there a way to allow individuals consciousness and intentional action, without assuming that there are free-wheeling individuals who are so unconstituted by their cultures that they can trade in cultural meanings without any restraint? Finally, is there a way to conceive a mediation of culture and the individual through historically determined intermediate groups, rather than through predetermined analytic categories like class and market?

As I noted in Chapter 2, Gandhi assumed neither an integral individual nor a determined culture, and therefore he did not posit a deterministic culture or an independent individual. For him, individual and culture were constantly interlinked by confrontation and struggle that limited and defined, constituted and enabled them both. Individual experiments in confrontation with the existing culture made for constant cultural innovations and, when successful, culture changes, which then constituted the basis for future individual experiments. The existing culture was born in opposition, but as it matured, it encoded forms of inequality and domination that had to be resisted by future experiments. Quite unwittingly, some recent scholarship fulfills these ideas about the individual and culture (much as Ricoeur's notion of utopia does). They translate what is in effect a Gandhian approach into more familiar Western scholarly terms and intellectual history. Roy Bhaskar, to begin with, shows how much a Gandhi-like approach differs from other perspectives on the individual and culture change.

Bhaskar's Transformational Model

Bhaskar contrasts four positions on what he calls the "society/person connection" (1979: 39). The "Weberian" position or "voluntarism" (Bhaskar uses both labels) holds that individuals create society or culture through their intentional social behavior. "Individualism" is the term I used earlier for the weak phrasing of this approach; the "Great Man" theory would be its strong form. Bhaskar labels a second position "Durkheimian" or "reification," which corresponds to what I have termed "cultural determinism." It conceives culture and society as external to and coercive of individuals. Scientific Marxism (Gouldner 1980 distinguishes scientific Marxism from critical Marxism), which pictured individuals as completely configured by the mode of production, also adopts a "reification" approach. Both the Weberian and the Durkheimian positions, Bhaskar argues, suffer from partiality (1979: 39–40).

The "dialectical" position, the third that Bhaskar recognizes, conceives culture and the individual as in continuous feedback. According to Bhaskar, Peter Berger and others adopting this position believe that culture constitutes individuals who, in turn, constitute culture, and so on in a continuing mutuality. This position must assume that individuals create culture, when, Bhaskar argues, it is evident that individuals are born into an already constituted culture. Individuals never make culture (including the system of inequality it encodes) afresh; they must always work with — and against — the cultural materials they are given. Nevertheless, insists Bhaskar, such work by individuals is essential, not epiphenomenal (as cultural determinism argues), because the culture can carry on only through individual social activity. Individual consciousness and intentions are significant because they motivate this social activity.

Bhaskar then proceeds to the fourth position, his own "transformational" model. The intentions and actions of individuals, as they bounce off the existing culture and society (including the production system and the system of inequality), can either reproduce or transform that culture, in ways usually unintended by individuals (Bhaskar 1979: 42–44).[1] Unintended consequences arise precisely because individual intentions must come up against an existing culture, including an existing pattern of inequality. The existing culture compels individuals and so is reproduced, or it enables individuals, in which case it is transformed. In either case, the outcome depends on individual intentions and the actions these intentions generate, as they come up against and rebound off the current set of cultural meanings, power relations, and economic conditions defining the society — and thus these intentions may never reach fruition.

Anthony Giddens (1984: 173) similarly speaks of the "constraints" and "enablements" simultaneously produced by any sociocultural system:

Each of the various forms of constraint are thus also, in varying ways, forms of enablement. They serve to open up certain possibilities of action at the same time as they restrict or deny others (Giddens 1984: 173–74).[2]

By extending an image that Giddens introduces (1984: 174), I can convey the "transformational" position that Bhaskar and Giddens appear to share (though Giddens uses the term "structuration" for his approach) and contrast it with the other three positions. The *69* image is of an individual in a room. The Durkheimian (and scientific Marxist) approach of "reification" would perceive the walls of the room as restricting the individual's freedom of movement outside, but within the room the individual would be unconstrained. The Weberian position of "voluntarism" would conceive of the individual's determining the room's dimensions as he or she wished. For Berger's "dialectical" approach, the individual would build the walls of the room, which would then restrict his or her mobility until the individual chose to step outside and rebuild it. The individual would always be able to renegotiate — and thereby recreate — the room's constraints on his or her movement. Finally, in Bhaskar's "transformational model" and Giddens's "structuration" approach, the walls of the room would not only limit the mobility of the individual, but they would also give the person certain spaces in which to exercise his wishes. Such openings may be likened to doors or windows; they are potential avenues of departure from the existing culture. To change the room's existing dimensions, the individual must find — and pass through — these doors or windows. Getting outside therefore depends on the openings provided inside. Once outside, the individual perceives the "iron walls" of culture from a new position; just getting outside therefore gives the individual a new vision by which it might be possible to reconstruct the room.

People must act within the existent even when they act against it, and in so doing they may preserve their existing culture or break out of it. In thus asserting that individual experiments with existing social conditions make culture, Bhaskar and Giddens come very close to what I take to be a Gandhian position. Two additional points will bring us even closer, however. First, whereas Bhaskar and Giddens emphasize that individuals may either reproduce or change their culture as they practice it, Gandhi was much more specific about the kind of cultural practice or social experiments that leads to change. Experiments must actively confront the existing cultural beliefs and social system. By simply practicing the existing culture, an individual would not be likely to find the way to change it. That is, there is not much chance that an individual would accidentally and unintentionally stumble up against — and out through — a closed door or window, even when the culture provides such potential openings. For Gandhi, as I understand him, in order to break out of the room and to renovate it, the individual must purposely knock up against the doors and windows, which, although they are weaker than walls, are always closed or locked. Then, after finding particular points of weakness, or potential openings, in the room and enough personal strength, the individual must throw them open or unlock them. Gandhi thus gave human consciousness and intentions a much more emphatic or decisive role in breaking through whatever passage points the culture provided.

The second point develops from the first. Even before breaking out of the room, an individual must have some incipient consciousness that leads to confrontation with the existing culture — that gives the individual the personal strength to search out the inside openings that may eventually enable breaking out. How does this personal strength develop? Bhaskar and Giddens maintain that it is enabled by the very culture and social system the individual eventually confronts — as the individual practices the culture, he or she may come to reject it and try to change it. Again, taking inspiration from Gandhi allows a more specific answer. Gandhi would probably not have conceived of a room containing a lone person; rather, the room would be filled with individuals mutually reinforcing their personal strengths and coordinating their efforts. Gandhi emphasized, in opposition to the Hindu notion of personal austerity as an end in itself, that individual effort, no matter how morally sound, was only self-serving until and unless it engendered mass support. Any experiment, any satyagraha, required a core corps of committed individuals that produced consciousness for itself ("soul force") while it pursued confrontation (nonviolent resistance). An individual, the reputed leader or author of a cultural breakthrough, might exercise authority over such a group, but at the same time that leader would find personal direction and social consciousness only from the collective effort. On the one hand, collective effort would facilitate knocking up against culture's "iron walls," finding the openings in the room, and then breaking through them. On the other, one individual's authority would facilitate making a composite floor plan and mapping the potential openings, drawing on the individual experiences and attempted breakthroughs of the others. Individual authority would determine which person was first out; collective effort would point that person in the right direction and give him or her the personal strength to push forward. Alvin Gouldner, to whom I now turn, takes a particular case of cultural innovation, authorship, to make the equivalent point: that group labor underlies so-called individual innovation even as the reputed innovator girds up and controls the innovative group.

71

Gouldner's Attack on Authorship

Gouldner (1980: 275) begins with a skirmish in Marxism's historiography: the tendency, which he deplores, to make Engels the author of vulgar Marxism while Marx remains "a demigod incapable of error." Gouldner then moves to a massive engagement against the simplistic notion of "authorship":

> The tacit but dubious methodological assumption is that we can properly impute differences . . . by comparing texts which bear Marx's name with those bearing Engels'. Differences between the two texts are then attributed to differences between the two persons because it is assumed that the names on each text indicate its *true* and *full* authorship, *and* that each of these is *independent* of the other . . . (Gouldner 1980: 276).

This notion of exclusive authorship is "a socially sanctioned illusion," enforced by a political economy that requires any item of intellectual production to be some *one's* property; it is a "societally standardized myth of origins" in an "individualistic" culture that believes some individual must be accountable for any text. Conceiving authorship in this fashion obscures the reality of intellectual production, which, Gouldner says, is always the product of collective effort:

> Behind each theory product, then, there is not merely the person whose name appears as author, but an entire group and tradition for whom the assigned author is merely the emblem . . . An author's name . . . is actually not the name of an individual person but of an intellectual work group (Gouldner 1980: 277).

For Gouldner, an intellectual work group consists of colleagues, comrades, students, spouses, and lovers, who inform the ostensible author in an immediate sense. Such a work group also includes others, distanced by time or space from the author, whose words or lives have had a more mediated influence. Often, authors appropriate the ideas of the work group, which are thereafter attributed to them. Gouldner speaks of the alienation of the work group's labor in this situation, because they gain "neither income nor repute" from their ideas, whereas the author profits. The likely victims of alienation would be the relatively powerless in the work group, perhaps often women. Sometimes there is partial "compensation" through acknowledgments or citations, although these too are at the behest of the author. More often, rather than outright appropriation, there is a complex authorship of ideas, which makes determining an exclusive pedigree impossible. Such an instance, Gouldner asserts, was the continuing interchange between Marx and Engels, perhaps most aptly illustrated by the fact that certain publications attributed to Marx were actually written by Engels.

An author is not an "inanimate puppet" whose articulation depends on the work group's ventriloquism (Gouldner 1979: 279). On this point, Gouldner improves on other critics of the authorship concept, as, for example, Lucien Goldmann,[3] who saw authors as relatively passive conveyors of the consciousness of their class (compare Routh 1977: 150; Williams 1971: 17). For Gouldner, the reputed author actively forges the work group: by recruiting helpful members; by dismissing unhelpful ones; by selectively appropriating the ideas of others; and by disciplining the members of a work group to effect better cooperation. Successful authors must enforce their domination and "authority" by securing the recognition of their rights of authorship within the group and ensuring the representation of that authorship as exclusive to the outside (Gouldner 1980: 278–80). They must also offer the work group "package deals" (adapted from Barth 1966: 19) that reinforce or strengthen the network and that cut off the possibilities of dissension, disaffection, and defection.

Just as an author is active, not passive, he or she is also not omniscient. Some collaborators may not be welcome, but the author may not be able to be quit of them. Furthermore, the outside world may assign an authorship the recipient would rather disown. Gandhi's hostility to the unwanted authority brought him by the title of Mahatma — "Often the title has deeply pained me" (Gandhi 1957 [1927]: xii) — echoes Marx's disclaimer, "I am not a Marxist" (quoted in Gouldner 1980: 278), that distanced him from unwanted collaborators.

Gouldner's critique of authorship is also relevant to understanding individual intentions. It reinforces the Gandhian attack on the notion of an integral selfhood. If we think of intentions only as integral to an individual, we simply authorize the idea that personalities, once constituted in childhood, thereafter give intentions to the person. If we think of an individual's intentions, however, in the way Gouldner understands authorship, as a product of a social network, we affirm the Gandhian notion of nonintegral and discontinuous personhoods in two senses. First, a person *over time* can undergo personal discontinuities and even revolutionary ruptures, and second, a personhood as we come to characterize it *at any one moment* is authored by a social network and does not exist independently of such a network. We see Gandhi's intentions and what they wrought in India, but these intentions, by which we define Gandhi, actually condense the ideas and actions of many others. Gandhi is a precipitate of these ideas, of this social network — not in a passive sense, but actively. He undertakes the leadership, dishes out the discipline, exercises the selectivity, and offers the package deals that authorize him as Gandhi, the author of Indian independence (see Chapter 7).

Culture and Individual "in the Making"

What then should be the relative weights of cultural constitution and individual intention in the production of cultural change? Let me now try to answer the question, posed in Chapter 1, in part by changing the question. The weights I propose will disappoint anyone expecting a quantitative judgment, a "how much" of one constituent as against "how much" of another. If such a measurement can be done, it can only be done in the context of history, where contingency — that is, the actual relationships among cultural meanings, the social inequalities they encode, and individual intentions — determines their weighting. To do so even in an actual historical situation requires a clear conception of "the individual" and of "culture." Therefore, my proposed weighting system is qualitative. It does not answer the question of "how much." Rather, it rethinks and redefines individual and culture to get a better understanding of the "whats," the relationships of culture and individual, that make up culture history and make for cultural change. The question becomes: what are these "whats" in any real historical case?

Following Gandhi's notions and also Bhaskar's transformational model, I suppose that culture is always concrete and always in a historical context — that is, it is always being made under particular conditions of time and place. Culture in this conception does not exist in advance of human action or social practice in history; it is not an immobile, oppressive, and consensual tradition or structure. Rather, it is a continuous outcome of individual and group confrontations, placed within a social field of attempts at domination and inequality. The anthropologist, after the fact, can construct a cultural pattern, but this pattern only exists in a specific

74

time and place and within a particular field of oppositions and conflicts. This does not mean that any cultural innovation is possible in a society at any time. The brake on cultural innovation is not, however, the deadweight of supposed cultural traditions; it is the entailments of the immediately pre-existing culture, the hard walls of the room that compel the individual.

The existing cultural meanings as they encode inequalities of power and wealth — that is, as they compel social relations based on current material conditions — compose these hard walls. Thus, existing cultural meanings are always weighted by material conditions; culture is always hegemony, or attempts to be (for this concept, see Williams 1977: 110–12 and Chapter 15), and, when hegemony is weak, domination and suppression. Cultural innovation is always a struggle against current cultural meanings but also against existing material conditions, because the cultural meanings are entrenched in relations of inequality. Thus, cultural innovation is always based on utopian experiment, in Gandhi's and Ricoeur's terms. Cultural reproduction is also always a struggle, but of a different sort. This struggle is to preserve current cultural meanings and their entrenched inequalities — cultural reproduction is always either a failed experiment, in Gandhi's terms, or an ideology, in Ricoeur's. Both sorts of struggle depend on individual intention, the last constituent to be weighted.

Following Gandhi and Gouldner, I have also employed in this research a conception of the individual very different from the "culture carrier" postulated by cultural determinism or the "individual manipulator" presumed in voluntarism. I have tried to see individuals as precipitates of social relationships with others; that is, as defined by their social practices and the webs of social relations these practices weave. The individual, rather than being preformed by early cultural indoctrination (as American, as Trobriander, etc.) or instinctual will (to power, to status, to wealth, etc.) gains consciousness, purpose, and self-definition only in social practice. Neither self-willed *ab initio* nor programmed by acculturation, the individual is always in the making, as chains of relationship and the ideas and actions that bind them (or break them apart) change. The intentions that we attribute to a Gandhi and by which we assign him authorship of a Gandhian utopianism can be properly weighted only when conceived as a condensation of wider social networks and the ostensible author's more active constructions of authority.

75

What, in sum, goes into making culture? One "what" is human intention. Intentionality is a complex product not only, or even mainly, of individual life-history, but of the life-histories, which are really social histories, of intellectual networks. The human intentions precipitated by such groups and the individuals in whom they condense butt up against the existing material conditions entrenched in cultural meanings, the two "whats" that make up culture and give it a constitutive character. Bouncing intentions off the existing culture compels certain outcomes and enables others, giving rise either to utopian experiments or to ideological legitimations. Cultural reproduction or cultural innovation then emerges, and, in either case, culture history is in the making.

Scientific Experiments and Innovations

As a general rule in scholarship, information used in creating conceptions cannot also corroborate them. The culture history of Gandhian utopia that follows this chapter is saturated with the conception of culture and the individual I have just summarized and with the weighting of material conditions, cultural meanings, and individual intentions that this conception carries. Furthermore, I have acknowledged that Gandhi, an important subject of this work, is also a significant source of the work's conceptions. Both the native's point of view, then, and my own author's point of view overdetermine the culture history of Gandhian utopia that follows. That history contains an intellectual "double exposure," or conceptual "supersaturation," that makes it now impossible (if it ever was possible) to disentangle the initial scholarly experimentation from the final conceptual outcome.

Would another culture history support these conceptions, however? In planning this work, I became convinced of the need for some supportive prelude to the supersaturated presentation of Gandhian utopia — a sort of prolepsis, coming in advance of that presentation, but also advancing it through comparison. Such a brief comparison would be in keeping with Gandhi's notion of experiment. Indeed, the more extravagant or exaggerated a historical case of continuing cultural innovation I could find, the more it might support the conceptions. But what other culture history would show sustained radical innovation, clearly manifested individual intentions, well-established systems of understanding, and deeply entrenched patterns of inequality? Again, Gandhi's thinking gave me direction.

Gandhi believed he was a social experimenter. He likened his dream and the experiments in truth it catalyzed to a scientific research agenda and the investigations it promotes. What better way to test a conception based on Gandhian notions of cultural innovation, of the individual and culture, than on the culture history of science? This history is commonly taken to show major innovations, in the form of theoretical breakthroughs or discoveries; the innovations are presumably based on experimentation; the intentions of individual scientists are said to activate the experiments; and these intentions and the experiments they engender confront existing scientific understandings and the scientific establishments that have a vested interest in them. Taking a look at how scholars see the culture history of science seemed a good way to preview the culture history of Gandhian utopia.

The first view of science I wanted was: what underlies and promotes scientific innovation, and is the process similar to the Gandhian understanding of utopian experiment?

Karl Popper and other philosophers of science have emphasized "contexts of justification," that is, the way in which scientific theories were tested, over "contexts of discovery," the initial creative insight that led to theory generation. This perspective, as Augustine Brannigan argues (1981: 5–7), shifts attention away from theory innovation, probably because Popper could not avoid acknowledging that theory is often generated by a scientist's vested intellectual (or other) interests, whereas he could argue that validation was objective (Brannigan 1981: 42). (Later on, I shall show that even the supposed objectivity of verification procedures has come under attack.)

Because contexts of innovation and discovery have been downplayed, inadequate individualist ("Great Man") or cultural determinist explanations of scientific breakthroughs hold sway. Individualist explanations sometimes simply assume that an innate personal creativity underlies scientific discovery. This view assumes precisely what needs to be explained. Another individualist explanation, convincingly demolished by Brannigan (1981: 27–32), argues that discovery occurs through "bisociation," that is, an event in one context, usually commonplace, is associated with another, novel context, as Watt did with teakettles and steam engines.

77

In this view, discovery comes through sudden flashes of insight. Brannigan argues, however, that not all bisociations or gestalt insights are correct and that not all discoveries seem historically to depend on such gestalt shifts. Therefore bisocation seems neither necessary nor sufficient (Brannigan 1981: 32). Brannigan (1981: 46–47) also disputes the cultural determinist explanation, that scientific innovations occur "when the culture is ready for them," because it too begs the questions of what a discovery is and how it comes about.

If scientific discoveries do not spring ready-made from innate creativity and are not predetermined by cultural necessity, how do they happen? Robert John Ackermann proposes a "technical" explanation. Although he recognizes that experiments are always theory-laden, the development of new experimental methods and instrumentation, he believes, may cause experiments to direct theory rather than the other way around (Ackermann 1985: 112–64).

Unfortunately for Ackermann's argument, scientists appear to dispute not only over experimental results, but also over what constitutes proper experimentation. In a review article on the sociology of science, Stephen Shapin (1982) discusses several empirical studies demonstrating that science has been filled with controversies over observations and interpretions of observational evidence. These studies also show that controversies break out over the nature of experimental methods themselves. Points of view infuse what is regarded as a competent experiment and what is not. For example, Martin Rudwick, in his monumental study of the mid-nineteenth-century Devonian controversy, finds that most of the observations made were not only theory-laden, but also "controversy laden" — that is, directed by the aim to persuade (Rudwick 1985: 431–32). Shapin (1982: 163) concludes, "reality. . .has no immediate compulsory force."

Not the physical reality they study but the social reality in which they work — such appears to be the compulsory force behind discoveries by scientists. Discoveries result from the confrontation between scientists holding opposing theories, especially when one group is established and rewarded and the other is not. Bruno Latour and Steve Woolgar argue that scientists direct themselves to an "agonistic field" rather than nature, and their agonistic field is like other arenas of contention in society. Contestation, negotiation, and confrontation over what constitutes a good experiment and adequate proof are like arguments among lawyers and politicians (Latour and Woolgar 1979: 237–38).

The "natives" themselves have at times appreciated this: for example, the participants in the Devonian controversy used the image of a military confrontation with a field of battle, maneuvers, routs, and the marshalling of resources. There were other images too, among them the image of a courtroom hearing or judgment. In science, then, there is always a field of competition, Rudwick says (1985: 435–37), even if open conflict breaks out only infrequently.

This work contests Thomas Kuhn's (1970) idea that reigning paradigms constitute a scientist's world view and make dissent extremely difficult. For Kuhn, normal science would see scientists working in near unanimity on the puzzles given them by a paradigm. Confrontations over ideas would be abnormal; they might be in evidence perhaps only at times of paradigm shift, when proponents of a new metatheory challenged an old guard's paradigm. Kuhn would thus see confrontations as epiphenomenal, the spin-off of periods when the empirical anomalies discovered in working a paradigm have doomed it. Those critical of Kuhn argue the opposite: that confrontations are endemic to science, that new thinkers continuously assail old guards, and that scientific establishments are routed not by empirical anomalies but by these very battles over ideas.

Ackermann, to begin with, says Kuhn overemphasizes the degree to which one paradigm replaces another as well as a paradigm's power to compel thought (Ackermann 1985: 47). I have already mentioned the discovery that one scientific community's empirical anomaly is another's incompetent experimentation. Acknowledging these points, Yehuda Elkana generalizes about the nature and course of scientific innovation. Knowledge progresses, Elkana writes.

> by a continuous critical dialogue between competing scientific research programmes with their competing scientific metaphysics and competing images of knowledge . . . in the flux there are no finished products, there is no elimination of the unknown, no strict separation of open problems from the solved ones and, consequently, no distinction between [contexts of discovery and justification] (Elkana 1981:45).

Discovery is an outcome of this social confrontation and opposition, just as justification is.   79

When Gandhi considered his social experiments akin to scientific ones, he perhaps did not realize that the likeness held true the other way as well; scientific experiments are also social struggles.

The vested interests of scientists promote this agonistic field. Confrontations over ideas are also competitions for position and reward, and the force of these material conditions compels intellectual battle positions. There is the same inextricable — and complex — mix of cultural meanings (for science, read "intellectual positions") and material conditions found in the wider culture. These vested interests and the material conditions that produce them go far beyond crude personal venality; they often involve visions of how science should proceed or what society should be. They are no less interested, however, for not being venal, as the following examples demonstrate.

In some cases, factors internal to the science may determine controversy, as when two groups of scientists take opposite positions because each group supports a theory or experimental practice that uses the particular technical skills in which it has invested (Shapin 1982: 166–69). At other times, external factors may be compelling, as when particular theories privilege certain classes. For example, eugenics was promoted by the British professional middle classes because it privileged meritocracy against hereditary aristocracy as well as against the laboring class (Shapin 1982: 186). Society's very composition may be at issue in scientific contests, as in the confrontation during the Restoration between Boyle and Hobbes. Boyle and his fellow experimenters at the Royal Society argued that the society should be open, with a privileged space for scientific work. Hobbes argued for a ruled society, where philosophy was free to follow any line in its speculations, but there would be acknowledged masters. This dispute about science was also a battle about the nature of public order and the political process (Shapin and Schaffer 1985).

Using the case of phrenology, Shapin shows just how compelling these vested interests can be. Nineteenth-century phrenology in Scotland represented not only a scientific position but also a program of social and cultural reform. It appealed to intellectuals outside the main positions of influence and authority, the established elite opposed it. Phrenology challenged the Edinburgh elite's commitment to Enlightenment environmentalism, which accepted the possibility of human perfectibility through adaptation. Phrenology pointed to what was innate and limiting in humans, especially the physiological limits placed on mental powers. Because there were innate limits to human plasticity, social reform could only proceed effectively after those limits had been measured — so said phrenology's proponents. They therefore heralded an observation-based method, in opposition to the elite's method of introspective philosophizing (Shapin 1979: 145–46).

Shapin shows how this social and intellectual confrontation compelled scientific investigations that superficially appear extremely esoteric. For example, phrenologists had to study human frontal sinuses because they seemed to contradict the phrenological notion that the exterior of the cranium reflected the interior of the brain surface (Shapin 1979: 149ff.). Much more recently, as an outcome of a political and intellectual confrontation in the 1970s, high-flux gravitational waves were deemed impossible, and by extension, this (intellectual but also status) "position" in science was compelled out of existence (Shapin 1982: 163).

Through such confrontations and by pursuit of such vested interests, scientific investigations are compelled in some directions, but they are also enabled by these very factors to push new lines of research or make new discoveries. It is the same pattern stipulated by the Gandhian idea of utopian experiments. By constantly contesting the existent, both social and scientific experiments may crystallize new truths. There is the example of the controversy between Pearson and Yule over statistical measures of correlation for nominal variables. His eugenics interests led Pearson to develop a particular statistical measure, whereas Yule, uninterested in such a measurement, did not (Shapin 1982: 190). Another example is the Devonian Controversy in the 1830s and 1840s, which involved two conflicting interpretations of geologic deposits and eras. The resolution did not come about by one of them proving triumphant — "it required the interaction of both," and this led to novel and unforeseen knowledge (Rudwick 1985: 405).

Scientific confrontations can compel but also enable quite unforeseen social outcomes, as Roger Cooter (1984: 265–70) shows for phrenology. As the nineteenth century progressed, phrenology lost its original middle-class base and became a popular, workingman's set of beliefs, although it still contained a strong antielitist element. This "do-it-yourself phrenology," as Cooter labels it, at times compelled the working class to attempt individualistic social mobility, which in effect endorsed existing social stratification. Other times, however, phrenology and its criticism of elitism en- 81 abled workers to recognize the system of inequality under which they lived.

If confrontations are the agencies of scientific innovation, it becomes important to understand who the agents of these controversies are. Historical and sociological studies of science demonstrate that the individual scientist is not the source of innovation, that some larger group is involved, but the limits and character of such a group are matters of controversy. Sociologists have used citation indexes and charted so-called "invisible colleges" to delimit a large-scale interactive scientific group (see Collins 1982: 44–46 for a review and criticism of this literature; also Rudwick 1985: 435). At the small end of the scale, scholars have done ethnographic studies of laboratory research teams (as, for example, Latour and Woolgar 1979: 237–38; also see Brannigan 1981: 87). The effort to set quantitative boundaries — to answer "how many" scientists constitute a group — seems futile, however. Much more promising are attempts to set qualitative, conceptual demarcations. Collins (1981), for instance, argues that "core-sets" of scientists — including those who agree or disagree with a particular research program, those who are actively engaged in experimentation and discovery on the topic, and those whose work will influence the scientific outcome — make up the significant scientific work units.

Several studies find what appear to be core-sets at work in the history of science. Robert G. Frank, Jr. (1980), for example, depicts the very strong scientific community centered in Oxford in the seventeenth century; it was the agency for the development of a new physiology. Although its members differed in specific orientation and temperament, they worked together to create a new scientific program of physiology. Rudwick finds a much less harmonious and integrated research grouping responsible for the solution of the Devonian controversy. "[T]he myth of the egalitarian research collective is in this instance as inappropriate as the myth of the lonely genius," he writes. The solution to the controversy came from "a collection of highly unequal individuals in far from harmonius interaction" (Rudwick 1985: 411).

Harmonious or hostile, large or small, co-resident or dispersed, egalitarian or stratified, long-standing or short-term — these variables define the characteristics of any core-set and determine that each is historically different. More to the conceptual point, Collins's core-set and Gouldner's intellectual work group — the terms label the same reality — both measure supposedly individual accomplishment in group dimensions.

In sum, science, like culture, is always in the making through experiments promoted by confrontations over what shall be the dominant orientation. Scientists motivated by a range of interests, just like cultural experimenters driven by utopian dreams, run up against entrenched understandings and powerful proponents of them. Bouncing off them, they are compelled to follow out certain experimental paths, but they are also enabled to follow those paths (or other ones) to unforeseen discoveries and innovations. In the process of their experimental journeys, scientists, and cultural innovators in general, only become recognized individual authors as their ideas and actions precipitate — even commandeer — the work of many others, in much the way that the white image on a photograph only exists courtesy of the black background. The culture history of science therefore confirms an image of culture and individual in the making. It also affirms a contingent culture history, based on the fact that struggle and confrontation, experiment and counterexperiment, have no determined outcome. As Elkana (1981: 5) puts it, if the assumption is that science could develop only in the way it did, then the research question has to be, How did what had to happen take place? But if the assumption is that whatever has happened could have happened otherwise, then the research question becomes of necessity, Why did it happen this way and not another? The culture history of science I have briefly presented would appear to allow the second question. By extension, this history has helped legitimate a conception of individual and culture in the making, which combines the singular and the structural to form a contingent history. In this way, it serves as both theoretical prolepsis and historical preview of the culture history of Gandhian utopia that follows.

FIVE

The World-System Laboratory

> What the missionaries seemed to achieve . . . was not the
> conversion of Hindus into Christians but the conversion of
> "heathens" into reformed Hindus.
>
> David Kopf (1979: 157)

Writing in the *Illustrated London News* for 18 September 1909, G. K.
Chesterton exercised his wit on the Indian nationalist movement.
Indian nationalism was neither very nationalist nor very Indian,
Chesterton asserted. He went on to give weight to his word play:
the Indians putting forth demands for home rule (they wanted an
independent, elected government for British India) belonged to an
elite that did not represent Indian opinion. According to Chesterton, they were a small and decultured group that existed in a false,
shadowed world — shadowed because they had been somewhat
enlightened by British education and civilization, yet they were
still partly darkened by India's obscure Oriental traditions.

These Indian nationalists therefore did not represent the true
India, and what they asked for in the way of nationalism was quite
inauthentic. After all, Chesterton argued, how could their nationalism be authentic when all they wished for was their own English-
style parliament, their own English-style elections, and their own
English-style liberties. Now, if they asked for a truly Indian independence, Chesterton maintained, the British should naturally
be required at least to listen to them seriously, but this sham nationalism hardly deserved credence.

84   Chesterton's fulminations profoundly convinced one reader,
who wrote home about them in 1909. This reader agreed with
Chesterton. He came to repudiate the brown Englishmen who ran

the nationalist movement — Macauley's bastards, as an Indian character in Anita Desai's novel *Bye-Bye Blackbird* self-deprecatingly calls them, after the mid-nineteenth century British official who wanted to produce a class of Indians British in all but their skin color — but this reader reproved them more gently than Chesterton. He came to repudiate the parliament the nationalists wanted; he agreed with Chesterton that it was not authentically Indian. And he grew to believe in a people's democracy that started in the little republic of the Indian village and built up in "oceanic circles" — village added to village — to form a national government. He also, because he was thorough to a fault, repudiated modern physicians and Western medicine (except for Dr. Kellogg's nut butter), trains, lawyers, printed books, telegraphy, and modern civilization in general.

Mohandas Karamchand Gandhi, not yet Mahatma, read Chesterton's diatribe while in Britain to plead the plight of South Africa's Indians. He wrote home excitedly, endorsing Chesterton's condemnation of an Indian nationalism that only aped the West:

> Indians must reflect over these views of Mr. Chesterton and consider what they should rightly demand . . . May it not be that we seek to advance our own interests in the name of the Indian people? Or, that we have been endeavoring to destroy what the Indian people have carefully nurtured through thousands of years? I . . . was led by Mr. Chesterton's article to all these reflections . . . (*Collected Works of Gandhi* [hereafter CWG] vol. 9: 426).

On the return voyage to South Africa, Gandhi reflected further and even more passionately embraced an Indian nationalism that claimed authenticity by declaiming against the West. In *Hind Swaraj, or Indian Home rule*, written aboard ship, Gandhi inscribed Chesterton's message as the credo for a different Indian nationalism. He went far beyond Chesterton's sarcasm and superficiality. Condemning ersatz Indian imitations of the West, as Chesterton had, Gandhi on the one hand broadened that condemnation into a fervid rejection of modern civilization and on the other hand used it as an acclamation of traditional India — and thereby as an apology for contemporary India's "backwardness." Gandhi first disowned a nationalism that

> would make India English. And when it becomes English, it will be called not Hindustan but *Englishtan*. This is not the Swaraj that I want (Gandhi 1982 [1909]: 30).

85

True nationalism, for Gandhi, had to disavow modern civilization and build on India's traditional strengths:

The tendency of Indian civilization is to elevate the moral being, that of the Western civilization is to propagate immorality. The latter is godless, the former is based on a belief in God. So understanding and so believing, it behoves every lover of India to cling to the old Indian civilization even as a child clings to the mother's breast (Gandhi 1982 [1909]: 63).

India needed no parliament other than the ancient village panchayat; no Western enslaving machinery when the peasant's plow had served well for thousands of years; no all-consuming Western materialism when India's wise ancients had counseled against luxuries and indulgence (Gandhi 1982 [1909]: 61–62). British colonialists, and the Indian nationalists who mimicked them, wanted to replace India's traditional strength with Western modern weakness precisely because they mistook strength for weakness:

It is a charge against India that her people are so uncivilized, ignorant and stolid that it is not possible to induce them to adopt any changes . . . What we have tested and found true on the anvil of experience, [however,] we dare not change. Many thrust their advice upon India, and she remains steady. This is her beauty (Gandhi 1982 [1909]: 61).

Disowning modern civilization in 1909, Gandhi already perceived his utopian vision in broad outline. What precisely brought him to this condemnation? Gandhi's personal development of resistance to modern civilization should typify the general process by which an alternative dream, such as Gandhian utopia, evolves. This chapter therefore begins with the compelling and enabling circumstances behind Gandhi's denial of modern civilization. We shall see that as Gandhi butted up against Western thinkers and their Orientalist stereotypes of India, both positive and negative, he developed a utopian resistance to British colonialism and Western civilization — in other words, he denied an existing system of domination and the cultural meaning it sponsored. We can then relate Gandhi's personal story — a history of the singular — to the general processes by which resistance to Western domination arises in what I conceive as the world system of cultural domination, with Europe (and, most saliently for India, Britain) at its core. This constitutes a structural history.

Englishtan versus Wisdom-land

Stephen Hay argues that Gandhi's rejection of modern civilization rested on the model of the Jain path to liberation of the soul, which was "so deeply imprinted on his mind that he did not even think of it as a Jaina one" (Hay 1978: 127). It is impossible to refute outright an argument that speaks of Gandhi's public espousals in terms of deeply rooted understandings from his early life.[1] Still, there are good reasons to question whether long-latent beliefs can explain Gandhi's resistance; put another way, the influence of the Jain religion is not a sufficient explanation for that resistance. Jainism, which counseled nonviolence and nonattachment, may have been an important early influence on Gandhi — but if its influence was indeed so early and so important, why did Gandhi wait to reject modern civilization and "Englishtan" until 1909, when he was forty years old? Even Hay allows that Gandhi's disenchantment with modern, rather than Western, civilization developed as he prepared a talk on "The East and the West" for a British pacifist society (Hay 1978: 125). Gandhi delivered this talk on 13 October 1909 (CWG 9: 477).

Let us look into Gandhi's immediately previous history to see if it throws light on what led to his supposed realization of his Jain imprinting. Gandhi stated right after his talk to the pacifists (CWG 9: 478) that "the thing was brewing in my mind," and in a letter of 14 October 1909, he maintained that his ideas were not "new but they have only now assumed such a concrete form and taken a violent possession of me" (CWG 9: 481).

Did Gandhi's "not new" condemnation in 1909 in fact go back to a Jain past brewing in his mind over many years? It does not seem so. Gandhi's condemnation of an Indian nationalism premised on modern civilization was rapid. In 1906 he thought he would rather live in London than anywhere else (Hunt 1978: 143), but by 1909 he was of a much different mind. Gandhi suggested that London might be necessary to visit, but "I am definitely of the view that it is altogether undesirable for anyone to . . . live here" (CWG 9: 389). What made London deplorable in 1909 was modern civilization:

> We have trains running underground; there are telegraph wires already hanging over us, and outside, on the roads, there is the deafening noise of trains. If you now have planes flying in the air, take

it that people will be done to death. Looking at this land, I at any rate
have grown disillusioned with Western civilization (CWG 9: 426).

Modern civilization had not just come to London between 1906
and 1909. What, then, had come to Gandhi over this short period
that enabled his disillusion? Perhaps one factor was the strong
influence of the vegetarian and Theosophist Edward Maitland during Gandhi's early days in South Africa. Maitland corresponded
with Gandhi and sent him books; in 1894 Gandhi advertised himself
as an agent for Maitland's Esoteric Christian Union in Natal. This
organization stood in opposition to "present-day materialism"
(Hay 1970: 278). Sometime after 1906, he reread Tolstoy's affirmation of nonviolence in *The Kingdom of God Is within You*, which
proved much more affecting the second time (Green 1983: 89). Still,
even as late as 1907, Gandhi continued to believe in the benefits
of British rule and Western education (Swan 1985: 143–45).

Then in the spring of 1908 Gandhi translated Ruskin's *Unto This
Last*, which he had read for the first time some years earlier. That
first reading had led him to set up his first experimental community, the Phoenix settlement, in 1904. Ruskin was an important
authority for Gandhi, as I indicated in Chapter 3. Gandhi played
off Ruskin's condemnation of capitalist political economy to argue
that British commercialism and industrialism were unsuitable for
India (Hunt 1978: 144). Introducing his translation of Ruskin (spring
1908), Gandhi allowed that imitating the West in some ways might
be necessary, but that "many Western ideas are wrong" (CWG 8:
239–41). In a talk to the Johannesburg YMCA in May 1908, Gandhi
distinguished modern technology from Christian progress, declining "to believe that it is a symbol of Christian progress that we
have got telephones . . . and trains" (Hunt 1978: 144). Although
he already regarded Western civilization as destructive, he also
viewed India as lethargic. Eastern civilization, Gandhi argued at
this late date, "should be quickened with the Western spirit," and
he saw mutual advantage in the meeting of the British and Indian
"races" in India (CWG 8: 244, 246).

His growing distrust of the West was further confirmed and
sharpened by what he read in London during 1909.[2] Gandhi absorbed Edward Carpenter's "very illuminating work," *Civilization,*
88   *Its Causes and Cure* (1921 [1889]), and its condemnation of modern
civilization. Carpenter, who called ancient India "the Wisdom-
land" (Carpenter 1910: 355), in recognition of its spiritual superi-

ority to the West, led Gandhi to see clearly and afresh the Indian nationalist problem. Gandhi warned his correspondent Polak in a letter of 8 September 1909 that during a previous trip to Bombay Polak had seen "Westernized India and not real India." Gandhi also said that he issued this warning upon reading Carpenter's book (CWG 9: 396). Shortly thereafter he read Chesterton's article, and then, about a month later, he wrote *Hind Swaraj* aboard ship. Chesterton and Carpenter, in different ways, clarified his belief that his resistance should be not to the British people, but to modern civilization, and that a truly Indian nationalism — not the simulacrum of the West that Chesterton rightly ridiculed — had to build on ancient traditions and had to be a swaraj of the spirit. They helped Gandhi distinguish his nationalism from the Indian "anarchism" adopted by expatriate groups he also met during his London visit (Gandhi 1972 [1928]: 211). These other Indian nationalists disowned Gandhi for his loyalty to the British, not understanding his more profound disloyalty to modern civilization (Yajnik 1950 [1934]: vii–viii; also see Secretary of State for India 1907: 56–59).

This history of the singular represents the genesis of one experiment with utopia, but it is also exemplary of the general pattern by which cultural resistence to domination emerges. In this example, Gandhi's new nationalism is compelled by Chesterton's diatribe against what Gandhi shortly thereafter labels Englishtan in India. Gandhi accepts the definition of an authentic Indian nationalism that Chesterton thrusts at him — and so he embraces an Indian nation without parliaments, physicians, lawyers, and trains. Chesterton's view of the authentic for India is obviously shot through with cultural stereotypes — the notions, for example, that parliaments and elections are inherently foreign to India or that the Westernized Indian is fundamentally decultured and unrepresentative. Confronting the domination encoded in Chesterton's stereotype, Gandhi can achieve an authentic Indian nationalism only by rejecting Englishtan. Chesterton also enables Gandhi, however. By saying what the goal of an authentic Indian nationalism cannot be, Chesterton gives Gandhi the space to say what it can be: if not Englishtan, then a Wisdom-land utopia built on the ancient cultural essentials.

In positing this utopia, Gandhi is again compelled and enabled, in a reverse way, by the critics of modern capitalist civilization, Ruskin and Carpenter. Through their resistance to Western ma-

89

terialism and mechanization, Ruskin and Carpenter enable Gandhi's rejection of modern civilization. Carpenter, however, compels Gandhi's nationalism by stereotyping India as a Wonderland of spirituality and anti-materialism. He is of course not the first to give a positive image of India, just as Chesterton is not the first to offer a negative one. Whether negative or positive, these stereotypes are equally Orientalist, as we shall see; that is, they are equally products of the cultural domination of India by the West. In addition, they equally compel and enable Gandhi's utopian resistance to that domination. Chesterton compels Gandhi against Englishtan, and Carpenter and Ruskin further enable that opposition. Carpenter, however, compels Gandhi into an Indian nationalism based on the traditional Wisdom-land, which Chesterton enables by denouncing Englishtan. What brings forth Gandhi's utopian denunciation of the West is not some long-latent Jain influence, although this influence may have entered into it. Gandhi's dream develops early in the twentieth century as he struggles with and "bounces off" the negative *and* positive Orientalist stereotypes of India encoded in existing Western domination. This same cultural "rebounding" motivates resistance to cultural domination in the world system generally, as I shall now try to show.

Cultural Domination in the World System

Immanuel Wallerstein (1974) posits a "capitalist world system" that began to develop in the sixteenth century as the capitalism evolving in northern Europe spread outward to engulf the rest of the world. Conquering and subduing the labor and productivity of the New World, then later Asia and Africa, and extracting their raw materials, the northern European core converted these other places into a subordinated periphery within an emerging unequal world economy. Anthropologists have amended Wallerstein by insisting that a variety of local outcomes emerged as European core capitalism engaged precapitalist societies. Europeans did not roll over the precapitalist political economies without struggle: as European core capitalism transformed the rest of the world, it also generally had to accommodate to it. Many cultures that earlier anthropologists accepted as pristine represent, in fact, such a local accommodation of the world system — fur-trading American Indians here, South Asian peasant cash-croppers there, slave-raiding African Kingdoms elsewhere (see Wolf 1982; Mintz 1977; Kahn 1980; Fox 1984).

For Wallerstein, the world-system concept has had greatest application to world production and labor relations. I believe it also can say much about cultural meanings and cultural domination, however.

Alongside the capitalist world economy that began to develop in the sixteenth century, there grew up a world system of cultural meanings, within which core regions culturally dominated the peripheries. Through regional specialization and global stratification, the spread of cultural meanings around the world paralleled the unequal division of labor spawned by the capitalist world economy. Cultural meanings emanating from the core of the world system, in northern Europe, served as ideologies for its inequalities, specifically its exploitation of the Asian and African periphery. They attempted to displace or transform existing indigenous systems of cultural meaning, as the world system enveloped new regions — much as precapitalist forms of labor and production were swept away or harnessed to the expanding world economy. Varieties of these dominating ideologies developed as the European core encountered different cultures in the periphery.

The notion of "hegemony" that Raymond Williams (1977) derives from Antonio Gramsci informs my conception of a world system of cultural domination. The hegemony concept was originally formulated to get away from crude notions of class oppression, especially intellectual dependence on an assumed mystification practiced by the dominant class, and the false consciousness supposedly suffered by the oppressed. "Hegemony" emphasizes that domination can so infuse cultural meanings and cultural practice that it ceases to be an exterior ideology legitimating oppression. It is now internalized and appears natural. A system of domination can come to "saturate" everyday life

> to such a depth that the pressures and limits of what can ultimately be seen as a specific economic, political, and cultural system seem to most of us the pressures and limits of simple experience and common sense (Williams 1977: 110).

For Williams (1977: 112), hegemony is a process, not a structure: "It has continually to be renewed, recreated, defended, and modified. It is also continually resisted, limited, altered, challenged."

91

On the level of the world system, cultural domination or attempted cultural domination represented a process of hegemony by the European core. A variety of ideologies, allied in their pejorative image of peripheral cultures, enacted this process. For India, an ideology of domination developed and became a worldwide commonsense view of Indian civilization as Oriental.

Cultural domination in the world system generated and spread the set of understandings about the so-called East — but by necessity also beliefs about the so-called West — that Edward Said (1978) labels "Orientalism." Orientalism — the notion that there are essentially different "Eastern" and "Western" cultures, moralities, psychologies, societies, sexualities, and even races — "is a political doctrine willed over the Orient because the Orient was weaker than the West," says Said (1978: 204). Orientalism is a hegemony in the making. The West, through its political-economic domination, through its placement at the core of an expanding world system, invented the Orient not only for itself but also for those it would call Orientals. In the end — that is, when the world system and its core dominating ideology have engulfed the periphery — the Orientals themselves come to define their own culture according to the "indigenations" asserted in Western Orientalism. Said (1978: 42, 94) only hints at this point, but it is essential for placing the concept of Orientalism within a world-systems framework. (Otherwise, we end up reifying the categories "Oriental" and "Occidental" in our analyses.) It is also essential for understanding the kind of resistance to its own compelling cultural domination that the world system enables.

Late in the eighteenth and throughout the nineteenth century, in Britain *and* in India, an Orientalist image of India evolved. The admission of Christian missionaries to India after 1813 gave it further impetus. Whether ultimately condemning India or affirming India (I deal with the latter in the next chapter), this Orientalism depended on the same stereotypes. In its negative version, this Orientalism categorized India as passive, otherworldly, tradition-ridden or superstitous, caste-dominated, morally degraded, unfree and despotic, and therefore weak, backward, and unchanging. It thus justified British rule and anglicization as the only hope for a culture under a "sentence of reprobation" from God (Bearce 1961: 86). A few examples will convey the quality and scope of negative Orientalism.

India Orientalized

The missionary Alexander Duff deftly catalogued the horror and degradation of India Orientalized in his 1840 volume, *India and Her Missions*. His table of contents alone made out a convincing case for the need to Christianize India. In it, Duff promises "practical sketches of some of the leading superstitions and idolatries of eastern India," such as "Hindu murders and suicides in the name of humanity and religion" or the Goddess Durga and her "free-will offering, bloody sacrifices and grotesque processions"; then "various self-inflicted tortures [will be] described" (Duff 1840: xix, also see 220–83; on Duff, also see Kopf 1969: 254–61).

Moral degradation was everywhere: in the hereditary associations dedicated to evil, like that of the Thugs, in the so-called self-immolation of widows (*sati*), in female infanticide, and in Untouchability. There were, furthermore, idolatry, indecent ceremonies, slavery, ritual murder, and many other vile practices that all went to show, as Southey put it, "that of all false religions, Hinduism was the most monstrous in effect" (quoted in Bearce, 1961: 104).

Politics was no less a sink of inequity. Despotism ruled India and, for James Mill writing in 1812, gave proof of its backwardness and incapacity for self-governance (Bearce, 1961: 71). India was fit only for an arbitrary government, which at least, when it was foreign, was leavened by European "honour" and "intelligence" (Bearce 1961: 68). Native despotism, without the European virtues, had broken Indians; it explained their gentleness and submissiveness. The social system was equally bankrupt, beset by indolence, avarice, uncleanliness, venality, and ignorance. Hindus were morally, economically, and socially untidy — "more engaged by frivolous observances, than by objects of utility." Indian art, literature, and history fared no better with Mill, who found only "absurd legends" and inferior techniques (Bearce 1961: 73–74).

The failure of the spirit in India, its backward and uncivilized condition, ultimately rested on the depravity of Hindu religion. William Wilberforce wrote in 1813 that "Our religion is sublime, pure, and beneficent. Theirs is mean, licentious, and cruel" (quoted in Bearce, 1961: 81). Charles Grant, who believed Hinduism was "rotten to the core" (compare Kopf 1969: 135ff.), observed in 1794 what marvelous consequences would come from first giving Indians the English language and then giving them the Christian religion: "Men would be restored to the use of their

93

reason . . . [would rise] in the scale of human beings" (quoted in Bearce 1961: 62). And Mill's highly influential *History of British India* denounced all Asian civilizations (Kopf 1969: 238) and was no less scathing about Indian religion. He found Hinduism "gross and disgusting," riddled with supersitition, dominated by overbearing Brahman priests, and taken up with harmful ceremonies rather than with moral uplift (Bearce, 1961: 72–73).

So foul a culture justified a harsh cleansing, which could come, in the opinion of colonial administrators like Macauley, only by turning India from the Brahmans to the British, from superstition to science, from traditional lore to European logic, from the otherworldly to the utilitarian, and from the backward to the modern. Macauley worried much more about introducing European technology than about Christianity; his India of the future consisted of an English-educated middle class, with the leisure, status, and wealth to benefit from Western knowledge (Bearce 1961: 163–71). Only their skin color would tell against their Englishness.

As the nineteenth century gave way to the twentieth, the excesses of this Orientalist condemnation diminished. Perhaps it was because the battle to introduce English education, administration, and social conventions was long over — English and Englishness officially prevailed — and the Christian crusade to convert Hindus and Muslims was also past — overall, a failure. By this time, however, the essential cultural difference between India and the West was taken as a certainty, even if it was not often buttressed by the Christian evangelism and Western chauvinism of the earlier period.

The amateur ethnologist and professional administrator Sir Herbert Hope Risley as late as 1915 could suggest that Hindu religion might swallow science in India. He could believe that elements of nationality were missing from India even as he maintained that "there is in fact an Indian character, a general Indian personality, which we cannot resolve into its component elements" (Risley 1915: 299). Still later, another administrator, Hugh Trevaskis (1932, vol. 1: 71) of the Punjab, "explained" the backwardness of India by the pessimism and fatalism of Hinduism and Islam. Would-be advocates of India perpetuated similar negative images in spite of themselves; even when they started out positively, the entailments of the Orientalist stereotype led them to the old pejoratives. For example, Max Müller, who instructed Europeans on what India could teach them, nevertheless maintained (1883: 122ff.) that the Indian

94

"character" developed the transcendent, "not the active, the combative, and acquisitive, but the passive, the meditative, and reflective. . . ." Even for Carpenter, India became a good deal less than Wisdom-land at times:

> The Hindu especially with his subtle mind and passive character is thus unreliable; it is difficult to find a man who will stick with absolute fidelity to his word, or of whom you can be certain that his ostensible object is his real one. . . . (Carpenter 1910: 330).

If even India's foreign defenders were unwittingly persuaded by the Orientalist stereotype (as Chapter 6 shows in detail), could Indians themselves escape it? Orientalism in fact Orientalized "Orientals" into a world system of cultural domination. Ashis Nandy (1983) and Partha Chatterjee (1986a) maintain that British exploitation of India dominated the cultural perceptions and identities of its inhabitants just as it deformed its economy. They show that even in their anticolonialism, early Indian nationalists employed and reinforced Orientalist stereotypes of India.

Bankimchandra Chattopadyaya (1838–94), for example, in his youthful Indian nationalism deplored the backwardness of India in Orientalist terms:

> The present state of the Hindus is a product of this excessive otherworldliness. The lack of devotion to work, which foreigners point out as our chief characteristic, is only a manifestation of this quality. Our second most important characteristic — fatalism — is yet another form of this otherworldliness . . . Because of this otherworldliness and fatalism . . . this land of the Aryans has come under Muslim rule. And it is for the same reason that India remains a subject country till this day . . . for the same reason again that social progress in this country slowed down a long time ago and finally stopped (quoted in Chatterjee 1986b: 69).

The underlying fault, according to Bankimchandra, was the philosophical foundation of Indian religious beliefs, namely the medieval Hinduism of Sankhya.

Early Indian nationalists commonly looked back on a Golden Age when India had been strong and progressive, but they accepted the Orientalist condemnation of contemporary India. Rammohun Roy, among the earliest nationalists, and many others after him saw true India in the ancient Vedic period, which supposedly lacked the idolatry, the superstitious priesthood, the caste inequities, the primitive technology, the ubiquitous poverty, and the other corruptions of the present day. For these nationalists, the only means to return India to glory was to turn to the West. India's resurgence would come from Europe's rationalism, secularism, and liberalism (Broomfield 1968: 15–18). Their idea was to bond the progressive materialism of the West with the ancient spirituality of the East in order to reform a contemporary India that possessed neither (compare Chatterjee 1986a: 50–51). With the intention of restoring the past, reformist organizations like the Brahmo Sabha (founded in 1828), the Brahmo Samaj (1843) and the Arya Samaj (1870s) accepted the condemnation of the present (see Kopf 1979, Jones 1976). Progressive members of the Brahmo Samaj, strongly influenced by Unitarianism's social activism, worked for the social reform of Hinduism on the basis of Western models (Kopf 1979: 35–37). Other members, more concerned with "denationalization," still accepted a Western-based rationalism as the way to recapture India's former glories for the present day (compare Kopf 1979: 173–85; Broomfield 1968: 15–18; Sarkar 1973: 31–35). For the Arya Samaj, reclaiming Hinduism meant establishing "Anglo-Vedic schools," which tried to reassert India's ancient scientific and scholarly prominence by imparting modern, European-style education. Their battle increasingly involved opposition to Christian proselytizing rather than denial of modern civilization (see Jones 1976).

Except for a short period early in the twentieth century when he embraced a cultural nationalism (Sarkar 1973: 53–54, 62–63), Rabindranath Tagore was a latter-day spokesman for this pro-modern viewpoint. Regardless of India's golden past, the country's present degradation, Tagore believed, argued for an Indian universalism that would create a symbiosis of West and East (Hay 1970: 309–10; Kopf 1969: 298). Tagore disliked Gandhi's rejection of Western civilization, and he persisted in believing that India could learn from the West even into the 1920s, when a new Indian nationalism, in part under Gandhi's inspiration, resisted his universalism (Hay 1970: 280–85). Roy, Tagore, the Brahmos, the Arya Samajis, and other nationalists and reformers like them wanted to pour "the new wine of modern functions into the old bottles of Indian cultural traditions" (Kopf 1969: 205), because the current Indian vintage had soured. They might revel in the old Vedic spirit, but they did not take joy from contemporary India, as Gandhian utopia did. Their thirst for improvement was to be quenched by an imported Orientalism.

Cultural Resistance

If by the late nineteenth century, there was a world system of cultural domination — that is, a set of dominating cultural meanings constructing identity and self-perceptions in most corners of the globe — then how could an effective resistance arise? How could a Gandhian utopia emerge as a vision of a future that contested the Orientalist hegemony (or, more precisely, the hegemony process) in the present?

Several scholars have already provided what would amount to the simplest answer. The Gandhian dream, they maintain, grew out of Indian cultural traditions that proved resilient to the world system's domination. Richard Lannoy (1971) asserts that Gandhi spoke to the poor in their own language of tradition, and he explains one of the major visions in Gandhian utopia, the avoidance of class conflict, as a faithful reproduction of that age-old culture. In the "highly structured society of India," according to Lannoy (1971: 395), "the instinctive aesthetic desire to preserve the stable equilibria and *status quo* of society is more developed than the rational desire to change the forces and relations of production." Chatterjee similarly argues that Gandhi's critique of modern civilization stood "outside . . . post-Enlightenment thought" and represents a

> standpoint which could have been adopted by any member of the traditional intelligentsia in India, sharing the modes and categories of thought of a large pre-capitalist agrarian society, and reacting to the alien . . . colonial rule (Chatterjee 1986a: 100).

Gandhi's was an authentic and effective resistance, Chatterjee maintains. It may have used European commentaries, but it was in essence unauthorized by British domination, although it never completely escaped its control (Chatterjee 1986a: 42).

Unlike Lannoy and Chatterjee, Nandy does not see Gandhi as the nearly perfect representative of deeply rooted Indian cultural values, but he does believe that Gandhi's dream creatively used them. For Nandy, Gandhi operated outside the shared system of ideas that configured both British imperialists and other Indian nationalists. The Mahatma was neither simply a "genuine son of the soil" nor a "totally atypical Indian" (Nandy 1980: 83). Nevertheless, Nandy agrees that Gandhi championed and transformed folk values that "had remained untamed by British rule" (Nandy

97

1983: 100), and he thereby constructed a denial of the West that was also not of the West (Nandy 1983: 100–106; Nandy 1980: 130–31 prefigures this approach).

Although Chatterjee and Nandy (much more than Lannoy) recognize how powerfully British colonialism (what I see as a world-systemic Orientalism) configured the self-perceptions of Indian nationalists, they assume that traditional culture or parts of it remained undominated or "untamed." Their preserve of cultural autonomy, personified in the Gandhian vision, can resist cultural domination from outside: Gandhi can build an effective nationalist resistance, a utopia, independent of British Orientalist stereotypes. Although they do not say so explicitly, Nandy and Chatterjee permit such cultural autonomy within the world system because they might otherwise find difficulty in explaining how a world system of cultural domination can nevertheless internally generate a true utopian resistance to its ideology. But then they confront an equally vexing problem: are there really cultural crannies that remain proof against the world system long after its uninvited arrival?

John Richards (n.d.), following Immanuel Wallerstein, argues that the world system had had major repercussions on India as early as the eighteenth century, which would mean that Gandhian utopia occurred not in the first flush of indigenous resistance but after nearly two centuries of the world system's penetration and domination. By the late nineteenth century, British colonialism, under whose aegis the capitalist world system gained a purchase on India, had introduced fundamental changes at all levels of Indian society and culture. The objective was to make India pay (for general descriptions of change under colonialism, see Fox 1967, 1985; Jones 1976; Seal 1970; Srinivas 1962; Rudolph and Rudolph 1967; Washbrook 1976; but for denial of change, see Sarkar 1983: 72).

Some British colonial practices destroyed or deformed India (see Fox 1985: 27–51). By this time, for example, the British had successfully subordinated Indian agricultural production and labor to world commodity markets and international currency ratios. Indian cultivators in favored regions like the Punjab might still labor with ox and primitive plow, but they were no longer subsistence peasants. They produced wheat that helped supply British laborers with cheap bread. Indebtedness to moneylenders, which grew rapidly with British commercialization of agriculture, often forced these cultivators into producing cash crops. Cotton, exported to supply the English cloth industry, was a major cash crop in Gujarat, where Gandhi was born. Even in regions with no commercial value, the world system reached down into peasant villages and fields. The marketplace rather than custom increasingly determined land values and wages, and British law regulated land tenures and tenancy on capitalist principles. In cities, too, the British had their way. Indian weavers, for example, suffered while British mills profited, as the colonial administration set conditions that favored goods imported from the "home" country over indigenous products (for an overview of economic change, see Charlesworth 1982; Stokes 1959; Tomlinson 1979). The British way also predominated institutionally in the urban centers: in schooling, court proceedings, office operations, government functions, even in speech and medicine. When the indigenous forms coexisted — as in the cases of languages and medical treatments — they occupied an inferior place, not only by official fiat but also often in the estimation of the Indian elite.

Colonial domination also generated a new indigenous occupational category. Termed the "educated classes" by the British, it consisted of lawyers, civil servants, teachers, and other Westernized Indians who fleshed out the colonial administration or helped their countrymen cope with it. These educated classes represented elite groups that had evolved under colonialism and that eventually — some of them at least — came to oppose it.

Indian culture and society were not entirely anglicized, however. By British design, India's exotic beliefs and worship were to be "respected" and not interfered with. The colonial administration also believed that the "real India" would prove resilient — which might be for good or bad, the British thought. Caste customs, for example, were said, with regret, to endure.

Yet even when Indian caste and religion appeared superficially resilient, even where the British chose not to meddle, Indian culture was in fact fundamentally displaced and distorted. At best, the benign neglect of the British only fossilized customs: they might look the same externally, but their essential social meaning changed in the new British India. For example, when indigenous rulers were also major religious benefactors, temples had not only been sacred spots; they were also nodes of secular status. In their very rituals, they apportioned spiritual merit in a manner that recognized and validated the claims of the powerful. The British "hands-off" policy, however, recognized separate state and sacred realms. The colonial authorities therefore respected Indian religion only in the most ethnocentric way. The colonial policy redefined the Indian concept of the sacred according to British expectations of what religion should be about (in India, anyway). Temple rituals now concerned persons, families, and perhaps even castes; they were definitely no longer matters of state (see Dirks 1987).

At worst, the colonial power unwittingly provided new social arenas in which supposedly old institutions took on radically different roles. The British colonial state, for example, no longer supervised and maintained the caste hierarchy as indigenous rulers once had. Formerly independent endogamous caste groups joined together to form new caste associations that clamored for preferment from the colonial government. They invented new names and pedigrees that the British inadvertently recognized and sometimes validated in their Indian censuses and gazetteers (see Cohn 1968). Meanwhile, some other functions of the pre-British caste system, such as outcasting, regulating food exchanges between castes, and occupational specialization, weakened and even disappeared.

By this time, too, British expectations of India and Indians had even come to dictate dress codes, invent etiquette, and dominate other basic cultural practices (see Cohn 1989). What sort of cultural autonomy could persist under these conditions and after so many years?

The more complicated answer, yet the one I believe to be true, is that indigenous resistance, in the form of Gandhian utopia, grew up within the Orientalist hegemony of the world system. Indigenous resistance outside the world system's domination, I suggest, takes place only in early contact situations and usually involves armed resistance under newly strengthened indigenous leaders, as, for instance, the prophets among the Nuer (see Evans-Pritchard 1940; Sachs 1979). Sumit Sarkar (1983: 5) makes a similar distinction between primary and secondary resistance. Indigenous populations, primarily intent on protecting their continuing or recently lost ways of life, undertake primary resistance in the earliest phases of domination. Secondary resistance occurs later, when the indigenous society has changed markedly under contact and the leadership and its goals are different. Primary resistance to the world system usually results in genocide or cultural destruction. A secondary resistance like Gandhian utopia, precisely because it grows up within, and is compelled by, the world system of domination, has better chances of success. Its unavoidable accommodation to hegemony allows such resistance to struggle against domination and even prevail. Following the precedent set in Chapter 3, I leave India momentarily to examine another historical case, with which to validate this approach.

African Socialism as Secondary Resistance

Wherever and whenever the world system spread its compelling hegemony, it also enabled secondary cultural resistance. In Africa, a somewhat later victim than India, nationalists built utopian visions on presumed cultural essentials, too. Even in its particulars, the premises of African socialism duplicated the dreams of Gandhian utopia. They struggled, after all, against a common world-systemic hegemony.

Julius Nyerere, Leopold Senghor, Tom Mboya, and other African nationalists wagered their futures and the futures of their countries on an African socialism superior to the West's (see Young 1982: 101; Munslow 1986: 25–30). How could it not be superior, they argued, when African traditional society had been essentially socialist? Julius Nyerere observed that "Both the 'rich' and the 'poor' were completely secure in African society . . . Nobody starved . . . he could depend on the wealth possessed by the community . . . That is socialism" (quoted in Young 1982: 98). Like Gandhi, Nyerere took the village as the core institution. He wanted to recommit Tanzania's villages to socialism based on the *ujamaa* ("kinship communalism") they had supposedly enjoyed before colonialism (Young 1982: 113ff.; see also Yeager 1982: 46, 48). Nyerere and also Leopold Senghor rejected class struggle as an alien doctrine for Africa; individualism and acquisitiveness were also foreign. They argued for a "communitarian ethos" as a heritage for Africa (Young 1982: 98; Senghor 1968 [1960]: 93–94). In 1965 the Kenyan government ratified its African socialist plans by portraying traditional African society as basically democratic. In this society, the portrayal averred, leaders were not owners, because class divisions did not exist. Leaders were only trustees of the community's powers and wealth. Individuals had easy political access and there was real grass-roots democracy. Religion provided a community moral code. The result traditionally was "mutual social responsibility," **101** and this the government of Kenya wished to reinstate as the modern (Mohiddin 1981: 67–80; see 203–4 for what actually transpired in Kenya).

African socialism differed from Gandhian utopia in particulars when the world-system stereotypes of Africa did not match the Orientalism applied to India. African resistance had to accommodate to the type of domination, the form of hegemony, applied to Africa. So too with cultural domination: cultural stereotypes differed by region; the put-downs were fit to the cultures the Europeans encountered. Savagery, emotionalism, and uncontrolled passion were the usual indigenations imposed on Africa, rather than spirituality and passiveness. In resistance, Leopold Senghor (1968 [1960]: 68–72) asserted a special "Negro-African" way of knowing that depended on deeply felt intuition and passionate concern for the Other. He distinguished this intuitive and participatory African reasoning from the analytical and categorizing reasoning of Europeans (1968 [1960]: 74).

"Conflicted Intimacy" in India

Neither the Gandhian vision nor African socialism, it seems, had the cultural autonomy from the world system that Chatterjee and Nandy posit. Cultural resistance in the world system appears to develop in the same manner that cultural resistance arises within a single society's hegemony: internally and as a spin-off from that domination. In nineteenth-century France, to cite an instance provided by Richard Terdiman (1985), cultural resistance arose from within the bourgeois hegemony. Terdiman says that this "symbolic resistance," as he labels it, uncovers and denies the domination encoded in the existing discourse, or hegemony. Symbolic resistance depends on the development of "counter-discourses," that is, ways of expressing resistance to domination. Terdiman's term "counter-discourse" is thus tantamount to the term "utopia." His label, however, emphasizes that counter-discourses are always spin-offs of the dominant discourse: "Counter-discourses inhabit and struggle with the dominant which inhabits them . . . counter-discourses are never sovereign" (Terdiman 1985: 18). "Conflicted intimacy" is Terdiman's expression for the entangled relationship between the hegemonic discourse and the counter-discourse that contests it (Terdiman 1985: 16). He maintains that in the very act of contesting it, a counter-discourse reinforces the dominant discourse (Terdiman 1985: 65).

Gandhian utopia is in conflicted intimacy with negative Orientalism. In meeting this Orientalism head-on and contesting it, the Gandhian dream fostered another equally stereotyped Orientalism, and therefore it never completely escaped cultural domination in the world system. The Gandhian vision did, however, build an effective cultural resistance in India.

Gandhian utopia built cultural resistance by accepting the pejorative indigenations of India encoded in the world system and making them affirmative. What appeared in Orientalism as India's ugliness now became India's beauty; her so-called weaknesses turned out to be her strengths. Otherworldliness became spirituality, an Indian cultural essential that promised her a future cultural perfection unattained in the West. Passiveness became at first passive resistance and later nonviolent resistance; the age-old Indian character thus provided a revolutionary technique by which to bring on that future perfection. The inability of Indians to govern themselves except through state despotism became India's inherent rejection of the state entirely. The backward and parochial village became the consensual and harmonious center of decentralized democracy. Absent national integration turned into the oceanic circle of a people's democracy, where integration flowed from bottom to top. Moral degradations like sati or Untouchability became latter-day perversions of a formerly well-functioning and harmonious social order; they were brought about by foreign conquest and colonialism. Insufficient Indian individualism became altruistic trusteeship, and inadequate entrepreneurial spirit turned into nonpossessiveness.

Gandhian utopia, which struggled against the dominating ideology of the world system, was not independent of the world system, however. Its resistance stopped short of contesting the basic notion behind cultural domination: that Indian culture was based on deep-seated, relatively immobile, and age-old principles antithetical to the West and encoded in religion (and mainly in Hinduism). In conflicted intimacy, it could only shift positive evaluation from modern (Western) society to traditional (Indian) culture. Gandhi and the intellectual work group that authored the Gandhian dream accepted the ultimate Orientalism thrust upon them — that India was, had always been, and would always be radically different from the West — and then claimed a superior   *103* nationalism and a more humane society as the possible outcomes of this India, spiritual and organic.

The complex condition of such utopian resistance — at once a creation of and a denial of the world system — puts a heavy burden of struggle on it. Many times, as Terdiman suggests, it inadvertently supports hegemony. At other times, however, bouncing *off* hegemony, resistance succeeds in bouncing *out* of its domination, at least partially, and in setting new circumstances for society. Chapter 8 shows that successful experiments with Gandhian utopia before independence set up circumstances that significantly compelled India's politics and society after independence.

Conflicted intimacy also means that the authorship of Gandhian utopia is a complex process set within the world system, a point I develop in the next chapter.

Early Experimentalists

Passage, O soul, to India!
Eclaircise the myths Asiatic . . .

Walt Whitman 1926 (1871)

Annie Besant believed her mission was to awaken India. Reflecting on her first passage to India, in 1893, she wrote, "when I came to India, Indians told me that India was dead; they smiled sadly at my statement that India was not dead, but sleeping" (quoted in Dar and Somaskandan 1966: 40; also see Besant 1917: 211–12). India's slumber was due to a severe spiritual sickness, as Besant diagnosed it, even as she prescribed the ministrations to ensure it need not be terminal. The disease that threatened was "despiritualization," and its symptoms were "national degeneracy" and loss of "national spirit." Indians had caught the disease, according to Besant, by copying "English ways [and] English manners," which proved so infectious that

> The crowds of the so-called English-educated class were followers of Huxley, Mill and Spencer, and they had entirely forgotten their own literature, were contemptuous of the past and hence hopeless for the future (quoted in Dar and Somaskandan 1966: 40).

Besant believed that she and the Theosophical Society she headed were to be instrumental in waking India from this sickly slumber. Besant might have called it a self-cure because it consisted of purging India of foreign ways and letting its ancient traditions hold sway. Although India would cure itself, Besant felt she had a special gift for diagnosis, without which India would not be

105

revived. Her self-perceived gift permitted Besant to lecture Indian youth about their nation; it also legitimated her preparation of elementary and intermediate textbooks on Hinduism, to make sure that Indian children understood their culture correctly:

> I wish in these lectures to hold up to you Ideals which may help in guiding your conduct, in inspiring your lives, for India can only regain her rightful place among the nations when her children learn to understand her genius . . . (Besant 1904: 1–2).

In 1909, under attack from Indian modernizers, Besant defended the emphasis she and other Theosophists (as well as, she might have said, many other Europeans) had put on what they took to be deeply rooted Indian traditions — essentially Hindu values — for reviving India. Accused of buttressing Hindu orthodoxy against progressive forces, Besant countered that Theosophy under Madame Blavatsky, Colonel Olcott, and herself had initiated a revival of religion. No bond of unity would be possible in India, she asserted, until the value of the ancient faith was recognized (Besant 1917 [1909]: 217). Whatever her reasons, Besant could not deny she had spread such notions as "India and Hinduism are one . . . Without Hinduism, India has no future" and "[religion] is the foundation as well as the crown of the national life . . ." (Besant 1904: 165, 197).

Besant evidently was not struck by the contradictory prescriptions she gave for India's health. Her regimen required that Indians give up English manners and ways. As late as 1925, she was to say that India had "sold her birthright . . . for a mess of western pottage" (Besant 1925: 4). Concurrently, however, Besant prescribed an English medicine to cure India's sickness, namely, that Indians must swallow Besant's stereotyped — and European — notions of India's past constitution for the nation's future health.

Besant's understanding of India and of her own role in India, which I will recount later in greater detail, is one instance of what Raymond Schwab (1984: 24) calls the "condescending veneration" of India by the West.

This veneration became a major source for what I referred to in the previous chapter as affirmative Orientalism. Equally stereotyping even though less pejorative than the Orientalism of India's detractors, this Orientalism developed out of the conflicted intimacy between Indian nationalism and the world system's cultural domination. This chapter traces the authorship of affirmative Orientalism though the combined efforts of European nonconformists and occultists, especially the Indians by persuasion like Annie Besant (1847–1933) and Sister Nivedita, née Margaret Noble (1866–1911), and of Indian nationalists like Swami Vivekananda (1863–1902), Sri Aurobindo (1872–1950), and Bal Gangadhar Tilak (1856–1920). Through their affirmative Orientalism, they experimented with cultural resistance to European domination and thereby anticipated Gandhian utopia in many of its aspects.

The authorship of this cultural resistance is complex, a process set within the world system. European and American nonconformists used their affirmative stereotype of India to negate capitalism at home, while Indian nationalists marshaled these utopian ideas against a foreign colonialism. The acknowledged and unacknowledged authors of India's resistance to cultural domination thus arose within the world system itself, and their forms of resistance resounded throughout the world system, not only configuring a utopian future for India but condemning the dystopian present in the core of the system.[1]

This singular history — of multiple authorship — defines the intellectual work group authorizing the Gandhian utopia that Gandhi, in Gouldner's sense, ultimately authored. I have earlier referred to this work group as a set of experimentalists with (what later became Gandhian) utopia, and thus this chapter records instances of such Gandhian experimentation in advance of Gandhi's acknowledged authorship.

Conflicted Intimacy and Affirmative Orientalism

Analyzing the West's rediscovery of India in the period from 1680 to 1880, Schwab finds that German writers like Schlegel, Herder, and Schopenhauer were taken with the notion of India's superior spirituality. India, importantly for them, was ancient and Aryan. That this culture had possessed an antique spiritual wisdom elevated her contemporary Aryan kin in Germany above the Latins and the French (Schwab 1984: 76ff.; see also Müller 1883: 31ff.). At first, the British did not participate in this veneration, according to Schwab, because such a high image ill fit their colonial interests. By the latter part of the nineteenth century, however, a passion for India had developed among the Lake School poets Shelley,

Byron, and Coleridge, and there was an equal fervor among some American transcendentalists. As Arthur Christy (1932: vii) puts it, "spiritual values were added to the silks and spices which Americans imported."

This importation went on among the many experimental and countercultural movements that appeared in the United States and in Europe's core capitalist nations as the nineteenth century ended (see Green 1983: 97–100; Shi 1985). Because Unitarians perceived ancient Hinduism as also embracing monism, they looked sympathetically on India during their battles with Trinitarians. Theosophists and other Western occultists also believed that India possessed an ancient wisdom (Campbell 1980: 19). For late-nineteenth-century vegetarian socialists like Henry Salt, a vegetarian India proved that an ancient and great civilization could be built by humans who neither feasted on their fellow creatures nor cannibalized by capitalist wage labor their fellow men (Salt 1921: 64). The anti-modernist Edward Carpenter (1914: 71–72, 82–83) not only found release from Western materialism in Indian's ancient Wisdom-land, but also escaped the aggressive masculinity of the West by embracing what he saw as India's mild androgyny.

Movements opposing capitalist society and modern civilization, which welled up in this period, took divergent forms but had overlapping memberships. A Henry Salt, G. B. Shaw, Edward Carpenter, or Annie Besant could be socialist, Theosophist, vegetarian, atheist, and sexual libertarian in various combinations, sequentially, or even all at once (see Mackenzie and Mackenzie 1977: 76–77; Morgan 1944: 29–33). Similarly, India either as vegetarian, spiritual, traditional (not capitalist), passive (not Western aggressive), or gnostic (not theist) — in any combination of these indigenations — affirmed in one way or another an attractive antithesis for all these movements.

Veneration, or what Hay (1970: 314–15) calls the "Orientophilia" of India's "Western allies" encouraged positive Indian self-conceptions. Hay strongly emphasizes this foreign authorship:

> Paradoxically, the idea that Asia possessed a uniquely spiritual civilization was essentially a Western idea, ancient in origin but transmitted in modern times to English-speaking intellectuals in the Westernized city-ports of the coasts of Southern and Eastern Asia . . . Their very insistence on the importance of Eastern culture as a counterweight to Western Civilization thus betrayed the depth to which

men like Rabindranath [Tagore] . . . had been influenced by Western ideas about the Orient (Hay 1970: 51).

Nirad Chaudhuri also makes European Orientophilia primary:

> Externally viewed, modern Indian culture was based on a fusion of two independent and unconnected cultures, the European and ancient Indian. But in reality, before the synthesis was undertaken in India by Indians, the ancient Indian element had become subtly transformed by being passed through the filter of European thought and scholarship (Chaudhuri 1951: 447–48).

Ascribing the authorship of affirmative Orientalism exclusively or predominantly to Europeans is too simple. So is viewing it entirely as an indigenous response to foreign rule. There was joint effort by Indian nationalists and their European allies. To be sure, both parties worked with an Orientalist stereotype, but that stereotype was just as much at home in India as in Europe; it resided, in fact, in the world system. Tilak, one of the most important cultural nationalists at the turn of the twentieth century and therefore no friend of Western civilization, recognized Indian agency but also this altogether complex authorship when he wrote:

> Modern times are so strange that. . .we need a mirror to know the importance of our eyes. . . It was the articles of Europeans who studied our ancient books which made them attractive to our own people. . .we began to recognize the importance of the contents of our own home only after the foreigners showed us these contents (quoted in Wolpert 1961: 64).

Similarly, Kopf (1969: 7) sees an "encounter" between the British and Indians in eighteenth-century Bengal, by which he means to emphasize the mutuality of their interaction, and especially the respect the British accorded Indian culture. Bipan Chandra, too, argues that Indians developed "myths" about their former Golden Age, their superior spirituality, and their Aryan purity to counter British colonial distortions. Their notions may have had European origins, but they served as foundations of nationalist resistance. Because the myths were based on Orientalist stereotypes, however, Chandra (1969: 36–53) labels the nationalism they produced as "vicarious" or "backdoor."

The geography of its conception is perhaps the strongest indication that the authorship of affirmative Orientalism was jointly Indian and European, and that it took place within the world sys- 109 tem. It developed neither exclusively in the core nor in the periphery. Sometimes its authors were Indians in India or Westerners in Europe or America. More often, its authors were Indians traveling to the West and confronting it, or Europeans living in India and affirming it. No matter the place, these experimentalists with cultural resistance everywhere authored experiments with utopia, more often as belief but sometimes as practice.

Among these experimentalists were Bengali landlords, British colonial officers, members of the new British salaried class or "salariat" that increasingly replaced the petty bourgeoisie (Mackenzie and Mackenzie 1977: 250), civil servants and businessmen in India, and the expanding professional class of teachers, lawyers, clergymen, and physicians in both countries. They formed a new, increasingly self-conscious elite in a world system evolving toward monopoly capitalism at the core, imperialism in the periphery, and bureaucratic colonial states almost everywhere.

Experimentalists in Britain and India commonly arose from groups thrown up by these massive changes in the mid-nineteenth-century world system. A new salariat in both countries achieved its position by servicing the needs of expanding government and expansive companies under monopoly capitalism. In India, where colonialism was paramount, there was a shift (sometimes quite a rapid one) from serving the needs of traditional rulers and states to filling positions in the British colonial service or in the ancillary educational, legal, and commercial institutions colonialism created. Gandhi's father and elder brother, for example, administered the domain of an Indian princeling, whereas Mohandas prepared for the (British) law (Devanesen 1969: 95–146 reviews the effects of British colonialism on the Gandhi family). Even the Bengali landlords, the *bhadralog* I discuss below, had just gained their property rights at the end of the eighteenth century, when the British colonial government had rationalized Indian land tenures in terms of capitalist economy.

Not only in social origins, but also in the way they sought intellectual authority, experimentalists were products of the world system. They tuned into the emerging world community of intellectual counter-discourse concerning religion, art, philosophy, politics, and society. In citing authorities for his diatribe against modern civilization in *Hind Swaraj*, for example, Gandhi (1982 [1909]: 105–10) mentions works by eleven Europeans (six by Tolstoy alone) and only two Indians, and both of the Indian pieces are in

English. This emerging intellectual community for India was in large part compelled but also enabled by British colonialism, which introduced a top-heavy educational system, biased in favor of universities employing British curricula. For this reason, British occultists and nonconformists and Indian nationalists read the same texts and spoke a common intellectual language. Another enabling factor was the emerging world system of reliable and relatively speedy communications and transportation. Tolstoy wrote a letter advocating nonviolent civil disobedience to an expatriate Indian in Canada; the letter was later published by another Indian (Gandhi) in South Africa; Gandhi probably had first learned of civil disobedience by reading a biography of Henry Thoreau written by Henry Salt, a fellow member of the vegetarian society Gandhi had joined during his education for the bar in Britain (Harding in Thoreau 1968: 332).

Experimentalists before Gandhian Authorship

One of the earliest areas and periods of joint authorship transpired, naturally enough, in one of the first regions of India to come under direct British domination. The encounter between the British and Bengalis in eighteenth-century and early-nineteenth-century eastern India led to what has been called the Bengal Renaissance, which, like the European Renaissance, depended on discovering a glorious past. British colonial administrators, who also served as amateur Oriental scholars, joined with Bengali *bhadralog* (large landholders), who also acted as an indigenous intelligentsia. Together, they found, or, what is much the same thing, invented a golden age for India in her ancient Vedic past. This age, to their minds so different from India's deteriorated contemporary condition, gave proof of her great civilization against the attacks of missionaries and the other agents of pejorative Orientalism (Kopf 1969: 156ff. presents the opposing viewpoints). Westernization was necessary, however, for these early Bengali experimentalists belonging to the Brahmo Samaj and Young Bengal, because India needed to be forced out of its recent decline (see Kopf 1969: 176, 200 on the Englishman Colebrooke and the Indian Roy; also Kopf 1979: 157–66, 173–76 on the Brahmos and Young Bengal).

Early in the nineteenth century, this emerging affirmative Orientalism began to champion Indian ways with much less equivocation, even tolerating or embracing the current customs that a previous generation had disavowed (Kopf 1969: 205–7). For example, Unitarian reformers had a profound influence over the pro-Western segment of the Bengali intelligentsia late into the nineteenth century. However, when the Unitarian reformer Annette Akroyd denounced members of this supposedly enlightened elite for very traditional treatment of their wives, she engendered much opposition. This issue of women's liberation, which was just as important to Unitarians as veneration for India, seems to have been the breaking point for many Bengali males ostensibly bent on Westernization (Kopf 1979: 35–39).

An alienation from the West evolved, and with it an affirmation of India progressed, now firmly in the hands of Bengalis. Often, like Rajnarain Bose and Swami Vivekananda in his youth, they had previously embraced reform through a thorough Westernization; these were Bengalis, in other words, who had participated with the British in the construction of a golden age for India as the first instance of affirmation. As the nineteenth century ended, they formed a camp of so-called "traditionalists," in opposition to other Bengalis, called "modernizers," who still adhered to the original affirmation they had constructed with the help of British veneration. Modernizers and traditionalists came closest at first in their condemnation of present-day India but differed about whether reform should be from within or imported. Later, they came to differ increasingly in their attitudes toward the present.

Traditionalists came to affirm India very differently, or, to put it another way, they affirmed a very different India. Idol worship in contemporary Hinduism now represented an effective way to fix people's minds on the divine; it was no longer to be disdained as a deterioration of pure Vedic worship. Sati (the immolation of a widow at her husband's cremation) could be defended as a valued tradition (Kopf 1969: 270–72). Even when these experimentalists deplored aspects of contemporary India, including popular Hinduism, they believed that reform should come from within India's own cultural legacy, rather than by a total replacement of the indigenous with the Western. Some Westernization was admissible to these reformers, but it could only be introduced with sufficient appreciation for Indian traditions and must be in keeping with them. Besides affirming sati, the Bengalis who founded the Dharma Sabha, for example, called for aid to the rural poor, Indianization of the civil service, and other social changes that were to take place within the context of indigenous, or what they took to be indigenous, culture.

Affirmative Orientalism in Bengal, which had first been motivated by confronting the disparagement of India by missionaries and colonials, now developed out of a confrontation between these Indian modernists and traditionalists (Sarkar 1973: 33–35), in which veneration *and* contempt for India in the world system were important factors. This confrontation was soon to be reproduced in Bombay, on the western side of India, and then throughout India as a whole. Out of confrontation came many experiments in cultural resistance that anticipated Gandhian utopia and many experimentalists who therefore coauthored it.

I now abandon this structural history for a brief singular account of some of these intellectual work groups. Even this account overemphasizes the authorship of single individuals, rather than the infinite regression of coauthors who helped authorize each of them. My purpose, however, is not to chronicle these intellectual work groups but to show how they preceded and precipitated Gandhi. Composed of both Indians and Europeans who "went Indian," these groups experimented with affirmative Orientalism and thereby presaged elements of Gandhian utopia. In the following account, I emphasize the specific elements they helped author.

Bengali Experimentalists

When Swami Vivekananda attended the 1893 World Parliament of Religions in Chicago, he was received as a "monk of the orthodox Brahminical religion." Contemporary accounts applauded him as a typical and influential representative of Hinduism, not as a spokesman for a new dispensation (French 1974: 55–56). He was to undergo a rapid spiritual evolution in the United States, however, which left him no longer simply the disciple of the Bengali saint, Ramakrishna, but now the initiator of a new religion of spirited and spiritual service, an invocation to Indians to affirm and then reform their own world.

In 1890, four years after his guru's death, Vivekananda traveled all over India (as Gandhi would later). In his journey, he may have encountered the poverty and backwardness that would later lead him to an activist spirituality (French 1974: 49). When he then went to Chicago, he confronted both defamation and veneration, which actualized his message to India and to the West about India. Before, 113 during, and after the Parliament, Vivekananda was exposed to the hopes for India's reform held by liberal Christians, which were friendly in intent, as well as the expectations of India's conversion put forth by Christian missionaries, which were much more hostile. Friend and foe alike drove him increasingly to defend India and Hindu society and to devalue the West. Vivekananda's "counterattack from strength," as French (1974: 58–59) calls it, depended on affirming India's ancient spirituality and her current advancement in spiritual wisdom, perhaps the most important component of Gandhian utopia. Vivekananda also denounced the materialism of the West and conceived of its modernity based on wealth as a degradation.

Vivekananda did not tell Americans in 1893 and 1894 that all was well with India, although he did underplay or ignore India's poverty and the plight of Indian women (French 1974: 58–59, 61). When he returned to India, however, he called for a new, national spirit of service to end poverty and to reform social life. This new dedication would emerge from India's inherent spirtuality, Vivekananda believed. All that was required was to change Indian spirituality from passive to active: from experiments with individual discipline, such as his guru Ramakrishna had practiced and prescribed, to experiments with active service, which were experiments in social and national discipline. Vivekananda required such spiritually derived social service from the other disciples of Ramakrishna, for devotees, above all, should have the spiritual depths to make such a dedication. Vivekananda thus foresaw the connection between individual discipline and national development later incorporated into Gandhian utopia, and he also gave an early authority to the idea that the welfare of all should proceed through individual service. Still another prolepsis was Vivekananda's emphasis on action, on confrontation with poverty and backwardness, rather than on passive and personal spiritual exercises. He once advised, "You will be nearer to heaven through football than through the study of the Gita" (Vivekananda, quoted in French 1974: 39). Vivekananda's emphasis on physical strength (along with action) was not authorized in the later Gandhian vision, but it became essential to Hindu nationalism, as I shall show in Chapter 12.

114   Vivekananda's mission encountered trouble among Indians and Europeans. In 1894 Christian missionaries, Bengali modernists, and

Theosophists all questioned his legitimacy as a spokesman for Hinduism (French 1974: 61). Orthodox Hindus had difficulty reconciling his belief that monks should be called to social service with Ramakrishna's more traditional message. After 1895, he followed his vision in private, by setting up small groups of converts in the United States and Britain and, in 1898, by founding a spiritual center (*math*) in Bengal (French 1974: 70).

A young Irish woman, soon to be a major experimentalist in Bengal, came under Vivekananda's influence during one of his foreign missions and left home in 1898 to join his center in India. The political sensibilities that Margaret Nobel took with her are in some doubt. Barbara Foxe (1975: 11–17) believes she left Britain supporting the British empire, in spite of her youthful socialism and the passionate support of her grandparents for Irish home rule. Foxe claims (1974: 48ff.) that Vivekananda forced Noble to reconsider her British patriotism after she was admitted to his religious brotherhood in 1898 and renamed Sister Nivedita. Other scholars, however, note her sympathy for anarchism, especially Kropotkin's idea of communitarian settlements and his evolutionary sociology that found cooperation, not competition, to be the basis of human progress (Majumdar 1986: 65; but also see Dasgupta 1986: 116–22). Kropotkin is said to have been a major influence on her from 1891 to about 1895 (Majumdar 1986: 65), and she did name him the "king of modern sociologists" in a 1912 letter to *The Modern Review* (Nivedita 1968: 395). In 1895, she opened a "Ruskin School" in Wimbledon (Reymond 1953: 29), which may indicate an early rejection of modern society. In the same year, when Nivedita was in London, she is said to have joined the "Free Ireland" group and begun working for Irish home rule (Reymond 1953: 28–29). Did she also at this time head the London center for Irish revolutionaries, as has been claimed (Burman 1986: 195)? At least by the early twentieth century Nivedita was acquainted with the writings of the Italian romantic nationalist Giuseppe Mazzini and with the history of Irish resistance (Foxe 1975: 169).

The European ideas Margaret Noble brought to India are significant because, as Sister Nivedita, she had an important role in the Bengali resistance to British colonialism and in Indian utopian rejection of modern society. Nivedita instructed Indian experiments in utopia in two ways. The first and better-known way consisted of the many lectures she gave throughout India, beginning in 1904. Her themes were the necessity of Indian unity at present — and the basis for such a unity, if only Indians would recognize their own traditions — and the possibility of Indian independence in the future (Foxe 1975: 165–66). An affirmative Orientalism and what appears to be a European-instructed organic nationalism urged her on. The other way in which Nivedita had influence is just as important, but much less clear. She seems to have directly instructed Bengali revolutionaries, like Aurobindo Ghose (later Sri Aurobindo), in their underground resistance to the partition of Bengal in 1905.

In her lectures and writings, Sister Nivedita espoused many themes of affirmative Orientalism that became important parts of the Gandhian dream. Not only could India instruct the West spiritually, said Nivedita, but it could also give good instruction on family bonds and individual refinement even in the face of abject poverty. In religion but also in social matters, then, "what changes are necessary you [Indians] are fully competent to make for yourselves, and no outsider had the right to advise or interfere" (Nivedita 1968, vol. 2: 460–61).

An abiding cultural relativism came easily to Nivedita. She used it to argue that India could become a unified nation and do just as well as the West if it followed its own cultural essentials (Nivedita 1968 [1909], vol. 4: 265–66). The mind of the Indian ascetic, she maintained, would prove especially capable of reaching scientific insights; beneficial to science, too, would be the Indian penchant for finding grand unities. The passivity inculcated in the Indian child (1968 [1911], vol. 2: 467–68) permitted deep and informal family bonds. Although caste and sectarian divisions existed, they made India stronger because her unity was organic, not mechanical (1968 [1909], vol. 4: 270, 291, 320). Nevertheless, a future Indian nation would have to be more than Hindu, because India's strength resided in the diversity of its society, although Nivedita (1968, vol. 4: 291) recognized an overall "unity in communal diversity." Passivity, otherworldliness, and organic society, all of which constituted an essential Indian (Hindu) cultural inheritance for Nivedita, figured importantly in later Gandhian utopia.

Nivedita expressed two other essentials of Gandhian utopia. From 1898 onward, the journal *Dawn*, with which Nivedita was associated, argued against Western industrialism as a model for India and championed handicrafts. Sarkar sees this plea as a rejection of the West (Sarkar 1973: 104–8). Nivedita also gave strong support to the swadeshi movement (the boycott of English goods), which she believed would earn India the world's respect and would prove still once more that

> Eastern people have always shown themselves to be vastly stronger than Westerners in their ability to unite for the affirming of a given idea. . .in surrender to a moral impulse. . .to endure discomfort for the sake of right (Nivedita 1968, vol. 4: 277).

In addition to lecturing and writing to Indians about India, Nivedita seems to have instructed Bengalis about revolution. Although the record is poor, there is some evidence that she took part in underground revolutionary organizations and espoused a more radical politics there than she could in her public lectures and writings. Sri Aurobindo, an experimentalist discussed directly below, claimed that early in the twentieth century he organized a central council of five people to unite revolutionaries in Bengal and that Nivedita was one member. The council soon disbanded, and Nivedita and Aurobindo had no further communications on the revolutionary movement, or so Foxe (1975: 169) claims. Whereas Foxe (1975: 204) also ridicules the idea that Nivedita worked underground to foment revolution, Majumdar (1986: 65) believes she was an active revolutionary. Even Foxe allows that by the early twentieth century, Nivedita had introduced Aurobindo and other revolutionaries to the writings of European romantic nationalists like Mazzini and to the history of the Irish movement (Foxe 1975: 169). She is said to have embraced revolutionary violence as a last resort and to have doubted that passive resistance would be effective in itself (Foxe 1975: 169; Majumdar 1986: 65). Perhaps Nivedita accepted violence because Vivekananda called for action and valued physical strength. Whatever the reason, her vision here contradicted what would later become the Gandhian dream.

Sri Aurobindo, baptized Aurobindo Ackroyd Ghose, might have read about Mazzini and the Irish resistance at the urging of Sister Nivedita, but it is just as likely he read about them during the years he spent in Britain. Believing Indian culture to be corrupting Aurobindo's father emigrated to England shortly after his son's birth, but not before bestowing on his son a middle name Aurobindo was later to drop — a middle name his father chose, it would seem, out of respect for the Unitarian reformer, Annette Akroyd (who may have been present at Aurobindo's baptism).

Aurobindo spent his first twenty-one years in Britain, during which he was probably raised a Christian, and when he returned to India in 1893 he spoke no Indian language. Ashis Nandy's (1983) contention that Aurobindo remained proof against Western cultural domination is therefore very hard to accept. Aurobindo was highly successful in the British university and concentrated on classical studies and European literature. Losing a career in the Indian civil service because he refused or was unable to qualify in horsemanship and failing to get a Cambridge degree because he did not have enough money, Aurobindo took passage to India like many impecunious Britons: to teach English in India.

Dietmar Rothermund, conversely, does not conceive the youthful Aurobindo as British. For Rothermund, Aurobindo represents a "rudimentary [Indian] bourgeoisie," formed by colonial rule. Aurobindo, Rothermund suggests, was typical of the "half-educated" among them, who failed to get lucrative jobs and then turned to nationalist protest and even terrorism (Rothermund 1970: 145, 148). Perhaps Aurobindo was both British and Indian — discontinously: perhaps the British emigré turned into the indigenous revolutionary soon after Aurobindo returned to India, his erstwhile homeland. In 1893–94, shortly after his repatriation, he wrote a series of eleven articles in which he turned against his English background and the Westernizers and modernizers in the Indian National Congress. By the end of that decade, Aurobindo envisioned a mass armed uprising to free India. It was not until 1907 that he embraced passive resistance, by which he meant boycotts, strikes, and other forms of noncooperation. Aurobindo also conceived of a form of trusteeship such as Gandhi would espouse later. Spiritually dedicated individuals would call on all castes to work together in common purpose and would convince the rich to fund public works and charity (Dixit 1986: 124).

Aurobindo adopted passive resistance expediently, however, and without a Gandhian moral commitment (Ghose 1972: 116, 119, 122, 126–27; Sarkar 1973: 31–35, 69–71), and soon after he urged passive resistance in print, he seems to have started planning violent revolution in private.

For Aurobindo, successful revolution required a deep spiritual commitment, and this vision brought him closest to Gandhian utopia. In 1907, in resistance to the partition of Bengal ordered by the British colonial administration, Aurobindo "glorified revolution as a religious duty." He and a small band of other Bengali "extremists" invoked the Hindu goddess Kali, who defended her kingdom through violence and destruction, and Kali in another manifestation, who avenged herself in blood (Broomfield 1968: 31–34). Aurobindo wrote,

> Liberty is the fruit we seek from the sacrifice, and the Motherland the goddess to whom we offer it; into. . .the fire of the [sacrifice] we must offer all that we are and all that we have, feeding the fire even with our blood and lives and happiness of our nearest and dearest; for the Motherland is a goddess who loves not a maimed and imperfect sacrifice, and freedom was never won from the gods by a grudging giver (Ghose 1972: 122).

As Aurobindo saw it, Kali was to serve as a symbol of the motherland and as a model for Bengali youth — and she did. By 1908, a terrorist campaign had started to protest the partition, and Aurobindo's involvement in this terrorism, presumed by the British but never proven, was to force him into permanent political exile in 1910.

Aurobindo's appeal for a religious dedication to Indian nationalism takes much of its inspiration from the "gospel of duty" enunciated by Mazzini earlier in the nineteenth century. Mazzini called on Italian patriots to turn their backs on materialism and egotism and to embrace self-sacrifice, duty, and love for the nation. He called them to the worship of God and Truth (Mazzini 1907: 2–3). Mazzini wanted to do away with the individualism that educated people in greed and egoism and to replace it with one law: that the object of life should be not individual happiness, but the benefit of all. This law would be to the individual's betterment as well (Mazzini 1907: 15–16). Similarly, Mazzini said, property cannot be abolished from human nature, but it must be made to serve the many, not just the few — as when all workers in an enterprise get shares of the profit (Mazzini 1907: 103–10).

Mazzini is the link between Aurobindo and Gandhian utopia. The religious dedication and revolution of the spirit, the association of God and Truth, the call for selflessness, the expectation of a rapprochement between the propertied and the poor — these means to revolution as set forth by Mazzini, both Gandhi and Aurobindo would have accepted. The Mazzini that Gandhi chose to ignore (although claiming his authority in *Hind Swaraj* — see Gandhi 1982 [1909]: 105) is the Mazzini that Aurobindo exulted in: the violent revolutionary. As with Vivekananda and Sister Nivedita, so with Aurobindo we see major anticipations of Gandhian utopia, as, for example, antimodernism, organicism, spiritual revolution, and passive resistance, but we also see what is missing: the moral commitment to passive resistance and the disavowal of violent revolution that were essential to Gandhian utopia.

Still another difference exists between the Gandhian dream and the revolutionary vision of these Bengali experimentalists, and this difference too is related to the idea of satyagraha they lacked. The Bengali experimentalists never launched a mass revolutionary movement like the later Gandhian uses of satyagraha. Beginning in 1907, they engaged in a terrorist campaign that was short-lived and unsuccessful. Sumit Sarkar (1973: 71–72, 79–83) argues that the Bengalis, because they were landlords, could not mobilize peasant anticolonial protest without possible damage to their own interests. Another problem was that Muslims became increasingly suspicious of the strongly Hindu character of the nationalism the Bengali experimentalists proclaimed.

The Bombay–London Core Set

In western India, too, anticipation of Gandhian utopia developed within an evolving affirmative Orientalism at the start of the twentieth century. Nationalism here, however, often contrasted sharply with Gandhi's vision; yet it also enabled that vision as Gandhi confronted — and rejected — the Bombay experimentalists. This "core set" of experimentalists included expatriate Indians or Indian students in Britain, and it was also intellectually nourished by English ideas, specifically the evolutionary sociology of Herbert Spencer.

Affirmative Orientalism in Bombay evolved out of the confrontation between modernizers and Westernizers like Ranade and Gokhale and cultural nationalists like Tilak. The modernizers put their effort into social reforms, like the education of women and the remarriage of widows. They petitioned the British colonial administration for greater benefits, but their expectation was that 120 political freedom would follow after social reconstruction.

Tilak and other cultural nationalists reversed these priorities. They pressed for political freedom first and foremost, and they finessed the issue of social reform thereby. Tilak used the term "swarajya" just as much as Gandhi, but he meant something quite different by it (and used a different spelling, too). Independence for India would come when Indians, not Britons, had power. Indians would elect councils and parliaments; Indians would control an English educational system in the villages; Indians would decide how to modernize their traditional institutions. Swarajya, self-rule, for Tilak meant that Indians would govern themselves rather than being governed by others (see Tilak n.d. [1916, 1917]: 205, 207, 235; Tahmankar 1956: 116). If Indian self-government proceeded through Western institutions, Tilak had no objection. For Gandhi, "swaraj" meant a very different self-rule: it referred to a personal and national discipline based on essential Indian cultural values, antithetical to the West's. Gandhi's noncooperation program, his boycott of English institutions like schools, civil service, and the courts, opposed Tilak's determination to make English education universal, his faith in responsive cooperation with the colonial administration, and his efforts toward constitutional reform, especially after 1916 (Cashman 1975: 212).

Cultural nationalism in Bombay came closest to Gandhian utopia when positively evaluating Indian religious and social traditions. Cultural nationalists defended many Indian customary practices, basing their defense on a consensual view of Indian's traditional society. Tilak, for example, defended caste as an ancient Aryan institution that had developed in association with an increasingly complex division of labor and had regulated social behavior in accord with cultural values. He believed that caste could once again become a living force in India — perhaps it could be made to protect contemporary India's working classes in the way it once had (Kumar 1968: 310–13). He also used popular festivals in honor of India's former rulers, like the Mahratta king Shivaji, as means by which to inculcate a modern national identity.

Tilak combined his defense of Indian traditions with an appreciation of revolutionary methods in Europe and elsewhere. In 1902 he editorialized on guerrilla warfare, comparing the methods the Boers had used against the British in South Africa with those the Mahrattas had employed against the Muslims (Wolpert 1961: 150–51). Some years later, he spoke approvingly of the Sinn Fein movement in Ireland, which had resolved that begging for concessions from Parliament rather than taking direct action was futile (Wolpert 1961: 180). On the Bombay side of India, as in Bengal, experimentalists did not shrink from contemplating violent resistance. The important difference was that Bengali experimentalists thought

121

violence would develop from spiritual dedication to nationalism, whereas in Bombay revolutionary violence was considered one among several secular techniques. As Tilak said, politics was a "game of worldly people and not of *sadhus*." Tilak's instrumentalism distressed Gandhi, who in 1918 disowned it as a Western importation (CWG 14: 261; Wolpert 1961: 291–92).

This difference is important because Gandhi came into confrontation with the Bombay experimentalists through their colleagues in England, but he did not directly lock horns with Bengali revolutionaries. Because Tilak and the expatriate Shyamji Krishnavarma (see below) did not couch their nationalism in the spiritual terms that Bengalis like Aurobindo used, Gandhi could disavow both their acceptance of violence and their secular revolutionary stance without denying spiritual revolution. Gandhi might have found it harder to separate cleanly his revolutionary vision from Bengal's justification of spiritually motivated violence.

Tilak's nationalism had its counterpart in the politics of expatriate Indians in Britain, the ones that Gandhi confronted during his visit to England in 1909. Shyamji Krishnavarma had settled in Britain, and his independent wealth permitted him to pursue his goal of complete independence for India in several ways. His publication *Indian Sociologist*, begun in January 1905, used the principles of Spencer's evolutionary sociology to argue for Indian home rule. Despotism, argued Spencer — and Krishnavarma concurred — limited individuality and therefore retarded the progress of society, so the British had to leave India. Krishnavarma required the departure of the British, but not necessarily of British institutions like Parliament. For Krishnavarma, Western despotism was the problem, not Western science and civilization. His masthead supported several "fundamental truths of [Western] social science," among them this idea from Spencer: "every man has freedom to do all that he wills . . ." (*Indian Sociologist* January 1905, vol. 1, no. 1: 1). Krishnavarma's scientific individualism and Gandhi's spiritual corporatism were obviously very far apart (see *Indian Sociologist* January 1908, vol. 4, no. 1: 2 and February 1908, vol. 4, no. 3: 11 for Krishnavarma's attacks on Gandhi's South African resistance) — as distant as Tilak's instrumentalism was from Gandhi's moral politics.

Further to advance his nationalist goals, Krishnavarma endowed (in December 1904) five Herbert Spencer Travelling Fellowships to help Indians study in Britain. The fellowships disallowed their

122

recipients from taking employment with the British colonial government when they returned to India (*Indian Sociologist* January 1905, vol. 1, no. 1: 3). Soon afterward, Krishnavarma set up an Indian lodging house in Highgate (London) that soon became a safe house for Indian revolutionaries and a launching pad for Indian nationalist propaganda. Another such locale in Acton was called Tilak House (Secretary of State for India 1907: 56–59). In February 1905, Krishnavarma established the Indian Home Rule Society (*Indian Sociologist* March 1905, vol. 1, no. 3: 1), and throughout 1906 and 1907 he publicly advocated passive resistance and peaceful civil disobedience (see, for example, *Indian Sociologist* June 1907, vol. 3, no. 6: 28; November 1907, vol. 3, no. 11: 44). Krishnavarma at this time put forward his *Principle of Dissociation*, which called on Indians to boycott government service, schools, and law courts, and to repudiate the public debt of India (Yajnik 1950 [1934]: vii–viii). By 1909, however, he had come increasingly to advocate violent revolution, and the *Indian Sociologist* began presenting this position very directly (see, for example, January and February 1909, vol. 5, no. 1, 2). Fearing British imprisonment, Krishnavarma absconded to Paris in 1909.

Gandhian utopia received comparatively less from the Bombay-London core set than from the Bengali experimentalists. There was less affirmative Orientalism in Bombay's notions and much more acceptance of Western models — of revolution, of social science, of modernity, of instrumental politics. There was, however, the defense of traditional social institutions like caste and the support for traditional folk festivals to build national consciousness. In addition, the Krishnavarma-Tilak axis importantly authored Gandhian utopia by providing negative instances. When Gandhi confronted their views in London in 1909 and found them wanting (and read Chesterton's lampoon of them), he butted up against an Indian nationalism he could not accept — even though by this time he was becoming an outspoken cultural nationalist — and, in opposition, constructed one he could.

Hindu Nationals, Made and Born

Even before Annie Besant arrived in India in 1893, Theosophists had industriously reminded the East of its ancient wisdom, as had, for example, Colonel Olcott's missions to the Singhalese Buddhists. Annie Besant's affirmative Orientalism reconstructed Hinduism

123

and operated on an all-India level. Crisscrossing the country, she broadcast her belief in India's great future — when India would rightfully claim a high place among the world's nations by following its ancient Hindu cultural traditions.

Besant sharply contrasted Western culture with Indian, the starting point of any Orientalism: Rome had achieved civic greatness, and Greece, intellectual advancement; India's contribution to world progress was spiritual greatness (Besant 1913: 2–10). For the West, Besant (1904: 12–14) said, the ideal was the self-reliant, free, and independent individual "over whom no one has any title to tyrannize," whereas India's ideal was based on duty and the recognition of the unity of all beings.

> From this naturally followed the view [in India], that each man was but a part of a whole; he was not isolated, he was not independent, he was a portion of a vast interlinked and interdependent order. He was not born free; he was born into numerous obligations, and by the very fact of living he was constantly adding to his debts (Besant 1904: 18–19).

It also followed that respective personalities differed, the Westerner being "aggressive, combative, tend[ing] to separateness" and the Indian "yielding, peaceful, and tend[ing] to unity" (Besant 1904: 20).

A consensual, hierarchical, and corporate civilization was another essential heritage of India, according to Besant. In the West, democracy, the rule of the many, evolved over centuries of struggle against state oppression. Ancient India also gave individuals liberty, but in a quite different way:

> Liberty was ensured to the individual by the careful ordering of society and the definition of the place and duties of each class by wise men . . . This was Aristocracy, the rule of the Best, growing out of the eastern Ideal as Democracy grew out of the Western (Besant 1904: 113; see also 136).

Besant maintained that India's political future could not depend "on struggle and the assertion of rights," in imitation of the West. A future "suitable to Indian genius and congruous with Indian history" would be based instead "on peace and on the enforcement of duties" (Besant 1904: 137). As Gandhi would later, Besant believed that India's solidarity began in the village — here was the core unit of India's future administration, where duties would be enforced and peace attained (Besant 1904: 138; Nethercot 1963: 215–16).

Besant also anticipated Gandhi's dream of a deep spiritual foundation for India's national life. Closer to Aurobindo than Gandhi, however, Besant was avowedly sectarian, asserting that Hinduism was India's essence and future (Besant 1904: 165, 197; see also Besant 1966 [1897]: 1–39). She did allow that Hinduism's inherent toleration toward Islam and other faiths promised a national "unity in diversity," but she also maintained that Hindu traditions would be basic. Besant defended Hinduism as a rational, even scientific religion. Its idol worship, for example, helped fix the believer on the essential divine Unity, which, in its abstractness, was otherwise difficult to apprehend (Besant 1919: 2–3). Not only, said Besant (1919: 58–60), did Hindu scriptures recognize biological evolution, but they also provided the reason for it: the gradual unfolding, or development, of the Self.

In very specific ways, too, Besant prefigured Gandhian utopia. As early as 1895, she (1913: 112–22) counseled Indians to maintain their native dress and to support Indian manufactures over foreign goods. In the same year, Besant (1913: 44) defended the ancient caste system as based on "natural" occupational divisions to be found in any nation; only later had it been corrupted and made overly rigid. Her dream also imagined a future India, perfected along an indigenous "line of evolution," as capable of instructing the world: India would become a "spiritual nation . . . the teacher of the world in spiritual truth," and Indians would serve as a "priest-people of the world" (Besant 1913 [1893]: 41: 1913 [1895]: 122).

Besant not only urged these experiments in spiritual nationalism on Indians through her many lectures and writings; she also directly experimented with them herself. In 1898 she founded Central Hindu College in Benares city (present-day Varanasi), dedicated to teaching young men the Hindu heritage — a counterforce, she hoped, against both secular government and Christian missionary schools (Dar and Somaskandan 1966: 41–42; Nethercot 1963: 62–63). Subsidies flowed in from various princely patrons, perhaps confirming Besant's belief in India's inherent rule of the Best. (She did not subscribe to mass protest, such as Gandhi's satyagraha, because it was not in keeping with her vision of India's corporate, elitist essence.) Three years after the college opened, Besant took

125

over the *Hindu Boy's Journal* published by her fellow Theosophist Colonel Olcott and renamed it the *Central Hindu College Magazine: A Journal for Hindu Boys*, "devoted to the revival of spirituality among Hindu boys" (Nethercot 1963: 68). In 1902 the college issued a series of textbooks on Hinduism called the Sanatan ("orthodox" or "traditional") Dharma Series.

By 1910, Besant hoped to experiment with "unity in diversity" by organizing higher education on this basis. She petitioned the British crown to establish a University of India that would affiliate colleges established by all indigenous religious groups, but would not affiliate secular institutions. The experiment failed when Muslim support waned as plans went forward to make the Muslim school in Aligarh into a university (Dar and Somaskandan 1966: 90–102). Besant then developed a scheme for a Hindu university with Madan Mohan Malaviya. Malaviya had written a brief for a Hindu university in 1905, but he held back from a joint effort with Besant, perhaps because he feared a Theosophical tinge to the Hinduism taught in Central Hindu College. In 1911, however, Besant and Malaviya together proposed a new University of Benares (the present-day Banaras Hindu University), in which Hindu culture would be a significant part of the curriculum (Dar and Somaskandan 1966: 105–17). This joint effort betokened the merger of affirmative Orientalism and an overt Hindu nationalism, which imagined a future Indian nation defined by Hindu cultural traditions.

Not yet anti-Muslim, this early Hindu nationalism represented a "liberal communalism," as Bipan Chandra (1984: 323–30) calls it. It was liberal, seemingly, because it held up a utopian image of an India free from imperialism. Besant and Malaviya and other Hindu nationalists of the early twentieth century defended Hindu cultural traditions against pejorative Orientalism from abroad, not against Islam or other Indian minority traditions within. Building a (Hindu) Indian identity butted up against a (British) colonial domination. "Liberal communalism" is just another term for "affirmative Orientalism" as undertaken by the Bengal experimentalists and some of the Bombay core set. In this respect, these groups were exemplary for Gandhi's own vision of an Indian Wisdom-land. Gandhi, however, was more guarded in his use of terms like "Hindu" and "Hinduism," and he much more forcefully pursued cooperation between Muslims and Hindus in the nationalist movement. Still, for Gandhi as for Malaviya, Besant, Tilak, Aurobindo, Nivedita, and Vivekananda, the miraculous India of the spiritual, of the village community, of organic caste society, and so forth was in most respects a Hindu India. By the 1930s and especially in the 1970s and 1980s, liberal communalism would give way to a more exclusive and uncompromising Hindu nationalism (discussed in Chapters 11 and 12), which saw India's enemies as the non-Hindu minorities living within the nation.

Coauthorship

Long before he accepted some of their experiments and rejected others, Gandhi had come to know of these laboratories of utopia. In the late 1880s, studying in Britain, Gandhi had read the Theosophists Besant and Blavatsky. Blavatsky "disabused [him] of the notion fostered by the missionaries that Hinduism was rife with superstition" (Gandhi 1957: 68). Other experimentalists did not make a positive impression at first. In 1896, still cherishing what he regarded as a unique loyalty to the British Constitution (Gandhi 1957: 172; 1972: 45–48), Gandhi visited Bombay and Poona. He met the cultural nationalist Tilak but chose the Westernizer G. C. Gokhale as his political guru. Three years later, Gandhi met Sister Nivedita in Calcutta and also found "there was not much meeting ground" (Gandhi 1957: 236). In his 1909 journey to England, Gandhi met up with many Indian "anarchists," as he calls them — they were probably militants adopting violent revolution as Krishnavarma had.

Years before his first Indian uses of satyagraha after World War I and even before his South African satyagraha campaign became a mass movement in 1913, Gandhi had an intellectual work group or core set, even if at this time it was unacknowledged — unacknowledged because when he met or read these people, he rejected most of their experimental ideas. Gandhi was fully to adopt affirmative Orientalism and the cultural nationalism it sponsored only after 1909. He did not completely abandon a Westernizing consciousness until his return to India during World War I and his rejection by other Westernizers and modernists in Bombay, as we shall see in the next chapter. Gandhi's late and rapid reversal confirms that Gandhi the public figure and Gandhian utopia as a public set of cultural meanings were precipitated by his ongoing experiences and by coauthors.

127

Gandhian utopia eventually and faithfully reproduced the affirmative Orientalism, especially the belief in India's inherent spirituality, found in Bengal and Besant. It accepted the cultural chauvinism found in Tilak's defense of the caste system or Besant's "proof" that Hinduism was scientific. It incorporated the commitment to spiritual revolution, indigenous manufactures, village government, and corporatist national spirit of Nivedita, Besant, Vivekananda, and Aurobindo. Gandhian utopia even denied what the Bengali experimentalists and Besant denied. In its opposition to Krishnavarma's "Indian sociology" and Tilak's instrumental nationalist politics, it rejected Western apologia for revolution, a secular nationalist spirit, and a modernist conception of development, much as the Bengalis and Besant did. A nationalism untrue to India was no nationalism — that was the root message of affirmative Orientalism as authored in Bengal, by Besant, and within a general "liberal" Hindu nationalism, and as absorbed by Gandhian utopia.

Gandhian utopia rejected and went beyond these anticipatory experiments in two important ways. Gandhi rejected the violent revolution countenanced not only by Aurobindo but also by Krishnavarma and Tilak. He also substituted nonviolent resistance and mass protest through satyagraha for either Besant's constitutional reformism, at the behest of an Indian elite, or Bengal's terrorism, also an elite undertaking. Are these innovative experiments in utopia due to Gandhi's sole authorship, his unique greatness? Yes and no — mostly no, because sole authorship and unique greatness are contradictions in terms, as this chapter has argued, but also somewhat yes, because individuals conspire to authorize themselves, as the next chapter shows.

SEVEN

Authorizing Gandhi

> *I was the author of the Satyagraha movement.*
> M. K. *Gandhi (1972 [1928]: 90)*

Gandhi left India for South Africa in 1893 not because he was shy or financially embarrassed, as is often supposed (see Swan 1985: 48), but because he had, unwillingly, experimented with British rule and gotten a "shock [that] changed the course of [his] life" (Gandhi 1957: 99). Although shyness had stymied his career in court, and lack of income had forced him to close his legal practice in Bombay, Gandhi had removed to the provincial town of Rajkot, where he was doing "moderately well" by drafting memorials and applications (Gandhi 1957: 98).

A confrontation with British colonialism then precipitated Gandhi's passage to South Africa, as well, perhaps, as his first outrage at British domination. Bullied and cajoled into it by his brother, Gandhi called on a British colonial officer he had known in England. He hoped to convince the officer that accusations of intrigue against his brother, arising from his prior service to an Indian princeling, were unwarranted. Although Gandhi hesitated to presume in India on an English friendship, in the event he found out just how much "Kathiawad was different from England." The British officer chastised him for abusing their acquaintance, had him removed bodily from the office, and replied arrogantly and unrepentantly to Gandhi's subsequent protest and threat of legal action. Sir Pherozeshah Mehta, in spite of being a leading nationalist, then told Gandhi to "pocket the insult," which was advice Gandhi found "as bitter as poison" (Gandhi 1957: 99).

129

Although Gandhi took the advice and pocketed the insult, he understood that the incident had serious consequences for his legal career in Rajkot. The offensive British officer presided over the court that would also be Gandhi's professional venue. Reflecting that the "quarrel with the *sahib* stood in the way of [his] practice," Gandhi, "without any higgling," accepted the job offer of a Muslim trading company in South Africa (Gandhi 1957: 100–103).

If Gandhi's departure for South Africa had been an outcome of his financial straits and professional failure, and if these difficulties, in turn, had developed from his extreme shyness, then we might readily argue that Gandhi's innate personal characteristics were determinative. The truth, however, is that his decision to leave India was precipitated by an experiment he entered relatively naively, in which he confronted the authority of British colonialism, and for his efforts was literally and mentally pushed about. The result of Gandhi's experiment was his physical departure from the British Raj in India, and perhaps also a mental departure, a moving away from quiescence and toleration of that rule (at least when supercilious and corrupt agents represented it). The result, in other words, was a spiritual disjuncture and a personal discontinuity. After several additional experiences with discrimination in South Africa, Gandhi came out a new, politically conscious person and began the long South African resistance, which he did not leave until 1914.

There is another instructive point in this history of the singular. The portrayal of a shy and impecunious Gandhi forced out of India represents him as passive in the face of his own (negative) personality characteristics. What really happened, however, was that he took the immediate circumstances in which he was set — namely, that he, a young lawyer, had become persona non grata with the local arm of the colonial power — and actively authored a location and situation for himself. Within the circumstances, that is, he recognized he had to go outside them, although he soon also recognized — and then actively confronted — the fact that Indians in South Africa were hardly "outside" of British domination.

The specific circumstances precipitating the Gandhi who departed for South Africa provide the departure for this chapter in general. Through a singular history of Gandhi in South Africa and India, I chronicle a case of cultural innovation and personal revolution.

The last chapter showed that several groups of Indian cultural nationalists had confronted British colonialism in India and that affirmative Orientalism had allowed them to develop a cultural resistance to that domination. It thus indicated the precedents for the Gandhian dream that developed early in the twentieth century. This chapter shows the way in which the major innovation of Gandhian utopia, the aspect of Gandhi's vision not anticipated by other Indian cultural nationalists, condensed in Gandhi as he incorporated other intellectual sources (mainly Tolstoy) and underwent formative experiences in South Africa. The ultimate outcome was a cultural innovation, as a new utopian vision arose out of the existing, constitutive ideology of society. At the same time, a new Gandhi developed. In the first two decades of the twentieth century, Gandhi underwent a revolution in personhood, as he mastered compelling circumstances through satyagraha and other experiments with Gandhian utopia — and as he gained authority first over the South African resistance and then over the Indian nationalist movement. By about 1920, Gandhi had been publicly credited with the invention of satyagraha and other elements of what I have called Gandhian utopia. He came out as a recognized cultural innovator, an accredited Great Person, the author of a utopian vision that broke with accepted canons. Neither India nor Gandhi was ever the same after that.[1]

Through this history of the singular, I emphasize two structural points:

1. Immediate circumstances condense individuals and set the compelling conditions that may enable discontinuous or even revolutionary personhoods from time to time. Individuals try to control compelling circumstances first by mastering themselves (as Gandhi did when he left for South Africa), and then by marshaling, even manipulating, the intellectual and practical labor of others. Butting up against the existing culture and the domination it encodes can encourage a personal discontinuity and an individual resistance — as Gandhi's confrontation with the arrogant sahib did. Then, bouncing off the thinking and actions of sympathetic others, an individual can come to participate in an intellectual and practical work group that transforms such a personal discontinuity into a revolutionary consciousness. Such collective labor — with both "hands and minds" — can radically alter individual intentions, and in doing so it can create utopian visions: as personal

discontinuity turns into revolutionary consciousness, collective labor can support immediate experiments with the imperfect present on the promise of a perfected future.

In everyday life, therefore, the making of cultural innovations and of cultural innovators is concurrent and intertwined, as we shall see in the specific instance of Gandhi's satyagraha in both its theory and early practice. Unlike many of the other significant experiments constituting Gandhian utopia, which were anticipated by other Indian cultural nationalists, satyagraha as a morally armed nonviolence and as a mass means of protest was unprecedented in Indian cultural resistance early in the twentieth century. Only the element of resistance through noncooperation and boycott has its precedents in the beliefs of Gandhi's nationalist contemporaries. Yet no less than other aspects of Gandhian utopia, satyagraha — and the Gandhi associated with it — condensed out of group experiences and thinking, mainly confrontational in character. Besides precipitating satyagraha, these circumstances also precipitated a Gandhi who rejected the modernizing and constitutional approach to nationalism, which he had earlier championed. He accepted, instead, the affirmative Orientalism that lay at the core of Gandhian utopia, which he had earlier rejected.

2. In pursuit of such utopian visions and experiments, an individual may consciously or unconsciously try to gain exclusive authority over the intellectual and practical labor of others. Authority successfully asserted by the individual or endowed on the individual by others equals authorship, in Gouldner's sense (see Chapter 4): that is, a collective effort becomes publicly assigned to individual creativity. Such individual authority is real, however, because the individual now has power over the utopian vision and experimental practices. Furthermore, maintaining that authority may require a further discontinuity or a continuing revolution in personhood, as individuals must more thoroughly master themselves in order to monitor others better, especially if with success the work groups grow larger and more divergent.

Because most of the precipitating experiences and informing beliefs came from outside the currents of Indian nationalism discussed in the last chapter, satyagraha, as Gandhi authorized it in South Africa, constituted a cultural innovation when he later experimented with it in India. I therefore show here the way in which Gandhi initially asserted authority over satyagraha as it precipitated, often quite independently of him, in response to South African circumstances. I also show how Gandhi later maintained control over this cultural innovation by modifying satyagraha, again in accord with immediate circumstances — namely, those he encountered when he took nonviolent resistance from South Africa to India in 1915. By his initial assertion of authority and his later control, although never fully successful, Gandhi came to claim authorship and in fact became acclaimed as the author of nonviolent resistance. In turn, satyagraha — coupled after 1909 with the presentiments of Gandhian utopia provided by Besant, Aurobindo, Nivedita, and others, and then further modified after 1917 — came to claim authority over the Indian nationalist movement.

This chapter, therefore, documents the forging and solidification of Gandhian utopia as a formative set of cultural meanings from about 1904 to 1920.

Inventing Nonviolent Resistance

When Gandhi reached South Africa, he found an Indian merchant community (mainly Muslims from Gujarat) that passively bore insult — or so he claimed. "They had therefore made it a principle to pocket insults as they might pocket cash" (Gandhi 1972: 39). Just as his year's employment ended and he expected to leave for India (1894), the Natal government introduced a bill to disfranchise Indians. Gandhi urged the Indian merchants to "strenuously resist this attack on their rights," and the merchants in turn beseeched Gandhi to stay on as their "guide" (Gandhi 1972: 40–41). Gandhi (1972: 40) therefore claimed to have inspired "the South African Indians' first experience of . . . agitation." He therefore asserted authority over the resistance in no uncertain terms.

Maureen Swan (1985: 38–43), however, finds that merchant resistance to official discrimination had developed as early as 1885 and "reached a peak of activity in the [pre-Gandhian] early 1890s." Gandhi seems to have walked in on an ongoing political struggle and then been enlisted into it. The same circumstances pertain to Gandhi's early Indian satyagraha campaigns, as I shall indicate later. He was not the movement's author, but its representative;

133

Gandhi's legal knowledge and fluency in English made him valuable to the merchants' cause (Swan 1985: 49).

As for the form of resistance he came to label "satyagraha," Gandhi sometimes claimed authorship, as in the remark that begins this chapter, and at other times spoke of it as a spontaneous invention (Gandhi 1972: 43). The earliest use of satyagraha, in 1906, consisted of the Indian community's refusal to re-register with the Transvaal authorities (who wanted to limit Indian immigration). It required picketing registration places, refusing to pay fines, and accepting imprisonment, and therefore its basic strategy was noncooperation. Gandhi first called for passive resistance in 1904 (Swan 1985: 117), and the initial campaign began two years later, shortly before Krishnavarma and Aurobindo publicly advocated such a tactic for India. Was it therefore without precedent?

Inventing Resistance

According to Gene Sharp (1979: 26–32), one major element of satyagraha was not Gandhi's invention. Its civil-disobedience aspect, the "resistance" in nonviolent resistance, developed from previous and contemporary examples of noncooperation that Gandhi imitated. Sharp mentions the nonviolent Irish resistance against the British in the late nineteenth century, the early-twentieth-century Chinese boycott of American goods in protest against discriminatory immigration laws, civil disobedience in the 1905 Russian Revolution, and the Bengal boycott of British goods in 1905. Gandhi referred to these instances in his contemporary publication *Indian Opinion*. There were thus multiple anticipations of what Gandhi at this time called "passive resistance." The very label, which he came to reject only in 1908, tells us that Gandhi's sources were the same as those Krishnavarma and Aurobindo tapped.

Sharp also finds precedents for satyagraha-style protest in South Africa before 1906. Indians had noncooperated with official attempts to sequester them in "locations" and to limit their movements with pass laws. There were also instances of African noncooperation before 1906 (Sharp 1979: 33–34). Although Gandhi after the fact believed moral discipline and strength of purpose made satyagraha unique, Sharp finds that, in its actual practice early on, it was hardly so (Sharp 1979: 37). Similarly, Gandhi's early understanding of satyagraha did not yet recognize these characteristics that he was later to say made it distinctive.

134

Gandhi's understanding of nonviolent resistance, therefore, grew out of immediate circumstances. It was neither his invention nor a product of his Indian enculturation. "Traditional" Indian forms of nonviolent protest, such as "sitting dharna," have been claimed as antecedents for Gandhi's satyagraha (Spodek 1971: 363–64; Irschick 1986). But the civil disobedience that Gandhi practiced in his early South African satyagrahas seems much more a response to the world around Gandhi than an echo from his Indian past.

Discovering Morality

The moral dedication that distinguished satyagraha from the expedient passive resistance of Aurobindo and Krishnavarma grew out of immediate circumstances and a complex authorship. It was also not Gandhi's exclusive invention. Here I am referring to the special morality that came to define the Gandhian commitment to the "nonviolence" aspect of nonviolent resistance.

The first investiture of nonviolent resistance with moral dedication caught Gandhi by surprise. Although Gandhi had earlier extolled self-sacrifice to the Indian community, it was a leading Muslim merchant named Haji Habib, rather than Gandhi, who called for a solemn oath of noncooperation at the mass meeting held in September 1906. Gandhi says he was in fact startled by it (Gandhi 1972: 96).

Gandhi did not invest civil disobedience with moral purpose until 1907 or 1908 (Swan 1985: 167–69). He may have learned about Thoreau's essay on civil disobedience in the early 1890s, because Henry Salt, his vegetarian associate in England, was Thoreau's biographer. It was not until 1907, however, that Gandhi used Thoreau's ideas to justify the South African resistance (CWG 7 : 211–12, 217–18, 304–5). This was shortly after he had taken a vow of celibacy (1906). Early in the South African struggle, Gandhi thought of the movement as passive resistance (Gandhi 1972: 102). Only later did he "realize" that passive resistance was a method of the weak; only later, that is, did he disown passive resistance as the expedient of the weak and adopt nonviolent resistance as the moral dedication of the strong. Again, Gandhi's "discovery" of a morally armed nonviolence condensed not only Haji Habib's earlier solemn oath but also the ideas of European nonconformists. He came to know of Ruskin and Tolstoy through European associates in South Africa like Henry Polak (Green 1983: 89). Gandhi's imprisonments after 1906 ironically gave him freedom to read or reread Ruskin, Tolstoy, and others who led him to affirm Truth and God as integral to resistance (Swan 1985: 167). Only in late February or early March 1908 did Gandhi develop a distinctive name, satyagraha, for his new discovery (CWG 8: 91, 131–32).

After reading Tolstoy's *Letter to a Hindu* in the fall of 1909 (see Green 1983: 91; CWG 9: 445), probably while in Britain, Gandhi seems to have fixed on his moral commitment. Tolstoy's open letter to an expatriate Indian revolutionary in Canada was filled with affirmative Orientalism. It was therefore ready-made for Gandhi. By attacking his erstwhile correspondent's acceptance of English institutions and revolutionary violence, Tolstoy gave replies Gandhi could also use in confronting the London branch of these Indian revolutionaries during his 1909 visit.[2]

In phrases that Gandhi's *Hind Swaraj* would shortly echo, Tolstoy enjoined Indian nationalists from imitating the West. Continuing Indian servitude, he said, depended on being duped into this mimicry. Tolstoy asserted that Indians (like everyone else) would find freedom only when they understood and accepted nonviolence as the highest moral law, "the eternal truth inherent in mankind":

> the great religious teachers . . . directed attention to the one inevitable condition of love: the enduring of affronts, injuries, and all kinds of violence, without resisting the evil by evil . . .
>
> The ancient simple truth that it was natural for people to help and to love, instead of torturing and killing each other, began to dawn upon the minds of men . . . People saw more and more distinctly . . . the absurdity and the immorality of the submission of their will to that of others like themselves [monarchs and other heads of state] who require of them acts not only contrary to their material welfare, but which are also a violation of their moral feeling . . .
>
> It is, therefore, perfectly natural that people who have lost faith in the divine authority of all manner of potentates should endeavor to free themselves from it (Tolstoy [1908]: 5).

Here then are the precipitating circumstances that armed Gandhian utopia with a morally committed nonviolence, quite unlike the passive resistance proposed by the Bengali experimentalists and the Bombay core set. In so many other ways, as we have seen, these groups anticipated the Gandhian dream. They never anticipated, however, the satyagraha that Gandhi condensed from his South African experiences and from his particular European intellectual work group, the satyagraha that he made a distinctive cultural meaning for India in his time and thereafter.

Catalyzing Mass Protest

Satyagraha as a means of mass protest also made the later Gandhian utopia distinctive. The precipitation of a mass movement only happened very late in Gandhi's South African experiences. Swan convincingly argues that before 1913 the satyagraha campaign was predominantly an elite enterprise (see her conclusions, Swan 1985: xvi). The resistance to disfranchisement, re-registration, and immigration restrictions, as well as the primarily "civil rights" concerns of the protests, reflected the interests of well-off Indian merchants and former indentured laborers who had successfully entered commerce and white-collar work (Swan 1985: 10–16). The great majority of the Indian population, the indentured laborers who worked in the South African mines or on sugar plantations, were left out of satyagraha until after 1913 (Gandhi 1972: 249). Their condition in South Africa was abject (Tayal 1978), and their servitude was obvious. By the late 1890s, Gandhi knew about their exploitation and humiliation, and a "regular stream of indentured labourers" came to him for legal aid (see Balasundaram's touching story in Gandhi 1957: 153–55).

Gandhi did not try to enlist indentured laborers into the satyagraha campaign until his political fortunes reached such a low ebb in 1912 that he fixed on "new goals" (Swan 1985: 234) in what Swan (1985: 245) calls a "last ditch stand." Opposition to his leadership had arisen among the Indian elite, and there was little support for continued satyagraha from traders or white-collar workers (Swan 1985: 225–26). Gandhi then introduced a new ground for protest. He came out against the annual head tax of three pounds levied against all former indentured laborers whose indenture had begun after 1895. His demand had been anticipated by other Indian political groups (Swan 1985: 192–95). A protest against the head tax appealed to the many still-indentured laborers because this tax crippled their chances for future independence and prosperity in South Africa; the tax had even forced reindentures (Swan 1985: 243).

Immediate circumstances precipitated Gandhi into implementing "a tactic which he was so ill-prepared to use that he was uncertain

137

of how successful it would be" (Swan 1985: 245). Gandhi's desperate tactic worked, however. A massive strike and mass protest march of indentured laborers broke out in 1913, and Gandhi led it physically (except when he was in jail) and spiritually (see Gandhi 1972: 274–84). In 1912, perhaps in a symbolic anticipation of the new mass and class basis of his upcoming satyagraha campaign, Gandhi permanently donned Indian clothing for the first time since childhood (Swan 1985: 236). This new image was so "radical and unfamiliar" that the Reverend Charles Andrews did not recognize Gandhi when he arrived in South Africa in 1913 (Bean 1988: 000). Gandhi changed his apparel when he changed his appeal, because the conversion to a mass campaign also converted Gandhi.

Gandhi left South Africa a year after the mass campaign, which had forced the government to rescind the head tax. Accompanying him on his return to India — and precipitating him as a new political force there — was his relatively recently constituted knowledge and practice of a form of mass civil disobedience based on moral commitment and discipline. It was the satyagraha of his utopian dream.

Authorizing Nonviolent Resistance

Before 1906, Swan says (1985: xvi), Gandhi was the representative of the Indian elite in South Africa; thereafter, she believes, it is only partly true to call him its leader. Almost right up to his departure for India, Gandhi continually tried to assert or maintain his authority over the satyagraha campaign. Early on, this assertion meant inserting himself into events he did not control; later, it meant protecting the partial authorship he had gained. Motivating these manipulations was his developing utopian vision. An important point is that Gandhi was politically "savy" — he may even appear wily in the following presentation[3] — in the interests of a revolutionary dream, not in defense of a status-quo ideology. Just as his utopian vision led him to discipline himself, so it required him to discipline others — and, as I shall try to make clear, he consciously pursued or protected the authority by which he could make his revolutionary discipline effective. Rather than a full chronological review, I give some instances to illustrate the general manner in which Gandhi built and exercised authority and through which he eventually won authorship.

138

For example, when Haji Habib called for the solemn oath of noncooperation at the 1906 mass meeting, Gandhi was quick to "explain" the oath's consequences at length to the audience (Gandhi 1972: 96–100). Haji Habib and H. O. Ally were the important conveners of the meeting (Swan 1985: 119), but Gandhi also asserted his authority: by explaining the nature and consequences of an oath, Gandhi stamped the initiative with his own interpretation and imprimatur.

Controlling the understanding of group action, as Gandhi attempted at the mass meeting, is a very important principle of authorship and was nothing new to him. Gandhi gained a much stronger voice in the resistance after he began publishing the paper *Indian Opinion* in 1903. It obviously served as a vehicle for his authority as well as for his ideas. He used its pages, for example, to solicit new names for the noncooperation campaign, once he had decided that "passive resistance" would no longer do. Then, not content with the prize-winning entry, Gandhi "corrected" it to satyagraha (Gandhi 1972: 102). By stating that he had *corrected* the name, Gandhi implied that there was a transcendent "right" one, and that only he had recognized it.

Giving a name to a movement is an important initial assertion of authorship. Giving the movement a permanent support group and command center is perhaps the next important claim to authority. Gandhi formed a loyal cadre at his rural communes (or ashrams, as he later called them in India): first the Phoenix settlement and then Tolstoy Farm, at both of which resistance strategy was also planned. Families of jailed satyagrahis were maintained at Tolstoy Farm; satyagraha recruits were held in reserve at Phoenix until they were committed to active noncooperation. The idea of such rural communes did not originate with Gandhi, of course. Ruskin and Tolstoy provided models in their writings, and there was a pre-existing rural commune near the Phoenix settlement (Swan 1985: 59). That the commune should also serve as a staging ground for protesters, however, occurred on Gandhi's own authority. Gandhi believed (for himself, most of all, but for others as well) that the self-sacrifice of a few could authorize action by the many, and he lived out this belief in the way he used his fellow communitarians in political action. He precipitated the mass strike by indentured laborers with the help of only sixteen women satyagrahis, the female core of his Phoenix establishment (Gandhi 1972: 253–56). These early protests and many of Gandhi's later acts of satyagraha started out as "ashrams-in-motion," to adapt Erik Erikson's phrase (1969: 445) for the most famous Indian satyagraha campaign, the Salt March in 1930.

The personal and communal discipline that Gandhi ordained in his settlements patterned a strong common consciousness and practice (see Gandhi 1972: 215–36 for a description of this well-developed patterning even in the early settlement, Tolstoy Farm). It prepared for dedication to the cause and commitment to the leader (of course, those who joined the settlements were self-selected for these qualities as well). Gandhi also used these loyal followers to effect a division of labor in the satyagraha campaigns: one follower could be sent to India to collect funds, while Gandhi himself petitioned Parliament in Britain and another back home in South Africa continued publication of the newspaper. Even when support waned externally or there was severe official repression, Gandhi could depend on a corps of supporters to staff the resistance campaign and therefore to maintain his authority over it.

Gandhi also claimed authority by representing (in both senses of the word) the protest abroad. As he moved across India, from Bombay to the United Provinces, Madras, and later Bengal, and as he joined delegations to Britain, he represented the plight of the South African Indians, but at the same time he represented his own leadership (for a later period, compare Wolpert 1984: 127). His Indian representations then enhanced his authority in South Africa — most obviously in the reputation he earned by accompanying his much more famous Indian political mentor, Gokhale, on tour in South Africa in 1912.

Having asserted his authority and formed organizations to support it, Gandhi also ensured an independent source of funds to maintain what he had authored. When his authority began to be challenged after 1909 and support for him declined among his merchant backers, Gandhi could fall back on funds from an Indian industrialist, Sir Ratanji Tata, to maintain his newspaper and his rural commune (Gandhi 1972: 212). These funds came from a successful fund-raising trip to India by Polak, one of his most loyal fellow communitarians (Swan 1985: 226). Another committed follower, Herbert Kallenback, donated the land for Tolstoy Farm in 1910 (Gandhi 1972: 214).

140   Authorship must first be asserted, then maintained, and, last of all, guarded. Throughout his last years in South Africa, Gandhi took great pains to discipline the satyagraha movement, to confine

it within limits that he, by now its recognized author, set. Without such pains, authors would lose authority over their "creations": the creations might become something quite different, or another person might try to assert authorship over them. Gandhi guarded most authoritatively where his authority was most strategic: in the rural communes. If his discipline did not reach there, it would not control the campaign anywhere. Therefore, Gandhi intervened in the smallest details of life at Tolstoy Farm: after getting common consent to a vegetarian regimen, Gandhi still helped out in the kitchen because his "presence acted as a check on petty bickerings" (Gandhi 1972: 216). Later, in jail and on the march with indentured laborers, Gandhi similarly doled out food, so that rations were equal. Gandhi certainly understood that authority over the spirit also involved control over the stomach. Gandhi's concern with disciplining everyday life did not stop with food, however. He taught the other Tolstoy Farmers sandal-making techniques, the precepts of various religions, nature cures, the necessity of making friends with snakes, and the recipe for coffee substitutes (it appears in Gandhi 1972: 225n.). Gandhi even convinced the young women to shave off their hair so that they would not provoke the emotions of the male communitarians. The motivation, we must remember, was not Machiavellian; it was utopian dedication: as Gandhi disciplined the supporters of satyagraha, he confirmed himself as a satyagrahi.

Outside the ashram, Gandhi also attempted to control misreadings of the movement. Swan notes (1985: 111–12) with disappointment that Gandhi blamed failures in the movement on deficiencies in individuals, rather than on problems of organization, of goals, or of beliefs. Gandhi perhaps emphasized the limitations of ordinary people to accentuate the importance of heroes to a movement (see Gandhi 1972: 119; Swan 1985: 115), especially the fact that they served as models and gave direction (read: discipline) to otherwise hapless followers. Such heroes were in fact indispensable: "wherever [a movement] has good men and true at its helm, it is bound to attract to itself the requisite funds," Gandhi said (1972: 119–20), and further reflected, "It is always difficult for followers to sustain a conflict in the absence of their leader" (1972: 135).

Gandhi's control could be quite palpable: an internal revolt by some Pathans, who believed Gandhi had sold out to South African authorities, threatened to radicalize (in Swan's opinion [1985: 163]) the satyagraha movement in 1908. The Pathans wanted to continue civil disobedience, whereas Gandhi had reached a compromise with the government that allowed Indians to fulfill the legal requirement to register, but to do so voluntarily. The Pathans, who saw little difference between voluntary compliance and legal coercion, contested Gandhi's authority in the most direct way: they assaulted him and beat him severely. Although Gandhi (1972: 155–56) says he refused to testify against the attackers, Swan (1985: 163) reports that he asked the government to deport the ringleader.

In 1913, on the protest march with indentured laborers, Gandhi combined authority and discipline. He had the indentured laborers, who had deserted their employment, sell their property or leave it behind. Stripped of almost everything except clothes and blankets, they were also almost completely stripped of independence. Gandhi promised them a daily dole, and they became Gandhi's "pilgrims," his satyagraha "soldiers." He even intervened in their sex lives, for, as adulteries happened from time to time on the march, Gandhi soon "arrived on the scene" to segregate the guilty parties (Gandhi 1972: 270). Gandhi also cooked, dished up, and did "sweeping, scavenging and similar work." He recognized that "where the leader himself becomes a servant, there are no rival claimants for leadership" (Gandhi 1972: 268).

A year later, the next experiment in authorship took place when Gandhi moved satyagraha to India, where, because it had few precedents, it could become more securely his. Gandhi, however, had to reauthorize himself under very different circumstances. Not only did he become a very different person, but also satyagraha changed considerably.

Authorizing Satyagraha Abroad

Authorship involves reputation, which can spread independently of the person. Gandhi's reputation, the reputed Gandhi who had condensed in the immediate circumstances of South Africa, preceded him to India. When he himself arrived in 1915, he probably confirmed the worst fears of the Westernized elite. He appeared at a party given in his honor wearing turban, *dhoti*, and rustic cloak because, he explained (1957: 374), "I . . . had lived my best life among indentured labourers" (but only in fact for a short period in 1913: again, Gandhi tells us, radical changes in personhood precipitate from immediate circumstances). He then left for Poona, Gokhale's home base, where he learned that the authorship of satyagraha in South Africa — his best life, as he put it — would hurt his political future in India. The Indian National Congress had split in 1907, and the two camps, of cultural nationalists and "extremists" like Tilak and of Westernizers and modernizers like Gokhale, were still at odds over goals and methods. Although Gokhale pressed Gandhi's case, the other members of the Friends of India Society would not have him as a member because they feared mass protest methods like satyagraha. The society's reaction was typical of the Westernizers. For them, legitimate nationalism consisted of petitions, debate, and constitutional modifications; any other protest was revolutionary and suspect. Shortly thereafter, Gokhale died, and Gandhi withdrew his name from consideration for membership.

Gandhi did nothing to alter his negative reputation as the author of satyagraha during the opening ceremonies of Annie Besant's Benares Hindu University at Varanasi in 1916. In his autobiography, Gandhi (1957: 230) made only a short allusion to this immediate circumstance, but it was one that led many Indian nationalists to join the Bombay Westernizers in fearing the authority of his South African experience. Gandhi was one among many notables invited (by Malaviya, Gandhi said) to address a large gathering of rajas, princelings, and other members of the indigenous gentry who had funded Besant's and Malaviya's project. Eleven years afterward, Gandhi recalled with great clarity — and great disgust — the ostentation of these Indian princes:

> pearl necklaces round their necks, bracelets on their wrists, pearl and diamond tassels on their turbans, and . . . swords with golden hilts hanging from their waistbands.
> I discovered that these were insignia not of their royalty, but of their slavery (Gandhi 1957: 230).

In his autobiography, Gandhi did not report the reception given his speech in Varanasi that day. The audience heard, or thought it heard, Gandhi condemn the Indian wealthy and condone extremist protest methods. Decorum completely broke down, as many dignitaries departed in protest and students shouted, and

143

the meeting evaporated in collective anger and embarrassment, even before Gandhi had finished (see Erikson 1969: 282–85 for a portrayal; CWG 13: 210–16 and following).

The lesson at Benares Hindu University on that day was quite clear. The Gandhi that had precipitated in South Africa and the satyagraha this Gandhi had authored there — an authorship, it should be remembered, that had been secured by bringing satyagraha out of South Africa and into India — would have to adapt to the immediate circumstances of India. This Gandhi and "his" invention inspired fear in India as revolutionary, as an instigator of the masses. Furthermore, this Gandhi's reputed authorship of extremist protest had cut him off from the Indian support base he had hoped to develop through his connection with Gokhale. Earlier, in 1901, Gandhi's wish to gain authority within the Indian nationalist movement had been stymied by Pherozeshah Mehta (Swan 1985: 91). Gandhi seemed even worse off after World War I began.

Between 1915 and 1922, however, Gandhi experimented with satyagraha in India and with his own authority in response to these immediate circumstances. The other elements of Gandhian utopia, which he had combined with his developing notions of satyagraha in the 1909 confrontation precipitated by his trip to Britain, presented few problems because there were so many antecedents for them in Bengal, Bombay, and Besant. The problem was how to authorize satyagraha as a suitable invention for India. The solution, as it condensed in the last years of World War I, was a clearly defined authority for Gandhi in India and a carefully delimited experimental practice for satyagraha in the Indian independence movement — and thus Gandhian utopia became constituted.

Satyagraha in Champaran

Champaran, as Gandhi himself admitted, was a little-known district in the backward state of Bihar. That made it ideal for Gandhi's purposes. Rejected by the nationalist elite, Gandhi conducted his first experiment with satyagraha in India in a region "cut off from the rest of India," where "the Congress was practically unknown" (Gandhi 1957: 411). Gandhi therefore did not have to compete with any existing Congress authority, and, since he made it very clear that he was on his own, he did not have to share authority with the Congress for his eventual success (see Gandhi 1957: 412).[4]

144

Though perhaps a backwater in India, for Gandhi Champaran was a beachhead into the Indian nationalist movement.

Gandhi said he was successful in Champaran, and he was generally acknowledged as successful by the nationalist movement. In this case, Gandhi authored his reputation better than he managed social reality, however. Stephen Henningham (1976: 73) finds that Gandhi was a "figurehead" in Champaran and that his role was of a "limited nature" in solving the dispute there. When Gandhi reached Champaran in 1917, he walked in on an existing conflict between British planters and a local Indian elite.[5] He had been invited by Raj Kumar Shukla, whom Gandhi saw as a gullible and simple peasant but who was not in fact the long-suffering and put-upon cultivator that Gandhi took him to be. Shukla and many of the other Indian protesters represented a class of rich tenants, who had actively lobbied against British planters for some time. These British planters leased large tracks of land from the local raja and made their tenants like Shukla, although well-off themselves, answer to the British landlords' needs. Earlier, the planters had forced their tenants to cultivate indigo. In Gandhi's time, aniline dyes had curtailed indigo cropping, but the rich tenants were freed from growing indigo only to have their British landlords impose other crops or increase their rents (Henningham 1976: 64). The tenants wanted these restraints on their pursuit of profitable agriculture lifted. Local professionals, like the lawyer Rajendra Prasad (afterward one of Gandhi's most loyal allies and first president of India), joined with the rich tenants against the British planters. They had often been employed to argue the tenants' case, or for other reasons joined with the tenants in common purpose against the British landlords. This coalition, Henningham believes, had the battle already nearly won before Gandhi's entrance; at most, Henningham (1976: 73) allows that Gandhi helped deliver the coup de grace.

These immediate circumstances precipitated Gandhi into leading a movement he did not control and perhaps did not understand (in terms of its class base); because he was reduced to a figurehead, his authority was manipulated. Gandhi, however, achieved authorship relatively cheaply and quickly, and Champaran provided him with a method of experiment suited to Indian circumstances. Gandhi's coup de grace consisted of mass demonstrations and a private inquiry into the tenants' grievances. The British colonial administration soon authorized an official commission of inquiry, with Gandhi sitting as the tenants' representative. The commission

145

advocated substantial reforms, which met most of the demands of the Indian cultivators against the British landlords (Henningham 1976: 68–69).

In Champaran, Gandhi learned that a successful satyagraha campaign came from confronting British domination — in this case, a British plantocracy. He also learned that mass support for satyagraha could be mustered out by working through local leaders — and perhaps only by working through them. In the Champaran case, the local leadership consisted of the coalition of rich peasants and the professional lower-middle class that had invited him in and supported him once he was on the scene. That is, Gandhi learned from the immediate circumstances in Champaran that "local subcontractors," as Judith Brown (1972) calls them, had to convey his authority to the masses. They were necessary intermediaries — necessary to Gandhi because they interpreted his message at the local level; intermediary because they used Gandhi's authority to enhance their local reputations while they mobilized the local support that authored Gandhi as a national leader.[6]

Champaran taught Gandhi what he could and must do. The next satyagraha experiment taught him what he could not and must not do.

The Ahmedabad Experiment

Early in 1918, with Champaran behind him, Gandhi intervened in a dispute between mill owners and laborers in the city of Ahmedabad, very near his first Indian ashram. Both mill owners and workers were Indian, and Gandhi found himself in a new situation: mediating a class confrontation between his own people. The class situation could not fail to have a direct, personal meaning for Gandhi because the leading mill owner was a major financial supporter of Gandhi's ashram, whereas that mill owner's sister, who had been Gandhi's friend even longer than her brother, represented the discontented workers.

Gandhi advised the workers to strike. Once the strike began, he held daily meetings to strengthen their resolve. Nevertheless, their determination weakened after several weeks, and Gandhi feared the strikers would capitulate. Gandhi then fixed upon a new experiment with satyagraha, a new way to discipline challenges to his authority. He undertook one of his earliest fasts, not so much to change the minds of the mill owners (although it had that effect)

146

as to control the workers. In the end Gandhi obtained a settlement that gave the mill laborers the wage increase that Gandhi had determined was just — but only for one day, after which the eventual wage would be left to arbitration (see Erikson 1969: 322–63 for an extended account of the strike).

The Ahmedabad strike left Gandhi feeling ambivalent. He worried that the fast had coerced the mill owners, and coercion, for him, did not belong in satyagraha. Gandhi's concern no doubt depended somewhat on his friendly and financial relations with the mill owners. Perhaps more important, this satyagraha saw Indians confront Indians in a naked class struggle, and Gandhi, although recognizing the exploitation of the mill owners, found it difficult to intercede with the same forthrightness as in Champaran.[7] Confronting equally exploitative planters who were also British colonials was probably much less ambiguous. Another powerful lesson for Gandhi was the indiscipline of the poor. There had been a near-riot at the public distribution of sweets sponsored by the mill owners as a peace gesture, after the strike and Gandhi's fast ended. The ensuing chaos had mostly involved the city's beggars and poor rather than mill workers, but it confirmed Gandhi's fear that the desperation of the poor rendered "them insensible to all feelings of decency and self-respect" (Gandhi 1957: 434).

Gandhi never again got stuck in the middle of an overt class confrontation between Indians, although he did continue to confront — and distrust — the dehumanization of the masses and their lack of discipline (see, for example, Gandhi's [1957: 470] admission of a "Himalayan miscalculation" in the anti-Rowlatt satyagraha of 1919). After Ahmedabad, he worked assiduously to direct Indians against the British. He told them to leave the differences between wealthy and poor Indians for solution later, in the postcolonial period. The immediate circumstances in Ahmedabad precipitated Gandhi's sharpened vision that class struggle did not "suit" Indian culture.

The Kheda Satyagraha

Gandhi's evolving experiment with "class conciliation," as Francine Frankel (1978: 38) calls it, dominated his next satyagraha, the Kheda protest in Gujarat. Here, Gandhi's opponent was not an 147 exploitative economic class, of either foreigners or fellow Indians, but the colonial administration itself. The issue was economic but

involved political domination, not class. The administration refused to grant remission of land taxes to the Kheda peasants, in
spite of widespread crop failure. The proper resistance, Gandhi
advised, would be to hold back payment of land taxes until the
government granted concessions. Gandhi made his appeal to rich
and poor peasants alike, even though the rich could weather the
forced sale of their assets (by which the British collected tax arrears)
better than the poor. Gandhi evolved the concept of trusteeship to
justify the need for common action: the wealthy had a moral obligation to use their riches in support of the poor (Frankel 1978:
39–40).

In Kheda, as in Champaran, Gandhi unwittingly represented the
interests of "substantial landowners," who were attempting to convert their growing economic and social importance into political
leverage against state taxation (Breman 1985: 366–67, but also see
Hardiman 1981). Crispin Bates (1981: 809) refers to them as a "rural
bourgeoisie," most of whom had no trouble paying up their revenue arrears once the colonial government got the political message
that Gandhi helped deliver.

The revolutionary Gandhi who disdained the raja's wealth at
Varanasi, who wore the clothes of the indentured because his best
life was with them, who pleaded for the poor mill worker against
his friends the mill owners, disappeared (except for the rustic clothing) and was replaced by a new Gandhian authority and a different
Gandhi personhood, both of which developed under the press of
Indian conditions. In India, the Gandhi of class conciliation, of
careful discipline of the poor (through the "good offices" of the
rural rich peasantry and the urban educated middle class),[8] and of
confrontation only with British colonialism was definitively authored. If, as Gandhi believed, the mobilization of indentured
South African Indians caused a revolutionary rupture in his life
and politics, then the Indian experiments newly authored Gandhi,
too: they dissuaded him from a politics of class and a direct appeal
to the impoverished, both of which might have led to an undisciplined, impoverished satyagraha and a Gandhi whose authority
was lost in a mass upheaval.

Recruitment for the Raj

In June 1918 Gandhi acknowledged that he had accepted "the
toughest job I have yet handled" (CWG 14: 473). He became a

recruiter for the Raj in Gujarat as world war raged in Europe. Gandhi toured districts, like Kheda, that he had only recently directed in antigovernment protests. Now he advocated "absolutely unconditional and whole-hearted cooperation" with the British war effort, and he issued pamphlets urging peasants to enlist (CWG 14: 428, 434, 439–43). Gandhi's idea was to prove to the British through good deeds that Indians deserved self-rule. He also hoped to show that he and other satyagrahis harbored no abiding ill will against the British, but only against their colonialism. He recalled his feelings later on:

> I recognize that in the hour of its danger we must give . . . ungrudging and unequivocal support to the Empire of which we aspire in the near future to be partners . . . I would make India offer all her able-bodied sons as a sacrifice to the Empire at its critical moment (Gandhi 1957 [1929]: 447–48).

Recruiting proved too tough a job for Gandhi. Other nationalist leaders and even otherwise dependable supporters like the Reverend Charles Andrews had chastised his recruiting all along (see CWG 14: 474–78). By early July, several weeks after he began his campaign, Gandhi had not a single recruit (CWG 14: 473). Peasants questioned his commitment to nonviolence, and they wondered why he now felt it necessary to help an oppressive colonial administration (Gandhi 1957 [1929]: 446). Under this attack, Gandhi admitted that he "nearly ruined [his] constitution during the recruiting campaign"; a physician, however, found nothing wrong with his vital signs and diagnosed a nervous breakdown (Gandhi 1957 [1929]: 450, 452; also see Wolpert 1984: 54–55).

Recruiting for the Raj did break down Gandhi's old constitution and reconstitute him, I believe. It brought to a virtual end the personal revolution that Gandhi had begun early in the twentieth century. That revolution had been in response to immediate circumstances and had been informed by an intellectual work group that Gandhi had in part fashioned. During that revolution, Gandhi had experimented with class conflict and class conciliation; he had cycled between confronting the colonial state and doing good works for it. He had tried out new personal diets and celibacy and tried on different sorts of clothing, as well. Thereafter, there were few new experiments and little personal discontinuity, and perhaps *149* it is fitting that Gandhi did write his so-called autobiography in 1927–29, as if — because? — his experiments had terminated.[9]

Thereafter, he was never to advocate unstinting and loyal service to the British colonial state. Just as he adopted class conciliation in response to class antagonisms within India, the negative reactions of his fellow Indians to the recruitment campaign made Gandhi abandon some of the moral entailments of his vision of satyagraha. One should not take advantage of an opponent, perhaps, but one should also not offer aid. The failed experiment with recruiting also told Gandhi that if he were to authorize a nationalist movement, he could not abandon class struggle *and* anticolonial protest. Subsequently, as he increasingly adopted class conciliation at home, he more directly and aggressively confronted the foreign British power. Indian circumstances did not permit Gandhi to join the British; therefore, he learned he had to beat them.

The later successes or partial successes of satyagraha — among the most important, noncooperation in 1922, civil disobedience and the Salt March in 1930, and the Quit India campaign in 1942 — confirmed nonviolent resistance and the other basic elements of Gandhian utopia as the program of the nationalist movement. Accepting satyagraha as it had evolved by the early 1920s meant embracing spiritual revolution, trusteeship, an organic view of society, the virtues of discipline, simplification, and most of the other elements of Gandhian utopia. It meant experimenting with class conciliation so that the primary experiment, confrontation with the British, could have priority. Although not completely constituted by the early 1920s, Gandhian utopia was already an acknowledged, labeled, and authored set of cultural meanings that closely defined the nationalist movement. When Gandhian utopia was challenged, it was sufficiently constituted and strong to resist, as in the first major test: B. R. Ambedkar's 1932 plea for electoral guarantees to Untouchables. Similarly, Gandhi's political authority and moral leadership survived challenges from the left, also noted in the following chapter. Even when commitment to Gandhian utopia or to Gandhi was weak, that utopia had to be dealt with or acknowledged as the reigning set of beliefs. Nehru, for example, admitted to grave doubts about where Gandhi was leading the nationalist movement, came near to ridiculing the idea of trusteeship, and certainly reacted negatively to Gandhi's distrust of industrialization (Nehru 1962 [1936]: 504–52). Yet in spite of his doubts, Nehru followed Gandhi. Moreover, when Nehru got out of line, Gandhi's authority forced him back into it, as I shall indicate in Chapter 8, which discusses how Gandhi's individual dream became India's vision.

EIGHT

The Gandhian Experiment

> At the end of every human labor-process, we get a result
> that already existed in the imagination of the laborer at its
> commencement. He not only effects a change of form in the
> material on which he works, but he also realizes a purpose
> of his own . . .
>
> Karl Marx (1967 [1867], vol. 1: 178)

What difference did Gandhi and Gandhian utopia make to Indian
nationalism? To ask this question is to move from a history of the
singular to a structural history.

No one can say what India might have been, had Gandhi not
been. One can say with somewhat more certainty what India did
not become because Gandhian utopia came into being. To the extent that what did happen was what the Gandhian vision wished
to happen, the outcome can be judged a successful experiment
with utopia.

From this perspective, I review in the following pages the structural consequences of Gandhi's incomplete assertion of authority
over the Indian nationalist movement. When his experiments
proved successful in the nationalist movement before independence, Gandhi's authority made for a real difference in the way
India achieved nationhood. He successfully disciplined the nationalist movement to nonviolent resistance and the other constitutive
elements of Gandhian utopia he had authorized by the early 1920s.
In these cases, Gandhi's intentions, at least to the extent I and
others infer them correctly from the history of what he said and
did, made new circumstances. In other cases, Gandhi's authorship
failed to control certain experiments, and he attracted collaborators
he did not want or bowed to their authority. In these cases, he
failed to control misreadings of his authority, even by himself. For,

151

after all, if individuals are precipitated by immediate circumstances, the consistency of any acclaimed author is always contingent and variable, as Gandhi himself recognized. In these circumstances, when Gandhi's authority proved unsuccessful, when the public Gandhi proved inconsistent, Gandhian utopia became an empty label or an ideology, and "Gandhi" — now condensed into a different individual authorship — spoke willy-nilly for vested interests or was turned into a hollow hero.

Successful Experiments

Today, in India and abroad, many people sadly discount Gandhi's lasting significance for his nation because, they assert, so few of his proposals and programs survived after independence. "Gandhi was too saintly for the real world," it is said, which is perhaps the cheapest way to deauthorize a utopian vision. Gandhi disliked his Mahatma reputation, not least of all perhaps because he found the trappings of sainthood inconsistent with a social revolutionary's mantle. It is true that after independence in 1947, many Gandhian social experiments were not implemented or underwent great change, as I will indicate in the next chapter. Other, personal, experiments, like celibacy and nature cures, were not even considered. By that time, however, Gandhian utopia had already helped constitute the future of the Indian nation through several successful experiments before independence. That is, the circumstances of India after 1947, including even the devaluation of further Gandhian experiments, were compelled by these earlier successful experiments. As saintly as the Mahatma may have been, as utopian as his vision was, the experiments I chronicle below were significant for what late British India became and for what early Nehru India therefore had to deal with.

Ahimsa

Satyagraha authorized Gandhi as a national leader, and Gandhi defended his authorship against interpreters and deviations that threatened it. Nonviolence, or ahimsa, was so important a part of nonviolent resistance that Gandhi was quite willing to abandon national protest when this principle was violated. In the most famous instance, he halted the noncooperation movement in 1922 because some Congress volunteers had murdered policemen in the village of Chauri Chaura.

We can gain a sense of what might have been the norm by looking at what was only the exception: shortly after the Congress adopted the Quit India protest in 1942, the British administration arrested the Congress leaders. Without their restraining hand, the most violent confrontation developed between Indian nationalists, who consciously abandoned satyagraha and adopted terrorism, and the British (see Frankel 1978: 63).

Gene Sharp (1979: 7) measures the authority of ahimsa in a more direct way: judging from casualty ratios in the Algerian revolution, he estimates that 3 million to 3.5 million Indians would have died in a hypothetical violent independence struggle, whereas only eight thousand are estimated to have been killed in the actual Congress campaign, governed, as it was, by nonviolence. Again, an exception shows the importance of the Gandhian norm: the communal frenzy that took place in the Punjab at the time of partition, in which Sikhs, Hindus, and Muslims each discriminately murdered the others, shows what might have happened more generally, if Gandhian utopia had not disciplined violence.

Satyagraha also curtailed the destruction of India's economic infrastructure, which had reached a high level of development even though, or sometimes because, India was a colonized society. In the interests of increasing the colony's revenues or for military reasons, the British had subsidized railroads, the telegraph, great irrigation works, and other modernizations. Beginning in the late nineteenth century but especially after World War I, the British introduced tariffs and trade policies that rewarded and protected indigenous industrialization. Factories and mills had sprung up, especially in western India, along with antagonistic classes of owners and wage laborers — as Gandhi could attest from his Ahmedabad experiment. By the time of independence in 1947, then, India already had a good start on industrialization and capitalist economic development (see Fox 1985: 14–26; Mukherjee 1986: 242–50).

Nonviolent resistance did not countenance blowing up railroads, cutting telegraph lines, sinking ships, dynamiting bridges, burning crops, destroying factories, or perpetrating other acts of revolutionary sabotage. The only mass destruction involved burning foreign cloth, which, if anything, increased demand for cloth produced indigenously. Revolutionary sabotage would have found many attractive targets, given India's relatively high level of de-

153

velopment for a colony, and the problems of capital formation and infrastructural growth in the post-independence period would have been that much greater.

This is not to say, however, that the nationalist movement accepted nonviolence because it was functional. Sumit Sarkar (1983: 46–50) shows that Gandhi's spirited defense of nonviolence had costs for Indian nationalism, too. According to Sarkar, the periodic halts Gandhi called to nationalist protest severely hurt the movement after 1922 and in the early 1930s, in spite of Gandhi's argument that the halts were necessary to keep the anticolonial forces intact. It was the desire to defend a principle and protect his authority, not utilitarian calculation of ends, that made Gandhi put the brakes on mass militancy (for another view, see Chandra 1985: 18, who argues that Gandhi's retreats were part of an overall, effective strategy).

Perhaps, too, it was not ultimately in the best interests of a future India to adopt the nonviolent vision. Many contemporary Congress leaders, among them Jawaharlal Nehru (1962 [1936]: 504–52), did not fully believe so, and there are many present-day Indians who still do not believe so (see the discussion of "deferred revolution" below). When Gandhi proposed nonviolence, no "distanced onlooker" existed who could have judged nonviolence as most beneficial, just as today there is no way to measure objectively whether nonviolence was most functional to India. The contingency of belief, not a conscious calculation of interest or an unconscious functionalism, precipitated the successful experiment with nonviolence, just as it did the other experiments to which I now turn.

Disciplining Peasant Militancy

Partha Chatterjee (1984: 184–87) argues that Gandhian ahimsa and satyagraha curtailed peasant protest and placed it under bourgeois nationalist control. The Indian nationalist movement therefore got all the benefits of a mass following without any of the revolutionary dangers that such mass mobilization usually entails. Noting Gandhi's deep suspicion of mob action, Chatterjee suggests that the concept of ahimsa subjected Gandhi's mass following to political discipline, which, in the Gandhian framework, was meted out by a confirmed leadership consisting of a few committed satyagrahis.

Shahid Amin (1984) substantiates the importance of Gandhi's discipline by giving an instance when it was only partially successful. Amin says that nationalists promoted the image of the peasant masses as politically inert. The masses, nationalists maintained, had to be goaded into action by an educated and middle-class political mediator, someone whom they could invest with saintly qualities and whose message they could follow religiously. When Gandhi visited Gorakhpur (a backwater district in eastern Uttar Pradesh, or the United Provinces, as it was then known) in 1921, local elites or "subcontractors" stage-managed and promoted him as a saint. The peasants were supposed only to worship him.

The peasants had their own ideas, however. Gandhi had promoted "an incipient political consciousness" among them. They ignored the subcontractors (Amin 1984: 48); they even ignored the nonviolence the Mahatma had enjoined. The peasants precipitated their own Gandhi: "not as he really was, but as they had thought him up" (Amin 1984: 54). Using their Gandhi, the peasants supported direct and violent action against the colonial government or against wealthy Indians — the very actions the "other Gandhi" had denounced. In this case, government repression administered the ultimate discipline to popular militancy, which had proved too strong for the Gandhian experiment. In many other situations, however, as Sarkar (1983: 44) maintains, satyagraha and ahimsa proved sufficient "as a brake on mass pressures."

One melancholy story sums up Gandhian discipline of the peasantry — in this case, an inadvertent discipline. At a mass gathering in 1921, Nehru spoke against the recent looting of a landlord. Filled with the spirit of satyagraha, Nehru asked the guilty peasants to raise their hands. When they did, they were promptly arrested by the police who were stationed in the audience (it is not clear that Nehru knew the police were present). These mass arrests crushed the agrarian movement, and Nehru came to regret his role in sending these peasants to prison, where, he lamented, they would spend their youth (Chatterjee 1986b: 149).

Nehru's discomfort does not obscure the fact that peasant agitations and protests sometimes threatened to go far beyond the effective control of Gandhian leaders. As Sarkar (1983: 45–47), following Gyan Pandey, argues, local protest often took the most radical forms when the Congress organization was too weak to discipline it. At such moments, the colonial authorities were often important agents of discipline, as they unwittingly maintained Gandhian authority over anticolonial and anti-landlord peasant protest. These breakdowns also suggest the converse: that when and where the Congress movement was strong, it played an important role in limiting the real threat of peasant militancy.[1]

"Secularism"

The Gandhian vision of an organic, consensual society validated a "secular" approach, which, in the Indian context, meant that all sectarian groups were to coexist harmoniously, and no religious community would be given preference. Gandhi, perhaps because of his positive experience with Muslim traders in South Africa, worked assiduously throughout his Indian experiments to join Hindus and Muslims in nationalist undertakings. The same vision of society disallowed special provisions for minorities — in a corporate, consensual society, the good of the many is also the good of the few. Gandhi therefore struggled with great enthusiasm to remove all the social disabilities that Untouchables suffered, but he was equally adamant in refusing them special privileges. Gandhi successfully suppressed a 1932 attempt by Untouchables, led by B. R. Ambedkar, to gain special electoral privileges similar to those Muslims held. Gandhi fasted until the Untouchable leadership reluctantly accepted his discipline. Ambedkar thereafter held Gandhi responsible for conserving Untouchable backwardness (see Ambedkar 1945). Only some twenty years later — and only after Gandhi's death — did Ambedkar finally get affirmative-action provisions for Untouchables accepted in now-independent India.

Ambedkar's eventual success was not the end of the Gandhian experiment, however. In the late 1970s, the Gandhian vision of a corporate and consensual society sponsored new social action. It became an important justification for an increasingly powerful social movement that opposed the government's affirmative-action program for Untouchables and other backward caste categories (see Chapters 11 and 12).

Voluntarism and Self-Help

Because Gandhi believed that personal dedication was the most powerful force for social change, he emphasized the importance of voluntary service by individuals. His ideas on this point condensed the thinking of many Indian nationalists. Vivekananda, for example, developed a brotherhood of activist monks in Bengal, and Gokhale organized a secular society of educated, middle-class social reformers in Bombay. Gandhi, however, took voluntary service out of the realm of the sacred and away from the exclusive control of the English-educated middle class. It was also no longer to be an armchair social reformism or a hands-off paternalism by the prosperous for the poor. It might require digging latrines at the annual meeting of the Indian National Congress, as Gandhi did, and it was to involve the masses. Although it necessarily started with individual dedication, voluntary service was to be a mass movement. Gandhi hoped it would become India's way of generating social change.

Gandhi's Constructive Programme for regenerating village communities, ending Untouchability, introducing basic education, and accomplishing other social experiments depended on voluntary labor. Volunteers, by their very acts of service, displayed the dedication and discipline that betokened a revolutionary change in mind. Their service, in turn, would change the minds of others. The greatest dedication of voluntary labor came in satyagraha campaigns, for in these circumstances individuals dedicated their well-being, even possibly their lives, in the interest of reforming society. The alternative to voluntary service was institutional coercion, which, given that it could not change inner being, depended on power and punishment. Voluntary service, because individuals dedicated themselves to it, was therefore "self-help" for society even as it helped individual selves to achieve self-regulation and worthiness; selfless service, in a typically Gandhian twist, became a means of self-help.

Belief in voluntary service — that it could be disinterested, that it could change society, that it could be more effective than institutional change — and, conversely, distrust of official action — because corruption and inefficiency plagued it and because policies pronounced from on high could be readily avoided down below — these beliefs constituted significant principles of Indian political consciousness by the time of independence. The contrast, and even confrontation, between government undertaking and voluntary labor from Gandhi's time continued on afterward. For Gandhi, before independence, the contrast was inextricable from the colonial relationship: it was an Indian voluntary movement confronting British government management. After independence, the   *157* contrast was just as sharp but the relations were less hostile: the early Five-Year Plans of the Nehru Congress government valued the Gandhian voluntary movement that persisted even after Gandhi's assassination. The plans gave the movement substantial rewards to continue its efforts, for example, to ameliorate the lot of Untouchables or to build up village industries and hand-loom weaving. Nevertheless, there was a continuing tension between programs of social revolution to be enacted by voluntary labor and the government's program of officially sponsored social reconstruction, a tension that state subsidies probably only exacerbated. In the 1960s, this tension led to a voluntary land reform and village development movement that ran concurrent with government undertakings, as I shall show in the next chapter. In the 1970s, the contrast turned into confrontation, as a voluntary movement for a "partyless" democracy threatened to overturn India's democratically elected Congress party government (discussed in Chapter 10). Without Gandhi's constitution of voluntary movements as alternative and superior to official programs, I suggest, neither of these developments would have been able to gain so much authority in India after independence.

Class Conciliation: Disciplining the Left

Gandhi experimented with coalescing the Indian population into a powerful anticolonial movement. Bipan Chandra (1985: 3, 30) maintains that Gandhi hypothesized correctly: the primary contradiction in colonial India was between British colonialism and the entire Indian population, not the class struggle between Indians. Gandhi's disavowal of class confrontation, his acceptance instead of class conciliation, helped authorize a coalition of Indian classes, although it also deferred any major accommodation of the poor and the landless until after the independence struggle (Chandra 1985: 49). This aspect of Gandhian utopia, then, had important consequences for the postindependence Indian nation. It led to "deferred revolution" (Sarkar 1983: 72) or "passive revolution," to use Gramsci's phrase (Chatterjee 1984: 155; 1986b: 51): colonialism was defeated, but a radical redistribution of wealth and power was not instituted.

158   Sarkar believes India deferred revolution because the Indian bourgeoisie, through the nationalist movement it controlled, successfully detached the issue of political independence from the

issue of revolutionary social change. In this view, India got free of the British in 1947 but remained under the class domination of an indigenous bourgeoisie, whose interests Gandhian utopia, because it deferred class confrontation, had always served. Chandra, although he accepts the fact of passive revolution in India, argues against the notion that Gandhi's vision and his nationalist movement inevitably served certain class interests. He sees no "direct or necessary or inevitable relationship to the bourgeoisie or the bourgeois class structure" (Chandra 1985: 38; also see Mukherjee 1986: 277ff.). Chandra thus rejects a class determinism of Indian nationalism, but he sees another sort of external necessity as determining it. The Gandhian nationalist program, according to Chandra, read the immediate circumstances of colonial India correctly and responded to them properly, through passive revolution.

Gandhian utopia did not represent class interests in some simple and determined way, as Chandra rightly argues, but it was not *only* a response to immediate circumstances, as he maintains. Through his authority, Gandhi worked hard to shape those circumstances and, when that was not possible, to control or discipline them. The multi-class coalition leading the nationalist movement was not just an already determined response to circumstances. Its very fragility argues that it had to be continually reauthorized — hardly what one might expect of an institution supposedly dictated by existing conditions. Again and again, Gandhi intervened to maintain the coalition against internal class conflicts and from the ideological prospecting of Communist and other political organizations on the far left. In this way, Gandhi's faith in Gandhian utopia helped author the passive revolution in India.

Gandhi, for example, strained to ensure that his Congress coworkers did not upset the class coalition. When Nehru in 1931 pushed through a no-rent campaign, in which tenants held back payments to their (Indian) landlords, Gandhi intervened to reassure the landlords that the Congress did not intend class struggle (Frankel 1978: 50–51). As late as 1939, when radicals had become even more powerful in the Congress, Gandhi was able to overturn the election of the revolutionary Subhas Chandra Bose as Congress president (Frankel 1978: 61–62).

Another telling argument: as opponents of Gandhi's class conciliation grew more threatening throughout the 1930s, Gandhi's struggle for authority over the nationalist movement became an ever more dubious battle. Trusteeship, nonviolence, and consensus came under increasing attack. For example, an ardent Marxist (at that time), Jayaprakash Narayan, dismissed Gandhi's "preaching" of class accommodation as bourgeois European thinking. Taking at face value Gandhi's statement that in the society of his dreams both prince and pauper would have justice, Jayaprakash disingenuously wondered why Gandhi dreamed of a future society where there were still paupers. His summary condemnation of Gandhi's trusteeship is contained in a chapter heading: "The Shark, a Trustee for the Minnow" (Prasad 1980: 36–40).

As leftist attacks on Gandhi in print became more strident, Communists and other revolutionaries increasingly organized peasant militancy on the ground. The *kisan* (peasant) movement, which won mass support for its anti-landlord program from the early 1930s on, was an important threat to the Gandhian vision of class conciliation (Frankel 1978: 55–60). When Communists decided to make common purpose with nationalist forces in the 1930s and became members of the Congress on an individual basis, the threat of a class-based revolutionary politics came close to home.

As Communist penetration and peasant militancy proceeded apace in the late 1930s and criticism of the Gandhian vision increased both within and outside the Congress, Gandhi more strongly emphasized his experimental Constructive Programme for rural uplift. Gandhi's program, in opposition to the Communist and kisan movements, disciplined peasant militancy. It emphasized self-help measures and labor-intensive means that would not require large investments of capital. Heavy capital outlays could be obtained in the Indian situation only by expropriation of the rural wealthy. Better to raise up peasants a little way by their own efforts than have them reach new heights by trampling their class enemies — that was the thinking behind the Gandhian experiment with the Constructive Programme. Gandhi's motives were principled and presumably for India's ultimate good, as Francine Frankel (1978: 47) notes, even though they sacrificed egalitarian goals in the short run.

Chandra (1985: 6–7) argues that Gandhi became increasingly radicalized from the 1930s on and began to champion the economic demands of the rural population. Here was another Gandhian experiment in carefully balancing — and therefore neutralizing — class forces. The threat of a Marxist socialist model, sponsored by the urban, educated middle class, explains Gandhi's apparent "radicalization" in his last years. As the rich peasantry became a more important political factor in the years just before independence (see Raghavan 1983), Gandhi embraced rural populism against the urban power base of Nehru and other Congress socialists committed to large-scale industrialization and class struggle (see Sarkar 1983: 68–69). Gandhi even reverted to his initial prescription of hand-loom weaving as a form of self-provisioning bread labor, rather than as a cure for rural underemployment (which implied selling hand-loomed cloth in the market) (Chatterjee 1986a: 117–21). That Gandhi continued to reinterpret his dream even into his last years indicates that his authorship was not a certainty. Instead, it was constantly contested and had to be reauthorized. The Gandhian dream therefore continued to be somewhat responsive to immediate circumstances, although within ever more narrow limits imposed by its own increasingly substantial existence. As Gandhi became typecast as the saintly Mahatma — a typecasting that he had to allow to some extent to keep authority over his nationalist subcontractors and to mobilize the rural masses — so his individual vision became fixed or constituted within the nationalist movement. Gandhian utopia, like any set of public, activated beliefs, lost its flexibility and became more compelling than enabling.

The best proof of this last point is that Gandhi's successes often promoted his failures — that is, by his authorization of some things, Gandhi failed with others.

Failed Experiments

Some of Gandhi's failures, or what he regarded as his failures, like Muslim separatism and the creation of Pakistan, have so many circumstances behind them that the Gandhian vision, even if it was contributory (see Sarkar 1983: 57–58; Chandra 1984: 297, 301 n.6), would probably not be the essential element. In such cases, the Gandhian experiment failed because it had insufficient authority to remake society completely. When it struggled against powerful circumstances and failed, as with Muslim separatism, Gandhian utopia probably made little difference to the outcome, therefore; and that outcome, in turn had little effect on the utopian vision.

The following section deals with a different sort of failure, those that were directly perpetrated through misuse of the utopian vision. Obviously, these failures depended on Gandhian utopia's

161

power to compel belief and practice, rather than its weakness. If it had not had some authority, there would have been little value in misrepresenting it. As that authority increased and the set of meanings constituted by Gandhian utopia became more and more common belief and practice, the payoffs from misrepresentation also went up.

This second sort of failure, those due to misuse and misrepresentation, had effects on Gandhian utopia. In these cases, Gandhi's utopia had insufficient authority to control interpretations or applications of its own vision. The result of such misappropriation was either that the utopia became an empty label, a public meaning with no real content in terms of social practice, or that the vision was converted into an ideology justifying vested interests rather than revolutionary dreams.

Political "Hijacking" of Gandhian Utopia

Hijacking (a term I "hijack" from Baxi 1985: 2) a utopian vision means converting it into a justifying ideology. It requires appropriating the utopia in name only and using it in the most opportunistic fashion to label practices that actually violate its vision. Gandhi's major failure was his inability to stop the Congress movement from hijacking satyagraha and class conciliation. Hijacking, however, had limited consequences. It only "ripped off" the Gandhian vision; it did not rip it apart. That is, hijacking used the vision expediently, while leaving its central meanings intact and still authoritative; it did not transform its meanings and reauthorize them for very different circumstances, as happened in the "ideological transplanting" I discuss in the next section.

David Arnold (1977: 186–89), for example, argues that although Gandhi's methods had the potential to be revolutionary, they were not actually so, as they were practiced by the Congress in South India before independence. The propertied classes in the Madras region were alienated from Gandhi in 1919, when satyagraha most threatened colonialism. They took to satyagraha later, as nonviolent protest was increasingly directed at local problems and limited constitutional reforms. By 1937, "satyagraha was being used by the Congress as a clamp from outside the constitutional system to exert pressure inside that system" (Arnold 1977: 186), rather than as a revolutionary hammer with which to crack the system wide open. British repression in part forced this hijacking of Gandhian utopia by the Congress, but it also happened because propertied Indians in Madras willingly accommodated with the British Raj against the threat of left-wing militancy. Power was therefore passing from the British to a Congress that had proved "safe." It paid lip service to the Gandhian dream but pursued quite a different vision in practice.

Hijacking, which was an ever-present problem throughout India, led to a strong tendency toward "institutional" Gandhism (compare Ostergaard 1985: 4–5) in the National Congress before independence and in the ruling Congress party afterward. At times, the Congress seems to have had no more use for the Gandhian vision than as a nationally acknowledged "brand name." Nehru, for example, reputedly rejected a plan for national reconstruction even though it was truly Gandhian (Kantowsky 1980: 25–27). Nehru could inaugurate a mass-production factory and claim that Gandhi would have approved had he been alive (Chatterjee 1986a: 154). These instances are part of a general pattern by which Congress leaders appropriated "the political consequences" of Gandhi's vision (Chatterjee 1986a: 153–55) without his Truth. They were content, once they had enough control over satyagraha and the other aspects of Gandhian utopia, to elicit disciplined mass protest. They thus appropriated Gandhi's mobilization and manipulated his saintly public presence, but only superficially appropriated his thought. Congress leaders probably emphasized Gandhi's image as a saintly Mahatma not only to speak out to the masses but also to silence Gandhi as a revolutionary experimentalist.

Hijacking had inherent limits, however. Congress leaders continued to need Gandhi the public figure and the effective mass leader. When they got him, however, they also had to take the authority of his utopian vision, which Gandhi enforced in no uncertain terms — on Nehru especially (as in the no-tax campaign previously mentioned), and on other potential hijackers. Turning Gandhi into the Mahatma — or into a "totem," as one Indian leader I interviewed in 1988 termed it — was much easier after Gandhi's death than while he lived. The living Gandhi required Congress leaders to hand-spin daily. It was, among other things, a symbolic enactment of his authority. It was a real acknowledgment that Congress could have Gandhi only if they also accepted Gandhian experiments.

Therefore, Congress leaders only hijacked the utopia, and even that was only partially successful while Gandhi and his authority were alive. The Congress movement failed, perhaps dared not try, to turn Gandhian utopia into an ideology or utopia justifying, for example, forced-march industrialization under centralized state socialism — which was Nehru's dream. This vision would have required wresting authority away from Gandhi, who was, after all, the ostensible author of Gandhian utopia. It was attempted only after Gandhi's assassination. Gandhi and Gandhians thus continued to exert independent authority, in spite of the hijacking. Even after independence, when the Nehru government tried very hard to go beyond hijacking the Gandhian vision, which now lacked Gandhi's authority, it failed to transform it completely (see the next chapter; for an opposite opinion, see Chatterjee 1986a: 132). The Gandhian dream endured and eventually provided the basis for a new utopian vision of India in the J.P. movement I discuss in Chapter 10.

Gandhian Utopia as Ideological "Transplant"

A far greater challenge to authority than from hijacking comes from transplanting a utopia. In an "ideological transplant" (I "transplant" this concept from Devdutt 1981: 204), there is a true appropriation, a radical misreading and therefore a deauthorization of the utopian vision, rather than just lip service emptily paid it. Unwanted collaborators appear, or, more accurately, desired collaborators turn into attempted coauthors, who challenge the authority of the reputed author. Utopian ideas may then be transferred to particular groups or classes, whose ideological property they become. The ideas themselves may not be reformulated, but they are reauthorized — that is, when the ideological transfer is successful. No longer do the ideas challenge the present by a vision of future perfection. Instead, they are made to legitimate existing vested interests or to rationalize current circumstances.

Before independence, Gandhian utopia served rich peasants and the Indian bourgeoisie as an ideological transplant. Both groups fell upon Gandhian ideas as these populations developed an increasing consciousness of themselves and their political interests. Gandhian politics appealed to the "peasant upper crust," to use Sarkar's (1983: 68) phrase, because it minimized class upheaval and violence in the countryside. The rich peasants, who were already well on the way to the political dominance they eventually achieved in independent India, found natural allies in the urban middle class

164

leading the nationalist movement (as in the Champaran coalition).[2] The Gandhian program often served unintentionally to further both these urban and rural interests. Similarly, by the 1930s, Indian big business was well disposed toward the Congress program because Gandhians disavowed class warfare and property confiscation (Marcovits 1985: 70–71, 97–98). Big business was sufficiently powerful to pressure Gandhi into ending the Civil Disobedience satyagraha in 1931, discussed in Chapter 3, "in a [sudden] retreat which at times became very nearly a rout" (Sarkar 1976: 139). In the late 1930s, provincial governments under Congress control (by this time, the British had relinquished provincial administration to elected Indian politicians) passed legislation giving capitalists great power over labor (Marcovits 1985: 168–69). In the case of the rich peasantry and business interests, then, the connection to the Gandhian vision and practice was sometimes very close, perhaps so close as to be suffocating.

However close, though, the connection was always contingent, never deterministic or inevitable. Business interests or rich peasants followed Gandhi only instrumentally and only as long as he made ideological "sense" to them. Conversely, Gandhi sometimes willingly collaborated in what were in effect purposeful misreadings of his authority — readings, that is, done in bad faith. In these cases, the utopian experiments that served Gandhi's vision also served the interests of these evolving classes, at least to a certain extent (compare Mukherjee 1986: 278–79).

Contingency, for example, ruled the connection between the Gandhian vision and big business in the 1930s. The business community never operated as a self-conscious class that then used Gandhi in its own interests (Marcovits 1985: 18–20; Sarkar 1983: 64). In the 1920s, the Indian business community was highly factionalized (Marcovits 1985: 37–39), and the factions adopted quite different political stances (Sarkar 1983: 64). By 1930, Indian business was much more united in support of the Congress. Yet still the connection with Gandhi was curiously contingent. Not class, but happenstance caste membership and sectarian allegiance linked them:

The link created between Gandhi and a large section of the business community was a link between Hindu *baniyas* [people from the merchant caste category, as was Gandhi, too] and a Hindu political leader, rather than a link between an emerging capitalist class and a national leader; it had a strong religious component and was also highly personalized (Marcovits 1985: 188).

Through this peculiar connection, business groups did use their influence to get Gandhi to call off civil disobedience in 1931. The business groups feared the new peasant militancy that had appeared, as in no-rent campaigns, which were not as easily controlled as the earlier forms of protest, like urban boycotts or no-tax campaigns. Fearing mass upheaval, business groups urged Gandhi to bring his campaign to an end (Sarkar 1983: 114–17).

Did Gandhi capitulate to this pressure because he was a pawn for bourgeois interests? Sarkar rejects this explanation and argues that Gandhi halted civil disobedience because he too feared an undisciplined mass upheaval and the violence and class warfare it might sponsor (Sarkar 1976: 142–45). Similarly, the alliance between business interests and Gandhians later in the 1930s was contingent on the increasingly militant leftists in the Congress. Fearing the leftists would initiate a new confrontation with the British, the Gandhians courted big business as an ally in their fight to keep control over the movement and to maintain the dominance of the Gandhian program (Marcovits 1985: 97–99).

Even though these classes provided a fertile ground, transplantation was never complete, because Gandhi and his fellow experimentalists (at least, Gandhi in certain public guises and some of the experimentalists) had to comply with the transfer to really make it work — and Gandhi used his authority to make connections only when they served his experiments. After Gandhi's death, which did not exactly terminate his authority but did make it easier for others to claim, and in the new circumstances of an independent India, hijacking and ideological transplantation gained the upper hand. Shortly after independence, Gandhian utopia had been almost completely hijacked by a state committed to heavy industrialization, centralized socialism, and the needs of upper-caste rich peasants and an urban lower-middle class. The ideological transplantation did not occur until later, in the 1980s, when Hindu nationalism appropriated Gandhian utopia.

Reauthorizing Gandhi

There are several ways to deauthorize Gandhi. One argument is that circumstances in India would have led to a similar nationalist movement and a similar independence in 1947 or thereabouts, with or without Gandhi. In this view, a passive Mahatma was conveyed along by geopolitical forces. Another argument, that Gandhi was only a mouthpiece for bourgeois interests and that his utopia simply rationalized bourgeois domination, similarly deauthorizes Gandhi. It also attempts to reduce individual intentions to cultural determination, in this case, by class.

Gandhi obviously butted up against world circumstances and often failed to make any impression on them. In some cases those circumstances even remade Gandhi, as affirmative Orientalism did. At home, Gandhi clearly had to confront class interests and incipient class consciousness, and in some cases he found it in the best interests of his utopian vision to connect with them. At other times, the connection was forced upon Gandhi, or he did not understand class dynamics well enough to avoid making damaging connections. Circumstances sometimes dictated; failures happened; class connections were forced, or were stumbled into naively. All this only says that Gandhi was human and fallible and not above his own times and circumstances. But also because he was human, Gandhi was a social animal who labored with symbols and with others. He had a complex series of experiences and a ramified network of collaborators and fellow experimentalists. These experiences and experimentalists precipitated Gandhi's intentions (changeable ones and sometimes serially contradictory), which he then tried to authorize. By authorizing his intentions into a utopian vision and by authorizing himself as its creator, Gandhi came to express Gandhian utopia, but Gandhian utopia also came to express the personhood of Gandhi. Gandhi was therefore not just the creature of his times or of his class. The Gandhi that most people know was also the creature of his own utopian dream. He was a condensation (to shift the imagery) of his individual experiences and fellow experimentalists — experiences and experimentalists that had become significant to him as he confronted his own times and circumstances and tried to master them. Gandhi therefore never rose above his times, he only bounced off them. His new dream of a "nowhere" India better than the Orientalized present was opposite to the present, not beyond it. Utopia bounces off, it does not rise above, the current ideological constitution of society.

Gandhi's failures put the lie to any tautological argument that he was only a product of his times or his class. To allow that he failed requires us to permit him to succeed — partially and not frequently, perhaps, but his successes were just as real as his failures. By the time the British departed India and not long before Gandhi departed this life, the successful experiments had made the Gandhian vision into a powerful set of cultural meanings and practices that configured the post-independence political identity of many Indians (secularism and satyagraha), compelled the character of the society they lived in (passive revolution and class conciliation), and constituted a dream so absorbing (the future welfare of all) that it might turn into a nightmare for any Indian government that did not control it.

NINE

Vinoba's Mild Experiment

I come to loot you with love.

Vinoba Bhave *(quoted in Scarfe and Scarfe 1975: 278)*

Was he Gandhi's heir or government's saint? Did Vinoba Bhave blinker the Gandhian utopian vision after Gandhi's assassination in 1948? Did he sanctify the Nehru government and its policies, even when they confounded Gandhi's dream? Or did Vinoba essentially keep faith with Gandhi? Were his experiments those Gandhi himself would have pursued in an India with a swaraj government but still without swaraj of the soul?

As Indians and Indianists look back on the first quarter-century after independence to judge the fate of Gandhi's dream, they ask these questions about Vinoba. Through diverse explanations — some say Vinoba was a more consistent anarchist than Gandhi (Ostergaard 1984: 84), others maintain Vinoba became too dependent on government subsidies (Rothermund 1984: 120), and still others blame the personal ties between Vinoba and Nehru (Shah 1979: 38, 94) — they reach this consensus: that the Gandhian experiment changed significantly once Gandhi was gone, and that the change was not for the good.

Yet Vinoba Bhave had good reason to claim that he was, and be acclaimed as, Gandhi's principal heir. Never a political crony, Vinoba served as spiritual acolyte to Gandhi the Mahatma. He became the paragon of the loyal ashramite, the most revered of that "re-

169

serve spiritual army" Gandhi mustered out in the initial stage of a satyagraha.

Born in 1895, Vinoba entered Gandhi's Ahmedabad ashram in 1916. Five years later, Gandhi sent him to manage the Sevagram ashram at Wardha, which remained Vinoba's permanent base thereafter and increasingly became Gandhi's principal retreat. In 1940, when Gandhi fixed on individual rather than mass satyagraha against the British war effort, he chose Vinoba to offer the initial self-sacrifice. First to go to jail, Vinoba was thereby marked as first among Gandhi's followers. In March 1948 at the Sevagram ashram — Gandhi had been assassinated little more than a month before — Vinoba and other Gandhian workers launched an association to coordinate the activities of the many organizations implementing Gandhi's Constructive Programme. The Sarva Seva Sangh, as this organization was soon named, became the main institution through which Vinoba hoped to continue Gandhi's experiments. Twenty years later, it became the major arena for struggle over what those experiments should be and whether Vinoba had undertaken them properly.

Did Vinoba fail as Gandhi's successor because the heirs of Great Men are generally lesser beings? Or was India after independence simply not ready for Vinoba, as it had been for Gandhi and his experiments? Neither Small Man theory not cultural determinism explains why the Gandhian dream lost its utopian character for twenty-five years after independence.

In this chapter, I explore the way in which Gandhian utopia turned into a daydream after independence. Its diminished state, I believe, was a result of contemporary confrontations over what it was and what it should be. Gandhi's anointed heirs, Vinoba chief among them but also including Nehru, and self-appointed heirs, like Rammanohar Lohia, for whom Gandhi probably foresaw no legacy — each of them labored with certain intentions toward Gandhian utopia. They disagreed about the sort of experiments that should be tried. They saw different somewheres in the future that such experiments with nowhere now would lead to. Yet they all claimed to be Gandhi's legitimate heirs because they needed the authority of his person and his program to justify their own experiments.

170   In the resulting confrontation, the Nehru government succeeded in hijacking Gandhian utopia: it carted it around like ideological

baggage but never had to unpack it. Instead, its mixed economy delivered the goods for an indigenous lower-middle class that took over when the British took off, as I make clear later in this chapter. Nehru and Vinoba jointly resisted an interpretation of satyagraha that would have conserved it as a means of revolutionary experiment in India after independence. In reaction to this interpretation and as reputed spiritual successor to the Mahatma, Vinoba pursued experiments so "mild" — unworldly, in fact — that they did not confront reality. Lacking any element of confrontation, of struggle — lacking, in other words, any way to experiment on existing society with utopian intentions — Vinoba's Gandhian utopia thus became a daydream. Vinoba's "experiments" were unintentional forms of escapism, not of revolution (see Ricoeur's concept of escapism, discussed in Chapter 2). The Nehru government paid lip service — and subsidies — to some of these experiments, like hand-spinning (khadi) and village industries and voluntary land reform (bhoodan), but in most other ways the government claimed as Gandhian what was patently not — most of all, the government itself. At its worst, the Gandhian daydream became a weak ideology justifying a regime based on the dominance of a lower-middle class. At best, this daydream simply tolerated existing conditions without protest (but also without necessarily legitimating them, either). Vinoba's Gandhians were taken up with fantasies about the future and the alchemy — for they no longer practiced a true experimental science — by which they supposed that future could be brought about.

Vinoba was not Gandhi's heir, if by that phrase we mean to say that he was a Great Man who unfortunately was unable personally to take Gandhian utopia forward. Neither was he government's saint, however, if by that we mean that Vinoba was entirely a creature of circumstances beyond his control and that these conditions co-opted him. This chapter shows that what became of Vinoba and what he helped Gandhian thinking become after independence was historically contingent. Given the constituted set of cultural meanings that Gandhian utopia had become by the time of Gandhi's death, there was a real struggle over what it should become thereafter. Individuals were compelled by what Gandhi had bequeathed and also enabled by it, and as they tried to adapt their interpretations of what Gandhi had left behind to what a *171* Gandhian might or should do in the present, they came into confrontation with each other, with the Indian state, and with the class conditions of independent India. A new Gandhism developed, especially a new form of the central experiment, satyagraha. It was no longer nonviolent resistance; instead, it became mild acceptance.

The general point is this: authority of a direct sort is not easily exercised from the grave (or the cremation ground), not even in societies that worship ancestors. When an author dies, his creation remains, and in most cases so does his reputed authorship. His work then becomes a testament and he, a founding father. While he was alive, Gandhi could restrain the hijacking of his authority. After he died, the issue changed: now some sort of disposition and transfer of Gandhian utopia was necessary. The salient questions were, to whom should it go and what would become of it?

A struggle often ensues over a founder's true heirs: who now possesses his authority? Is this one really of the founder's school? Does he conserve the founder's ways and methods? Authors, like kings, worry and appoint successors — sometimes, also like kings, their designations are disputed after their death. Furthermore, it is not at all certain how these heirs, anointed or self-appointed, will treat their legacies. How will they react to the immediate circumstances of their worlds, necessarily different from the founder's? How will they struggle for but also struggle with and even against their inheritance under these changed conditions?

In 1948, Gandhian utopia was a rich testament to India. By its provisions, India was to launch a set of fundamental experiments with society and with the spirit. Even before independence, as the last chapter showed, there were attempts to manipulate the legacy in favor of the Congress party or certain classes. There were attempts to make Gandhi a figurehead without authority, a saint without substance. Even these attempts, however, recognized the compelling character of Gandhi's vision, or, if not the vision itself in all its aspects (because peasants misinterpreted and reinterpreted), then the compelling character of Gandhi as Mahatma, a condensed personhood that was also manipulated before independence. The heirs, designated or self-proclaimed, could try to accept the legacy as given or attempt to use it for other purposes, but in no case could they refuse to acknowledge the fact of inheritance. It was Gandhi's authority that made most of India claim to be his heirs — and that made them have to.

Vinoba, Lohia, and Mild Satyagraha

Vinoba believed that satyagraha could not remain the same in India after independence. He differentiated two types of satyagraha: negative or harsh satyagraha, *duragraha* (see Bondurant 1965: 43), aimed to coerce the opponent, while mild satyagraha hoped to convert the opponent. The nonviolent *resistance* of Gandhi's preindependence struggle was to give way to nonviolent *assistance* in Nehru's free and democratic India (Ostergaard 1985: 15–16). Vinoba's satyagraha therefore consisted of communicating a message — hardly even a warning, only "assistance in right-thinking" — to opponents, in order to change their hearts (Prasad 1984: 106; Bhattacharya 1984: 150; also see Ostergaard 1984: 83, 94). To resist British colonialism, Gandhi had to employ harsh satyagraha, Vinoba maintained. Once India was freed, Vinoba believed that satyagraha tactics could be relaxed. Instead of needing the confrontation that was uppermost in the old satyagraha, a democratic society in independent India would respond to his mild satyagraha. For Vinoba, resistance, if that term could even be applied any longer, should proceed from mild to milder to mildest. By this means, India, now having achieved Gandhi's goal of swaraj, could proceed to the next point of evolution, the attainment of sarvodaya, or welfare for all. Vinoba and his followers often used the term "sarvodaya" to distinguish the Gandhian program after independence from what it had been before.

Some commentators criticize Vinoba for deauthorizing Gandhi's satyagraha, for turning a true weapon of social revolution into a plaything, for "undoing the essential Gandhi" (Devdutt 1984: 176; also see Nargolkar 1974: 9–10; 1975: 110–14). If Vinoba did bury the Gandhian patrimony, as these and other critics maintain, he did so because he thought he was protecting it from a rival claimant.

Rammanohar Lohia (1910–67) agreed with Gandhi—and with Vinoba after independence—that satyagraha had to prevail, otherwise "the gun and the bullet will" (quoted in Arora 1984: 55). Like Gandhi, too, Lohia felt it required a great and life-long discipline, although he did not rest it on a belief in God. Lohia called himself a "heretic Gandhian," however, because his idea of satyagraha was affected by Marxism. Rejecting Gandhi's class conciliation and trusteeship concept, Lohia embraced satyagraha as the poor man's way of obtaining social justice and economic equality.

For Lohia, satyagraha was a form of class struggle, and therefore what Vinoba distinguished as harsh or negative satyagraha was as essential for rectifying social inequality in independent India as it had been for dislodging British colonialism.

As early as 1952, Lohia called for socialists to incorporate Gandhian techniques, and two years later, he called for the "renunciation of force as a revolutionary weapon" (Arora 1984: 134–57 provides a chronology). Subsequently, as leader of the Socialist party, Lohia launched what he thought of as a "permanent" satyagraha from the middle 1950s through the middle 1960s. He agitated (nonviolently) to "Remove English [language]," "Fix [consumer] Prices," "Break Castism," and "Save Himalayas [from pollution]" (Sharad 1972: 272). He also protested corruption and Portuguese rule in Goa through nonviolent resistance. Although Nehru tried to work out compromises, Lohia dismayed him (Dutt 1981: 221–23). Soon after independence, Lohia settled into what became a permanent state of opposition to the sitting government.

Unlike Vinoba, Lohia maintained that satyagraha's most salient characteristics were nonviolence *and* confrontation. Lohia believed that satyagraha provided an alternative to constitutional reform (which might not be forthcoming) and violent struggles (which created terrible suffering). Whereas Vinoba advocated his voluntary program for social reconstruction and mild satyagraha as sufficient to change minds and thence society, Lohia pressed for satyagraha as "peaceful class struggle." Satyagraha would change minds not by being mild, Lohia asserted, but by being militant: by organizing and mobilizing the demands of the poor forcefully and directing them, nonviolently to be sure, against the wealthy and powerful. Lohia's formula for achieving an egalitarian social order was "the prison, the spade, and the ballot box" (Nargolkar 1978: 9). By this equation, Lohia accepted Nehru's democracy (the ballot box) and Vinoba's voluntary Constructive Programme (the spade), but also mass struggle through satyagraha, and the consequences thereof (the prison).

In contrasting Lohia's nonviolent socialism with Vinoba's mild social reconstruction (and with Nehru's Congress government), Francine Frankel perceptively notes,

174   Ironically, the differences that kept them apart were, to a large extent, rooted in a common legacy—the thought and practice of Gandhi. The question they all tried to answer was how best to adapt Gandhi's

technique of nonviolent resistance against foreign rule to India's internal struggle against social and economic exploitation (Frankel 1978: 107).

As Vinoba and Lohia confronted each other, each claiming to be Gandhi's true heir, they divided up the original experiment with satyagraha. Lohia disdained Vinoba's sarvodaya, his social reconstruction, his politics of truth and love, as ineffective (Nargolkar 1978: 8). Vinoba distrusted Lohia's power politics, his encouragement of social dissent (Ostergaard 1985: 15–16). Before independence, Gandhi's practice was sometimes harsh, as when he tried to bring British India to a halt with civil disobedience; at other times, mild, as when he embarrassed the British by making his own salt; and at still other times, mildest, as when he attempted to win respect from the colonial authorities by becoming an army recruiter. Vinoba and Lohia each took one part of Gandhi's satyagraha and claimed, if not to have inherited the whole, then at least to have gained the essential part.

Vinoba's claims persisted and then prevailed during the 1950s and 1960s in terms of mass support, whereas Lohia's increasingly floundered and then were abandoned by the Indian masses. There were two major reasons for Vinoba's superior authority. First, Vinoba enjoyed strong institutional support, including financial support, especially from the Congress party and the Nehru government, as the legitimate heir of the Gandhian movement and therefore the true authority on satyagraha (see the next section). Lohia, conversely, got nothing but political defeats or jail sentences from the Congress and the government, respectively.[1] The second reason was that Lohia lacked a secure organizational base for his claims. He worked through political parties without strong grass-root cadres and incapable of major political success, and these parties were further handicapped by factionalism, ideological disagreements, and indiscipline. Vinoba, however, had inherited the strongest base for Gandhian authority, control over Gandhi's ashram and over the many Gandhian voluntary workers. Vinoba strengthened this authority by organizing a single institution for oversight and coordination, the Sarva Seva Sangh, in 1948. From this base, he continued to authorize his Gandhian legacy as the proper starting-point for all further experiments. Vinoba was especially effective in getting his experiment in voluntary land reform, the bhoodan movement, accepted as the true Gandhian experiment with sarvodaya of the 1950s and 1960s, a point I detail later in this chapter. As Vinoba's authority grew and mild satyagraha prevailed, a third claimant, Nehru and the Congress party, could effectively hijack Gandhian utopia, convert mild to meek, and turn utopian dream into unworldly daydream.

Vinoba, Nehru, and the Congress Government

That Vinoba became Gandhi's reputed spiritual successor — the custodian of the ashrams and what they stood for — indicates how much Gandhian utopia changed once India gained independence but lost its Mahatma. Like the country itself, the Gandhian legacy was officially partitioned after independence. The main claimants agreed, as I shall show shortly, on this division: a spiritual heir, Vinoba, was soon appointed, and the secular successors, Nehru and the Congress government, were already in situ. Lohia was effectively disinherited; even his status as a legitimate heir was denied.

Because he claimed Gandhi's spiritual mission, grounded as it was in the ashrams and voluntary workers, Vinoba inherited not only the most authoritative Gandhian institution, but also what had become the most commanding aspect of the Gandhian vision, its saintliness. The Congress had promoted a saintly Gandhi and, by extension, a sanctified Gandhism, in its precipitation of the Mahatma image. Nehru and the Congress took the tangible in Gandhi's bequest: the new nation's state power and economic assets.

Unlike the partition of India and Pakistan, the division of Gandhi's legacy provoked no violence. Instead there was intimacy and subsidy, as the Congress party and the Indian government under Nehru's direction attempted to undergird Vinoba and his Constructive Programme, which, by distinguishing and then renouncing harsh satyagraha, had proved it would be no threat. Furthermore, Vinoba eschewed politics, and no member of the Sarva Seva Sangh could hold electoral office or join in party politics. Here was another partition of the Gandhian legacy: saintly service passed to Vinoba; secular politics went to the Congress. At most, Vinoba used his Congress connections to admonish the government, and sometimes he succeeded in getting policies rescinded through such "jawboning." Vinoba's dissent thus worked to tie him up with the Congress even more. In 1965, more than half the Sarva Seva Sangh leaders agreed that "the movement has become too closely identified in the public mind with the Congress Party" (Ostergaard and Currell 1971: 233).

Vinoba's thinking did not actively justify the Nehru government, but neither did it contest it. He foresaw a peaceful evolution from state rule (*rajniti*) to a people's government (*lokniti*). As independent India increasingly decentralized government and democratized society, Vinoba believed, the state would no longer be necessary and would disappear (Ostergaard 1985: 13–14). Class, caste, or sectarian conflicts, just as confrontations between the state and the people, were not inherent in this evolution, but they could be elicited by a power politics that battened on them. Vinoba, therefore, hoped to avoid mobilizing dissent by committing the country to a "politics" of mildness and to welfare for all (sarvodaya).

Conflict between the Congress and Vinoba's spiritual authority was also not inherent. Quite the opposite: there were many close ties, especially through the Gandhi National Memorial Trust (Gandhi Smarak Nidhi). In April 1948, sorrowful over Gandhi's assassination and hopeful of continuing his Constructive Programme, Congress leaders, among them Congress president Prasad, Nehru, Patel, Rajagopalachari, and Jagjivan Ram, planned for an autonomous memorial trust and launched a fund-collecting drive. A year later, by which time the trust was a reality, more than one hundred million rupees had been donated. The Memorial Trust thereafter became a major source of funds to a multitude of Gandhian voluntary organizations, including the Sarva Seva Sangh, and to many of Vinoba's special projects, such as voluntary land reform (Gandhi Smarak Nidhi 1976: 1–9).

The Gandhi Memorial Trust not only deeply involved the Gandhian voluntary campaign with the Congress party, but it also entangled it with big business. The trust was to expend the contributions it had received by the Gandhi centenary in 1969, but by the middle 1970s, it still had a balance of nearly 50 million rupees. Trust managers invested the major part of that sum in the shares of Indian companies, the interest from which — rather than private donations — continues to endow the Memorial Trust (Bhatt 1982: 16; also see Gandhi Smarak Nidhi 1976: 11). The anomaly, as one Gandhian expressed it to me in 1988, is that Gandhi's dream of the small-scale, decentralized, self-laboring, and nonmechanized society now depends financially on its nightmare antithesis, capitalist big business.

Government subsidy was another major source of funds, and, because the Congress party ran the government (until 1977), such subsidies only reinforced the connections between the secular and spiritual heirs of Gandhi. For example, the Gandhi Peace Foundation received a grant of 1.5 million rupees from the central government between 1974 and 1976, and state governments subsidized it with 225,000 rupees from 1977 to 1979 (Bhatt 1982: 15). The major conduit for official subsidies, however, was through various government agencies authorized to fund "village industries" such as hand-loom weaving, oil pressing, manual paper making, leather working, and country sugar making. Although ostensibly intended to fund an activity, the subsidies from these government agencies went to the Gandhian organizations that coordinated such village industries and promoted their products. Long after independence, at a time when the government viewed Gandhian associations as inimical and perhaps even as subversive, Indira Gandhi rued the large amounts of money previous governments had given them (Modhumita Majumdar 1986: 9). For example, the First Five-Year Plan, proposed in 1952 by her father's government, committed 150 million rupees to village industries (Government of India 1951: 82). Subsequent plans, the Second Five-Year Plan in 1956 and the Third in 1961, continued to recognize special reasons to assist village industries, although there was also increasingly concern about the level of subsidy and the lack of gains in productivity (see Government of India 1956: 26; 1961: 426–31).

These planning documents also continued to praise the role of voluntary organizations in social reconstruction and to judge them as worthy of government support. The First Plan argued that Vinoba's volunteer movement had "considerable moral value and should be supported" (Government of India 1956: 96). The Third Plan was transparent about the reason. Subsidizing Vinoba was an investment in social consensus:

> Uneven distribution of the fruits of progress . . . gives rise to a sense of deep resentment and frustration . . . greatly heightened by the spectacle of fortuitous incomes and gains from anti-social activities . . .
>
> Explosive situations do not develop suddenly and when outbursts occur, they are only symptoms of a malaise which has existed and grown over a period of time . . . It is through the quiet influence of

voluntary workers steadily engaged in acts of selfless service . . . that the voice of reason can prevail . . .

Voluntary organizations can help to create a sense of oneness and common outlook (Government of India 1961: 292–97).

That government subsidies underwrote Vinoba's mild version of Gandhi's vision, that they therefore served the ideological goals of the Nehru government, that they paid off the national debt to Gandhian utopia rather than paid it up — all these points are summed up in the story of khadi production after independence.

Khadi

Home-spun cloth and yarn production (khadi) was a major experiment in Gandhian utopia. Cotton, silk, or wool is hand-spun into yarn using a *charkha*, or spinning wheel, which is set on the floor. The vertical spinning wheel was in common use in village India, and it was the first type Gandhi adopted. A spinning wheel of this sort formed the central motif in the flag of the Indian National Congress until Indian independence. The image of Gandhi at the vertical spinning wheel is quite familiar, thanks no doubt to Margaret Bourke-White's famous photograph, taken a year or two before his assassination. Gandhi also spun on an improved, horizontal spinning wheel.

Initially, the experiment with khadi was to test whether people could perform "bread labor" for themselves and thereby avoid wage slavery and the market economy. Although this purpose continued to inform khadi production, its greater significance came as a test of the Gandhian belief in small-scale, decentralized industrial production. Since Indian independence, khadi production has passed into the hands of specialists, who spin and weave khadi for their livelihood. The Indian government provides long-term loans and grants to such khadi producers, making it a paying proposition for them to hand-spin yarn and weave it into cloth. Special shops, operated by Gandhian organizations and subsidized by the government, retail the khadi as yard goods or as tailored garments: long shirts (*kurtas*) and loose-fitting trousers (*pyjamas*) for men, saris for women. Hand-spinning makes khadi cloth coarse and irregular. It is also more expensive than cloth from Indian mills. For these reasons, few Indians wear khadi nowadays. Although khadi became chic among Bombay's jet set in the early 1980s, it is currently in common use only among India's politicians,

179

who wear it as a badge of identity with the nationalist movement, and among Gandhian voluntary workers. Nevertheless, after independence, it became one of the essential experiments in Vinoba's sarvodaya campaign, and among Sarva Seva Sangh voluntary workers it was generally considered second in importance only to the bhoodan land reform efforts.

Nehru supported the khadi program even though he believed it was an outmoded form of production. He saw other benefits from it: it fit in well with the rural production system of India's peasantry, it helped organize that peasantry, and it served to check price-gouging by Indian mill owners (Paranjape 1964: 1). At first, government subsidies seemed to pay off. Between 1953/54 and 1962/63, the production of all forms of khadi (cotton, silk, and wool) more than doubled, and the value of this production nearly tripled (computed from Dagli 1976: table 5), as the table opposite indicates. Over the same period, the population employed in khadi production expanded to more than 1.5 million, an increase of more than 100 percent. Khadi production and employment continued to rise until the late 1960s. Between 1963/64 and 1972/73, however, the average annual production fell by 23 percent from the previous five-year period, and employment dropped by 40 percent. In the late 1960s, the government began to sponsor improved spinning wheels and other innovations to increase the per-capita output (Government of India, Khadi and Village Industries Commission 1967 *passim*, 1968: 12). The result has been to stabilize the numbers of khadi producers while increasing the value of their production — khadi has become an activity of expert artisans, not an employment for the rural masses. Thus, the five-year period 1973/74 to 1977/78 saw a further reduction of 16 percent in khadi workers from the previous five-year period, whereas the amount of khadi produced rose slightly. In 1980/81, there were only 1.2 million workers in khadi, some 37 percent fewer than the high point reached in 1964/65, but they produced about 11 percent more khadi. Over roughly the same period, the average annual government subsidy per khadi worker increased by more than 500 percent. Furthermore, khadi production still provides less than 1 per cent of India's textile output, and it has yet to become price-competitive with mill-made cloth. The government must offer a standard rebate on khadi purchases throughout the year, and during certain months it gives additional price concessions to honor Gandhi's memory. Khadi workers have become an artisan aristocracy, a small and subsidized

180

craft group —therefore, a Luddite version of a "labor aristocracy," protected by unions and government wage guarantees.

Neither as an experiment in bread labor, nor as a major employer of India's rural underemployed, nor as a check on mill owners' greed, but only as a destination for government funds has khadi succeeded.[2]

The Khadi Program, Five-Year Averages

Period	Production	Sales	Employment	Subsidy*	Per-Capita Subsidy
1953/54–1957/58	27.31	47.2	.71	45.1	63.17
1958/59–1962/63	62.23	144.9	1.65	104.3	63.09
1963/64–1967/68	75.88	228.3	1.77	108.0	60.91
1968/69–1972/73	58.25	265.1	1.07	86.5	80.99
1973/74–1977/78	60.79	513.5[†]	.89	143.2	160.54
1978/79–1980/81 (three years)	81.60	919.1	1.12	369.2	329.64

SOURCE: computed from Dagli 1976: tables 5, 9; Government of India, Khadi and Village Industries Commission 1980, 1981, 1982: tables 10, 11.

Figures for production are in millions of square yards. Figures for sales and subsidy are in millions of rupees. Employment figures are in millions of persons. Per-capita subsidy is in rupees.

*Subsidy is computed by adding the annual amount of government grants with the annual increase in outstanding government loans and subtracting that amount from the total loans outstanding from the previous year. The latter computation gives a figure for the net of government loans per annum.

†In 1975/76, the government began recording the value of khadi sales in terms of the list price, which, because it did not take into account additional price concessions offered during the year, enhanced the reported value of sales.

Ostergaard and Currell (1971: 252) admit that khadi production is uneconomical but justify it in terms of the social reconstruction it has accomplished. At the same time, they acknowledge the strange contradiction in Vinoba's Sarva Seva Sangh and its experiments, including khadi: an organization that claimed to be revolutionary undertook programs that appeared to be extensions of the Congress government's programs. The question is: was the government subsidizing khadi, or was it girding up Vinoba and his voluntary associations? Kantowsky scorns the way in which *181* government support for khadi "honored" Gandhian principles. It produced hand-loomed material worn mainly by the political elite — it was too expensive for the villager. Donning khadi produced through official subsidy, Congressmen adorned themselves with Gandhi's mantle. Support for khadi cloaked other development efforts that proceeded along un-Gandhian lines. Kantowsky argues that the political elite used Gandhian labels for programs that in actuality "devalued Gandhian principles" (Kantowsky 1980: 79–80). He leads us to consider the way in which the Nehru government hijacked Gandhian utopia.

Official Hijack

The First Five-Year Plan (1952), the major policy platform of the Nehru government, made clear how far India would depart from Gandhi's vision while claiming to follow it. Eschewing property confiscation and other forms of coercive wealth redistribution, the planning statement called for a "middle way" toward social equality,

> which, while avoiding a violent overturning of society will, nevertheless, enable the State to promote rapid changes in the social structure . . . class hatred and violence in the guise of reprisals against those sections of society which are associated in the public mind with the inequalities of the older order . . . are far removed from the traditions and ideas of this country. They are inconsistent with the basic premises of democratic planning (Government of India 1951: 17).

To implement the middle way, India must have a "rapid expansion of the economic and social responsibilities of the State" (Government of India 1951: 18). For India, the plan envisions not the Gandhian oceanic circles of village democracy but the pyramid of centralized state power. The government would be so commanding, in fact, that it could even afford to subsidize its Gandhian alternative.

The Second Five-Year Plan could claim that "many of the basic ideas of Gandhiji have become part of the national heritage" but at the same time maintain, "the most important single factor in promoting economic development is the community's readiness to develop and apply modern technology . . . " (Government of India 1956: 143, 6). Would such twisted reasoning have sent Gandhi spinning?

182

The Third Five-Year Plan began with a fanfare for India's age-old virtues and the great spirits, like Tagore and Gandhi, that they produced. The ethical and moral values that have governed Indian life must now be synthesized with modern technology, the plan goes on to say. The State will have to take on more responsibility for the synthesis: the State must make sure that rapid urbanization and industrial growth do not introduce new inequalities. It must not shift its responsibility for social welfare onto private voluntary associations. It must rapidly expand the public-sector (state-run) economy to discipline private wealth accumulation and to eliminate backward sectors (Government of India 1961: 1, 13, 14).

Chatterjee (1982: 51, 132) asserts that Gandhian thinking became a state ideology under Nehru, who used it to legitimate a heavy role for the state in development, welfare, and social control. To call Gandhian thinking an ideology implies that Nehru's government had some commitment to a particular way of thinking, if only to manipulate it better and use it more effectively as a justification. But the Congress government under Nehru used Gandhian thinking in the most transparent and superficial way. "Gandhian thinking" served not as a justification, but as a handy label. When there were matters that really counted, as in the government's program of community development, or panchayati raj, Nehru and the Congress hardly bothered even with the label.

Panchayati Raj

Drafting the Indian constitution in 1948, B. R. Ambedkar, the Untouchable leader who had fallen out with Gandhi over minority rights, also showed his distaste for the idealization of the village community that Gandhi and others had put forward. He wrote, "what is the village but a sink of localism, a den of ignorance, narrow-mindedness and communalism" (quoted in Kantowsky 1980: 90). Ambedkar chastised those who championed the village community but decried communalism and provincialism, as if these did not emanate from the village. In this criticism, Ambedkar seconded Nehru. In a 1946 letter replying to Gandhi's request for a return to the simplicity of village life, Nehru argued that everyday rural life did not necessarily embody truth and nonviolence, and he noted that villages usually were intellectually and culturally backward (Shiviah et al. 1976: 49–56). Not surprisingly, the Indian constitution did not contain any provision for democratic decentralization, as Gandhi might have wished. An amendment, passed during the debate over the constitution, did enjoin the state

183

to create village panchayats (councils) as units of local self-government.

Many years later, Balwantray Mehta, the Congress leader most associated with the ensuing village panchayat and community development program (panchayati raj), echoed Ambedkar and Nehru:

> I would like to point out that villages have never been as they have been depicted by poets and men of letters in their works. They have been what they are. What we find today has been there all throughout the ages. Factions are there, conservatism is there and superstitions are there . . . (Mehta 1969: 87–88).

Rather than affirming the village as the basis of Indian society, Gandhi-style, the panchayati raj program in effect made the village the lowest tier of centralized state administration and gave it responsibility for implementing development goals that mainly originated at higher levels. In 1956, Balwantray Mehta was appointed to a study team whose charge was to develop ways of ensuring the most economical and efficient implementation of Five-Year Plan projects. It recommended a reorganization of local government in three tiers — the village panchayat, the (development) block-level *panchayat samiti,* and the *zilla parishad* at the district level — linked by indirect elections. These were adopted in April 1958 (Shiviah et al. 1976: 82–87). This program of "democratic decentralization" resonated with Gandhian notions to some limited extent, but in fact the Mehta Report set its sights on development priorities, not a Gandhian vision. From its inception, panchayati raj was a plank in the statist policies of the Nehru government, although it also appeared as a promising experiment to Gandhians like Jayaprakash Narayan, who by this time had left Marxism (Shiviah et al. 1976: 319–22; Ostergaard and Currell 1971: 247–48).

Jayaprakash soon had misgivings. In January 1964 the All-India Panchayat Parishad, a voluntary association of panchayat organizations across India with Jayaprakash as its president, held a seminar to discuss the nature and direction of panchayati raj. In his presidential address, Jayaprakash called for clarification of the concept of panchayati raj. He contrasted two views of it: one was that the various levels of village, block, and district were simply extensions of the state government; the other view, which he endorsed, was that the panchayats were primarily self-governing bodies and only secondarily agencies of state government. Jayaprakash also

184

argued for an expansive view of panchayati raj, related to Gandhi's concept of a nation composed of oceanic circles and his desire to minimize state oppression (All-India Panchayat Parishad 1964: 34–42). In the ensuing discussion, Balwantray Mehta denied that the panchayati raj program was primarily meant to implement development goals. He intended it also as a plan for local self-government. Jayaprakash remained unconvinced (All-India Panchayat Parishad 1964: 48–49).

His skepticism was well founded. An official seminar on panchayati raj soon followed, at which Iqbal Narain distinguished four approaches to panchayati raj: Jayaprakash's Gandhian notion; the approach adopted by leaders like Nehru, who saw panchayati raj as responsible local government; the bureaucratic view, which looked at panchayati raj as simply an agency of administration; and, finally, the developmental view, adopted by Balwantray Mehta and a more specific version of Nehru's approach, namely, that panchayati raj would become the main means of community development, economic planning, and modernization. Narain found, however, that panchayati raj had mainly served as an agent for implementing planning by higher levels of government (Narain 1969: 19–34). At the same seminar, T. K. N. Unnithan (1969: 42–49) reviewed the Gandhian ideal of panchayats and indicated that neither in the government's policy nor in their operation did existing panchayats fit the Gandhian image.

These evaluations flew in the face of official government assertions of support for the Gandhian vision, as in Mehta's statement noted earlier, or as when, at the same seminar, Asoka Mehta, the head of the Planning Commission, denied that panchayati raj existed mainly to implement state development programs. Instead, he claimed, it was created as an institution of transformation, "going into the very bowels of our system and trying to change it" (reported in Narain 1969: 3).

Although panchayati raj had many positive benefits for state centralization and national politics, such as forging links between the Congress and village-level leaders, it did not create an organic, democratic rural community. Almost all case studies reveal that the rich and the powerful monopolized village government and resources (Bhargava et al. 1982: chapters 4, 5; Chaudhury 1981: 112; Kantowsky 1980: 99–100; Kihlberg 1976: 96; Raghava Rao 1980: 48; Ram Reddy 1974: 85; Singh 1969), and even a government report declared that the "weaker sections" of the village "community" were being misused (Government of India, Ministry of Agriculture and Irrigation 1978: 79ff.). Panchayati raj turned the oceanic circle of Gandhian utopia into a quagmire of the venal and the well-connected.

Vinoba was always wary of panchayati raj, probably because he doubted that true Gandhian experiments could be carried out under the aegis of the state. Vinoba put his hopes into a program of voluntary land reform that he pursued with the same deep and utter commitment that Gandhi had given his experiments. Yet because the bhoodan ("land-gift") program was utterly fanciful in execution — because it included no real confrontation with existing society, only mildness toward it — it was not a utopian dream with which to confront reality, but rather a daydream by which to escape it.

The Daydream of Land Reform

Vinoba started the experiment with bhoodan in 1951, during a walking tour of Telengana, a region in southern India where class warfare had broken out between landlords and tenants (Mishra 1972: 5). Communists had been actively promoting a violent peasant revolution in the region since 1948 (Ostergaard 1985: 5–6). Vinoba went to Telengana on a peace mission. He hoped to counteract class conflict in the short term by an experiment with the Gandhian idea of trusteeship, and his ultimate objective was to build an organic rural society. Vinoba therefore called upon landowners to give a gift of some part of their agricultural land to the poor. It was to be given from love, not force, and it was to build a rural society in which land was an object of social reciprocity, not a marketable commodity. Landowners would donate the land to Vinoba or to the voluntary workers of the Sarva Seva Sangh, who would then redistribute it to the needy. Later, Vinoba began an appeal for *gramdan*, the gift of a village. Here the objective was to make the village one family, in control of its own independent economy and polity. Once landowners had made a gift of their private property to a village corporation, it would be managed to ensure the welfare of all. Vinoba traversed the countryside of India, hoping to revolutionize it through such gifts.

186

The initial response to Vinoba's appeal was enormous. By 1970, Vinoba had obtained about 4 million acres in bhoodan donations (although most gifts came before 1956) (Kantowsky 1980: 82–83; Tandon 1984). By 1971, more than 168,000, or very roughly 30 percent, of India's villages had been pledged to gramdan (Mishra 1972: 108; Tandon 1984; also see Ostergaard and Currell 1971: 11 for other figures).

The Congress government responded just as favorably. In 1957, Nehru urged close cooperation between the community development program and the gramdan movement. "Gramdan has come to stay," he said (quoted in Shah 1979: 256). Two years before, the Congress party had passed a resolution at its annual session conveying deep appreciation for Vinoba's work and appealing to all members of Congress to give full support to the movement (Shah 1979: 227–28). Congress and the government soon became so entangled in the bhoodan effort that it was not clear who were the supporters and who the supported. I have already mentioned the heavy financial subsidy that the Gandhi Memorial Trust, with strong informal ties to the Congress party, gave bhoodan and gramdan. The Congress government at the center also gave subsidies, and state governments sometimes took an even more active role: in Bihar, for example, not only did the government grant subsidies to voluntary associations soliciting gifts of land, but it also took over redistribution of the donated land (Barik 1977: 35).

By the early 1970s, large subsidies and aggregate statistics could no longer hide the failure of Vinoba's appeal to revolutionize agrarian relations in accord with the Gandhian vision of welfare for all. More than 40 percent of acreage given in bhoodan donations proved uncultivatable, and only about 30 percent of the total had been redistributed by July 1975 (Tandon 1984: 58ff.; Ostergaard and Currell 1971: 14). Even when land was redistributed, it often did not go to the poor and landless (Oomen 1972: 70ff.). An impressive number of villages were committed to gramdan — more than 168,000 in the early 1970s — but they existed only as pledges, "paper commitments" (Tandon 1984: 58ff.), and in most places a village council did not exercise legal proprietorship (Ostergaard and Currell 1971: 14.)

Vinoba himself had helped empty gramdan of any true revolutionary character. Responding to opposition from wealthy peasants, Vinoba redefined gramdan in the middle 1960s to make it "simpler." *Sulabh gramdan,* as it was called, permitted landowners to "surrender" their entire holdings to the village community, but allowed them to retain effective possession of all but 5 percent of them; that small parcel of their lands would be the only acreage actually redistributed to the poor — that is, if it could in fact be cultivated (Oomen 1972: 30). This "simplification" was consistent with Vinoba's idea that difficult matters must be met by ever gentler methods. Even within the Sarva Seva Sangh, many workers thought Vinoba was too soft on the landowners (Ostergaard 1985: 23–25).

Vinoba seems to have been more interested in the numbers of pledges than in the program's actual performance. He emphasized the act of changing minds alone, and he did not distinguish between lip service and true change of heart. With the Gandhi centennial year (1969) approaching, Vinoba in 1965 launched a "whirlwind" (*toofan*) campaign in Bihar to enroll enough new gramdan villages to declare the entire state as pledged to his program (Ostergaard 1985: 23–25; Narayan 1980 [1970]: 302–19).

In the aftermath of the whirlwind campaign, which narrowly missed its goals, Vinoba's movement stalled. Its satisfaction with pledges gave way to a sense of failure. One study found that the village democracy that Vinoba hoped to establish in gramdan villages was a very "far cry" away; village leaders used gramdan to cement their control over property and power (Oomen 1972: 125, 152). Another study, in the Muzzaffarpur district of Bihar, found that total bhoodan land redistribution averaged less than an acre per village, that it was not always the poor who received land, and that when it did go to the poor, it went to households that were in bondage to powerful village landlords. Bhoodan, then, actually strengthened the semifeudal bondage of the landless and poor (see *New Age* 1975: 5). Landlords in Bihar, where the movement was strongest, supported gramdan superficially and in bad faith. They hoped to avoid the class warfare that had riven Telengana (Barik 1977: 35). Government support may also have had the same motivation — Nehru's socialism regarded class struggle as alien to India's traditions, after all. Vinoba's movement failed even at this avoidance of conflict, however. In 1969, the Naxalites, a radical underground party pledged to revolutionary violence and sabotage, began to succeed in enlisting the impoverished and exploited in rural Bihar, where Vinoba ostensibly had had his greatest success (Kantowsky 1980: 22).

By the early 1970s, problems were emerging within the movement itself. Vinoba increasingly retreated from worldly matters as he pursued a new goal of "entry into abstraction." The Sarva Seva Sangh recognized the difficulty of converting the bhoodan pledges into reality without some means of confrontation, such as the satyagraha Vinoba considered negative. Finally, in 1974, Vinoba recognized the de facto situation of the previous five years and advised that the movement be officially halted.

The failure of Vinoba's movement brought about a crisis in the Sarva Seva Sangh, which then helped precipitate a major new utopian experiment in India, as I shall detail in the next two chapters. Vinoba's failed experiment showed that confrontation was inherent in the Gandhian vision. When Vinoba buried this part of the Gandhian legacy, he enabled the Congress hijack — he had nothing with which to prevent or protest it. Disavowing confrontation also made the voluntary land reform movement a daydream: it depended on well-meaning or bad-faith resolution, and it had no means by which to transform this consciousness, whether well intentioned or not, into revolutionary social practice. Vinoba's mildness made his program unworldly, whereas Gandhi, no matter how spiritual, never abandoned confrontation in the real world (compare Devdutt 1984: 179).

While Vinoba daydreamed, the government hijacked, and wealthy peasants took empty pledges. These contingencies developed from the compelling nature of Gandhian utopia and Vinoba's accepted claim to Gandhi's spiritual authority: neither the government nor the wealthy peasants could ignore him. The question remains, however: what other force existed to make government resist Vinoba's efforts or, more correctly, subsidize them to death? Clearly, the Nehru government followed a different vision of India's future; its image was of a highly technological and centralized modern state. As it worked out in postindependence India, this vision became an ideology legitimating certain interests.[3] It became the existing set of cultural meanings with which Vinoba's mild satyagraha and voluntary land reform unsuccessfully tried to coexist. In whose interests did the Congress government act? Why were Vinoba's thinking and programs useful to government and the rural wealthy only in so far as they were not actually implemented? The answer to these questions emerges from the nature *189* of the postindependence regime and the class interests it willy-nilly served.

The Intermediate Regime

In India after independence, a lower-middle class came to form the ruling, or dominant, class, and the Congress program of a mixed economy and nonaligned state served to a large extent to represent its consciousness. It was in this class's interests for the state to hijack and neutralize the main Gandhian heir, Vinoba, and stand in opposition to the disinherited claimant, Lohia. This class profited greatly from the postindependence Congress regime in the 1950s and 1960s — a regime that some scholars (Raj 1973; Mitra 1977; Jha 1980; Fox 1984), following the ideas of the Polish economist Michael Kalecki, characterize as an "intermediate regime."

Kalecki (1972: 162) proposed that under conditions prevailing in former colonies, regimes might emerge that (primarily) represented the interests of the lower-middle class. Such an intermediate regime differs from a capitalist state, with a dominant bourgeoisie, and also from a socialist regime, where the proletariat rules in theory or there is state capitalism in fact. Intermediate regimes, because of their colonial histories, do not have a well-developed indigenous bourgeoisie or proletariat, and they are therefore dominated by a lower-middle class, which has arisen or at least grown dominant under colonialism.

By the term "lower-middle class," Kalecki referred to occupational groups that were neither wage workers nor large-scale capitalists. They might own some means of production, like capitalists, but they primarily used their own or their family's labor for profit, like wage workers. The lower-middle class therefore included merchants owning and operating family businesses and small factories, contractors, moneylenders, rich peasants (those producing a surplus for sale), skilled artisans, professionals like lawyers, teachers, and physicians (whose special skills, sold in the marketplace, represent a means of production), and venal bureaucrats (who traffic in their official powers like independent contractors) (also see the discussion by Raj 1973: 1189–92 and Jha 1980: 111ff.).

Although an indigenous industrial bourgeoisie existed in India before independence (see Mukherjee 1986, Marcovits 1985, and Chapter 8), the lower-middle class formed the mainstay of the Congress movement. They were the rural and urban "subcontractors" who helped authorize and interpret Gandhian utopia and brought satyagraha to the masses during the independence struggle. Although the lower-middle class was neither fully conscious of its class interests nor organized to pursue them before independence or shortly after it, there were consistent attempts to use Gandhi and satyagraha to discipline the left and peasant militancy — and, when Gandhi's dream proved recalcitrant, there were attempts to turn Gandhi into an otiose Mahatma. The lower-middle class was also the main profiteer of the deferred or passive revolution that brought independence to India. The British were out, and the lower-middle class could move in. They became the dominant factor behind the Congress party and its rule until the late 1960s, and Nehru's centralized state and mixed economy served their interests.

To maintain its position, a lower-middle class must avoid subordination to an industrial bourgeoisie, either foreign or indigenous, as was the historical pattern in Western capitalisms. It must eliminate "feudal" elements — patrimonial landlordism — from control over agriculture so that productivity can increase. It must increase industrial productivity, too, but without letting a powerful indigenous industrial bourgeoisie emerge and without permitting foreign capital to take over. Unless it expedites productivity gains, the opportunities for subsequent generations of the lower-middle class will not expand.

How to increase agricultural productivity and eliminate feudal remnants? How to expand industrial productivity without losing out to foreign capital or indigenous big business? How to augment employment to ensure the reproduction of the lower-middle class in the next generation? The Congress government gave suitable replies to these concerns up to 1969. It absorbed the many princely states of British India and pensioned off their feudal rulers. Through provincial governments, it instituted *zamindari* abolition, a form of land reform that eliminated the very large and usually absentee patrimonial landlords but left alone the rich peasantry, which formed the rural lower-middle class, or even augmented its wealth. It limited foreign capital's penetration (Bardhan 1984: 44) and regulated indigenous large capital (Vanaik 1985: 59) to preserve the dominance of the lower-middle class. Economic development, especially industrial growth, came from a large "public sector" under government control or a "private sector" licensed and supervised by the bureaucracy — in this way, productivity would increase but the lower-middle class would remain protected from large capital.

This mixed economy with ostensible socialist leanings but a true capitalist tilt was the lower-middle class's dream. As government necessarily burgeoned, so too did employment opportunities for the lower-middle class. Other "opportunities" — for bribes, kick-backs, underhanded university placements, job payoffs, and other forms of corruption and chicanery — also increased, creating en-tangling but profitable alliances among bureaucrats, politicians, traders, manufacturers, lawyers, wealthy peasants, and the other constituents of the lower-middle class. The result was, in Salman Rushdie's phrase, a land of *chamchas* ("spoons," nested front-to-back) — in the American idiom, a land of back-scratchers. More formally, an Indian economist typifies it as "a patron-client regime fostered by a flabby and heterogeneous [class] coalition preoccu-pied in a spree of anarchical grabbing of public resources . . . " (Bardhan 1984: 70).

How to deal with Gandhi's legacy? How to harness Gandhian utopia to the interests of the lower-middle class? These too were important questions for the lower-middle class after independence. Gandhi was dead, but the Gandhian vision did not disappear — Lohia's use of satyagraha for organizing the poor and his heretic Gandhism could not be ignored. Vinoba's confrontation with Lohia helped provide the answer. Once the official spiritual successor mildly acceded to the loss of satyagraha, once he was caught up with daydreams of voluntary land reforms, there was little effective opposition from experimentalists to the intermediate regime. Fail-ing confrontation, hijacking Gandhian utopia was sufficient — lip service, labels, and subsidies allowed the Congress to claim Gandhi for itself until the late 1960s. Then historical contingencies enabled another utopian vision, claiming to be Gandhi's but in fact some-what different, to appear.

${\mathcal{T}}$EN

Experiment with Total Revolution

> Bihar has become a laboratory for a new political experiment.
>
> *Atal Behari Vajpayee (1974)*

The 1969 centenary of Gandhi's birth commemorated a major event long past, but it also heralded some major events to come. By the late 1960s, it was hard to deny India's mounting problems as well as the momentous changes brought about by independence. After Nehru's death in 1964, the government's implementation of income equalizing and development policies became even more laggard and may actually have exacerbated inequality (Frankel 1978: 389). At the same time, natural disasters brought India famine and food-grain dependency on the outside world. Industrial growth was stagnant (Jha 1980), whereas the Naxalite revolutionary movement, embracing violence, assassination, and wealth confiscation, grew apace in the countryside (Frankel 1978: 378–81). The 1967 general election returned the Congress party to power at the Center, or national level, but with a greatly reduced parliamentary majority. Its record in state assembly elections was even more dismal. By the late 1960s, then, various compelling developments, including the lack of economic development, portended some change in India.

To many people, including Indira Gandhi and Jayaprakash Narayan, it seemed that too many things were going badly in the country and with the Gandhian vision a hundred years after the Mahatma's birth, and something would have to be done about it. What they and others did either intentionally or unintentionally in

193

the early 1970s sponsored a new utopian vision and experiment in India, which, although heavily indebted to Gandhi's dream, was not identical to it.

This chapter begins with a structural history: it reviews the contingencies at the national level and within the Gandhian voluntary movement that enabled a new utopia. It also chronicles the response to these immediate circumstances by one Gandhian experimenter, Jayaprakash Narayan, or J.P. as he was most often called (and as I shall call him). These circumstances precipitated his intention to abandon mildness and work for "total revolution" (*sampurna kranti*). Other circumstances, which this chapter also details, compelled J.P. and his experiment with utopia. They were ultimately to limit the authority he exercised over the utopian vision as it became a vehicle for mass protest in 1974 and 1975. This chapter thus ends with a history of the singular: it details the way in which J.P. reimagined the Gandhian vision and then lived it out with the help of many other individuals. The chronicle continues in the following chapter, which shows how J.P.'s vision became what Gandhi would probably have called a nightmare. It became an ideology justifying Hindu nationalism.

Contingencies

In 1969, Indira Gandhi, who had been prime minister for three years,[1] broke away from the Congress party leadership to form her own party, Congress (R).[2] She also broke with the old rhetoric and practice of class conciliation, the ostensible dedication to the idea of sarvodaya (welfare for all). She constructed her own political following by personalistic and populist appeals to the poor, such as her famous slogan of *garibi hatao!* ("End Poverty!") (see Mayer 1984: 144; Church 1984: 236). The national "political idiom was quickly transformed from one of conciliation to one of conflict" (Frankel 1978: 433). Mrs. Gandhi[3] welcomed many socialists and communists into her new party, and she worked to strengthen ties with the Communist party of India (CPI).

Political expediency no doubt partially motivated Mrs. Gandhi's class-based rhetoric and her opening to the left. She may also have been responding to the fact that the Indian masses had demonstrated a new political consciousness and political participation in the 1967 elections (Mayer 1984: 145–46). She may even have honestly tried to speak to the needs of India's disadvantaged (Church 1984: 236; see Wood 1984: 197–223 for a case in point). Whatever her motivation, Mrs. Gandhi destroyed the power of the old Congress leadership, or as P. B. Mayer (1984: 145) puts it, destroyed the Congress party itself, and substituted a highly personalistic and populist politics, centered on herself, for party rule.

The End of Congress Hijack

Switching to a class-based appeal, Mrs. Gandhi ceased to hijack Gandhian utopia. These were ideological goods no longer needed or wanted. In the event, Gandhian utopia became her chief opponent, and she showed increasing hostility to Gandhian associations, especially after 1975, as the following chapter shows. One lifelong Gandhian worker I interviewed in 1988 claimed that her hostility arose because the Gandhi Memorial Foundation refused to appoint her a trustee after she became prime minister in 1967. Many Gandhian workers had strong Congress sympathies going back before independence. They disapproved of Mrs. Gandhi's treatment of the old Congress stalwarts on her way to becoming prime minister, and they worried about her authoritarianism. Furthermore, there was a strong sense that she had no commitment to the Gandhian program. Another liberating contingency was the demise (although it was a lingering death) of the old Congress leadership, as Indira Gandhi's new Congress grew stronger, especially after the 1972 elections. Because many of the Congress old guard retained positions of influence on the governing boards of associations like the Gandhi Memorial Foundation, there was another reason for a new official relationship with the Gandhian movement. The split Congress, Mrs. Gandhi's changed rhetoric, her rebuff by the old-line Gandhian organizations, and the weakened Congress old guard disarrayed and then scattered the institutions of party and government that had interlocked to hijack Gandhian utopia in the years after 1947. Mrs. Gandhi would put some of these institutions together again in 1975 and for a few years thereafter, during the period in which she suspended civil rights and jailed opponents in what has come to be known as the Emergency (1975–77). Even in these years, Indira Gandhi made no attempt to hijack the Gandhian vision again. That is, during the Emergency, Gandhians — a portion of them — personally endorsed Mrs. Gandhi's policies, at the very same time that their

195

activities came under increasing scrutiny and censure by Mrs. Gandhi's government.

The official hijack having ended in the early 1970s, the question was: who would reclaim the goods?

Vinoba and the Sarva Seva Sangh were logical choices to recover the Gandhian vision, but the many years of official hijack had adversely affected their ability to do so. Vinoba's accommodation to that hijack, his ever milder experiments, had compelled a split in the sarvodaya movement almost at the very moment that the Congress was dividing. Geoffrey Ostergaard (1985: 26–27) refers to the years 1969–73 as a period of crisis for the movement. The failures of bhoodan and gramdan had to be faced. The khadi and village industries program had fared little better, and there was increasing pressure to introduce new techniques that would lower costs and raise productivity. Leadership was also a problem because Vinoba had retired from public life in 1969 (although his authority was still paramount in the Sarva Seva Sangh).

When Vinoba refused to sanction satyagraha as a forceful means to redeem gramdan pledges, he dramatized the movement's failure for many activists within the Sarva Seva Sangh. In 1970, they abandoned Vinoba's experiments in conciliation and adopted the use of satyagraha as a means to redress social injustice and inequalities (Ostergaard 1985: 28–33). In the early 1970s, too, there was concern that official sponsorship had compromised the movement's goals, and this negative attitude toward the government seems to have been heightened by the split in the Congress Party and Indira Gandhi's alliance with the Communist party of India (Ostergaard 1985: 36–42, 48).

The split soon widened, and two factions appeared, each one claiming a leader and proclaiming certain Gandhian experiments. Vinoba had his following, composed of those who continued to value mildness. The other faction, which increasingly collected around Jayaprakash Narayan, favored active — what Vinoba would have deemed harsh — satyagraha to redress social wrongs. They also wanted to sever the ties to government that they blamed, in part, for Vinoba's satisfaction with mild — what the J.P. group would have referred to as tame — satyagraha (I return to these differences later in this chapter).

196   By late 1973, J.P. and his following within the Sarva Seva Sangh intended to put their theory of satyagraha to a test (Ostergaard 1985: 70; Nargolkar 1974). What had compelled J.P. to join up with

Vinoba but now was compelling him to break away from him? J.P. would undoubtedly have said he intended to follow the Gandhian dream even if it meant splitting off from other Gandhians. Some of those others would undoubtedly have said that J.P. was unintentionally reverting to what he had been before, a Marxist revolutionary.

Intentions

From committed Marxist to mildest Vinoba follower and then to activist Gandhian — Jayaprakash Narayan would probably have so described his public life. In the extent of J.P.'s transformations and in their relative suddenness, we see perhaps one of the most impressive vindications of Gandhi's belief in discontinuous personhoods. J.P.'s self-intentions, as they stood in 1974, significantly enabled a new utopian vision and experiment.

Born in rural Bihar in 1902 to a civil servant, J.P. came under Gandhi's influence when he was still quite young (for accounts of J.P.'s life, see Scarfe and Scarfe 1975; N. K. Singh 1975; Barik 1977; and Nargolkar 1975). In keeping with Gandhi's noncooperation movement in 1922, J.P. renounced an education in Indian schools because they enjoyed British subsidy, and he left for the United States. At the same time, J.P.'s wife went to live in Gandhi's ashram. (She had come under Gandhi's influence during the Champaran satyagraha, in which her father had served as an important "subcontractor.") While studying at several American universities, where he was inspired by radical students and faculty members, J.P. became a committed Marxist. Working for wages in factories and on farms, as he was forced to do in the United States, also heightened his revolutionary consciousness.

Soon after he returned to India in 1929, J.P. made clear his strong disagreement with Gandhi. He ridiculed Gandhi's idea that trusteeship by the rich would improve the lot of the poor. J.P. also put little stock in Gandhi's claim that trusteeship was in keeping with Indian traditions. The theory behind trusteeship — that capital and labor are interdependent, that revolution is wasteful — "these are the commonest ideas of the west preached by smug bourgeois professors, thinkers, and churchmen," J.P. wrote in 1936. Trusteeship, he added, is "a system of clemency and charity instead of a system of justice" (Narayan 1980 [1936]: 36–40). J.P. worried that

Gandhism might stymie a true social revolution (Narayan 1980 [1957]: 183–184) because Gandhi refused to condone the elimination of private property (Narayan 1980 [1936]: 36). For J.P., Marxism had a much stronger commitment to economic equality and a "surer and quicker" revolutionary method (Narayan 1980 [1936]: 40; [1957]: 183–84). J.P. also mistrusted Gandhi's singular devotion to nonviolence; J.P.'s belief was that institutions would have to be changed before hearts, and sometimes only force was effective.

Until 1952, J.P. remained committed to a materialist world view and to a democratic socialism that envisioned the forceful removal of inequalities through government action. He consistently disowned Gandhian utopia (although, except for a brief period in the 1930s, he also disavowed Soviet Communism) (Narayan 1980 [1957]: 183–84). Before independence, he organized a socialist caucus within the Congress that tried to radicalize the movement away from Gandhian goals. During World War II, he joined a guerrilla organization that attempted to sabotage colonial rule in India (Barik 1977: 32) and issued underground revolutionary appeals calling for violence against the British (Scarfe and Scarfe: 146–50). After independence, he formed a socialist party to contest elections against Nehru's Congress, which J.P. came to see as corrupt, ineffective, and only superficially committed to socialism.

Around 1950, J.P. began to change his mind about politics and the world. There had been the partition riots and Gandhi's assassination; the socialists had been thrown out of the Congress and suffered a devastating defeat as an independent party in the first general election (1952); Nehru seemed to be abandoning his commitment to socialism; and J.P.'s comrades in the socialist party bickered bitterly (Scarfe and Scarfe 1975: 273). In 1952, J.P. fasted, considered, and then abandoned materialism. Reborn, as his wife put it, or converted, as many others believed (Scarfe and Scarfe 1975: 273), J.P. embraced Gandhian utopian thinking and in 1954 left party and power politics to dedicate his life to Vinoba's sarvodaya program, especially to bhoodan land reform (Narayan 1980: 181–208). J.P.'s biographers, the Scarfes, discount conversion: they maintain that he had always been sympathetic to Gandhian thinking "below the surface," and they write that "no man changes completely in such a short space of time" (Scarfe and Scarfe 1975: 274). No doubt there were anticipations of the change earlier in J.P.'s career. For example, Kantowsky argues, J.P. in 1940 pictured a future society that had moved beyond material satisfaction alone (Kantowsky 1980: 25–28). In 1948, J.P. called for spiritual leaders to guide the Indian people (Nargolkar 1975: 58). After the fact, J.P. himself recognized that he had been moving closer to Gandhi through the early postwar years, but the important point, which he also admitted, was that he was unaware of his development (Narayan 1980: 181–208). The revolution in his consciousness, his novel intentions toward Gandhian utopia, did not come about until 1952, and his consciousness was to undergo another revolution in the early 1970s.

After 1952, many Gandhian understandings, like trusteeship, were neither alien nor abhorrent to J.P. It now seemed reasonable to him that the rich would come to serve the interests of the poor — and that if they did not, the poor must noncooperate with them. For the new J.P., India could succeed with revolutionary experiments in the present, like trusteeship, even if they contravened Western experience, so long as the current experiments grew out of India's past traditions. The village was the point of departure, as much for J.P. as it had been for Gandhi. In 1959, J.P. wrote,

I have pleaded for our present political institutions to be based on the principles that had been enunciated and practiced in the ancient Indian polity.

"Community" in ancient India had two forms. The first and basic form was the territorial community, the village or township . . . The democracy of the village communities was so stable and efficient that it continued well into the British period . . . The other form of community was the functional or occupational community, the varna . . .

The concept of dharma [duty] was of great importance in ancient India . . . This concept . . . is another example of that synthetic, organic, communal organization of Indian society . . . Dharma has . . . declined and ceased to exercise any influence . . . upon present polity, which is a wholly foreign implantation and has no roots in the Indian soil . . . Unless life in India is again organized on the basis of self-determining and mutually co-ordinating and integrating communities, that organic self-regulation of society, which the concept of dharma represents, will not be possible . . . The ancient concept of dharma has to be revived and the appropriate dharma for a democracy has to be evolved (Narayan 1980 [1959]: 216–17).

"Partyless democracy" was the vision of India's future that J.P. said was possible given India's past (Ostergaard and Currell 1971: 199

234). Taking this phrase from the Communist M. N. Roy, J.P. gave it a Gandhian meaning. Parliamentary democracy did not fit India well; in 1974 J.P. was to call it "dead democracy" (*New York Times* 1974, 4 November). It led to corruption, divisive political struggle, and a nonrepresentative government. A vital democracy would have no political parties and no highly centralized state government over which politicians competed. There would be instead a five-tier organization of governance, starting with the village panchayat and rising eventually to a national parliament (Pulparampil 1975: 178–82).

Village self-government (*gramswaraj*), which J.P. believed he developed from the ideas of Besant, Das, Roy, and Gandhi, was the centerpiece of partyless democracy and the starting point for J.P.'s current experiments. In villages, committees of the whole adult population, and in cities, neighborhood councils of adults from about a hundred families would deliberate and reach decisions by consensus. They would elect representatives to the next higher level of administration, but no one belonging to a political party could be a legitimate candidate. The village would thus become a very extended family (Ostergaard 1985: 8–11); the village would form the basis of a decentralized state, just as the extended family constituted the base of Indian society.

When J.P. abandoned materialism, he began to concentrate on converting the people's spirit, as Gandhi did, rather than changing the institutions under which they lived. Disciplining wants was a major priority. Again, as for Gandhi, the idea was to lower needs to a minimum rather than raise all to equal, maximum consumption. "The aim of economic development should be Man . . . Standard of living: minimum," he was to write in his prison diary in 1975, after Mrs. Gandhi's government interrupted his utopian experiment (see Narayan 1977: September 9 entry). Aiming economic development at Man also meant decentralizing economic planning and depending on small-scale or medium-scale technology. It meant loosening state control over the economy and getting rid of government licensing and controls, which led to the growth of corruption rather than national growth (Johnson 1981: 483). J.P. said he now wanted a people's socialism, not a state socialism.

200   Whereas earlier J.P. had strongly doubted Gandhi's commitment to equality, he came to feel that socialism could not achieve the freedom and equality that sarvodaya could. Materialism provided

no incentives for ethical conduct, he claimed, but Gandhism and later Vinoba's program of mildness did. He committed his whole being, giving *jeevandan* ("life-gift") to Vinoba's bhoodan movement because it promised to abolish private property without violence (Narayan 1980: 181–208; Ostergaard 1985: 8–9). He became "entranced" with Vinoba (*New York Times* 1975, 7 March) and "submerge[d] his ideas and his vitality in Vinoba's personality" (Scarfe and Scarfe 1975: 285). J.P. dedicated about fifteen years of his life to Vinoba's mildness.

Then, in the early 1970s, another J.P. surfaced. The precipitating circumstance seems to have been the failure of bhoodan and gramdan. In his home state of Bihar, which was overwhelmingly pledged to gramdan, peasants brought J.P. out of Vinoba's daydream. Naxalite revolutionary cadres had moved into Muzzafarpur district in 1970 and sent execution notices to two sarvodaya workers in May. The same month a bomb exploded in the Gandhi Peace Foundation at Jamshedpur. By this time, Vinoba had retreated to his ashram, and J.P. had taken charge of the bhoodan effort. He soon arrived in Muzzafarpur to deal with the circumstances. As he saw it then, it was not a conflict with the Naxalites, but a challenge to the sarvodaya movement (Narayan 1980 [1970]: 302–19; see also Narayan 1980 [1969]: 279–96).

The bhoodan program, J.P. concluded a few months after his arrival in Muzzafarpur, had become too soft.

High sounding words, grandiose plans, reforms galore. But somehow they all, or most of them, remain suspended in midair. They hardly touch the ground — at least not here [in rural Bihar]. Or touch it very lightly . . . what meets the eye is utter poverty, misery, inequality, exploitation, backwardness, stagnation, frustration, and loss of hope (Narayan 1980 [1970]: 307).

J.P. absolved the Naxalites. The fault was with the landowners, officials, moneylenders, and politicians who had evaded and set aside reforms. They banded together, J.P. noted, to evade the laws protecting the poor and guaranteeing them a minimum wage — and the courts were too slow and costly to provide any remedy. As for the Naxalites themselves, who were mostly educated young men from middle-class families, J.P. faulted the educational system that produced an "ever-expanding army of ill-educated, frustrated, and unemployed youth" (Narayan 1980 [1970]: 310).

201

J.P. recognized that the bhoodan program had not confronted these realities, and he abandoned Vinoba's mildness for a steadily evolving activism from this point on (see Kantowsky 1980: 33–35). J.P. did not revert, however, to his former self: he did not fall back on materialism or parliamentary politics, nor did he alter his commitment to nonviolent revolution. Instead, J.P. became another self. He began to confront reality actively with his version of the Gandhian vision, which was an experimental procedure that had been absent from Gandhism for more than twenty years. Specifically, he launched an active campaign to make good on the bhoodan and gramdan pledges in selected regions of rural Bihar. He engaged in active field work to redistribute land, establish a village council, organize a "peace army," and develop a labor cooperative. He also attended to the legal work necessary to ensure that whatever the poor villagers gained would not be taken away from them (for details of the Muzzafarpur program, see Narayan 1978 [1970]: 230–53, or 1980 [1970]: 302–19). In December 1970, six months after his arrival, J.P. reported some progress, although he recognized that further gains would depend on the villagers themselves. He even allowed that satyagraha might have to be used in future against the "forces that are likely to thwart our work" (Narayan 1978 [1970], 1: 253; see also Nargolkar 1974: 10).

In 1975, J.P. looked back on Bihar and pinpointed the reason for the failure of bhoodan. His program had achieved a more fundamental reconstruction of rural society than bhoodan or gramdan because of the "atmosphere of struggle": in this atmosphere people became committed, accepted challenges, and thereby changed themselves and others. Vinoba's "spiritual and moral appeals" might change some minds, but "they never became a social or psychological force" (Narayan 1977: August 18 entry).[4]

During the early 1970s, J.P. publicized his increasing alarm at India's deterioration: corruption abounded, Mrs. Gandhi's government was becoming more authoritarian, and public morality had virtually disappeared (see, for example, Narayan 1978 [1972], 4:1–6; 1978 [1973], 4: 7–31). By 1973, J.P. seemed to be groping for some means through which to actively resist India's deadline, such as he had developed in rural Bihar to counter bhoodan's failure. He spoke of "citizen's action" — nonviolent, unselfish, and apolitical (that is, outside party politics) in character — but he could not say what specific action to take and which citizens should take it. Like Gandhi long before, J.P. invited suggestions from readers of his journal (Narayan 1978 [1973], 4: 32–34). Late in 1973, he took up a suggestion from an unlikely source. At an international youth conference, Indira Gandhi had alluded to a new political force in the world, called "youth power" (Narayan 1978 [1973], 4: 43–45; see his earlier admiration for the 1968 French student revolt in Narayan 1980 [1969]: 279–96). Appropriating her term, J.P. soon applied it to showing Mrs. Gandhi just how powerful a force it could be.

Compelling and Enabling Experiments

J.P.'s first experiment, however, consisted of a confrontation with Vinoba over the Gandhian legacy. It was a struggle over ideas and over people. J.P. wanted the Sarva Seva Sangh to recognize or reauthorize Gandhian satyagraha, so that voluntary workers could take part in what he later called "citizen's actions." Vinoba resisted him because he found J.P.'s ideas about satyagraha harsh, not mild, and he feared losing his voluntary workers to power politics.

The future of Gandhism, especially the course of Gandhian experiments in the near future, was at issue. J.P. wanted to use the voluntary workers as loyal and committed shock troops in the early days of mass nonviolent resistance, just as Gandhi had used his ashramites. If J.P. had gained full control over these workers, their participation would have enabled his experiment very directly. The workers would have provided a sizable all-India support base, and he would not have had to solicit substantial additional support. Of even greater importance, their "official" participation as the cadre of the Sarva Seva Sangh would have authorized J.P.'s experiment as a true Gandhian satyagraha. There would have then been much less risk that his satyagraha would be deauthorized as harsh or not Gandhian, as had happened to Lohia's "permanent satyagraha" ten years earlier.

Neither J.P. nor Vinoba won an outright victory because the very nature of decision making in the Sarva Seva Sangh compelled an impasse. The Gandhian rule was that decisions should be reached by consensus. By 1974, only a few years after the initial split noted earlier in this chapter, the activist followers of J.P. and the mild supporters of Vinoba had moved too far apart for consensus. J.P. had already started his experiment with mass protest in Bihar, which I shall shortly describe, and the issue before the Sarva Seva

Sangh at its 1974 meeting was whether it was proper for Gandhian voluntary workers to take part. One faction, Vinoba's, opposed participation, whereas the majority faction, J.P.'s, wished to approve. Because no consensus was possible, Vinoba pronounced a compromise: workers should feel free to join J.P.'s protest, but they need not go. Vinoba himself took a vow to remain silent for a year. By indirection, Vinoba refused to commit the Sarva Seva Sangh to J.P., just as his year's silence in effect avoided any personal commitment. As an organization, the Sarva Seva Sangh would authorize neither J.P.'s ideas nor his experiment in Bihar as true to the Gandhian legacy. In addition, it would not allow J.P. to deploy its cadres as such (Ostergaard 1985: 100–109; also see *Organiser* 1974, 27 July; Nargolkar 1975: 120–22).

In 1975, when J.P.'s Bihar experiment was even more advanced, the confrontation broke out again. This time Vinoba's compromise was even harsher, although it superficially appeared more mild: all members of the Sarva Seva Sangh would remain silent concerning J.P.'s mass protest until Vinoba's own period of silence ended; therefore, nothing about it would be said in the name of the Gandhian movement (see *Times of India* 1975, 15 March: 1, 4; Ostergaard 1985: 168–74). Because it could not speak as one, the Sarva Seva Sangh ceased to speak at all, and J.P. failed to achieve unqualified Gandhian authority. Although the support of large numbers of voluntary workers as individuals did enable J.P. to get his experiment going, J.P.'s ability to mobilize many voluntary workers, especially outside his home state of Bihar, was handicapped (Scarfe and Scarfe 1975: 424). Thus, even though government hijack of Gandhian utopia had ended, J.P., as he developed his utopian vision, could not easily lay uncontested claim to the Gandhian legacy because Vinoba hushed up the issue.

The silence of official Gandhism compelled J.P. to look for authority and mass support elsewhere, much as Gandhi had been forced to do shortly after he returned to India from South Africa and met a generally hostile reception from nationalist leaders. In early 1974, the first opportunity to employ "youth power" — J.P. was later to say that the equivalent of class struggle in India was student protest (Ostergaard 1985: 297) — arose in western India, in the state of Gujarat. The Gujarat protest began, early in 1974, as a strike by students in the engineering college in Ahmedabad city over mess bills; it then quickly spread to other college students. At the time, food prices had gone up considerably and there was a food shortage. Students boycotted classes and set up an action committee, which laid out specific goals for the protest. Because they blamed government for corruption, inflation, and poor education, the students targeted the political system for protest, and, by extension, their actions condemned Indira Gandhi's Congress and her government. The students wanted to bring down the state ministry and to dissolve the legislative assembly, and by the middle of March, through marches, strikes, and other forms of mass protest, they had accomplished both these goals — but not before 103 people were killed, 310 were injured, and more than 6,000 were imprisoned. They had aid from the leaders of opposition parties, who joined their spontaneous movement after the fact as a way to confront Mrs. Gandhi's rule (Barik 1977: 46–52; Wood 1975).

Although J.P. went to Gujarat to encourage the student protest, the movement petered out after the government's concessions in March. It was clear to some contemporaries (whether they approved or disapproved) that J.P. was looking for a cause and an occasion, and Gujarat beckoned, but he reached there too late and therefore failed to assert his authority (*Mainstream* 1974, 23 February; Nargolkar 1974: 10). In Bihar, too, he arrived after the start, but soon enough to turn youth power into his version of Gandhian utopia: total revolution.

Total Revolution

J.P. never claimed that he started the mass protest in Bihar (Narayan 1977: August 21 entry), but he did maintain he turned it into an experiment with total revolution. At its outset, in fact, the concept of total revolution (*sampurna kranti*) did not exist, nor did it seem likely that violent student agitation would ever give way to nonviolent revolution. As J.P. said, a revolution "writes its own book" (quoted in *New York Times* 1974, 4 November: 6). By this phrase, he seems to have recognized that many aspects of his utopian vision fully developed only in the course of the mass protest (or even afterward, when he was in jail): ideas he had been developing since the early 1970s (or earlier) fully condensed only in reaction to the immediate circumstances of the protest. This phrase may also have signaled J.P.'s recognition that his authorship of the mass protest was never secure. From April 1974 through June 1975, he gained substantial authority over the mass movement in Bihar, which then catalyzed agitations elsewhere in northern India and even threatened to bring down Mrs. Gandhi's government. Although substantial, J.P.'s authority never fully dominated the movement, which continued to be partially compelled by collaborators who eventually "rewrote" public conceptions about J.P.

Beginning the Experiment

In March 1974, Mrs. Gandhi capitulated to youth power in Gujarat and dissolved the state government. Bihar students next showed their strength. A month before the Gujarat settlement, on 17–18 February 1974, 500 students from 135 colleges all over Bihar assembled in the state's capital city, Patna (Barik 1977: 52). This meeting was in the wake of a *bandh* ("general strike") called by the Bihar branch of the Communist Party of India for 21 January, in protest against inflation and corruption in Mrs. Gandhi's Congress government. Most of the other non-Communist opposition parties had joined the protest. At the student assembly in February, however, the joint movement split between left and right. Students who were members or sympathizers of the Communist party and other leftist parties walked out to form one student organization. Other students, belonging to a range of opposition parties — from democratic socialist to Hindu nationalist ("communal"),[5] but in the main associated with the Hindu nationalist Jana Sangh party — formed a protest association, the Student Struggle Committee (Chhatra Sangharsha Samiti) that J.P. was eventually to lead (Das 1979: 71; Ostergaard 1985: 93). From the very beginning of the movement, then, J.P.'s future leadership cadre had political affiliations, mainly with the non-Communist opposition to Mrs. Gandhi.

J.P. exercised little or no authority over the first phase of the Bihar protest. On 16 March, the non-Communist Student Struggle Committee organized a mass protest in Patna against high prices and unemployment.[6] Police fired upon the demonstrators, killing three persons. Two days later, the students *gheraoed*, or "mobbed," the Bihar legislative assembly in Patna, not harming legislators outright, but surrounding them and refusing them free passage. Again, the police intervened; this time five people died and sixty were wounded. Widespread rioting and pillage followed in Patna city, in which 10,000 student-led demonstrators burned hotels and government offices (*New York Times* 1974, 19 March: 6). The killings and property destruction spread to other cities in Bihar (*New York*

Times 1974, 20 March: 9). That evening J.P. agreed to support the student movement and called upon the state's chief minister to resign. On 30 March, after another general strike in Patna (23 March), J.P. tested his authority. He called for a silent procession on 8 April, to protest government repression of the students. Under his leadership and with the support of members of the Sarva Seva Sangh youth wing (the Tarun Shanti Sena), the procession was held (Barik 1977: 52–57).

The silent procession probably convinced J.P. that he could successfully discipline the student movement, for he subsequently took increasing control over it. His formal entry marks the second phase. On 12 April he agreed to participate in the protest movement if the students accepted the principle of nonviolence and if they agreed to remain politically nonpartisan. J.P. then led a large procession on 21 April protesting Mrs. Gandhi's decision to allow Bihar's chief minister, Abdul Ghafoor, to form a new government (in capitulation to student demands, the chief minister had resigned on 11 April). He demanded that the Bihar legislative assembly be dissolved, and, if that were not forthcoming, that members of the legislative assembly should resign their seats to show their opposition to Ghafoor's allegedly corrupt and repressive government.

In June 1974 the third phase of the movement began, when J.P. called for total revolution. Communists had marched, 100,000 of them, on 3 June to express their hostility to what was becoming known as the "J.P. Movement" and their support for the Ghafoor government (Das 1974: 1223–24; for the attitude of the CPI and other leftists toward J.P., see Sinha 1974; *Mainstream* 1974, 23 February: 4–6; Chitta Ranjan: 1974: 10–12; *Janata* 1974, 15 August: 42; Gulati 1974: 5–6). The Congress party had expressed similar distaste for J.P. and his "Fascist forces" on 29 April, and on 4 June the Bihar government marched military and police troops through Patna in a so-called "flag march," to show official strength and determination. J.P. held a procession the following day, and that evening, in Patna's Gandhi park, he exhorted the public to what was in effect a utopian experiment. He called for total revolution (Barik 1977: 52–57; Das 1974: 1223–24).

Total Revolution

J.P.'s dream was to take the passive revolution accomplished by independence from Britain and make it an active revolution, a fundamental reorganization of Indian society, along what he understood as Gandhian lines. J.P. asserted that there had been no fundamental social, economic, or political change since independence and that none would take place until there had been a total revolution, a "revolution in every sphere and aspect of society." This revolution could not come about simply through democratic elections, legislation, and government administration. It would require "people's direct action," in the form of "peaceful" civil disobedience and noncooperation — "satyagraha in its widest sense" — to change both minds and institutions (Narayan 1977: 23 August entry; 1978 [1974] 4: 115–20).

Many contemporaries chided J.P. for being vague about total revolution (see, for example, Khuswant Singh 1975: 15). He was never unclear, however, about its two major aspects, "people's power" and "permanent revolution." By "people's power" (an obvious extension of youth power), J.P. meant that total revolution required direct action by citizens, even if that action confronted duly elected democratic governments and national (that is, no longer colonial) state policies. People's power would lead to people's government, the reorganization of the nation from the bottom up that J.P. dreamed of in his "partyless democracy." Starting from below, there would rise up "an all-round revolution — political, economic, social, moral and cultural" (Naryan 1978 [1974] 4: 116).

By "permanent revolution," J.P. understood that the goals of people's power would change over time as the movement progressed toward a just, equal, and moral (sarvodaya) society. A "continuing revolution" (another term he used) would have fluid, not fixed objectives, which would be set only in the course of doing "satyagraha in its widest sense." For example, the first "installment" in Bihar had been the student demands; the next would be his announcement of a short-range economic policy (Narayan 1978 [1975] 4: 126); after that, there would be other objectives. The movement's future might appear vague to some, but its course had to be determined by action, not by armchair theorizing. An interviewer who compared J.P. to Bertrand Russell must have regretted it when J.P. replied:

> did I ever strike you as a philosopher? . . . I hope you remember your Marx. The passive philosopher who goes on interpreting the world has no place in Marxism . . . In my humble way I am trying to alter the world, while Russell merely interpreted it. Have I been able by

now to command your respect as a better Marxist than Russell? (Narayan 1978 [1975] , vol. 4: 142).

Whether he took his belief in permanent revolution from Gandhi's idea of experiment or from Marx's notion of praxis was never clear, and sometimes J.P. teased those trying to find out, as the above exchange indicates.

In the spring and summer of 1974, J.P. outlined what had to be done to get "continuing revolution" going. Peaceful protest would continue, using the techniques of satyagraha as J.P. understood them. The objective would be to cripple the Bihar government. There were to be mass marches, general strikes (bandhs), blockades of buildings (dharnas), mobbings (gheraos), fasts, and other forms of protest that in some cases were innovations on Gandhian techniques. The mobbings and blockades, especially, had a threatening and coercive quality — even though they were nonviolent — that Gandhi might have forsworn (compare Chitta Ranjan 1974: 10–12; Ramachandran 1974: 139–42; Ostergaard 1985: 81–82; for J.P.'s defense, see Narayan 1980 [1975]: 348–54). Perhaps this quality also explains why J.P. often used the term "peaceful" rather than "nonviolent" to describe the protests.

After June 1974, J.P. adopted an overtly political and antigovernment course of action. He not only accepted the support of opposition political parties, but also tried to unite them in common cause against the government (Narayan 1977: 21 August entry). Even though J.P. protested that his movement aimed at no one in particular, Mrs. Gandhi could hardly mistake that the direction of total revolution after June 1974 was against her and her government.

J.P. also began the reconstruction of society from the bottom up in the summer of 1974. Colleges had been closed for some time; now J.P. called on students to boycott their schools for a year, or at least not to attend classes. Most students agreed that the colleges should not reopen until the "muscle-flexing" extra police forces brought into Bihar to muzzle them had been removed (Das 1974: 1224). In August, J.P. called on his supporters to stop paying taxes, and he sent out student leaders to form People's Struggle Committees (Jana Sangharsha Samitis) across Bihar. Not many were formed before the movement ended, but some, the most advanced, did refuse to pay government taxes (Narayan 1980 [1975]: 348–54). **209** Other students, at J.P.'s request, volunteered for constructive work and social service. They picketed wine and opium shops, supervised government food-rationing stores, organized mass vaccination drives, and opened a free university (Singh 1974: 4).

In August 1974, J.P. set his sights far beyond the reform of colleges and the dissolution of the local government. He forecast that the movement would spread across the nation within a year. "The day will come when I will ask policemen and others not to obey their officers but to obey the leaders of the movement," he said (Narayan 1980 [1974]: 338–41).

Revolution Discontinued

In early October 1974, J.P. learned that the day for persuading the police had not yet come. He had called a three-day general strike in Patna to force the legislative assembly's dissolution. Although the strike was nearly total and therefore quite successful, police action left 17 people dead, 300 injured, and 3,000 arrested. After inconclusive talks with Mrs. Gandhi on 2 November, in which she refused to dissolve the Bihar government, J.P. returned to Patna to lead a mass demonstration against the chief minister on 4 November (Das 1974a: 2049–51; Barik 1977: 52–57). The police dispersed this march with tear gas and *lathi* ("cudgel") charges, and, in the melee, they set upon J.P. and injured him (*New York Times* 1974, 5 November: 5; 12 November: 17). Afterward, J.P. took the movement into a new phase — the final one, as it turned out, perhaps because he realized the strength of the forces against him. The fact was that the police still obeyed their officers.

On 18 November 1974, J.P. asked the political parties behind his movement to form a coalition and to prepare to fight Mrs. Gandhi's Congress in the upcoming national elections (Das 1974a: 2049–51). From this point on, J.P.'s long-term vision of partyless democracy took on a short-term experiment with electoral contest. J.P. asserted that partyless democracy was an ideal for the future, and that even if he currently worked through political parties, the goal was still people's power (Narayan 1974, 21 July: 3–4).

Henceforth, J.P. seems to have become increasingly precipitated as the spokesman for the opposition parties arrayed against Mrs. Gandhi's government. He moved across northern India hoping to write new chapters in his revolution's book: in December 1974, he went on a "reconnaissance mission" in eastern Uttar Pradesh (*Times of India* 1974, 10 December: 1) and traveled across the state; in

210

January 1987, he told an audience in Madhya Pradesh that revolutions were like volcanoes, which no force could prevent (*New York Times* 1975, 5 January: 8); in February crowds "went mad" for him in Gujarat (*Organiser* 1975, 8 February: 7); in the same month, he told government workers in Bihar, Haryana, and Uttar Pradesh that they need not obey illegal orders (*Organiser* 1975, 8 March: 4). Leading a peaceful mass march of 100,000 people in New Delhi in early March, J.P. called for a month-long agitation across India to support overhaul of the educational system, an austerity program for government, and dismissal of corrupt officials (*New York Times* 1975, 7 March: 2). Outside Bihar, however, he did not seem able to mobilize mass support without the help of the established opposition parties (for Uttar Pradesh, see Kala 1975: 4; for Madhya Pradesh, see N. K. Singh 1975: 691–92). In February, J.P. announced the plans of many non-Communist opposition parties to launch a nationwide civil disobedience campaign against Mrs. Gandhi's "growing authoritarian trends" (*New York Times* 1975, 18 February: 3). In April, J.P. gave lemonade — and his support — to a leader of the opposition, Morarji Desai. J.P.'s lemonade symbolically broke a protest fast Desai had undertaken, but the fast really ended because Mrs. Gandhi had capitulated to Desai's demands for early elections in his home state of Gujarat.

At about the same time, Indira Gandhi was getting squeezed in other ways, as well. The CIA had just destabilized the Allende government in Chile, and Mrs. Gandhi evidently feared there might be American money from dubious sources behind J.P. and some of the Gandhian associations, such as the Gandhi Peace Foundation, which was considered J.P.'s "resort" (Ostergaard 1985: 183; Barik 1977: 72). The railways minister had been assassinated in January while addressing a rally in Bihar (*New York Times* 1975, 5 January: 8). Mrs. Gandhi asked J.P. to halt his movement now that it had turned violent, but he refused (*Organiser* 1975, 18 January: 3). In March, she had dismissed the minister of works and housing, who had urged her to make contact with J.P. (*New York Times* 1975, 6 March: 11). On 14 June, while her Congress party in Gujarat was losing the state elections to an alliance of opposition parties, Mrs. Gandhi was found guilty of corrupt election practices, stemming from events in 1971 (*New York Times* 1975, 14 June: 1). J.P. joined opposition leaders in "anti-Indira" rallies, and he denounced her decision to remain prime minister as "shameful" (*New York Times* 1975, 15 June: 3). Ten days later, when the Supreme Court of India permitted Mrs. Gandhi to retain her post, three opposition parties met in Delhi to form the People's Struggle Committee (Lok Sangharsha Samiti), which was to organize an all-India protest campaign against Indira Gandhi. The committee held a mass rally in old Delhi on 25 June. At the rally, Nana Deshmukh, leader of the Jana Sangh party, announced the coalition, and J.P. charged Mrs. Gandhi with taking the country toward dictatorship and fascism (*New York Times* 1975, 28 June: 8; Deshmukh 1979: 73–78). He also seems to have reiterated his belief that civil servants and the military owed loyalty to the constitution and need not carry out unjust orders (*New York Times* 1975, 2 July: 8).

Indira Gandhi then moved quickly to terminate the experiment with total revolution. On 26 June 1975, she had the president of India declare a national emergency, under whose terms civil rights were suspended and almost all opposition leaders, including J.P., were summarily imprisoned (*New York Times* 1975, 26 June: 1). The Emergency, as it has come to be called, lasted until 1977.

No one, least of all J.P., believed that his movement accomplished fundamental changes, except perhaps in the unintended consequence that it precipitated Indira Gandhi's declaration of emergency. Circumstances before and after the Emergency, which the next chapter details, confined J.P.'s utopia almost as much as the government's jail imprisoned J.P. during it.

Gandhian Utopia and the J.P. Movement

J.P. claimed Gandhian authority for the Bihar protest, and almost from the beginning of the movement, that claim was taken seriously, even when it was disputed (see, for example, Chitta Ranjan 1974; Mohen 1974; Ostergaard 1985: 81–82, 116ff.; Ramachandran 1974; *New York Times* 1974, 21 April: 4; Sethi 1975). During the Emergency, J.P. did not abandon the proposition that his total revolution was Gandhian satyagraha in its widest sense (Narayan 1977: 23 August entry; also see 9 September entry). The constitutive power of Gandhian utopia, its ability to compel social action and thought in India, was therefore still intact through the middle 1970s. No one disputed that J.P.'s claim to being Gandhian was powerful; they could only dispute its validity. Indira Gandhi therefore asserted that J.P. undermined faith in democratic institutions in the same way that the Nazis and Fascists had (*New York Times*

1975, 28 January: 4). For some leftists, he was "the Bonaparte of the RSS [Hindu nationalist] army," deploying majority Hindu chauvinism against a government representing minorities and the poor (*Mainstream* 1975, 8 March: 4–7). For others, his "saintly camouflage" barely covered up right-wing adventurism and CIA support (*Link* 1975, 13 July: 10–17). J.P. replied by reaffirming his Gandhian roots. He recalled that "Gandhi was [seen as] an agent of the capitalists, too" (quoted in *New York Times* 1974, 23 July: 2). In the same spirit, the supreme head of the Hindu nationalist Rastriya Swayamsevak Sangh (RSS) asserted before ten thousand people that "Jayaprakash is fulfilling the mission of noble leaders like Mahatma Gandhi, Acharya Vinoba Bhave and Guruji Golwalkar . . . who seek to serve the people selflessly" (*Organiser* 1974, 7 December: 1). As Gandhi had been before independence, J.P. was now "the symbol of the people's revolt" for the leader of the Jana Sangh party (*Organiser* 1974, 17 August: 3).

Both the disparagements and the encomiums assume that J.P. controlled the direction of the mass movement with his intentions. The commentators then evaluate those intentions: they were either noble or perfidious; J.P. was either a true Gandhian or a Napoleon camouflaged in khadi. The fact of the matter is that J.P. was neither so heroic nor so devilish — or, more precisely, whatever his intentions were, they were not directly reflected in the mass movement. Like Gandhi's and Vinoba's before, J.P.'s utopian vision butted up against existing circumstances, but unlike Gandhi J.P. did not effectively authorize his utopia in those circumstances, nor did he adapt it easily to them. Instead, the circumstances refashioned J.P.'s utopia and made him adapt. J.P. after the fact recognized and apologized for what had happened. After a summer's imprisonment, he confessed to his diary that involving political parties in mass movements, as had happened in the experiment with total revolution, necessarily compromises the movements. Under party direction, J.P. lamented, people fail to see the problems for themselves, and they do not come to take responsibility for their actions. According to J.P., however, no other choice had been possible: there had been no way to keep political parties out and still have a mass movement (Narayan 1977: 6 September entry).

Although J.P. underwent a radical discontinuity in personhood in the early 1950s and then again in the early 1970s, he did not achieve authority over the sarvodaya movement, which he tried to wrest away from Vinoba's exclusive authorship, or over the Bihar protest, which he hoped to turn from party politics to total revolution. Individual utopian intentions, sponsored by discontinuous personhoods, often fail to master social circumstances. These failed utopian experiments nevertheless do have consequences, which the next two chapters chronicle. Before the Emergency and even more so after it, J.P. became a personal vehicle, and his utopian experiment an ideological tool, by which Gandhian utopia became transplanted into Hindu nationalist ideology.

ELEVEN

Deauthorized Utopia, Transplanted Ideology

| *Has my revolution been as total as you wished it to be?*
| *Cartoon of J.P. speaking to a peasant (New York Times, 24 March 1977)*

When a policeman bore down on J.P. during the Patna march of 4 November 1974 and readied his truncheon to strike, it was symbolic that Nana Deshmukh should take the main force of the blow. Just as J.P. would probably not have survived the blow from which Deshmukh shielded him, so the experiment with total revolution would have died out quickly without Deshmukh and his cadres from the Rastriya Swayamsevak Sangh (RSS), the Hindu nationalist cultural association, and its affiliated political party, the Jana Sangh.

Because J.P. had to assert authority over a movement controlled and staffed by others, there was always something "theatrical," as Arvind Das perceptively notes, about his experiment. J.P. tried to authorize his Gandhian utopia not only to the Indian masses but also to his own cadres (excluding perhaps the Sarva Seva Sangh workers who chose to follow his lead). Therefore, what Das (1979: 138) says of the movement — "it lived on symbolisms and images and it died with them" — is even more true of its erstwhile leader. J.P. depended on symbolism because his authority over the actions of his cadres was limited. For example, J.P.'s ostensibly peaceful "mobbings" of legislators and civil servants often degenerated into actual mass manhandlings (Barik 1977: 52–57). His appeal to students to leave their colleges and take up constructive work for a year also failed. Through these images and exhortations, he hoped to revolutionize his followers away from the party affiliations that

215

had originally brought them to him. Through images and exhortations, he hoped to protect his utopian vision from misappropriation by the very cadres who were supposedly transfixed by it. He broadcast them forcefully — even, according to Barik (1977: 62), in an authoritarian manner — precisely because he had few other ways to enforce them.

As this chapter will show, J.P. was not successful. Even before the declaration of emergency made sure his total revolution would fail, his Gandhian utopia had been uprooted and transplanted as ideology in a foreign terrain. J.P.'s symbolisms and images therefore did not die, as Das suggests, with the declaration of emergency, nor did they die with J.P. in 1979. They continued to be nurtured into the present day by a Hindu nationalism that uses them — and therefore Gandhian utopia, too — to legitimate the notion that the Indian nation will be nothing unless it be Hindu.

This chapter traces the singular history behind the conjuncture of J.P.'s Gandhian experiment with Hindu nationalism in 1974–75. It details the existing circumstances that J.P.'s experiment confronted and failed to overcome. We thus see the singular history by which a failed utopian experiment can be converted into an ideology, despite human intentions and action. The chapter also chronicles the subsequent contingencies by which Gandhian utopia was abandoned — and J.P.'s Gandhian voluntary organizations persecuted — by the Congress government in the 1980s. Abandoned by the Congress that had once claimed authority over it, lost to the delegitimized Gandhian organizations that had once experimented with it, Gandhian utopia was readily hijacked by the political opposition, to become transplanted within a Hindu nationalist ideology. The next chapter then provides a structural account of the ideology of Hindu nationalism, its appropriation of the Gandhian vision as an ideology, and the social inequalities it justifies.

Hindu Nationalism's History

Until the 1920s — that is, until Gandhi and Gandhian utopia became dominant in the Indian nationalist movement — Hindu nationalism was a theme running through much nationalist thought. Early in the twentieth century, nationalists in Bengal and Bombay commonly argued for India's future capacity for self-rule in terms of the Hindus' ancient cultural and social accomplishments (see Chapter 6). Hindu nationalism's proponents usually came from the high castes; in particular, they were predominantly Brahmans, whose traditional role as custodians of Hindu civilization undoubtedly made this expression of nationalism attractive. Hindu nationalism, then, was part of affirmative Orientalism and therefore initially served as a form of cultural resistance to Westernization and British colonialism. This early Hindu nationalism represented a "liberal communalism," to use Bipan Chandra's phrase (1984: 323–30) once again, because it looked forward to an India free from imperialism and was not yet avowedly anti-Muslim. Those I have called experimentalists, like Vivekananda (French 1974), Sister Nivedita (Foxe 1975), Aurobindo (Broomfield 1968: 31–34), Besant (1904, 1913), Malaviya (Chandra 1984: 328–30), Tagore briefly (Hay 1970), even Savarkar (Raghavan 1983) and other staunch Hindu nationalists of the early twentieth century, defended Hindu cultural traditions against a pejorative Orientalism from abroad, not against Islam or other Indian minority traditions within.

Hindu nationalism turned against perceived indigenous enemies, especially Muslims, beginning in the 1920s. Gandhi's evenhanded policy toward minorities, the joint efforts of Muslims and Hindus in the 1920s noncooperation satyagraha campaign, British attempts to woo Muslims politically — all these undoubtedly contributed to the sectarian chauvinism that now appeared. As Hindu nationalism increasingly justified Hindu interests after 1920, it moved further away from Gandhian utopia. Even though both had their roots in the affirmative Orientalism that had nurtured resistance to cultural domination in the world system, their subsequent growth was very different. Out of the Gandhian vision, a utopia struggling against colonialism and the Indian status quo developed; from Hindu nationalism, an ideology defending that status quo emerged. A voluntary society called the Hindu Mahasabha, for example, had been founded in 1915 to support worthy Hindu causes, such as banning cow slaughter or spreading teetotalism. Soon turning moribund, the Mahasabha stayed that way until it was revived in the early 1920s with a new purpose: it was to safeguard Hindu rights against Muslim inroads (for the Hindu Mahasabha, see Anderson and Damle 1987: 28–29; Raghavan 1983; Dixit 1986: 131–35).

One important means of safeguarding the Hindu would be to define a future Indian nation in his image; in other words, to make

Indian nationalism synonymous with a Hindu nationalism. Perhaps the most influential and certainly one of the earliest statements of such a Hindu nationalism came from a future leader of the Mahasabha. Vinayak Damodar (also know as Veer) Savarkar attempted to define what a Hindu was and thereby what an independent India would be in his 1923 pamphlet, *Hindutva*. Savarkar, influenced in his student days by Shyamji Krishnavarma, tried to define the essence of a Hindu, and from that to argue that there was enough basic unity in India to form an independent nation. Savarkar rejected sectarian identity as such a base. Being Hindu, for Savarkar, was a totality of racial, geographical, and cultural identities, not merely sectarian allegiances: a Hindu lived in a geographical region, India; came from a racial stock, Indian; and followed a cultural tradition, Hindu, broadly conceived. By Savarkar's definition, India was a single (Hindu) nation in spite of its many castes and sectarian groups. The minutiae of their differences set aside, they shared this much: that India for them was both fatherland and holy land. They therefore could be trusted to have or develop a national patriotism and cultural allegiance to India.

Some sectarian allegiances, Savarkar warned, led to internationalism rather than nationalism: Muslims, Buddhists, and Christians, even if they were descended from India-born, Hindu converts, did not accept India as a holy land; their allegiances lay elsewhere. Addressing a 1937 all-India convention of the Hindu Mahasabha, Savarkar asserted that Muslims cherished "fanatical designs" to establish Muslim rule in India (Raghavan 1983: 595–600). The leaders of the Hindu Mahasabha, chief among them Savarkar and Bhai Parmanand, were increasingly harried by this fear of Muslim domination, as the British in the 1920s and 1930s brought Indians ever closer to home rule, but with very strong electoral guarantees to the Muslim minority. Besides exposing supposed Muslim perversity, the Mahasabha also hoped to gain its ends by reconverting Indian Muslims to Hinduism and by adding Untouchables to the ranks of Hindus. (High-caste Hindus often refused Untouchables privileges, such as the right to enter temples, that other Hindus enjoyed.)

Another Hindu nationalist association that was to prove more lasting and influential than the Mahasabha began in 1925. The Rastriya Swayamsevak Sangh (RSS) started up as a cultural association working for Hindu revitalization. A Brahman, K. B. Hedgewar (who headed the organization from 1925 to 1940), founded it in the central Indian city of Nagpur (Anderson and Damle 1987: 34). Although its leaders also feared Muslims and shared the Mahasabha's Hindu nationalism, the RSS avoided political engagements or public espousals of its cause. Instead, in keeping with its definition as a "cultural" (not "political") organization, the RSS worked assiduously to develop grass-roots cadres of committed and disciplined Hindu nationalists, as I shall discuss shortly.

Although Hindu nationalist associations became increasingly militant in the quarter-century before independence in 1947, a Hindu Indian nationalism proved relatively unsuccessful in comparison to the Congress nationalist movement. In the 1930s the politically active Hindu Mahasabha had failed to gain mass support, and by the 1940s it was inert (Cleghorn 1977). At independence and afterward — in fact, until about 1980 — Hindu nationalism enjoyed little political legitimacy and suffered under much state repression. Hindu nationalism was blamed for the assassination of Mohandas Gandhi and for the partition-period communal riots. Also, its image of a modern India could not have been further from the Nehru government's commitment to secular democratic socialism and from the Indira Gandhi (pre-Emergency) government's emphasis on the poor and the low castes.

Through these vicissitudes, the cultural activities of the RSS continued, even though the Nehru government banned the organization for more than a year right after Gandhi's assassination. The second RSS *sarsanghchalak* ("supreme guide"), M. S. Golwalkar (served 1940–73), argued that the ban should be lifted precisely because the RSS was a cultural, not a political organization (Anderson and Damle 1987: 52). In reality, however, the membership of the politically activist Hindu Mahasabha and the RSS overlapped considerably at independence and shortly afterward, just as their ideas were usually congruent (Khanolkar 1980: 13–14; see Golwalkar 1966: 53–54 on the ideals of Savarkar). Yet there was truth in Golwalkar's claim. The RSS mobilized potential political recruits through cultural activism. In this respect (but in little else) the RSS resembled Gandhi: he too had created a disciplined core group of political followers out of his ashram converts. The RSS operated with a similar sense of conversion and with at least as much discipline, but on a much wider scale.   *219*

The RSS leader Golwalkar (1966: 10) best expressed this cultural mission:[1]

> The Rastriya Swayamsevak Sangh has resolved to fulfill that age-old national mission by forging, as the first step, the present-day scattered elements of the Hindu Society into an organised and invincible force both on the plane of the Spirit and on the plane of material life.

The RSS works toward this spiritual revolution by organizing local-level *shakhas*, or branches. These cadres wear uniforms, drill army fashion, learn to wield cudgels (lathis), sing patriotic songs (which are also devotional), often share a clubhouse, and study Hindu traditions (Anderson and Damle 1987: 1, 84–86, 89–98; Mishra 1980: 52–55). Caste is no bar to membership, even though the RSS leadership has always been from the Brahman or other upper castes. Indeed, the shakhas work hard to break down caste barriers, as, for example, by requiring all members to take food in common (rather than separated by caste). The intent is to develop a national physical and mental discipline to make all Hindus and the whole of India strong and independent (see Balasaheb Deoras, present supreme guide of RSS, quoted in *Organiser* 8 March 1975; also see Golwalkar 1966: 52–54).

A complex, highly centralized, and authoritarian chain of command links the local branches up with the supreme guide of the RSS, through several intervening levels of organization (Anderson and Damle 1987: 86–89). Central to this chain are the *pracharaks*, or "full-time workers," who dedicate themselves to an austere existence — simple clothing, vegetarianism, bachelorhood — in the service of the RSS. Pracharaks are assigned to various duties, such as organizing and advising local branches within the RSS, or they are sent to work with other affiliated Hindu nationalist organizations (Anderson and Damle 1987: 87–88). The RSS newspaper *Organiser* (1975, 22 February: 3) summed it up succinctly: "there are only three organized forces in India: the Army, the CPI [Communist party of India], and the RSS."

The branches of the RSS spread not only upward but also outward; they reach out to many other organizations, in theory autonomous but in actuality supported by RSS shakhas and led by RSS pracharaks. The Jana Sangh party, from its inception in 1951, was closely associated with the RSS. Walter Anderson surveyed the Jana Sangh in 1968–71 and found that 90 percent of party workers had an RSS background. Anderson also found that advancement in the Jana Sangh followed from advancement in the RSS (Anderson and Damle 1987: 189–90). Another important RSS "affiliate," as Anderson and Damle label such organizations, is the Akhil Bharatiya Vidyarthi Parishad (All-India Student Association, hereafter referred to as Vidyarthi Parishad). Founded in 1948, its membership totaled 160,000 in 1974 and had grown to 250,000 by 1982; during the same period, the number of full-time workers increased from 24 to between 80 and 125. Although most students in the Vidyarthi Parishad do not have RSS connections, almost the entire senior leadership does (Anderson and Damle 1987: 119–23). Both the Jana Sangh and the Vidyarthi Parishad were to be compelling forces in J.P.'s experiment with total revolution.

The Conjuncture

Hindu nationalism and Gandhian utopia arrived at an unforeseen conjuncture during J.P.'s 1974–75 mass protest in Bihar. Before then, however, few people would have imagined such a coalition as possible. In 1948, the Hindu Mahasabha and the RSS were widely blamed for Gandhi's assassination, and although that accusation was never proved, there was no doubt that Gandhi's killer had been an RSS member and that he and his accomplices subscribed to Hindu nationalism (Anderson and Damle 1987: 50–51). Their belief that Gandhi had always favored Muslims — that he had therefore weakened Hindus, permitted partition, and stymied the chances for a strong, united, and Hindu India — led them to the assassination.

Ashis Nandy (1980: 76–84) recognizes certain similarities between Gandhi and his assassin, Nathuram Godse. They were both strongly nationalist, hostile to caste, ascetic, and celibate. Nandy emphasizes the differences between them, however. Gandhi challenged not only the colonial order but also the society of contemporary India. Whereas Gandhi in his nationalism looked forward to a future utopia, Godse used Hindu nationalism to defend an India in the past, some part of which continued to exist in the present. His ideal was the past glory of the Brahmans (specifically, the Chitpavan subcaste of Brahmans), from which caste Godse and most leaders of the RSS came. As colonialism ended, this former glory was under attack. New caste and sectarian populations challenged Brahmans for access to high-status jobs in government and

221

the professions. They demanded greater access to the educational advantages that had enabled Brahmans to monopolize these occupational opportunities. The new groups' secularism or reformed Hinduism often questioned Brahman cultural authority and control over Hindu traditions (compare Nandy 1980: 84). For Godse and many others who joined the Mahasabha and the RSS, Hindu nationalism legitimated the superiority of Hindu traditions and the superior place of the high castes, which served as custodians of those cultural traditions. Although they shared Gandhi's commitment to an independent India, to discipline, and to the simple life, many Hindu nationalists opposed Gandhi and some even hated him. For them, his nonviolence was cowardly, his benevolence toward Muslims compromising and perhaps even traitorous, his nonsectarian faith in God as Truth apostate, and his distrust of authoritarian relations anarchic. Their ideology thus led Hindu nationalists to be hostile to Gandhian utopia.

Unexpectedly, then, the Gandhian J.P. fell in with the Hindu nationalist groups, the Jana Sangh and Vidyarthi Parishad, in 1974–75. Some contemporaries, mainly those with Hindu nationalist sympathies, applauded the joint effort (*Organiser* 1975, 18 January: 3; 1975, 22 February: 3). Others, primarily the left but also Mrs. Gandhi's government, condemned it (see *Janata* 1975, 28 September: 7–11 for government; for the left, see Mishra 1974: 8–9; Krishnan 1974: 11–12; Tarakeshwan Sinha 1974: 9–10). No one doubted that it happened, however. Without the endorsement and full support of Vinoba's Sarva Seva Sangh, J.P.'s mass protest continued to depend on the students in the Vidyarthi Parishad, which had provided the movement's original organizational base before J.P. intervened (Ostergaard 1985: 93; *Organiser* 1974, 16 November: 3). The movement also depended on the local branches of the RSS and the membership of an ultramilitant and violent Hindu sect, the Anand Marg (Banerjee 1984: 14–18; *Times of India* 1975, 5 July: 5, 6 July: 1). Only these Hindu nationalist groups had the ground-level cadres to muster out for extensive and long-term protest action. N. H. Sanghavi (1977: 10) and Radhakanta Barik (1977: 62–65), from opposite ends of the political spectrum, make this point.

The Hindu nationalist politician L. K. Advani (1979: 8–11) even asserted that J.P. "enthusiastically welcomed" RSS participation. J.P. may not have been quite so overjoyed as Advani claimed; he had denounced Hindu nationalism as recently as 1968 (Narayan 1980 [1968]: 272–75). Nevertheless, J.P. himself admitted indirectly that RSS and other Hindu nationalist cadres were taking part in the protest, and the role of the Jana Sangh he acknowledged publicly:

> To my knowledge, there is no Anand Margi in any of the Sangharsha Samities . . . As for RSS, it too is not formally part of the movement, though I daresay there are many members participating. The Bharatiya Jana Sangh is certainly a constituent . . . the Vidyarthi Parishad, too . . . If all these add up to the RSS being a part of the movement, I have no quarrel with it (Narayan 1975: 5).

The leaders of Hindu nationalist associations publicly endorsed J.P.'s movement. Balasaheb Deoras, the supreme guide of the RSS, likened J.P. to both Gandhi and the recently deceased RSS chief Golwalkar (*Organiser* 1974, 7 December: 1, 2, 16). Nana Deshmukh, former RSS pracharak and a power in the Jana Sangh at the time, was literally at J.P.'s side throughout the mass protest. He later argued that India needed leaders dedicated to social construction, as he believed J.P. clearly was (Deshmukh 1979: 146–48). Reciprocally, J.P. endorsed the Hindu nationalist groups: he attended the Jana Sangh's 20th all-India session held in Delhi in March 1975 and said, "If Jana Sangh is fascist, then I, too, am a fascist" (*Mainstream* 1975, 15 March: 6). A month earlier, he had opposed the government's purported consideration of a ban on the RSS.

A story existed to charter the affiliation of the Gandhian J.P. with the RSS. Whether it was myth or fact is perhaps less important than that it was told by the head of the RSS. Balasaheb Deoras related that six years before the movement for total revolution, J.P. saw the relief work the RSS was doing in Bihar and noted especially that no distinction was made between Hindus and Muslims. That experience ostensibly changed his impression of the organization (*Organiser* 1975, 8 March: 7).

Some commentators see J.P. as a puppet of the Jana Sangh and RSS, and others see him as taking over an ongoing social movement and harnessing it to the so-called fascist right. Clearly, J.P. out of necessity initially accepted the support that existed "on the spot" in Bihar. As the movement went on, he found he could not revolutionize the students away from their previous affiliations, and instead, just to keep the movement going, he would have to come closer to affiliating with these organizations himself. Perhaps he also believed there was protection against a rampant Hindu nationalism in the four-party coalition, although he must have recognized that the Jana Sangh (with the RSS behind it) had the most grass-roots support. At its end, whether that end is considered the declaration of the emergency in 1975 or the dismissal of the Janata party in 1979 (which I will come to shortly), the utopia of total revolution had been appropriated in the interests of party politics and sectarian appeals. J.P. no longer authorized the movement, as he had when he agreed to lead the early student demonstrations; on the contrary, the parties and associations that constituted the movement now authorized J.P. He had to define his own authority in terms set by others — as, for example, when he declared that if the Jana Sangh was fascist, so must he be too. Soon, it seems, J.P. could not easily distinguish his former Gandhian utopia from the Hindu nationalism of the Jana Sangh and RSS. After the Emergency ended in 1977, J.P. believed that the Jana Sangh had lost its Hindu chauvinism (Ostergaard 1985: 263). He exhorted the RSS to "fulfill [his] dream":

> I have great expectation from this revolutionary organisation which has taken up the challenge of creating a new Bharat [India]. I have welcomed your venture wholeheartedly. Sometimes I have offered you my advice and have even criticised you, but it was as a friend (Narayan 1979: 5).

The friendship had been costly, however. Because it depended on the Jana Sangh and RSS, J.P.'s writ for total revolution did not travel well or far. His authority, limited even from the beginning, stopped almost altogether with the young, the urban, the lower-middle class, and the high caste — in other words, the segment of the Indian population that generally supported the Jana Sangh and the RSS. Much more than his utopian vision itself, the background of J.P.'s supporters brought on recrimination from the left. Reading the book of J.P.'s revolution perhaps more insightfully than J.P. himself, the left in general labeled the movement fascist, and the Communist party of India opposed it in the streets. In 1974–75, the leftist reading was that J.P.'s Gandhian utopia was becoming an ideological transplant for Hindu nationalism and other so-called right-wing forces, a legitimation of the class and caste interests that these associations represented. Their reading was generally correct, as I shall show, but the process of transplantation was still only beginning.

224

From Total Revolution to Gandhian Socialism

When Indira Gandhi ended the Emergency in 1977 and called for new national elections, J.P.'s vision of Gandhian utopia resided with the same coalition of social democratic, centrist, and Hindu nationalist parties that had supported the protest movement.[2] All of them could legitimately claim a Gandhian character, because each of them could authoritatively employ J.P. as their link to the Mahatma. Individual ownership of the Gandhian legacy was not an issue at first, for the parties decided to unite formally (in May 1976, before the Emergency ended), and the resulting Janata coalition party successfully disputed the 1977 national election against Mrs. Gandhi's Congress. Just three years later, however, the Janata had dissolved, Indira Gandhi had come back into power, and Hindu nationalism had successfully appropriated a Gandhian ideology, no longer a utopia, for itself.

The Janata Party: Failure and Split

The Janata *Manifesto* published in February 1977, after the Emergency ended but before the election took place, did not reflect the views of the constituent parties so much as the Gandhian vision of J.P. The Janata stated a commitment to the decentralization of government, honesty and simplicity for public servants, equality of opportunity, and the elimination of prejudice. It gave high priority to social welfare for the poor, subsidy of cottage industries, and promotion of rural development. It set out an independent foreign policy and expressed wariness about foreign investment and military dependency on other countries (Johnson 1981: 483). This Gandhian aspect, chiefly owed to J.P., had been present in the earliest Janata pronouncements (see *Janata* 1975, May Day Number: 23–30; 1976, 30 May: 1–12). Later on, the Janata gave this aspect public expression in the term "Gandhian socialism."

The Janata coalition won a devastating and unexpected victory over Mrs. Gandhi's Congress in the 1977 elections, with one constituent, the Hindu nationalist Jana Sangh, getting the largest share of victory. (Parliamentary constituencies were assigned to each of the formerly independent parties within the Janata coalition; their major cooperative act was to avoid contesting elections against each other.) Almost from the moment of its victory, however, the Janata

225

party began to fail and splinter. Implementing J.P.'s Gandhian vision receded as an issue, while competition for office and quarrels among the constituent parties came to the fore. What must concern us are not the specific charges of corruption, the personal squabbles over power, or the intraparty feuding, but the factors that by 1980 had left the Gandhian vision in the charge of only one of the constituents, the Hindu nationalist Jana Sangh, now renamed the Bharatiya Janata party.

In 1978, the chief minister of Bihar proposed a program of affirmative action to benefit "Other Backward Classes"[3] in the state, mainly middle-ranking Yadavs, Kurmis, and other rural cultivating castes that had been major beneficiaries of land reform and the Green Revolution (Blair 1980: 64). Notwithstanding their new wealth — indeed, as I shall show in the following chapter, because of this enrichment and the new political power it brought — the Bihar government set out to institute this policy.

In India, affirmative action generally consists of the "reservation" of college and medical school admissions, civil service and government jobs, and other perquisites for the designated castes (Galanter 1984: 179–87). To the extent that education and employment are reserved in this fashion for ostensibly backward castes, Brahmans and other upper castes must accept reduced opportunities.

The prosperous cultivators belonging to the Other Backward Classes naturally supported the chief minister's initiative, while the urban upper castes stood opposed. In this dispute, J.P., representing the Gandhian vision, sided with the anti-reservation forces. He argued that caste should not be the criterion for backwardness, as was the current policy; income should also enter in. That is, J.P. maintained, affirmative action benefits should flow only to the really poor among the members of castes designated as backward (see *Times of India* 1978, 13 March: 1). Even when the Bihar government adopted an income requirement, it was set at such a high level that 90 percent of the people belonging to Other Backward Classes would have qualified (Jha 1978: 6), and J.P. therefore was reluctant to endorse it (*Times of India* 1978, 23 March: 6). As a result, J.P. became increasingly identified with upper-caste and urban interests, the same interests generally behind Hindu nationalism and the Jana Sangh.

226   In the spring of 1978, J.P. seemed to be propelled into leadership of an upper-caste backlash against the reservation policy, a movement that could be called "total reaction." As a token of how little

J.P. controlled it, this movement took a violent turn. His authority was taken in vain, for example, during a violent clash in the town of Aurangabad. The anti-reservationists shouted out for J.P. as they attacked proponents and left three of them dead. Elsewhere in Bihar, they stopped trains, stoned police, and committed arson (*Times of India* 1978, 1 April: 1). As in the time of total revolution, the colleges closed: most students, from the upper castes, strongly opposed reservations (*Times of India* 1978, 7 April: 1). The leader of the Backward Classes Federation accused J.P. of encouraging the resistance of the upper castes, who had been, so he argued, the mainstay of the earlier movement for total revolution (*India Today* 1978, 15 April: 15–16).

In response to what was happening in the streets, the Janata party in Bihar began to fly apart. One wing, including the majority of the legislators, the chief minister, and most of his cabinet sided with the Other Backward Classes — in fact, many of them were members of these castes (see Blair 1984: 70). The others, mainly from the upper castes, used J.P.'s income requirement as a basis to resist the reservation policy (see P. C. Gandhi 1978: 6/7–8; *Times of India* 1978, 2 November: 1). These events in Bihar anticipated a similar split at the national level. In December 1978, a massive (prosperous) peasants' rally in Delhi showed that well-off rural cultivators, mainly from the Other Backward Classes, could vote "with their feet" in a different way from the one Marx imagined (Mohan 1979: 26–29; *The Call* 1979, January: 5–7; Byres 1988: 162). They marched in the tens of thousands to demand credit, subsidies, commodity supports, and other advantages from a coalition government that ostensibly represented their interests. By this time, in fact, legislators and party members within the Janata who represented these rural interests had begun to follow an independent political path. Attempting to build up the wealthy peasants as a voting bloc, they rhetorically pitted rural India against urban. They denounced rural poverty and called for official guarantees of equal opportunity. Urban leaders countered by speaking of voluntary action and spiritual revolution from the village up rather than from the government down. A call for self-help, not government props like commodity price supports or credit facilities, was their rhetorical gambit. For these urban interests, Gandhian thinking justified such a position, just as it did their opposition to the government's reservation policy. In this way an ostensibly Gandhian rhetoric came to serve urban upper-caste interests well, against the demands of rural cultivators. When the members representing rural interests finally left the Janata to form a separate party, they also left behind much of the Janata's Gandhian rhetoric, which had been so effectively employed against rural cultivators' interests.

Still another contingency in the last days of the Janata helped make a Gandhian ideology the preserve of Hindu nationalism and the urban upper-caste interests it represented. In 1979, the democratic socialist contingent within the Janata took strong exception to the "dual membership" of many Hindu nationalists within the party — that is, the fact that they were often members of the RSS as well as of the Janata. Many democratic socialists regarded the RSS as a fascist organization, staffed by bigots and pledged against secularism. Fearful of RSS influence over the party, the democratic socialists demanded that dual membership end: abandon the RSS, they urged Hindu nationalists, and openly embrace the secularism and socialism for which the Janata presumably stood. J.P. himself, in his last days, was enlisted to authorize these demands (see, for example, *Janata* 1979, 8 April: 4; 13 May: 2; Jagannatham 1979: 6–9).

Rather than recant, the Hindu nationalists walked out and organized a new party, the Bharatiya Janata party, which was not troubled by its roots in the RSS. Wanting some legacy from the Janata party, but not attracted by either secularism or democratic socialism, the new party's leaders fixed on the term "Gandhian socialism" from the old Janata rhetoric. This ideology permitted the Bharatiya Janata party to embrace a socialism that was purportedly indigenous, not a Western import — Gandhi was said to have sired it just as he had fathered Indian independence. In this scheme of things, as we shall see later in the chapter, Gandhi became a good Hindu and his socialism became a ground plan for an incorporative Hindu nation. Opposed by rural interests, lost to the democratic socialists, and appropriated by the successor party to the former Hindu nationalist Jana Sangh, Gandhian thinking submerged more deeply into Hindu nationalism until it was covered over as a utopia and became entrenched as an ideology.

There were two other possibilities — which might have happened, but did not. Why did the Gandhian vision have to be hijacked by a political party? The Gandhian voluntary movement still existed; what prevented it from regenerating a Gandhian vision? Or, if only a political party could exercise authority over Gandhian

228

utopia, why was it an opposition Hindu nationalist party? What prevented the ruling Congress party from hijacking Gandhian utopia, as it had before 1969?

Protection of Gandhi, Destruction of J.P.

Vinoba had taken a vow of silence in opposition to the J.P. movement, but Mrs. Gandhi, shortly after the Emergency, recognized that it was J.P.'s following among the Gandhian volunteers that had to be silenced, whereas Vinoba, mild toward the government, should be made to speak. Her subsequent actions showed the increasing hostility of the Congress government to all but the most subservient Gandhian organizations and impeded any rehijack of Gandhian utopia by the ruling party. Furthermore, her actions even further eroded the authority of Gandhian voluntary organizations and therefore their control over the Gandhian vision. After the Janata fell apart in 1979, the Gandhian organizations were in no condition to contest Hindu nationalism for the legacy, and Indira Gandhi's Congress did not wish to.

One of Mrs. Gandhi's tactics was to reauthorize Vinoba as the spiritual head of the Gandhian sarvodaya movement and to get him to speak out in favor of the Emergency. Vinoba's following within the Sarva Seva Sangh, a minority before the Emergency, became dominant after it. When his vow of silence ended in December 1975, Vinoba labeled the ongoing Emergency an "era of discipline." He was widely understood by this comment to have set his approval on Mrs. Gandhi's actions. Two months before, she had announced several measures in aid of prohibition, which was one of Vinoba's pet projects. About the same time, the head of the Gandhi Memorial Foundation called a meeting of Gandhian voluntary workers to discuss the opportunities for constructive work provided by the Emergency (Ostergaard 1985: 221–22). All this activity by Vinoba and his associates while J.P. and many others remained imprisoned also seemed to betoken acceptance of the Emergency.

Vinoba's reputed approval of the Emergency hurt his reputation, especially when Mrs. Gandhi's government was defeated by the new Janata party in 1977. The new goals that Vinoba set for the movement during the Janata period only exacerbated the decline in authority and vision of the Gandhian voluntary movement. In December 1978, more than two thousand Gandhian workers, from

229

both J.P.'s and Vinoba's followings, assembled under Vinoba's direction and settled on a one-point program to accelerate the pace of the Gandhian experiment with village development: they decided to concentrate all their efforts on cow protection (Bherwani 1979: 4). The integration of the two followings was in fact minimal (Ostergaard 1985: 310–14), perhaps because it would have been hard for J.P.'s followers to see the connection between cow protection and village development.

After Mrs. Gandhi returned to power in 1980, Vinoba's direction was even clearer: there was not to be another forced hijack of Gandhian utopia by the government, as had happened at independence; rather, it would be an amiable takeover, on terms set by Mrs. Gandhi. In 1982, Gandhian workers met in New Delhi on Vinoba's birthday to repledge their loyalty to Gandhi's Constructive Programme but also to dedicate themselves anew to a 20-Point National Programme that Mrs. Gandhi had set out shortly before. Geoffrey Ostergaard (1985: 328) characterizes this development as an attempt to "incorporate [the Gandhian movement] as a 'non-political' agency of the state's ruling elite."

While Indira Gandhi beckoned to Vinoba, her government bore down on J.P. and his followers in the Sarva Seva Sangh, who carried on whatever vital and utopian aspects remained in the Gandhian voluntary movement. In July 1976, during the Emergency, Mrs. Gandhi ordered an investigation into various Gandhian organizations associated with J.P. A member of Parliament had written her son Sanjay suggesting that foreign sources had paid off J.P. and the Association of Voluntary Agencies for Rural Development (AVARD), which was closely associated with J.P. Mrs. Gandhi alluded to the large government subsidies enjoyed by Gandhian organizations and asserted that "this money has been used against the government and sometimes even against the purposes for which these institutions were formed" (quoted in Modhumita Majumdar 1986: 9). Her government issued instructions halting central and state subsidies to the Gandhi Peace Foundation, AVARD, and other Gandhian associations (Government of India, *Lok Sabha Debates* 1981: 348). Nothing came of this inquiry because Mrs. Gandhi soon passed temporarily out of power, and the successor Janata government withdrew these instructions.

230   The matter was resumed in April 1981. A member of Parliament introduced a private bill that sought penalties for anyone "tarnishing the image of Mahatma Gandhi." An amendment, which

was supported by Mrs. Gandhi's government, altered the bill considerably by calling for a committee of inquiry to look into the finances and activities of Gandhian organizations, like the Gandhi Memorial Foundation, the Gandhi Peace Foundation, AVARD, and others. The amendment implied that the Gandhian associations tarnished Gandhi's name by selling out the country he had fathered. There were accusations in Parliament that the Gandhi Peace Foundation received funding from foreign espionage agencies and that government subsidies went for antigovernment and perhaps even subversive undertakings (see Government of India, *Lok Sabha Debates* 1981: 306–54; *Secular Democracy* 1982: 23–30 repeats many of these charges in detail). The motion passed on 28 August 1981; a commission of inquiry, named the Kudal commission after the judge who presided over it, was given six months in which to investigate the affairs of the Gandhian associations and report back to Parliament.

Six months turned into six years of scrutiny and supervision, as, by the government's request, the commission received annual extensions of its inquiry — over the objections of opposition M.P.s, like Madhu Dandavate, who argued that the government was attempting to destroy all organizations associated with J.P. and a Gandhian approach (see Government of India, *Lok Sabha Debates* 1984: 426–27). The Gandhian organizations sometimes refused to cooperate with the commission (*Hindustan Times* 1983, 31 July: 8) and accused it of being "an instrument of vendetta" (*Hindustan Times* 1986, 4 August; Bhatt 1982: 14–17). The Gandhian organizations found official repression was so severe that they jointly published two pamphlets of press clippings attacking the government's commission of inquiry (see Gandhi Peace Foundation et al. [c. February 1986], [c. August 1986]).

The Kudal commission finally reported to Parliament in February 1987. It suggested that organizations using Gandhi's name should not be permitted to tarnish the Mahatma's image, nor should the management of such organizations be allowed to use his name for "vested interests." Voluntary organizations that had "digressed" from Gandhian aims should lose their official recognition as charitable organizations, along with the benefits therefrom, and their officers should be punished. It reported that some Gandhian associations had misused and misappropriated funds and recommended that foreign funds received by these organizations should be monitored (*Hindustan Times* 1987, 4 February: 4).

Ostergaard (1985: 328) suspects that the policy of the Gandhi government — initially Mrs. Gandhi's government and then, after her assassination in October 1984, her son Rajiv's — aimed to split the Gandhian voluntary movement. One segment, Vinoba's or his successors' (Vinoba died in 1982), would grow strong under government subsidy and would strongly support the reigning Congress government. The other, J.P.'s successors' (J.P. died in 1979), might continue to oppose the government, but it would be weakened by constant official oversight. That was the way in which Gandhian workers described the situation to me in the spring of 1988. Some few Gandhians were with Rajiv Gandhi's government; some wanted to mobilize people against the government; the majority were unhappy with the current situation but not sure what to do. Rajiv had proved no more receptive to Gandhian ideas, they said, than had his mother, and top Gandhian leaders had not been able to get through to him.

By patronizing Vinoba and policing J.P., Mrs. Gandhi succeeded in further abridging the authority of the Gandhian voluntary movement — "further," because J.P. had started the process when he was forced to accept the aid of the opposition parties during the Bihar protest. The next step was for the parties to become the sources of Gandhian legitimacy. Once the independent authority of Gandhian associations was effectively diminished, this development was inevitable. Mrs. Gandhi took the process further, and with a vengeance: she helped deauthorize Vinoba as a government yes-man and J.P. as a pseudo-Gandhian, a prop of opposition parties or, worse, a puppet of the "foreign hand" — and along with them went their organizations. Could the Gandhi Peace Foundation disinterestedly speak of Gandhi, when its reputed foreign funding and antigovernment attitude spoke of power politics at its worst? Could Vinoba and his following truly represent the Gandhian image, when they seemed to mirror Indira Gandhi's policies so faithfully? If the Gandhian legacy and its heirs could no longer be legitimated by their own independent associations, their authority must come from their standing with political parties. As the leaders of the Gandhian movement were willy-nilly politicized, so too was the supposedly apolitical voluntary movement itself. The upshot was that Gandhi's image and some aspects of his vision were no longer controlled or legitimated by their old institutional base in the sarvodaya movement. Neither were they authorized by the Congress. From 1980 on they became fixed to Hindu na-

232

tionalist ideology. By 1984, political parties and their leaders did not bother to battle for control over Gandhian ideas; instead they competed over a Hindu nationalism that had come to incorporate a subordinate Gandhian ideology.

Gandhian Socialism and the BJP

When the Hindu nationalists withdrew from the Janata party coalition in April 1980, they wanted to preserve the connection to J.P. and, through him, their identification with Gandhi. The new party they formed, the Bharatiya Janata party (BJP), carried over the term "Gandhian socialism," used by the former Janata party, to express its goals (*Times of India* 1980, 7 April: 1). Its socialism was Gandhian, BJP leaders said, because it focused on economic and political decentralization and it eschewed class and caste warfare. Its Gandhism was socialist because it aimed for equality of opportunity — the "poor man to be the centre of all economic activity," as BJP president Atal Behari Vajpayee said (quoted in Sharma 1981: 5–6). There were a good many hedges, however, to ensure that benefiting the poor did not threaten the welfare of "all." The BJP therefore supported job reservations only when eligibility depended not only on caste membership but also on a stringent income ceiling (see early policy statements in *Times of India* 1981, 15 April: 1; 26 April: 5; *Organiser* 1981, 11 January: 2).

The new party also carried over the strong affiliation with the RSS that the Jana Sangh had previously enjoyed. A survey in a Bihar district, for example, found that the BJP recruited followers in a "peculiar" way. Family, caste, ethnic, or regional connections did not serve to recruit a following for the BJP, as they did for other parties. Rather, most BJP recruits joined because they had participated as adolescents in RSS local branches — where they had learned a Hindu nationalism consonant with BJP objectives. In this district, the survey found, BJP party members who came from the RSS were considered superior, and almost all the local party officers had an RSS background (Singh 1982: 65–78). A major segment of the national leadership also had strong ties with the RSS and were proud of them (see the statements of the party secretary and later president, L.P. Advani, in *Times of India* 1985, 10 October: 1; *India Today* 1986, 31 March: 19).

Could a party saffron-colored by Hindu nationalism become dyed-in-the-homespun-wool Gandhian? The idea struck many as anomalous. Doubters, such as the journalist A. S. Abraham (1981: 8), opined that the meaning of socialism seemed stretched to the breaking point. Even more critical detractors maintained, for example, that "the credentials of the RSS-dominated BJP to invoke either the name of Gandhiji or the concept of socialism are open to serious question . . ." For them, it was "patently a gimmick" (*Mainstream* 1981, 3 January: 3–4); elsewhere it was called a "Gandhian veneer" (*Link* 1981, 21 June: 16–18).

What really bothered critics of the BJP, its apologists insightfully argued, was their sense of a "loss of property or trespass" when the new party took over the term "Gandhian socialism" (Godbole 1981: 7). Could there be a more open admission of a transplant?

Curiously, the strongest doubters came from the ranks of the BJP and RSS themselves. Throughout the early 1980s, while one faction within the party propounded Gandhian socialism, the other faction, closer to the RSS, distrusted it (see *Times of India* 1980, 25 December: 9; Chitta Ranjan 1982: 1–3).

In this way, a Gandhian ideology became embedded within the BJP and, by association, within Hindu nationalism in the early 1980s. The Gandhian vision ceased to have much independent authority. It lost an independent institutional base as the Gandhian voluntary organizations suffered under official repression. Its charismatic authority died with J.P. Even subsidy by way of official hijack had ended, except the government grants to jejune experiments like khadi and village industries. The Gandhian vision was now subordinate to a Hindu nationalist view, for which it served as an ideological charter. Indeed, the Gandhian legacy had been so deauthorized that the BJP's secretary Advani could argue that the "Gandhian" in the formula "Gandhian socialism" had been added only to make sure no one took it for the Marxist variety (compare Chitta Ranjan 1982: 1–3). An ardent Hindu nationalist told me in 1988 that Gandhi had simply become a "totem," an object of empty adulation. Gandhian utopia, now grown into an ideology, had its future grafted onto the prospects of Hindu nationalism. As Hindu nationalism prospered and produced offshoots, so would the Gandhian ideology, which was intertwined with it and which no longer sustained a healthy, separate existence.

TWELVE

Hindu Nationalism: Failed Experiment or Future Utopia?

> If Gandhism is "reactionary" in that it wants to revive
> the highest human values, we have no objection to being
> bracketed with Gandhiji as "reactionaries."
>
> M. S. Golwalkar, RSS supreme guide (1974 [1949]: 160)

The new Curiosities of the Orient, on display in independent India two generations after Gandhi's death:

A novel nonviolent resistance appeared in India in October 1987, a month after a young upper-caste woman willingly committed sati in rural Rajasthan. According to antique Hindu tradition, the voluntary immolation of a widow on her husband's funeral pyre is a sanctified act; by current Indian law, it is a crime. After this sati, the state government took a further legal step against it: the government outlawed public rituals, processions, and other public demonstrations that glorified widow sacrifice. In Jaipur, Rajasthan's capital, seventy thousand people, mainly from the upper castes, marched in civil disobedience; perhaps it might be called an experiment with faith, if not with truth. They marched in protest against the law and in defense of sati. They regaled the helpless officials and police who watched the mile-and-a-half-long procession pass by with salutes to the dead woman and protestations of their Hindu faith (*India Today* 1987, 15 October: 58–61; 31 October: 18–20).

During the first quarter of 1985 in Gandhi's home state of Gujarat, upper-caste opposition to the government's new program of job reservations for the lower castes gathered force. Besides burning buses and boycotting classes, students observed fasts before statues of Gandhi. Then more violence erupted: bus riders along with buses were set afire. The leaders of the anti-reservation campaign nevertheless insisted they were following Gandhi's way. The violence, they said, was incidental and no one's fault (Baxi 1985: 5–6).

The Deendayal Research Institute, an affiliate of the RSS, invoked Gandhi's image as an ancestor-figure at a 1983 conference on "grass-roots experiments" in village development. Gandhi's smiling portrait, garlanded as a token of homage, served as a background to the proceedings, while the head of the RSS and other major figures in it looked on (see the photograph in *Manthan* 1984: 13).

In India since the early 1980s, a strong Hindu vision and a nationalism that conceives India as a Hindu nation have been in the making. This Hindu nationalism has appropriated and transplanted Gandhian thinking as an ideology justifying its stern beliefs and militant social action. The "curiosities" with which this chapter begins illustrate the way in which Gandhi and Gandhian-like experiments are taken to mandate an aggressive Hindu nationalism. In the previous chapter, we saw how Gandhian ideas and Hindu nationalist ideology became entangled. This chapter describes the reconstitution of Gandhian ideas by Hindu nationalists, who thereby commandeered and then disarmed potent public symbols. It also analyzes the existing system of social inequality in which Hindu nationalism, surcharged with a Gandhian ideology, has developed. For this purpose, I pursue a history of structure, quite different from the history of the singular found in the preceding chapter. Through this structural history, my aim is to explain the existing social inequalities in India since the mid-1960s that Gandhian utopia came up against. As re-envisioned in J.P.'s movement for total revolution, Gandhian utopia bounced off these conditions and changed in character, moving from a utopia to an ideology.

I begin this chapter with the ideology structuring Hindu nationalism and the manner in which Gandhian thinking is embedded in it. I then proceed to show the social interests that this ideology serves and legitimates. At the end of the chapter, I consider the possibility of a new utopian vision arising from, that is, bouncing off, current Hindu nationalist ideology.

Hindia and Hindian

"The majority appears to have developed a minority complex" announces *India Today* (1986, 31 May: 32). Since about 1980, the public media and the "educated classes" in India have increasingly recognized a growing Hindu nationalism, and many Indians have begun living it — or at least, living with it. While some Indians lead crusades to reclaim what they consider Hindu sacred land now occupied by mosques (Van Der Veer 1987), others organize mass meetings across the country for Hindu unity (see list in Seshadri 1984: 143–57), and still others decry "the thundering voice of arrogant Hinduism" (Chitta Ranjan 1981).

Hindu nationalists maintain that "Hinduism is in danger" (*India Today* 1986, 31 May: 30) and that India is endangered, too. Many Indian Hindus believe their nation grows increasingly weaker under Sikh, Muslim, Untouchable, and Christian demands. Bullied by these ethnic groups, it is said, the state capitulates and the just expectations of the majority go unfulfilled. At a grass-roots level, new associations espousing Hindu nationalism have sprung up, and existing ones have grown more militant. There have been numerous confrontations between them and Sikhs, Muslims, and Untouchables, even in places, such as the Punjab, where Hindu nationalist associations had been weak (for the Punjab, see *India Today* 1986, 15 April: 14–15; for Hindu-Muslim conflict in Gujarat, see Sayed 1986, Fera 1985, Baxi 1985 and, in Bombay, see *Economic and Political Weekly* 1984; for massacres of Untouchables by Hindus in Bihar, see *India Today* 1986, 31 December). The number of local branches of the RSS more than doubled between 1975 and 1981, with expansion especially pronounced in southern India, where the RSS has hitherto been weak. A 1981 government report stated that regular attendance at RSS local branches came to nearly one million people and that contributions exceeded a million dollars (Anderson and Damle 1987: 215). Government estimates in 1987 placed the number of communal organizations (including Hindu, Sikh, and Muslim associations) at more than five hundred, whereas in 1951 they numbered less than a dozen. They had an estimated membership in 1987 of several million. In 1961 only 61 Indian districts (out of 350) experienced communal violence, but by 1979 there were 216 districts affected by it, and the estimate for 1987 was 250 districts (*India Today* 1987, 15 June: 17, 19). Political parties are said to exploit Hindu nationalist sentiments, and even to compete for electoral support on this basis (*India Today* 1986, 30 November; Vanaik 1985: 78). As nonviolent participants in Hindu unity processions (*yatras*) crisscrossing India; as trident bearers (the trident, or *trishul*, is a symbol of the Hindu god Shiva) in general strikes; and, at the worst, as militants who will even kill in defense of their creed — in these various roles, Hindu nationalism involves a large and committed population.

Hindu nationalist ideology is still so much in the making that no popular indigenous usage exists as a label for its image of India and Indians. Hindu nationalists often use the two terms *bharat* and *bharatiya*, however, to express their vision of the Indian nation and population. I translate these terms as "Hindia" and "Hindian," respectively, and use them to refer to the India that Hindu nationalist ideology projects into the future in order to legitimate the India of today.

The Discovery of Hindia

Since the early 1980s, the old-line Hindu nationalist associations like the Hindu Mahasabha and the RSS and its affiliates have had to make space for many new sibling organizations, primarily private "armies," or *senas*, like the several regional Shiv Senas and the Bajrang Dal that enlist paramilitary volunteers. These militant societies, often blamed for violence against Untouchables, Muslims, Sikhs, and other Indian minorities, may have some connection with the RSS, but it is not clear of what sort (*India Today* 1986, 15 October surveys these senas and speculates on their connections).

These diverse associations, I believe, share a basic ideology. (Perhaps their agreement is one instance of the "unity in diversity" they espouse as an essential Indian characteristic.) Their guiding notion is that India must be a Hindu nation, in keeping with its essential cultural tradition, or else it will never achieve national integration and security. The call for a *Hindu rashtra* ("Hindu way") and a *bharatiya* ("Hindian") society is not sectarian, however (compare the statement by RSS member and BJP leader Advani 1979). *Bharatiya*, as used by Hindu nationalists, refers to India at once as a geographic region and as a cultural realm with deep-rooted traditions (compare Raghavan 1983 and Dixit 1986: 131–35), in much the way the Hindu nationalist Veer Savarkar defined India (see

Chapter 11). It thus combines what the English terms "Indian" and "Hindu," as a cultural, not sectarian, label, imply. I try to translate this meaning by the neologism "Hindian." Hindu nationalists maintain that underneath the superficial diversity of India's sects and castes lies an essential cultural unity, "a unity in diversity." Anyone who recognizes India as a geographic homeland and as a cultural heartland is a true Indian, that is, a Hindian. Hindu, Muslim, Sikh, Untouchable, and Christian Indians, no matter their superficial sectarian identities, partake of this essential Hindian unity, if they would only put aside their squabbles and recognize it.

The former head of the RSS gives a good example of the way in which the concept of Hindia lends Hindu nationalism an aggressive attitude toward Indian minorities. G. S. Golwalkar maintained that a devout Hindu must show respect for other ways of worship. Therefore, he claimed, the RSS respected Islam and Christianity as religions, but required that Christians and Muslims remember that they are children of the soil of Bharat, which is the nation of the Hindu. They must serve the Indian nation and not be loyal to foreign lands (Golwalkar 1966: 127–28). They should "come back and identify" with the Hindu way of life "in dress, customs, building houses, performing marriage ceremonies and funeral rites and such other things" (Golwalkar 1966: 131).

National success will ultimately depend on development in accord with inherent national characteristics, Hindu nationalists assert. A cultural essentialism underlies this notion — that a nation must have a character, that this character derives from some cultural underpinning, ancient and deeply rooted, and that India's must rest on a Hindian one (Deendayal Upadhyaya, perhaps the most thoughtful RSS leader, spoke of a nation's *chiti*, or essence. See Upadhyaya 1974 [1965]: 36–39; Upadhyaya et al. 1979: 34ff.; also see Golwalkar 1966: 1–10).

As stated by former RSS supreme guide Golwalkar (1966: 1–10), the Hindu solution to national identity and human welfare could not be based on materialism as all previous "isms" were. Ancient Hindu philosophers discovered, Golwalkar claimed, that each nation had a distinctive character, and that it was only by each pursuing its particular characteristics and making its special contribution that a harmonious world society could be accomplished. The RSS had accordingly taken on the mission of reorganizing the "Hindu People," so he said, in terms of their "unique national

239

genius." This reorganization not only would help the "true national regeneration of Bharat" but also would be the precondition for world unity and social welfare. Knowledge of the Inner Spirit will urge humanity to toil for the common good, and "this knowledge is in the safe custody of Hindus alone." According to Golwalkar, this divine trust was given to Hindus by Destiny.

Karan Singh, founder of the Virat Hindu Samaj, a Hindu revivalist society, argued the case with a more sectarian thrust. Hinduism has persisted over the ages because of its capacity for reinterpretation to fit new world conditions, he said. Singh called for a Hindu renaissance to "optimize the creativity of the Indian nation." Because it inculcates spirituality, he believed, Hinduism is probably the only world religion capable of coming to terms with the nuclear age (Singh 1983: 14–18).

Hindu nationalism posits two primary Hindian cultural essentials that will see India and the world through the nuclear age. One is a deep spirituality growing out of stern physical discipline, in contrast to the crude materialism and unrestrained consumerism of the West (compare RSS leader Nana Deshmukh 1979: 16). There must be an "intense rejuvenation" of this "ancient culture value," according to Golwalkar. For him, attaining the heights of national glory does not depend on the provision of food, clothing, shelter, or other material requirements, but on the organization of social life. By this he meant that people should be trained to common endeavor, to loyalty, to unselfishness. The first training should be for physical strength, so that no one can intimidate the nation. Other training must be given to inculcate purity of character, common sense, concentration, fearlessness, and devotion (Golwalkar 1966: 39–45).

The other Hindian cultural essential, according to Hindu nationalists, is that the corporate body, family, village, or nation is placed before and above the individual, so that loyalty to the nation should be based on consensus, not self-interest (Upadhyaya et al. 1979: 16–22). By pursuing the common good, individuals, no matter how imperfect they may be, attain a collective, national perfection (Golwalkar 1966: 38).

Given these essential cultural differences, "therefore both democracy and socialism need to be Indianized" (Deshmukh in Raje 1978: 36). The chairman of the RSS affiliate Deendayal Research Institute, Nana Deshmukh writes:

The RSS is not opposed to socialism as an egalitarian philosophy, but to the materialistic aspect of it which does not accord with our culture or our ethos, or the essential values of life we believe in (Deshmukh 1979: 16).

National development toward a future utopian Hindia must sponsor individual spiritual revolution first (Seshadri 1984: 80) — it must "inculcate mental and physical discipline," according to current RSS head Balasaheb Deoras (*Organiser* 1975, 8 March: 7) — before it can worry about institutional changes, such as redistribution of property and wealth. In praising the RSS founder, Dr. Hedgewar, Golwalkar summarized his hopes for India in this way:

> Doctorji concluded that a total revolution in the mental attitude of the people was the vital need of the hour . . . a total transformation in the attitudes and thought-processes and behaviour of the whole people, by taking individual after individual and moulding him for an organised national life . . . National reorganisation means fostering those traits which build up national character and cohesion. It is directed towards awakening a passionate devotion to the motherland, a feeling of fraternity, a sense of sharing in national work, a deeply felt reverence of the nation's ideals, discipline, heroism, manliness, and other noble virtues (Golwalkar 1966: 332–33).

To accusations that the RSS program of national reorganization was reactionary, Golwalkar (1966: 23–24) replied that the only true direction for India consisted of rejuvenating "eternal and ennobling values." Golwalkar left no doubt that this set of values, the "imprint of culture" to which he alluded, was synonymous with what he also called "ancient Hindu blood."

Hindia for the Hindians

For Hindu nationalism, India's current wounded condition rests on the nation's failure to recognize Hindian cultural essentials: consequently, it is a rag tag nation of many sectarian and special interests. For example, Sikhs and Muslims confuse their sectarian practices with their essential cultural identity, which is Hindian, whatever *they* may think (Golwalkar 1966: 81, 84, 87). Lack of patriotism is another national problem, as, for example, among Indian Muslims, whose primary loyalty, Hindu nationalists maintain, is

241

to Islam (Deshmukh 1979: 17; Golwalkar 1966: 168, 171–72). The misguided mimicry of Western culture also victimizes India. Educated Indians especially are alienated from their own traditions (Deshmukh 1979: 12, 19). Not unexpectedly, the policies of national leaders whose cultural identity has been twisted by foreign influences have proven bankrupt, as, for example, Nehru's commitment to a Western socialist model inappropriate to India (Upadhyaya 1969: 129–32). Still another problem stems from the contemporary machinations in India of America and the Soviet Union. Overall, India suffers from a rampant national corruption and personal selfishness, due to the lack of spiritual discipline and national commitment.

Hindu nationalists foresee a future, perfected Hindia arriving through a new spiritual dedication. Their intent is to develop a national physical and mental discipline to make Hindia strong (see Balasaheb Deoras, quoted in *Organiser* 1975, 8 March; also see Golwalkar 1966: 52–54). Some Hindu nationalists believe the 1983 Ekatmata Yajna, which consisted of Hindu processions crisscrossing India, achieved a major national spiritual revolution. Trucks carrying holy Ganges water (said to cleanse one of sin) along with Hindu nationalists traversed the country's major highways. They stopped often at shrines and other places to distribute the holy water. The idea was to unify and purify India symbolically, but the boundaries of this reunited India were significantly marked off as Hindu only. One Hindu nationalist claims that the Ekatmata Yajna entirely changed the cultural meaning of pilgrimage: Hindu pilgrimages have generally been for individual or family merit (*punya*). In the Ekatmata pilgrimage, he argues, personal merit was "sublimated into" social and national merit "towards giving a social and national direction to the people's devotion." Another revolution was that the "numberless" pilgrimage places were identified not only as "*Punya Bhoomi*" or holy land, but also as "*Matru Bhoomi*" or motherland (Seshadri 1984: 174–75). Whether or not the Ekatmata Yajna accomplished all this, Hindu nationalists labor hard at raising what they take to be such a revolutionary consciousness.

Along with such spiritual undertakings, Hindu nationalists adopt a secular program by which to attain the Hindia of their dreams. Here I speak of articulated policies, rather than the violent program in the streets that some Hindu nationalists adopt, as we shall see later. These policy directives, arranged in order of practical significance, include the following demands:

The government program of reservations, or affirmative action programs, for Scheduled Castes and Tribes and for Other Backward Classes must be curtailed or even stopped. The reservation policy, it is said, continues caste identities and strengthens intercaste hostility and brutality. *Manthan,* the journal of the RSS-affiliated Deendayal Research Institute, prefaced an issue devoted to the reservation question with a strong anti-reservation editorial. It spoke of a cutthroat race among castes to grab more of the limited benefits India has. It regretted that Backwardness had now become a sought-after designation rather than an embarrassment. The editorial traced reservation policy back to British colonial policies that aimed to divide and rule: the British artificially separated social classes, like the Scheduled Castes, out of a unified Hindu caste hierarchy. Gandhi, the editorial argued, worked hard to offset this imperial policy in his anti-Untouchability campaigns — as the editorial portrayed it, Gandhi labored to reintegrate Untouchables into the Hindu social order, against the British program of "divide and rule." It said little about Gandhi's labors against Hindu mistreatment of Untouchables, however. The editorial concluded that the current reservations policy only helps a small, urban, English-educated segment of the Backward classes, who "gobble" up all the perquisites (*Manthan* 1982: 5–9).

The state's involvement in social welfare programs, such as rural development, must be limited, and greater use should be made of private initiative. This policy takes instruction from Gandhi's desire for decentralization and his voluntary program of social reconstruction. At a workshop on "Development: Concept and Grassroot Experiment" held in 1983 under the auspices of several RSS affiliates, Nana Deshmukh made reference to these among Gandhi's intentions, while another workshop organizer and devoted Gandhian, J. D. Sethi, chastised the government for responding to "destitution in the villages" by building "five-star hotels in the cities" (*Manthan* 1984: 11–13). At a subsequent workshop on "Strengthening the Movement for Constructive Work in India," Nana Deshmukh argued that government had taken over too much and people had become too dependent on it and on political parties. What was now needed, Deshmukh asserted, was a "People's Movement" (*Manthan* 1986: 70).

As a corollary of decentralization and private initiative, "Russian-style" socialism, that is, excessive state centralization, must be avoided. Furthermore, there is a strong suspicion of entanglements with the Soviet Union and of joint political action with Communists in India (compare *Times of India* 1981, 14 April: 1).

Hindu temple sites must be reclaimed from the mosques and the Muslim congregations that now occupy them. The best-known case involves the Ramjanambhumi site along the Ganges River in Uttar Pradesh. Regarded as the birthplace of the god Rama by Hindus, it is now the location of a mosque founded by the Mughal emperor Babar some five centuries ago. Hindus, organized by the Vishwa Hindu Parishad, another RSS affiliate association, began demanding access to the mosque precincts for their worship in 1984. Although Muslims regarded Hindu observances as defiling, the grounds were opened by government order in 1986 (Weisman 1986: 3; Van Der Veer 1987).

Christian, Muslim, and Communist conversions of Untouchables and tribal members should be resisted because they weaken Hindian identity and national cultural integration. The ardent Hindu nationalist H.V. Seshadri deplores the "Missionary-Muslim-Marxist combine" and applauds the efforts of RSS *sevavratis* ("missionaries") to resist Christian and Muslim incursions in southern India (Seshadri 1984: 10–14, 33–35, 46, 62). The idea today is to avoid creating any more "Padrestans," as occurred among the Naga tribal population of eastern India in the 1960s (Golwalkar 1966: 182–83).

In the same spirit, separatist movements, such as the Khalistan agitation by Sikhs, must be destroyed because they threaten the nation's integrity. Hindu nationalist organizations and the BJP have instigated numerous mass protests against what they consider official inaction on the Punjab crisis and the government's inability to suppress Sikh violence. Many times these demonstrations have themselves degenerated into street violence (see, for example, *Times of India* 1986, 17 June: 3; *New York Times* 1986, 27 July: I, 3; Weisman 1986: I, 3; *Times of India* 1986, 1 December: 1, photograph of RSS peace marchers; *Times of India* 1986, 3 December: 1).

English education should be deemphasized. More resources must be committed to primary schooling, where "Indian religiocultural content, quality, and spirit" could be inculcated (*Manthan* 1986: 4–7).

A common civil code must be legalized to cover all Hindians. Muslims are not now covered by the Indian civil code because otherwise, the government believes and Muslims agree, Islamic religious law would be infringed (Seshadri 1984: xv).

Hindu cultural traditions, such as sati, should be given respect, even if they continue to be restricted or even outlawed (see *India Today* 1987, 15 October: 60–61).

Gandhian and Hindian

Hindu nationalism overlaps Gandhian thinking in many respects. Both accept an Orientalist notion that East and West are innately different. They share the view that India has been and must be spiritual, organic, and incorporative, as opposed to the materialist, individualist, and competitive West. Both therefore champion an indigenous scheme of development, one that eschews class conflict and promotes instead spiritual revolution and social discipline. Gandhism and Hindu nationalism agree that such an indigenous development will rest on political decentralization, economic development from the bottom up, voluntary action, and the subordination of the individual to the nation. The incorporative view of society they share means that both distrust special privileges for minorities, which may perpetuate separatist identities. Even on the issue of nonviolence, there is agreement, at least in principle if not necessarily in action. RSS chief Golwalkar (1966: 248–49) embraced a nonviolence from strength, obviously modeled on Gandhi's satyagraha; his successor, Deoras, reaffirmed this commitment in 1979 (*Organiser* 1981, 25 October: 15).

There are also major differences, perhaps most fundamentally in the conclusions drawn from the common view of Indian society as having "unity in diversity." For Hindu nationalism, this idea subsidizes the belief that underneath sectarian and caste differences, all Indians are Hindus in essence — Hindians, as I have called them. If Muslim and Sikh Indians do not recognize the Hindian substrate, they threaten the nation, and they must be either (forcibly) reminded of it or removed as a threat. For Gandhi, too, there was one Indian nation underneath the many separate caste and sectarian identities. At base, however, was consanguinity — all Indians were kinfolk — and, at an even deeper level, they shared a common humanity that even transcended India and linked them to people around the world. Thus, for Gandhi, Truth and God as human universals of belief and knowledge, not Hindu cultural essences, would make for indigenous development in India — India's history of spirituality, Gandhi believed, only gave the nation a head start in a global effort to perfect humanity. Gandhi's favorite devotional song speaks of God's name as both Allah and Ishwar, and, although Gandhi may have opposed special protection for minorities, his spiritual revolution required Hindus to recognize God and Truth in Muslims, Untouchables, and other minorities.

Hindu nationalism redefines what Gandhi spoke of as God and Truth and makes it a Hindu truth alone. On this basis, it is intolerant of all social identities other than Hindian. What it recognizes in Sikhs, Muslims, and Untouchables is an inherent Hindian identity — an essence that these populations themselves do not recognize or that they even deny. Gandhi respected these other beliefs and believers because of what they said they were — different segments of humanity pursuing Truth and God in their own ways; Hindu nationalists respect them only for what they are not overtly or what they claim not to be — closeted and converted Hindians. Gandhi's belief in an essential humanity supported toleration and a revolutionary humanism. Hindu nationalist belief in an essential Hindianness subsidizes aggressive attitudes toward other populations and a proselytizing sectarianism.

Perhaps as an outcome of its aggressiveness, Hindu nationalism often does not follow the principled nonviolence that Gandhi did, if it follows it at all. Gandhi did not overlook the violence that sometimes traveled alongside his mass protests; it was enough to lead him to call off the 1920s noncooperation movement. With Hindu nationalism, violence seems wedded to the movement. Although it is disowned in principle, its constant presence is overlooked and perhaps even tolerated. Even in its authorized protests, Hindu nationalism reconstructs Gandhi's notion of nonviolently shaming an opponent into capitulation (*ahimsa*) into physically intimidating an opponent short of violence (as in "mobbing" an opponent).

The Rhetoric of Transplant

Because Hindu nationalist ideology denies Gandhian utopia in basic ways, it must legitimate the transplant through ideological ploys. One device is to portray the RSS as truly Gandhian in spirit:

if the RSS could be so denominated, then its creature in the early 1980s, the BJP party, could be too.

The RSS mouthpiece, *Organiser*, made that clear:

> Nor need anybody be surprised by BJP's adoption of Gandhian Socialism. Gandhi was not a "socialist," and socialists are not "Gandhian." But a marriage of these two concepts could convey the sense of humanity of the one and that of equity of the other. It is an attempt at humanising socialism and making Gandhi intelligible to the "modern" mind.
>
> That the attempt should have come from BJP, is singularly apt; for no other party is as close to Gandhi as BJP (*Organiser* 1981, 11 January: 2).

Was Gandhi antithetical to the RSS? Indeed not, an *Organiser* article argued. When Gandhi visited an RSS camp near his ashram in 1934, he came away "tremendously pleased." He realized that the RSS, like him, engaged in quiet, constructive work. "Such is the congruence of RSS, grandfather of BJP, and Gandhi, Father of the Nation," the article went on to say (*Organiser* 1981, 25 October: 18). As for Gandhi's nonviolence, the RSS had conscientiously embraced it, or so it was argued. The cudgels wielded by RSS branches are instruments of physical culture and discipline, not weapons, and Gandhi, the article reminded readers, often carried a cudgel larger than any the most ardent RSS supporter sports (*Organiser* 1981, 25 October: 19).

For many Hindu nationalists in the RSS and BJP, however, Gandhi had appeased Muslims (compare Godbole 1981: 7), and his allegiance to orthodox Hinduism was also in doubt. Having adopted Gandhian thought, the BJP and RSS had also to assuage these doubts about Gandhi from within. Another ploy was to reauthorize Gandhi as a good Hindu and his thinking as entirely indigenous, which, by extension, accredited him as a Hindu nationalist. An *Organiser* article, for example, admitted that Gandhi had met "Muslim demands more than half way" and given them a "blank cheque," but after his policy failed, he admitted his mistake. Moreover, Gandhi repeatedly described himself as a "staunch" orthodox Hindu, the article asserted, and thought it would be "the most natural thing" for Indian Muslims, almost entirely converts, "to revert to their ancient faith." By such remarks, the article maintained, Gandhi identified himself not only as an orthodox Hindu, but also as a Hindu nationalist (*Organiser*

247

1981, 25 October: 15, 18). Two sketches accompanying this article showed Gandhi in 1934 and 1946 chatting with RSS leaders. Another proof of Gandhi's Hindu nationalism was to assert that his socialism was very different from the West's because it rested on India's essential cultural traditions:

> Mahatma Gandhi accepted the historical analysis of Marx about poverty and riches. He accepted that unequal division of wealth between the people to be a man-made and not a god-given reality. But he did not accept the glorification of centralisation or of the state as the only agent of change . . .
>
> Gandhian socialism emphasises decentralisation . . . [Centralization is] against the basic Hindu ethos of our country . . . While believing in one Brahman at the ethereal level, the manifested form in the shape of idol . . . has been decentralised in every household by Hindus . . . [Decentralization] is what Gramswarajya is all about."
>
> In the area of economic thought the Gandhians have done a good deal of preliminary work. They have developed some concepts [that] consist of a pure Bharatiya ["Hindian"] Theory of Socialism after absorbing Marxist thought (Godbole 1981: 7).

There were other ways to prove that Gandhi was a good Hindu and that Gandhism was in keeping with India's essential Hinduism. Karan Singh (1983: 14–18), founder of a Hindu nationalist association, asked the question, "Why did Gandhiji start his prayer meetings with Ramdhun [a devotion to the Hindu god Ram]?" and then answered it: "because India is a nation that has always nurtured religion . . . [it is] something in the soil." By implication, Gandhi too had to nurture religion because he was from the soil of India. Elsewhere, Karan Singh (1984: 24–27) declared Gandhi a "devout Hindu" and explained the Mahatma's secularism away as the outcome of the Hindu reverence for all religions.

In these ways, Hindu nationalism does violence to Gandhi and Gandhian thinking, as it transplants utopia as ideology. In most other ways, however, Hindu nationalism benignly husbands Gandhian thinking rather than harming it. Hindu nationalism embeds Gandhian thinking by intertwining certain strands of it and discarding others. The resulting Gandhism is a new but insubstantial growth, weaker and smaller than the original, in which utopia is not sustained. No longer is there a comprehensive view of Truth and God and revolutionary experiment that supports a set of particulars for India: personal discipline, decentralization, village development, indigenous and primary education, and other aspects

248

of what once was Gandhian utopia. These experiments, still called Gandhian, are implanted in a wholly different ideological scheme and one that serves very special interests, which I shall now describe.

Hindian Identity, Class, and Caste

Historical contingencies underlie the split in the *sarvodaya* movement, J.P.'s total revolution, Mrs. Gandhi's Emergency, and the creation of the BJP. But there was a solid base of support for J.P.'s appeal, and afterward the conjunction of Gandhism with Hindu nationalism served as a vehicle for the growing consciousness of particular elements in the Indian population. Support for the J.P. movement in the mid-1970s and for Hindu nationalism has usually come from Hindus rather than Muslims or Sikhs; from the urbanized rather than the rural; from young people, especially students; from the lower-middle class — that is, professionals, teachers, petty manufacturers, traders, civil servants, and the like; and from the "forward castes" rather than the "backward castes" or the Scheduled Castes. Collectively, these attributes define the social basis for an emerging Hindian consciousness and its subordinate Gandhian ideology.

One attribute, caste, requires some clarification. The Indian caste system never consisted of the four or five "castes" that Westerners often take as typifying it. This misperception rests on equating caste with the four varna categories (Brahman, Kshatriya, Vaishya, and Shudra), each actually composed of many castes, mentioned in ancient Hindu scripture. The caste system, as it was lived in precolonial India, consisted of numerous — one estimate is of some three thousand — highly localized, endogamous, commensally restricted, hierarchically ranked, and occupationally specialized social groups called *jatis*. The varna category "Brahman," for example, consisted of many different castes, each of which claimed priestly calling as its traditional occupation, and, by extension, high status in a local region. Therefore, people called Brahmans were found all over India, but they belonged to many different castes that would not necessarily intermarry, eat together, or otherwise socially interact. One such Brahman jati might not even recognize another as truly belonging to the Brahman category.

Colonialism further complicated the caste system. Among its many effects, it destroyed the Hindu customary law and the integrity of Indian village society that had supported the highly localized jati system. It also introduced new occupations and discarded old ones, thus attacking the economic rationale of the caste system. By 1947, therefore, jatis had lost many of their former functions, such as outcasting, commensal regulation, and even control over marriage.

Caste — or what looked like caste — lived on in colonial India in other ways, however. Responding to the new unity of India under the British and to the modern means of communication and transportation that existed by the late nineteenth century, novel forms of "caste," that is, caste associations, burgeoned. These associations joined together many localized jatis that shared a roughly similar social or political status. They came together for political and social-welfare purposes. I refer to the populations these new caste associations addressed and hoped to enlist as forming a "caste category." At this point, the Indian caste system came closer to the Western perception of a small number of castes than it ever had before, although there were still many more than four. Still, labels like "Brahman" or "Rajput" or "Untouchable" took on a political and social reality at a national level that they had never previously had. The constituent jatis might still not intermarry or might even refuse to eat together, but they would join together under the leadership of the caste association to "uplift" the caste. The caste association might fund caste schools, endow scholarships for caste members, and make claims to a more distinguished caste ranking. The association might also try to use political leverage with the government to get better access to colleges and civil service appointments, or to get their new statuses semi-officially corroborated in the census reports. Untouchables even advanced claims to special electoral consideration, to ensure that they were represented in the new legislatures the British allowed Indians to elect. Increasingly, caste associations competed with each other for such preferment and recognition, and caste took on a political aspect at a national or "all-India" level, as it is said, that it had never had before. Even when no association existed, caste categories tended to develop in response to modern means of communication and to the new unified political arena created by British colonialism.

This process of "nationalization" did not stop with the formation of caste categories, however. New labels or categories developed that classified the caste categories into still broader categories depending on shared political position. For example, in southern India, a strong so-called "non-Brahman" caste movement formed in the 1920s. Its adherents were drawn from caste categories that united in their opposition to Brahman precedence in the civil service and higher education. They also shared a roughly similar rank in the precolonial caste system, below Brahmans but above Untouchables.

Independence accelerated the formation of this new caste system, whose reality has to do with national and regional politics, vote banks, and competition for government benefits. Caste labels in contemporary India — like caste itself — are therefore quite complex because of the intersection — and sometimes interference — of folk perceptions, legal classifications, and political rhetoric. Often the labels take on social reality, as the caste categories referred to become real social or political groups — for example, when they form discernible and self-conscious vote blocs, when politicians and parties set out to "represent" their interests, or when the government gives them preference for jobs or education.

I use three such supra-caste labels, "Scheduled Castes," "forward castes," and "backward castes." These terms are in common use in India today to refer to broad collectivities made up of caste categories. These collectivities or supra-caste categories represent segments of the Indian population, which, on the basis of their caste position, share a roughly similar political and social position. The three collectivities I describe below differ, however, in the degree to which they are incorporated as political groups with sharp social boundaries. They therefore also differ in the extent to which their "members" share a common consciousness. The officially designated Scheduled Caste category is the cleanest cut: it generally consists of castes once called Untouchable or Harijan, now "scheduled" (that is, "listed") by the government for affirmative action benefits, and often at present self-labeled "Dalit." "Backward castes" and "forward castes" are much more ragged categories. The designation "Other Backward Classes," which is often synonymous with the label "backward castes," is a legal classification used in many Indian states to refer to castes above Scheduled but still deserving of affirmative action (Galanter 1984: 179–87). These castes are generally rural and intermediate in caste rank, and they have a long history of political action. They took to social and political activism earliest in southern and western

India, where they were a large proportion of the population and were more urbanized than in the north. In these areas, they fostered "non-Brahman" movements, combining castes ranking between upper castes like Brahmans and the Untouchables. Most recently (since the Green Revolution in agriculture) backward castes have mobilized in the north, where their political and economic ambitions have often led to violence. For example, backward castes like Koeris and Kurmis in Bihar have attacked Scheduled Castes, on whom they depend for agricultural labor; other backward castes, like the Sikh Jats in Punjab, have attacked urban upper castes, which in this state are predominantly Hindu.

The "forward castes" — the caste base for Hindian identity — are, roughly speaking, the "educated classes" of Brahmans, Kayasthas, Khatris, and other urbanized upper castes, which obtained English education and staffed the British colonial enterprise and have continued to dominate government and the professions even after independence. It also includes the somewhat lower-ranking and less-educated castes of merchants, moneylenders, and small-scale entrepreneurs, collectively known as "Vaishyas" or "Baniyas," who dominate trade, manufacturing, banking, and other commercial activities.[1]

The population that now avidly embraces Hindian identity therefore represents the urban/lower-middle-class "forward"-caste population that took control of India's postindependence intermediate regime. Christopher Bayly (1983) shows that this population forged its own institutions and identity before and during the British reign and that it was attracted to a politics based on Hindu nationalism from the onset of the nationalist movement. Since the mid-1960s circumstances have turned much less favorable for these Hindians, as I shall subsequently refer to the urban forward-caste lower-middle class, and the Hindia they would like to maintain. Other emerging classes, whose consciousness is often envehicled in sectarian or caste identities (on this point, see Fox 1985: 163–64; Sarkar 1983: 31), have now come to the fore. Hindu nationalism, with its embedded Gandhism, increasingly serves as an ideology for urban lower-middle-class/forward-caste interests under this threat. Emerging Hindian consciousness and the Hindia it legitimates would continue to privilege the urban lower-middle-class and forward-caste population. Thus, the identity "Hindian" pretends to be a cover-all term for all Indians in the future, whereas it actually covers up current class differences in India.

Against the Kulaks

Perhaps the most potent threat to these Hindians has been the growth of a vocal rural rich farmer class, usually drawn from middle-ranking or so-called backward castes (commonly, the official Other Backward Classes) like the Jats in Punjab and Uttar Pradesh, the Patidars in Gujarat, or the Yadavs, Koeris, and Kurmis of Bihar (Blair 1980: 64, 1984: 66–68; Breman 1985: 433; Bardhan 1984: 54; Brass 1983: 331). This rural lower-middle class was on the rise in favored agricultural locales even before independence. Land reform (*zamindari* abolition) in the 1950s also served these cultivators' interests by eliminating large, absentee owners and making their property available. Since the mid-1960s the Green Revolution, first in the wheat-growing regions of the north and then in eastern and western regions cultivating rice, has swollen the ranks of these wealthy cultivators. It has brought them increased wealth and also given them great political leverage. They therefore have recently come to threaten the domination of forward-caste cultivators in the countryside as well as the power of forward-caste urbanites.

The rich cultivators from backward castes belong to the lower-middle class, just as the Hindian urban forward castes do, because they stand between rural wage laborers and large landlords. Because they are rural, however, they often strongly oppose urban Hindian interests. This agrarian class/caste category goes by various names, including "kulak," "rich peasant," "farmer," "rural bourgeoisie" and "capitalist farmer" — all of which point to both wealth and commercial agriculture as its defining characteristics (for early descriptions of this rising class, see *Eastern Economist* 1978, 21 April: 775–76 and *Economic and Political Weekly* 1978, 29 April: 717–18 for southern India; Mohan 1979: 26–29; Joshi 1979: 9–10; *Times of India* 1980, 18 November: 1; Mathur 1981: 8–13; Roy 1981: 154–55; Shakir and Sonalkar 1981: 11–13 for all India; Gill and Singhal 1984: 1728–32 for Punjab).

Sharad Joshi, the Maharasthrian farm leader, glossing over class differences in the countryside, talked of an emerging war between "Bharat" and "India," by which he meant a conflict between rural India, for him the real India, and the urban population. Charan Singh, representing Jat farmers in Uttar Pradesh, spoke against high castes, urban lobbies, and a parasitic intelligentsia (see Byres 1988). These wealthy cultivators, fully committed to the market, and their spokesmen therefore see urban forward-caste interests

253

as antithetical to their own. Rural and urban movements, for example, fight over the terms of trade between rural agriculture and urban manufacturing or over the urban salariat's cost of living. The level of commodity supports has been a hot political issue for all parties, even though the government purchase price seems to have exceeded the cost of production since the mid-1960s for wheat and since the mid-1970s for rice (Bardhan 1984: 54–55). Massive *kisan* ("farmer's") rallies have taken place in New Delhi, bringing as many as a million cultivators to the capital in a vivid display of the power of the rural lobby against urban interests (see *Times of India* 1981, 17 February: 1; *India Today* 1981, 15 April: 42–43).

This confrontation is therefore not a class struggle but a competition within a class.[2] The newly empowered rural population of backward castes sometimes demands concessions on agricultural inputs like fertilizer, commodity subsidies, or price supports for their commercial agriculture, most of which would have to come out of urban lower-middle-class pockets—as, for example, in higher costs for their own foodstuffs and higher wages for their urban service sector. At other times, especially in Bihar and other regions where the Green Revolution occurred in rice and recently, the kulak backward castes want freedom from government and the law, in order to exploit Untouchable landless laborers. At still other times, the children of these backward-caste cultivators agitate against their lack of access to education and urban employment. The most significant of these rural movements led by rich farmers belonging to the backward castes is of course that of the (Sikh) Jats of Punjab, which by its own sectarian form authorizes an equivalent Hindian backlash.

When Hindu nationalists extol a Hindian essential identity, underlying superficial sectarian and caste differences, they quite obviously deny the validity of political lobbies and mass protests based on appeals to Sikh separatism or backward-caste status. Gandhi's disavowal of class struggle, his advocacy of an incorporative and consensual India, which has become so significant an aspect of emerging Hindian identity, also serves to admonish these recent rural movements that threaten the urban forward castes.

Against Muslims

Petrodollars, earned by Indian Muslims through wage labor in the Gulf states, provide an economic base for another conflict with urban forward-caste interests, in this case, a class conflict. Muslim artisans and skilled laborers are pitted against their Hindu urban lower-middle-class employers and consumers. In the 1984 riots organized by the Shiv Sena against Untouchables and Muslims in Bombay city, the main targets were immigrant workers. The flight of these workers to other locales resulted in an acute shortage of manpower for the city's textile factories (*Economic and Political Weekly* 1984, May 19–26: 826–28). Political alliances involving Muslims, backward castes, and Untouchables, such as in the state of Gujarat (Wood 1984: 197–223), have also heightened sectarian feelings of forward-caste Hindians against Islam.

Extramural remittances have helped subsidize a rising sense of injustice among Muslims in India (see Weisman 1986: IV, 3/1; *India Today* 1986, 15 October; 1987, 15 June: 17, 19), and also a forceful suppression by Hindians on the defensive — especially in Gujarat and Bombay, where the new Muslim wealth has been most apparent, but also in other developed regions, such as New Delhi and western Uttar Pradesh, where Muslim populations are concentrated. An aroused Muslim consciousness, broadcast, as one Hindu nationalist put it, by "Muslim petro-dollar-wallas" (Seshadri 1984: 129), lies behind the mass conversion of Untouchables to Islam at Meenakshipurum in southern India during February 1981 — which engendered a strong Hindian backlash (see Seshadri 1984: 7–9; Singh 1984: 24–27). There are accusations that newly rich Gulf states export their wealth for Islamic proselytizing in India (Singh 1983: 14–18). In response, Hindu nationalists press for a Hindu revival to match the Muslim resurgence; they recall Gandhi's reputed statement that Hindus are by nature cowards, whereas Muslims are inherently bullies (see its use by the Hindu Manch in Deshpande 1981: 33–34; also *Organiser* 1981, 25 October: 15) to energize this revival. The sentiment is that "the Muslims are breathing down our necks" and that the Hindus must stop being so tolerant of Muslims and protect themselves, as several correspondents replied to the *Illustrated Weekly of India*'s (1980, 31 August: 20–23) public query, "Should India Be a Hindu State?"

Anti-Affirmative Action

The class threat from Muslims and Untouchables and the intraclass   *255*
threat from the rural backward castes come together in the most direct and quotidian attack on urban forward-caste interests: the

reservation policies originally introduced by the Nehru government in the 1950s. This, the most extensive affirmative action program in any nation, reserved places in colleges, civil service, and government for Scheduled Castes and Tribes. At the state level, the reservations program expanded in the 1960s and 1970s to include more supposedly deserving caste communities, the Other Backward Classes, which usually represented the newly wealthy backward-caste farmers alluded to above (Galanter 1984).

By the 1970s the first generation to profit from these reservations had begun to argue for greater concessions. Indira Gandhi's program to end poverty also made reservations an important policy plank. As the urban forward castes perceived or feared that reservations deeply cut into their educational access and occupational possibilities, there was an obvious attraction to one of the main clauses of Hindu nationalism, its strong reservations about reservations. Reservations, so Hindians argue, enshrine sectarian and caste differences that are only superficial, so they should be eliminated — or at least a stringent income qualification be added to ensure that only the really poor profit from them. As a corollary, the argument that the government should leave social welfare to voluntary organizations also articulated a Hindian concern to get government out of legislating against their interests.

What has ensued over the last decade in parts of India has been at times a class and caste confrontation pitting Hindian forward castes against Untouchables and Muslims. At other times it has been an intraclass competition between urban forward castes and rural kulaks (compare the state-by state survey in Church 1984: 240). Because the Hindian population is at the center of both these confrontations, the conflicts often overlap. Sometimes, therefore, a confrontation over reservations that initially involved backward-caste kulaks against Hindians has later led the urban forward castes and their Hindu nationalism into conflict with Muslims and Untouchables.

Events proceeded in this manner in the state of Gujarat during 1985–6. Early in January 1985, the Gujarat government decided to reserve considerably more civil-service jobs and engineering and medical school admissions for backward castes in the state (*Times of India* 1985, 18 January: 8; Abraham 1985: 8). Forward-caste Hindus, especially dominant in Gujarat, responded quickly: they boycotted government functions, closed colleges, and burned buses. Other violence against persons and property followed. Most of the anti-reservation forces came from the forward caste of Patels, many were connected with the Vidyarthi Parishad, and they had RSS support (Gurjar 1985: 157–63; also see Yagnik and Desai 1985: 38–39). Eventually the government abandoned its reservation plans.

Resistance from the forward castes continued in a new form, however, because, as the social activist Achyut Yagnik has noted, anti-reservation protests and communal riots have a symbiotic relationship (Vaid 1985: 35–36). In July 1986, Hindus rioted against Muslims in Gujarat and especially in Ahmedabad city. Seven Muslims were burned alive after being doused with kerosene by rioters; others were thrown from hospital windows (*New York Times* 1986, 15 July: I, 8). In all, the communal rioting accounted for fifty deaths in six days. A general strike called by a Hindu nationalist association in Ahmedabad even mobilized the textile workers belonging to the union Gandhi had started right after World War I. It was the first time in its history that the union rank-and-file had become involved in agitational politics (Sayed 1986: 5).

From confrontations with the backward castes, forward-caste Hindus seem to move easily to pogroms against Untouchables and Muslims. Upendra Baxi (1985: 1–2) finds that the reservation policy in Gujarat did not threaten the forward castes very much in reality, but he sees the street violence against Muslims and Untouchables as "anticipatory class warfare" and a "symbolic politics" of repression. This symbolic politics, which depends materially on street violence and murder, is clearly more easily expressed against mostly defenseless Muslims and Untouchables than it is against the affluent and influential backward castes. The confrontation between urban forward castes and rural backward castes, by comparison, has been relatively benign except in the Punjab, where wealth and sectarian differences have greatly heightened the violent encounters between rural Jat Sikhs and urban Hindus (for the Sikhs, see Jeffrey 1986: 177–79).

Besides symbolic enactments in street violence, Hindu nationalists have also offered gestures of peace. By creating an ideology of Hindia and Hindian, they beckon to Muslims and Untouchables. As an alternative to immolation and defenestration, they offer them redemption and benefaction in India's future. The strenuous efforts of Hindu nationalist organizations to reclaim Hinduism's lost castes and tribes, especially in regions like Maharasthra where they are politically conscious and economically advanced (Contursi, personal communication), their desire to undertake Gandhian voluntary work among Untouchables and the rural poor, are instances of the Hindian ideology of "unite and rule."

Threats from Above

Threats to the forward castes come not only from below (Untouchables and Muslims) or alongside (backward castes). They also come from above, in the form of attacks on the lower-middle-class position of the forward castes. An intermediate regime, with the lower-middle class dominant, cannot continue indefinitely. Its very success in keeping foreign capital at bay eventually leads to the formation of a powerful indigenous bourgeoisie. Even though the Indian government has slowed the growth of big capital through public-sector development, licensing, and other controls, indigenous large capital has been growing slowly (Vanaik 1985: 59), and there is increasing alliance between big business and big bureaucracy. Pressed by this development, the urban lower-middle class finds Hindu nationalism's emphasis on "Gandhian" economic decentralization, small-scale enterprise, "appropriate" (to the lower-middle class) technology, and government deregulation most appealing. If such measures were implemented, they might retard the erosion of the lower-middle class's perquisites or at least pay them off in consumerism for their loss of political power.

Hindian Ideology and Utopia

After independence, as other nationalist ideologies became more radicalized, were hijacked by other interests, or failed in practice, there was no longer any strong ideological justification for the forward caste or lower-middle class. Nehru's democratic-socialist nationalism, which had earlier legitimated the intermediate regime, became much more radical as Indira Gandhi manipulated it after 1967. She was responding to the Indian poor's demonstration of a new political consciousness and political participation in the 1967 elections (Mayer 1984: 145–46). Gandhism, as interpreted after independence by Vinoba Bhave and the Sarva Seva Sangh, had, if not legitimated the intermediate regime, at least tolerated it. By the late 1960s, Vinoba's version of Gandhism had quite obviously failed, and violent movements were growing apace in the countryside. Because it no longer effectively kept the poor mild, it also no longer legitimated the intermediate regime. Hindu nationalism

and Hindian identity, as put forward by the "ideological professions" like lawyers, doctors, and college professors (Baxi 1985: 2),
are a substitute. The substitution has succeeded so well that alienated youth, the "educated unemployed," or "semi-literates" as
Vanaik (1985: 65) calls them, have flocked to the RSS, even from
ultra-left parties.

Hindu nationalism, with its intertwined Gandhian ideology, no
longer passes simply as the rhetoric of the BJP; it now discourses
as if it were India's national belief. The Sikh agitation, beginning
in the early 1980s, for a separate nation in the Punjab set off a set
of contingencies that freed Hindu nationalism from the BJP: Sikh
separatism led to the Indian army's attack on Sikhism's holy shrine
in Amritsar, the Golden Temple complex, in June 1984, which then
led to Mrs. Gandhi's assassination that October, which then led to
the current guerrilla warfare in which Sikh terrorists murder Hindus (and Sikh "collaborators") and the Indian police murder Sikh
terrorists.

For several years before her assassination, Indira Gandhi had
responded to the Sikh agitation in the Punjab by increasingly plug-
ging Hindu appeals into her political rhetoric (Vanaik 1985: 78;
Seshadri 1984: 138). Her son the successor and her party took such
appeals even further in the 1985 election (Brass 1985, vol. 2: 19;
Organiser 1985, 27 January). Hindu nationalist organizations like
the RSS realized they could fellow-travel with the Congress party
in power (*India Today* 1985, 15 January). There was even talk of a
"subterranean connection" between Indira Gandhi and the RSS
(Abraham 1983: 8/3–5). After Mrs. Gandhi's death, her son Rajiv
won massive support from Hindus in northern India, in what BJP
chief Vajpayee characterized as a Hindu backlash. Nana Deshmukh
endorsed Rajiv Gandhi, and numerous other RSS stalwarts deserted the BJP and supported him to prove that a Hindu majority
elected the government (*India Today* 1985, 15 January: 16–29, 31
January: 32–39). The once-secular Congress courted this vote
openly, and the irony was that the BJP's construction of a Hindu
Way and a Hindian political rhetoric now benefited its archrival.[3]

No longer exclusively representing Hindu nationalism, the BJP's
executive committee in 1985 decided to abandon Gandhian socialism as its electoral rhetoric (*Times of India* 1985, 10 October: 1).
Although soon reversed by the party's national council (*Times of
India* 1985, 13 October: 7), this decision indicated how much Gandhism had been emptied of message and appeal for the BJP, which

from 1980 had claimed sole custody over it. Gandhism in the particular aspects adopted by the BJP had become so entwined in burgeoning Hindu nationalism, so much an ideology legitimating it, that the party might choose to discard it or to retain it. The important goal for the BJP was to retrieve its connection to Hindu nationalism and its Hindu "vote banks" (*India Today* 1986, 31 March: 19); to be retained, transplanted Gandhism had to prove attractive for that purpose. Gandhism even as an ideology could not stand on its own. It was only a prop — perhaps, the BJP executive thought, not even a very strong one — for Hindu nationalism.

Is this the end of Gadhian utopia, perhaps even of Gandhian ideology, as a constituted and constitutive set of beliefs and practices in India? I have chronicled the singular and structural history of India since independence that stripped Gandhian thinking of its utopian vision, that then reduced it to an ideology in defense of certain interests, and that ultimately, in the 1980s, subordinated and marginalized it even as an ideology. Once parts of it had been transplanted and closely intertwined with Hindu nationalism, Gandhism dwindled. It lost much of its independent compelling and constitutive character in Indian social life.

Is the future only to see an empty Gandhism, hardly worth a hijack, thoroughly wilted as a transplant? Will Gandhi come to remain only as the distant father-figure of the country and the world's patron saint of noble but ineffective nonviolence?

Just as J.P.'s reaffirmed version of Gandhian utopia arose from the quietism of Vinoba, so human intentions may again butt up against existing cultural beliefs and social inequalities to envision a new Gandhian utopia, perhaps one only minimally associated with the Mahatma's dream, but claiming the legacy nevertheless.

One path of development seems quite plausible but may not be likely. Voluntary workers pledged to a Gandhian vision continue constructive and village-development work throughout India. During the 1980s, the voluntary movement inspired by J.P. set up People's Committees across India to keep the government honest while the movement worked toward total revolution. These committees, which have become increasingly antigovernment and antibureaucratic, allow the use of satyagraha against state corruption, and they champion the rights of landless laborers and poor villagers. Although the number of people's committees increased from 500 in February 1980 to 15,000 in December 1981 and the number of full-time workers went up from 200 to 350 over the same period, the movement has yet to become a major undertaking (Ostergaard 1985: 331–34, 335–39, 343–45).

The Gandhian workers I interviewed in March 1988 gave no promise of a future regeneration of utopia, however. At the Gandhi Peace Foundation and the Gandhi Memorial Foundation in Delhi and at the Gandhian Institute of Studies in Varanasi, people bemoaned the substitution of welfarism for revolutionary mission in the Gandhian movement. They admitted that the failure of the Janata's would-be Gandhian program in the late 1970s and the subsequent official repression by the Kudal commission had damaged morale, commitment, and even the subsistence of constructive workers. One Gandhian said that voluntary workers were a "confused lot." Another chastised the majority of Gandhian workers for their lack of revolutionary purpose, for their satisfaction with patchwork social welfarism. Although the regeneration of Gandhian utopia within the old-line Gandhian voluntary movement is plausible, it is not likely, or so it would seem.

Deendayal and Integral Humanism

A much less plausible path, but a more potent one should it develop, would be for a new utopia to arise out of Hindu nationalist ideology. It is important to consider this development. Otherwise, we disallow this possibility: that human intentions can butt up against existing cultural ideologies and, no matter how much these ideologies legitimate existing social inequalities and try to maintain them, that these human intentions can bounce off them to create new utopias. The questions become: could Hindu nationalism in future regenerate the Gandhian utopia it has subordinated at present? Could a new utopian dream develop from what many Indians see as a nightmare of bigotry and violent intolerance?

A prolepsis of utopia already exists in Hindu nationalism's recent past. In the 1960s, Deendayal Upadhyaya, a lifelong RSS pracharak and president of the Jana Sangh party after 1967, developed a set of concepts that he labeled "integral humanism." In these concepts, Deendayal paid homage to Gandhian utopia and, even further back in time, to the utopian thinking of the experimentalists who were Gandhi's coauthors. For example, in the policy statement he wrote for the Jana Sangh in 1965, Deendayal asserted that national development — "realization of National Self" — depends on overall

261

human development. By this integral humanism, he did not mean developing only the material side, predominant in the West, nor only the spiritual, at which India was said to excel, but also the physical side of people and their emotional lives as well (Bharatiya Jana Sangh 1973, vol. 1: 13–14). In this formula, Deendayal returned to Annie Besant's prescription (perhaps unconsciously — he did not cite her) for Indian education: that because human nature depends on the body, the emotions, the intellect, and the spirit, so there must be physical, moral, intellectual, and religious education (Dar and Somaskandan 1966: 41–42).

Deendayal's thinking continued many themes in Gandhian utopia — how could it not, given the constitutive character of Gandhism after independence? For Deendayal, as for Gandhi, a nation's development must be consonant with its cultural traditions. Deendayal reflected that India's problems came about because "the leadership has been prone to ignore the nation's real 'self' and to adopt recklessly foreign patterns." He rejected the notion, which he ascribed to several Western ideologies, that conflict between the individual and society is inherent. He called for an indigenous national development and educational plan in India (*Bharatiya Sanskriti* and *Maryada*), which would emphasize interdependence, cooperation, and concord over conflict, contradiction, and discord. Like Gandhi, too, Deendayal recognized "the individual [as] the chief instrument of society," by which he meant that the spiritual and material advancement of the individual led to general social welfare (Bharatiya Jana Sangh 1973, vol. 1: 8–9; Upadhyaya 1974 [1965]; for other comparisons of Deendayal and Gandhi, see Vajpayee in *Times of India* 1985, 14 October: 1/4–5; speeches by Desai, Chandra Shekhar, and Muley in Raje 1978: 14–16, 23–24, 25–30). Deendayal also accepted nonviolent resistance, and, again like Gandhi, feared indiscipline. Public agitations, he wrote,

> . . . are the media and expressions of social awakening . . . these agitations should be made instruments of a constructive revolution and not allowed to become violent or Adventurist (quoted by Walter Anderson in Raje 1977: 47).

Indigenous national development for Deendayal, just like Gandhi's swaraj, required breaking away from India's existing situation. Here what might be taken as the utopian aspect of Deendayal's thinking, inspired by his Hindu nationalism, becomes most obvious: he condemned what India currently was and spoke

262

about a "revolutionary element" in India's traditions (Bharatiya Jana Sangh 1973: 13–14). Some of the breakthroughs Deendayal hoped to achieve could easily pass as specific Gandhian experiments. Although he accepted modern machinery, he distrusted over-mechanization (Raje 1978: 25–30, 33) and believed in small-scale industry and in decentralization or collective ownership of large firms. Private versus state ownership of industry should be decided pragmatically, not ideologically, according to Deendayal (Chandra Shekhar in Raje 1978: 47; Upadhyaya 1974 [1965]: 77–78). He denounced Hindu nationalists who wanted to conserve Indian traditions at all costs. Untouchability, caste discrimination, mistreatment of women, and the dowry system struck Deendayal as signs of India's decline and degeneration. Although increased national productivity was a major goal for Deendayal, he also emphasized disciplined consumption and denounced consumerism (Upadhyaya 1974 [1965]: 64–65). He also believed every Indian should be guaranteed work — "meaningful employment" he also called it — and therefore a minimum standard of living, as well as a basic education and medical treatment (Upadhyaya 1974 [1965]: 68–69, 77).

Other breakthroughs Deendayal proposed modified or augmented Gandhian utopia. He accepted the necessity, in this "less than perfect era," for the state to direct and regulate the economy and even to own and manage economic assets. He thought the idea of trusteeship admirable, but he believed individuals should profit from their efforts. Deendayal therefore affirmed the right to property, but only when private ownership did not make an individual indolent and parasitical and when it did not limit the independence of others. He proposed a ratio of no more than 20:1 between the highest and lowest incomes (Thengadi in Raje 1978: 54).

Although he condemned Western capitalism for its view of "economic man" and socialism for its equivalent materialism, Deendayal insisted on appraising both Western and indigenous thinking to find the best way (Bharatiya Jana Sangh 1973: 11–14). Accepting class conciliation, Deendayal also recognized its limits. Political democracy without economic development and social equality was bogus (Bharatiya Jana Sangh 1973: 4–5, 8–9; Anderson in Raje 1978: 47).

Would Deendayal have constituted a new Gandhian utopia (or Gandhian-influenced utopia) out of Hindu nationalism, had he lived beyond 1969? Was he assassinated during a train trip, as his followers sometimes claim, because he was too revolutionary within the RSS, or was he only an ideologue? — and was his murder only a case of railway robbery, as an official inquiry concluded? Deendayal's thinking certainly eased the conjuncture of Hindu nationalism and total revolution in 1974–75, but, had he lived to see it, would the revolutionary experiment have succeeded?

What if Deendayal had lived, and what if Gandhi had lived? This is the kind of question we commonly ask of history when we take the past as exemplary of the future. We worry about what might have been, if only someone had not died and someone else had not lived, or some event had or had not happened. We try to read a simple chain of determination, a structure, from the past, out of the many contingencies that have made the present. Asking the question, "what if . . . ?," we naturally come to doubt what the past can tell us about the present and future. Even had Deendayal lived, his integral humanism might not have germinated into a Hindu nationalist utopia in the India of the middle 1980s. Even Gandhi himself might not have been able to prevent ideological hijack. In asking such a question and getting no answer, however, we might overlook what the past does say. If the past is not exemplary, at least it may be promissory — in this sense: that what has happened once may happen again, although undoubtedly it will appear in somewhat altered form. If Deendayal foresaw a utopian vision in the unpromising ideology of Hindu nationalism, then human endeavor in the future will perhaps make it be seen again, and perhaps the next time it will achieve more authority and success. Individual intentions may be socially aborted in the present, yet still promise and propose what is humanly possible for the future.

Conclusion

> One cannot climb the Himalayas in a straight line.
>
> *M. K. Gandhi, 1918 (CWG 14: 516)*

The problem has been that great persons and great ideas were supposed to rise above the common and ordinary even though it was hard to imagine how they could do so. The sticking point — for cultural innovation as well as for the Great Men supposedly doing it — was culture. If culture constituted the individual's perception of reality and social being, how could any individual rise above this conditioning?

Grounded under the weight of culture: this view of the individual has essentially been anthropology's understanding until very recently. Individuals were therefore always in a crunch — a crunch conditioned by culture. Anthropologists a generation ago commonly juxtaposed Great Cultures to Great Men: cultural change depended not on great individuals, rising high above their worlds, but on culture itself. Whenever it was ready or readied (by ecological necessity, for example) for change, a culture had the ability to rise above its present constitution and to change itself.

Great Cultures proved just as problematic as Great Men, however. If great persons could not rise above their cultures, by what means or agency did cultures exercise their supposedly inherent capacity for self-adjustment? Could cultures equivalently rise above the individuals who made them up? That cultures could completely dispose of individuals was no more convincing than that the individual could at will be dispossessed of culture.

265

Individuals are not butterflies, flying carefree above their culture, but neither are they ants, grounded by the weight of cultural tradition. We know that cultural innovation occurs, often in response to individual human intentions and purposeful action. We also know that cultural understandings are compelling and condition human intention and action. An ant image of humanity recognizes the compelling character of existing cultural beliefs on the individual. The butterfly image asserts the power of human intention and purposeful action to break free from this cultural conditioning. How to reconcile the two?

The reconciliation, it seems to me, is proceeding from two directions. Scholars lately have had greater concern for the way in which culture gets practiced by individuals. There is also much recent interest in what underlies the formative nature of cultural beliefs and what makes them compelling on the individual. Anthony Giddens (1984: 173) and Roy Bhaskar (1979), two scholars whose work has informed this book, speak of the way in which culture compels human activity but also enables it. They assert that human activity, that is, practicing one's culture, is necessary in order to carry culture forward in either reproduced or altered form. Most anthropologists a generation ago saw culture as compelling only. Individual practice therefore was only epiphenomenal or artifactual.

An anthropology of cultural practice, which Ortner (1984) heralded as the orientation of the 1980s, means we look at how people live with their cultural beliefs and how these beliefs are "envehicled" (to use Geertz's term) in daily existence (see also Bourdieu 1977 and Sahlins 1981, 1985). The major questions become: in what way are existing cultural beliefs compelling on individuals, and in what way do they enable cultural innovation? Recent studies of cultural practice conceive of the relationship between the individual and culture in terms of scenarios, templates, scripts, or habituations. These cultural scenarios or scripts provide individuals with predefined but not necessarily predetermined courses of action. Human intentions and ongoing experience work on these cultural settings. Individuals may apply these scenarios to cope with the circumstances they meet, or they may embellish and improvise on them, as circumstances demand (compare Ortner n.d.).

266   Looking at the way in which culture gets practiced makes anthropology more capable of dealing with issues of cultural domination and social inequality. Anthropologists can conserve the idea

that culture constitutes individual perceptions of reality even as they recognize that cultural beliefs incorporate and reproduce inequality.

In the past, recognizing that cultural beliefs legitimate domination or exploitation has made the formative character of culture problematic. It was all too easy to reduce culture to a set of manipulative or repressive strategies practiced by powerful individuals or privileged classes. The difficulty lay in linking social inequalities to the formative capacity of culture: how could we recognize that individuals and classes pursue advantage, and manipulate cultural meanings to that purpose, without denying culture's ability to define the way all individuals (not just the subalterns) see the world? The answer that seems to be emerging is to allow that just as culture is always practiced, it is also never neutral. Cultural beliefs integrate and constitute inequalities that may be taken as natural by all members of a society. Because inequalities lie behind cultural integration and constitution, the formative character of culture is a variable related to the degree of successful domination in a society. My reference here is obviously to the recent use of the concept of hegemony, derived from Antonio Gramsci, but more often used in the reading Raymond Williams (1977: 110) gives it. Hegemony happens as the system of domination and inequality in a society becomes so culturally encoded — that is, lodged so deep in cultural belief — that it comes to appear natural and inviolate.

Some troublesome issues remain, nevertheless, in relating the individual to cultural innovation. Can the cultural scenarios be completely recast by human experience? If they can, under what circumstances and by what process does recasting occur? One answer, unsatisfactory, I believe, is to allow that cultural innovations — new cultural scenarios — appear as individuals live out their existing cultural beliefs. Practicing their old cultures under new circumstances, individuals find they must come up with new scenarios to accommodate novel experiences, or so this argument maintains. Marshall Sahlins, for instance, relates individual practice to cultural innovation by asserting that

In action, people put their concepts and categories into ostensible relations with the world . . . Having its own properties, the world may then prove intractable. It can well defy the concepts that are indexed to it . . . Besides, as action involves a thinking subject (or subjects) . . ., the cultural scheme is put in double jeopardy . . .:

subjectively, by the people's interested uses of signs in their own projects; objectively, as meaning is risked in a cosmos fully capable of contradicting the symbolic systems that are presumed to describe it (Sahlins 1985: 149, see also x–xv).

Sahlins provides two somewhat contradictory reasons for why culture may change in practice. The first, the objective reason, is that an individual's cultural concepts may be at risk because the world does not conform to them. This answer basically conserves the ant image of the individual in relation to culture; it allows for humans no more than what we know to be true of ants, that they can modify social behavior to accommodate to changed circumstances.

Is culture change simply the result of practicing one's culture, and in the process coming up with new lifeways as the old scripts and scenarios cease to do well in practice? The concept of hegemony argues against the ready and expedient disposal of old scripts and scenarios. Existing cultural beliefs and the social inequalities they deeply encode clamp down on individuals too strongly for empirical testing by itself to recast culture. Very like Sahlins, Thomas Kuhn (1970) maintains that scientific innovation occurs when empirical anomalies require practicing scientists to reconstitute the paradigm within which they work. The history of science, as I reviewed it in Chapter 2, provides much counter-evidence: that anomalies are ignored or written off in scientific practice and that scientific investigations are no more necessarily "burdened with reality" — in the sense of being contradicted by it — than is cultural practice. Cultural innovation, like scientific discovery, proceeds from a quite specific cultural practice, very different from taking risks with reality.

Rescripting cultural beliefs, casting new scenarios, can only result from the individual's active struggle against the existing culture, as Gandhi well understood. Although culture is formative and hegemonic, it is not ever completely so. The very inequalities culture encodes create discontent, opposition, compliance without conviction, and sometimes even active resistance in society. Cultural practice never makes perfect. At any moment, a culture consists of imperfect scenarios and contradictory cultural practices, with the potential to come into active confrontation. Similarly in science, no paradigm is ever so dominant as to exclude all others.

268   Individuals and groups, bearing culture, therefore practice that culture with and sometimes against each other, not against an

empirical, that is, a culturally unconstituted reality. Because existing cultural understandings are ideologies confirming or legitimating or protecting current social inequalities, resistance to them must be a struggle, for resistance denies not only their formative character but also the domination that cultural meanings empower. Again, scientific procedure reflects cultural practice: confrontations over ideas and struggles among practitioners — the "agonistic field," as Bruno Latour and Steve Woolgar (1979) term it — propel science onward to novel discoveries and new paradigms. We struggle with ourselves and against each other — both in science and in a culture, as Gandhi clearly recognized. The risks taken with reality by scientific or cultural practice are checked by the real world, as Sahlins asserts, only ultimately and "in the final analysis": witness how far the human and environmental degradation that Gandhi feared has proceeded unchecked in the modern world.

My struggle with Sahlins over cultural practice discovers a remaining question: how do individuals or groups develop an active resistance to cultural hegemony; how does an agonistic field come about? Any culture may breed discontent as it legitimates disadvantage, but by what act of human intention does the misfit and malcontent individual become the revolutionary innovator? Sahlins, not taking any risks, contradicts the ant image of humanity in his first, objective, reason by a butterfly image in his second, subjective, reason: if cultural innovation does not occur because reality denies cultural understanding, he asserts, it happens because individuals, given their specific intentions and particular projects, may subjectively reevaluate their cultural categories. People "cease to be the slaves of their concepts and become the masters," Sahlins (1985: x) says. Which slaves break the chains of culture, what intentions and projects give mastery over it? That Sahlins does not say. Must we then fall back on the butterfly image of cultural innovation? Must some great individual rise above cultural constitution and hegemony and, after active struggle with them, fly free and clear?

Conflicted Intimacy and Utopian Intentions

At times Gandhian utopia accomplished significant cultural innovation; at other times it attempted cultural innovation and failed;   269 at still other times, it served as an ideology and worked against cultural change. Neither the ant nor the butterfly image, neither Sahlin's objective nor his subjective reason explains this complex culture history.

Gandhian utopia grew out of the Orientalist stereotypes of India that were part of Western cultural domination in the late-nineteenth-century world system. Its authors, Indian nationalists and Western nonconformists, did not easily discard the pejorative cultural scenarios constituting Orientalism. Gandhian utopia, as a new scenario of cultural resistance in the world system, did not readily arise as its authors practiced their hegemonized culture in ant-like fashion. It was a struggle, as I have shown, that took considerable time, involved a complex and contingent authorship, and gained authority only with great difficulty — because it butted up against powerful cultural understandings in the world system and the cultural domination they encoded. Once authored and authorized, ostensibly by Gandhi, Gandhian utopia still did not fly free of that cultural domination. By the very beliefs Gandhian utopia constituted, it showed a "conflicted intimacy" — to use again Richard Terdiman's (1985) illuminating phrase — with the cultural domination from which it had arisen. Gandhian utopia reversed the Orientalist pejoratives by which India was colonized and Indians dominated; it turned them into affirmative attributes. But they were no less stereotypes of India for that. The cultural essentials on which Gandhian utopia based its hope for India's future perfection — spirituality and consensus — were only the old Orientalist pejoratives — otherworldliness and a lack of individualism — stood on their heads. Gandhian utopia as a set of cultural meanings that was to constitute Indian nationalism was therefore enabled in certain directions by the very system of domination it resisted.

Even bearing this weight, Gandhian utopia, under Gandhi's authority from the 1920s until Indian independence, was able to spring free of Orientalist cultural domination and to spring India free. In his view of conflicted intimacy, Terdiman does not allow that an effective cultural resistance, a true cultural innovation, can emerge from it. For him, cultural resistance always ends up confirming the hegemonic (Terdiman 1985: 65). Yet under contingencies that beset and informed Gandhi in South Africa and India, as I have endeavored to show, just such a cultural innovation occurred. That was not the only possible outcome, and it was not the only one that happened. Cultural domination often succeeded by making educated Indians all but British in spirit, as Macauley and other Westernizers wanted. In such cases, there was much intimacy and little conflict. Even when conflict was uppermost, the resistance did not necessarily envision revolutionary cultural innovation for long. Hindu nationalism also grew out of the conflicted intimacy between Indian cultural resistance and Orientalism in the world system. In this case, its early utopian intentions, challenging the present through a vision of the future, were soon lost; with them went the possibility of cultural innovation. Hindu nationalists, almost from the beginning, denied Orientalist ideology only to intentionally legitimate an ideology serving the interests of the Indian upper castes.

For cultural innovation to occur, therefore, it is not enough to butt up against the existing cultural beliefs and resist them. The struggle must take place around utopian intentions; otherwise one ideology of domination gets replaced with another, as happened with Hindu nationalism. Gandhi may have deferred a specific kind of change, a class revolution, for the sake of achieving the immediate goal of national independence; he never worked to preserve or protect the status quo, as Hindu nationalists continue to do. Here is the essential difference between cultural resistance based on utopian intentions and that based on ideological justification.

Even with active struggle based on utopian intentions, however, individuals have often found the battle against existing cultural beliefs dubious at best. Gandhi's success with his utopian vision was perhaps the least limited of the several versions of Gandhian utopia I have discussed, but it was not fully formed at the outset or ever completely perfected. Gandhi's utopian vision and his authority over the resulting social protests in South Africa and India went through a lengthy development and frequently endured serious challenges. Gandhi not only suffered — and survived — threats of deauthorization from the left and from the nascent bourgeoisie. He also suffered under his own sanctification into a figurehead Mahatma by the Congress nationalist movement.

Other individual versions of Gandhian utopia fared worse. Sometimes, the utopian vision was so "out of nowhere" that it failed to confront the existing culture and became an otherworldly daydream. Vinoba's version of Gandhian utopia after independence in 1947 appears to me to have been such a daydream. The sarvodaya movement Vinoba authored was so intent on spiritual revolution that it took empty pledges of land reform, for example, as tantamount to real social revolution. At other times, conflicted intimacy proved too strong for utopian intentions, which were appropriated, or hijacked and transplanted, to serve other interests. Although Jayaprakash Narayan was intent on total revolution in 1975, he was not able to authorize his version of Gandhian utopia independent of certain existing class and caste interests. Very early in Jayaprakash's movement, these interests proved dominant, and the Gandhian vision with which J.P. worked was entwined and later strangled by Hindu nationalism, the ideology representing those interests.

New cultural scenarios sometimes grow out of the old, in a relationship of conflicted intimacy, as a result of struggle by individuals intent on utopian visions that contest present culture. Sometimes utopian intentions avail, at least partially, against the existing culture, and at other times they fall short. Sometimes utopian intentions meet such strong resistance from the existing culture that they are quickly reduced to ideologies. At other times, they may persist in an uneasy relationship with the existing culture, alternating between accommodation and resistance. What course any particular utopian vision will take depends on the historical contingencies of cultural hegemony and individual intentions in a historically particular time and place. That course results, in other words, from a specific combination of the structural and the singular, as Paul Ricoeur (1986) puts it. To chronicle this combination in an instance such as Gandhian utopia is to produce what I have called a culture history.

What then does this culture history of Gandhian utopia say about the relationship between the individual and cultural innovation? In our expectations of butterfly-like human innovation as well as in the converse, our acceptance of ant-like cultural compulsion, we seem to have greatly exaggerated the power of human intention, on the one hand, or cultural constitution, on the other. We have invested individuals with the power of flight they do not have; at the same time we have made culture more ponderous and crushing than it is. This chronicle of Gandhian utopia recommends another image of the individual and cultural innovation: that of the grasshopper. There are individual leaps, not flights, of cultural innovation, but they are of short duration, and they are propelled by bouncing off the resistance offered by the dominant cultural beliefs. The cultural innovation produced by human utopian intentions is therefore never fully free from the existing culture, but by the same token it is never fully compelled by existing cultural beliefs. Furthermore, human utopian intentions, like grasshoppers, intend to move forward, yet as they bounce up against cultural resistance, they sometimes inadvertently fall back in the same spot or only barely go forward. At other, perhaps especially fortuitous times, human intentions, again like grasshoppers, bounce off the existing culture and then bound ahead ot it, appearing almost to fly free as they traverse much new ground.

Grasshoppers are likely to bound further forward, the more contact they make with a resistant surface. This image helps me address the questions left over from my confrontation with Sahlins earlier in this chapter: which individuals master their culture rather than remain slaves to it, and under what circumstances? If all individuals confront their culture in daily practice, nevertheless some individuals are in better circumstances to leap away from it. Some groups and individuals experience greater intimacy with the inequalities and domination built into the existing culture. Greater intimacy compels them into hegemony — or enables them to bound forward into a cultural resistance that may lead to cultural innovation. Gandhi represented an educated and Westernized class of Indians who for that reason experienced Orientalist cultural domination most intimately. British colonialism undoubtedly exploited the Indian peasantry, but there was rarely conflicted cultural intimacy in their relationship. In special situations, as when Sikh peasants and Sikhism were enlisted into the British Indian army, conflicted intimacy developed and could be turned into anticolonial protest (see Fox 1985). The conflicted intimacies that beset Gandhi and the other experimentalists behind Gandhian utopia, however, were much stronger and more constant. I have shown that Gandhi's experience of cultural domination in South Africa and India inspired his experiments with cultural resistance and enabled his utopian vision. The experimentalists who preceded him — European nonconformists like Tolstoy, Salt, and Carpenter; Indian cultural nationalists like Aurobindo and Tilak; and Indians by persuasion like Besant and Nivedita — all enjoyed similar intimacies that engendered anticipatory struggles.

Those individuals most able to bound away from the existing culture come from groups which by their very circumstances are also the least likely to leap at all. This is the paradox of conflicted intimacy, and the cause of the self-struggle that Gandhi understood to be the starting point of any experiment with truth. When Gandhi mastered Orientalism, he also renounced its benefits, not only for himself, but for his family. Gandhi's sons, for example, explained their poor condition in society as the result of their father's failure to provide them with English education. Furthermore, one generation's mastery may not save subsequent ones from slavery. I have shown that Gandhi's utopian vision, as a constituted set of cultural meanings, resisted Orientalism and helped make Indians masters in their own land. Gandhian utopia thereafter served as a legacy that compelled later experiments, such as Vinoba's mild satyagraha and J.P.'s total revolution. Given circumstances in India after independence in Vinoba's case and after Indira in J.P.'s, they bounced off the legacy, but not very far. They failed to remaster Gandhian utopia into a new vision that was more than momentarily free from the existing culture and the inequalities it encoded.

In the butterfly image of the individual and culture, cultural innovation is contingent on individual human genius. In the ant image, it comes about when an all-constitutive culture is ready. In either case, cultural innovation is not contingent on the relationship between the individual and culture. The grasshopper image restores the contingency of culture change to this relationship: as individuals bounce up against and off the existing cultural beliefs and hegemony, they develop a conflicted intimacy that may enable utopian visions. As individuals try to master the existing culture through these utopian visions, cultural innovation may or may not happen.

The grasshopper image also argues for a change in our conception of the individual and of culture. Culture has too often been taken to be a long-standing and consensual set of traditions or an ecologically adaptive and coercive set of institutions. Even in the recent guise of cultural scenarios, culture is taken to set the terms of social action in advance of individual cultural practice. Similarly, the individual is often seen as an assemblage of personality traits set in childhood socialization and subsequently compelling the adult's life-course. Influenced by Gandhi's concepts of the individual and culture, I have tried to break with the foregoing conceptions in this volume. In my view, culture is constantly being produced through individual and group confrontations (what Gandhi called experiments) over beliefs and practices. In a similar manner, individuals over a lifetime may go through several different and contradictory personhoods; in unusual cases, they may even

274

be revolutionized as persons through their confrontations with existing cultural beliefs and through their collaborative labor within intellectual "work groups." Bouncing off the current culture, individuals can thereby revolutionize their intentions. By experimenting with these utopian intentions, they may then effect major cultural innovations without being completely outside or above the existing culture.

Experiments with Truth

Gandhi certainly recognized the significance of utopian intentions for culture change. Because he believed he was no different from the laboratory scientist — only the laboratories were different — Gandhi would also probably have expected that utopian intentions in scholarship, just as they did in "real life," would sponsor struggles or experiments, and that these, in turn, might sometimes help the scholar leap forward to new knowledge.

Many scholars who adopt a reflexive or postmodern stance, as I have discussed it in Chapter 2, would not agree with Gandhi. They have come to believe that what we presume to be knowledge is only ideology, or even just personal fictions, not even embellished by the need to serve certain larger interests. Often, their epistemological relativism seems to point to ontological nihilism. Only a deafening silence greets the question: is there a reality independent of our personal fictions and social constructions, a reality that — albeit with much difficulty — we can learn something about?

I have discussed the way in which Gandhi's thinking informed the very orientation toward individuals, toward culture, and toward culture history that runs through this book. To the extent that I have here made some sense of Gandhian utopia in large measure by using his ideas, this book also testifies to the worth of Gandhi's understandings on the larger issue of truth. Gandhi's belief in struggle — in experiments with truth — valued confrontations, nonviolent ones to be sure, not only between people, but also over ideas. His thinking valued intellectual struggle, then, even though its outcome was never certain, its findings were rarely provident, and its applications were sometimes even destructive. Gandhi, as I understand him, held to the idea that there was some truth to be obtained, some truthful understanding of the social

275

world and of the human condition in general. That truth was never absolute or certain, but such experiments with truth, Gandhi believed, produced knowledge that could be taken as certain — indeed, had to be taken as certain, if humanity was ever to make progress toward utopia — at least until the next experiment either confirmed or condemned it. The radical relativism, the reflexive accounts that start anywhere and go nowhere, the unwillingness to venture beyond the statement that all intellectual ventures are fictional and methodologically problematic, the unwillingness to take intellectual responsibility under the guise of destroying scholarly authority — these intellectual stances commonly associated with the postmodern critique of scholarship and science, Gandhi would have found self-indulgent and undisciplined, or so I believe.

Martin Rudwick insightfully compares science to mapmaking. Maps are social constructions based on symbolic conventions and therefore hardly depict reality literally. The mapmaker decides what are the principal roads and which are the major cities to demarcate, and these decisions are all either individually biased or culturally informed. At the same time, however, they are representations of a physical reality that exists and will exist no matter what mapmakers plot and where map readers journey (Rudwick 1985: 453–54). If we wish to get from one place to another — and always depending on our ultimate intellectual direction and destination (compare Elkana 1981: 54–55) — some maps will prove more truthful than others (see Campbell 1986: 118). Although they may be culturally constructed and therefore misleading, making flawed maps is better than despairing that "you can't get there from here" — unless you have no intention of progressing anywhere.

Gandhi might have put it differently: he disliked some inventions because they dehumanized people; others — sewing machines, watches, and electric lights — he admired because he felt they served humanity well.[1] No one can tell beforehand what service or disservice to humanity a particular invention will bring. Precisely because the outcome of human invention is never predetermined, we must constantly pursue experiments with truth in science, just as much as in society.

A reinvigorated culture history better able to comprehend human agency and cultural domination — the ultimate experiment I have pursued in this book — charts one future course for anthropology, I hope, out of the postmodern no-man's land.

New knowledge, like new culture, does not simply emerge from (scientific) practice, however. New or refined instruments and the craft of scientific experimentation in themselves do not lead to altered knowledge and new theories (for this view, see Ackermann 1985: 112–64); neither do empirical anomalies. Observations are rarely free of internal or external interests, and the findings of instruments can be disputed; anomalies need not be recognized or acted upon. What propels new knowledge, what makes for better maps are experiments that contest with others as they contest with truth (compare Elkana 1981: 45). We require "disputatious communities of 'Truth' seekers" (Campbell 1986: 119). So, too, Gandhi's notion of experiment meant struggles against others or against oneself, but it did not simply mean practice. The truth could come only from being a satyagrahi, which meant being both an experimentalist with future truth and a visionary who struggled against current falsehood. Such experiments and struggles, I am thankful, are not limited to Great Souls.

Notes

Chapter 2

1. Although I say "anthropology's purpose," I should note that anthropology's own way of knowing has come under attack as biased. For example, Abdallah Larouie (1976: 49–59) disputes the application to Islam of the anthropological concept of culture as an Orientalizing stereotype. Talal Asad, himself an anthropologist, has attacked the practice of anthropology as insufficiently sensitive to the world matrix of power in which the field operates. See, for example, his critique of the naive anthropological notion of cultural translation (Asad 1986: 163); He shows anthropology's all-too-common lack of concern for power inequalities in the world system. Furthermore, Third World scholars — the "natives themselves" — have not waited for a revelation from anthropology to attack Western epistemology. Partha Chatterjee (1984: 155–156; 1986b: 69) has analyzed the adoption of the Western epistemology of rationalism by Indian nationalists, and he has tried to write the history of Indian nationalism without this way of knowing (1986a). Although these criticisms are significant and the new ways of knowing proposed are useful experiments, I believe a self-conscious and self-critical anthropology is, by its very concern with other cultural forms and lifeways, well qualified to undertake the critique as well (see, for example, Overing 1985).

2. I provide later an extended discussion of Gandhi's vegetarianism as an example of successive "individuations" that are misinterpreted as part of a consistent pattern of individual identity constituted in childhood. The concept of an integral individual, to which I take exception, has been applied to Gandhi and the cultural innovations he authored in Erikson (1969) and Rudolph and Rudolph (1967).

3. In this case and the following, Gandhi's notion of cultural innovation through confrontation, I anticipated some of my current understandings in a work on the Sikhs (Fox 1985: 196–206). Reading Gandhi and

about Gandhi helped clarify certain aspects that I left too ambiguous in the Sikh material, namely, the constitutive character of existing cultural meanings and their simultaneous role as enabling and compelling.

4. As an example of the importance of distinguishing *"one* indigene's" point of view (such as Gandhi's) from a supposedly "indigenous" viewpoint, let me note that the Gandhian notion that opposition and struggle are prerequisite to the search for truth is now claimed as typically Indian. A convinced, self-proclaimed Hindu nationalist quotes *"Vade vade jayate tattwabodhah"* — "through arguments and discussions emerges the Truth," as "the Hindu approach" (Seshadri 1984: 81). Another Hindu nationalist organ, the journal *Manthan,* commits to this view in its very title, which means "churning." Do these instances argue that Gandhi's notion is an indigenous cultural meaning rather than simply the idea of one indigene (as I have treated it)? Not so, according to Thomas Pantham (1986: 12), who believes "classical" Indian thought was nondualistic and nondialectical and did not see politics in terms of antagonisms and dichotomies. Pantham also quotes an Indian authority to this effect. It is probably true that current Hindu nationalists' acceptance of opposition and confrontation is a "Gandhi-come-lately," just as they have taken over so much else of the Mahatma's message. But is this now an indigenous cultural meaning? I would prefer to use the concept "indigenous," like the concept of "other," as always lowercase, always singularized, and always located in the context of historical systems of inequality and domination.

5. My position differs from that of Sahlins (1981: 35, 38) who speaks of a "structure of the conjuncture," in which as people practice their culture, they change it to fit the conditions they encounter.

6. The fact that Gandhi anticipated various understandings about history, the individual, and culture, which I show for Ricoeur's thinking in this chapter and for Bhaskar's and others' in the next, only indicates the complex authorship of ideas in the modern world system. Provenance — meaning whether the ideas are "Western" or "Eastern" — is moot, just as I shall later show it to be for Gandhian utopia. Another instance of a recent Gandhian-like intellectual phrasing, one not discussed in this work, is the notion of "punctuated equilibria" put forward by Stephen Jay Gould and other paleontologists. The notion that organic evolution proceeds through sudden leaps punctuated by static periods, rather than steady accumulations of organic change, would fit well with Gandhi's notion of revolutionary experiments, although the resemblance is analogic rather than historically real (because organic evolution does not proceed through any organism's consciousness and intention). See Gould (1980: 260).

7. Ricoeur argues that ideology is integrative and that there are some basic shared cultural assumptions in a society. He assumes the need for this sort of ideological integration, however. He does not seem to say why it is necessary or where it comes from. For example, he discusses the

collective ideology of the U.S. and singles out the belief that unemployment is the fault of the individual, whereas in Europe it is conceived as the system's fault (Ricoeur 1986: 265). This may be true, but surely these attitudes rest ultimately on the outcomes of struggles involving various classes, the state, or both. They therefore grow out of systems of domination. I take Ricoeur's argument that ideology is integrative, but I do not see this integration as a necessary function of society. Ideological integration always operates within a field of domination and inequality, even though it may not be a simple distortion in the interests of certain classes.

Chapter 3

1. The label "Gandhian," as I use it, includes not only organizations and individuals formally recognized as such, but others, such as certain Hindu nationalist associations, that have adopted all or many Gandhian notions. It therefore includes groups and individuals espousing Gandhism in its utopian form and as an ideology.
2. Irschick, however, (1986: 1279–82) feels that there is a strong continuity between older forms of protest and Gandhian satyagraha. The exact characteristics of satyagraha, especially whether it was to have a coercive or "meek" nature and whether certain protest forms like the gherao were admissible, not only entered scholarly debate, but also led to divergent and then hostile positions within the Gandhian movement after independence, as I shall show in Chapters 9 and 10.

Chapter 4

1. Bhaskar's position should not be confused with a now widely accepted position in anthropology to the effect that people build their worlds with the cultural tools at hand. The anthropological position is only a weak phrasing of cultural determinism. This position differs from Bhaskar's in that it does not allow for any change in the cultural tools; all that alters over time or from generation to generation is whatever the tools are used to construct. Bhaskar, like Gandhi, would argue that over time individuals not only construct new lifeways but also may alter the cultural tools with which they build.
2. Throughout this work, I have adopted the concept of "enabling" in keeping with Giddens's usage. Instead of "constraining," however, I prefer to use "compelling," which for me communicates more actively the way in which culture "activates" the individual than the term "constraining."
3. Like Goldmann, the anthropologist Pierre Bourdieu also sees individuals as only structural variants of the group or class they belong to. Bourdieu makes the individual "the trace of a class trajectory," as Stephen Greenblatt (1986: 33) says.

281

Chapter 5

1. It is not at all clear how long-standing Gandhi's presumed "deeply rooted" Jainism was. Hay (1988: 70–88) notes the influence of a young Jain friend, Raychand, on Gandhi's thinking shortly after Gandhi went to South Africa in 1893. To give Gandhi deeper roots in Jainism, Hay then posits that he imbibed it earlier from his mother, who practiced Jain-like austerities and took counsel from a Jain monk. There is no good evidence that Gandhi understood Jainism in any detail before his correspondence with Raychand. Therefore, to the extent that Jainism did influence him later in life, I believe that that influence was a contemporary, immediate construction, made up no doubt of maternal recollections as well as Raychand's instruction, but combined in a new way. Gandhi's Jainism was not a legacy from a past self; rather, it reflected another discontinuity in his personhood.
2. In 1909 Gandhi read a work that was very influential on him, Tolstoy's plea for nonviolence, *Letter to a Hindu*, which is not discussed here. I deal with this work in the context of the invention of satyagraha in Chapter 7.

Chapter 6

1. Perhaps the most meaningful modern instance for most Americans is the adoption of an avowedly Gandhian nonviolent resistance by Martin Luther King in the Birmingham bus boycott (see King 1958).

Chapter 7

1. Here I am trying to distinguish between persons who are publicly acknowledged as great mainly because of the offices they occupy at important historical moments and those who are Great because they have asserted authority over circumstances that have precipitated new visions of the world. In the first case, the "great person" is mainly a product of the existing culture; in the second case, the great person, although not the socially autonomous innovator and integral individual assumed in Great Man theory, is innovative in gaining authority over a new vision produced by a much larger intellectual work group. As the conception of the "individual" changes, so too must the notion of "Greatness" change.
2. For the other immediate circumstances that proved so influential on Gandhi during his trip to Britain in 1909, see Chapter 5.
3. Gandhi's political acumen and savvy, which were so apparent to his contemporaries (see, for example, Viceroy Wavell's judgment in Wolpert 1984: 276), often go unrecognized or are even denied. This trait seems to have been deleted from popular representations of him by his later saintly or Mahatma image, or perhaps the deletion is the result

of a former Western notion, now belied by recent preacher-politicians, that saintliness and political action are antithetical. Wavell summed it up, albeit very negatively, when he characterized Gandhi as an "exceedingly shrewd, obstinate, domineering, . . . single-minded politician; and there is little true saintliness in him."

4. Gandhi even refused to vote for a resolution on the Champaran situation at the annual Congress meeting (See Gandhi 1957: 404; Scarfe and Scarfe 1975: 38).

5. Gandhi walked in on existing conflicts in all his Indian satyagrahas (see Sarkar 1983: 45–47), just as he did in South Africa.

6. My interpretation of Champaran avoids a scholarly dispute between a "top down" and a "bottom up" interpretation of Gandhi and the early satyagrahas. The "top down" approach sees Gandhi's mass mobilization of peasants as the result of the promotion of Gandhi by the educated nonpeasant middle class (as, for example, Brown 1972). A "bottom up" approach argues that Gandhi spoke directly to the peasantry, who converted his message into terms they understood (and ones often more revolutionary than Gandhi intended), without the mediation of the middle class (see Sarkar 1983: 25). Henningham (1976) shows that in Champaran the local educated middle class and the rich peasants formed a coalition of local subcontractors who used Gandhi's authority to raise a mass following. The separation of a "top down" from a "bottom up" approach appears artificial when a class analysis is done: rich peasant and middle-class professional shared a similar relation — and reaction — to British domination in Champaran, and elsewhere. No doubt as Gandhi's authority over the nationalist movement spread and grew, he was increasingly able to author appeals to the Indian masses without the intermediation of local subcontractors (for example, see Amin 1984: 6–7), but, as I shall shortly show, there was much less control over mass response under these circumstances, and Gandhi often had to repudiate the undisciplined movements that developed under these circumstances, in order to maintain his authority.

7. Gandhi similarly hesitated to take a strong position in class confrontations between Indians a few years later, when another conflict in the Ahmedabad mills pitted mill workers against owners. The ensuing arbitration award found the workers' demands for a living wage worthy, but in spite of this, it did not recommend that such a living wage be paid them, citing loss of profitability in the industry. Although he had hoped that the full wage demands would be met, Gandhi was satisfied that the arbitration award had recognized the principle of a living wage, and he was glad that this "agreement" could be reached without a strike (Frankel 1978: 83).

8. Nehru with great insight contrasted his and Gandhi's ultimate revolutionary design for the poor. Nehru wanted to raise up the poor and make them like the wealthy, whereas Gandhi wanted to reduce the

wealthy and make them like the poor — thus Gandhi rode in third-class rail carriages and wore the clothing of poverty, whereas Nehru worked for class struggle and wore rich clothing. Nehru (1962 [1936]: 515, also 518) once referred to Gandhi's socialism as "muddled humanitarianism." Nehru (1962 [1936]: 533) also contrasted Gandhi's condemnation of the Indian princes at Varanasi in 1916 with his later policy of conciliation toward them.

9. What makes Gandhi's last days so tragic is that he began to doubt himself and to redo long-past experiments. He re-experimented with his vow of celibacy by sleeping (literally) with women in his entourage (see Bose 1953: 154–60, 174–78). It was Gandhi's way of testing whether his own weakness had all along doomed the independence struggle and made the partition of British India into India and Pakistan inevitable. It was a desperate personal retesting, not a revolutionary personhood in the making.

Chapter 8

1. I have here adopted the approach of the "subaltern" school — to the effect that the political message broadcast by the Gandhian leadership of the nationalist movement might be given a very different interpretation by subordinate groups like the peasantry. My approach therefore does not assume any necessary continuity between Gandhi and the peasantry — it makes no assumption that he spoke "their" language without any struggle, or that peasants internalized his commandments without any reinterpretation. Bipan Chandra (1985: 3) argues for such an uncomplicated internalization, based on recent retrospective interviews with low-level nationalist cadres throughout India. It may be that these cadres represent the "local subcontractors" among the peasantry, in much the same way that the Champaran tenants discussed in the last chapter represented them. I do not adopt, however, the notion of the subaltern school that the peasantry, had they only been given their own voice, would have necessarily spoken out for true revolution.

2. The next chapter has an extended discussion of the class basis of the nationalist movement, in terms of the "intermediate regime" that came into existence after independence.

Chapter 9

1. As an instance of the role of historical contingency in Lohia's lack of authority over the Gandhian inheritance: until 1949, Lohia was a member of the Indian National Congress. He belonged to the Congress Socialist party, which had been permitted to join the Congress. After Gandhi's assassination, Congress leaders decided to purge all members of other parties, and Lohia, in spite of his desire to stay within the Congress and work to make it progressive, kept company with many

other socialists who left it to form a separate political party (see chronology of Indian socialism in Arora 1984: 134–57).

2. In recognition of this fact, Gandhians have recently begun promoting local programs of *asirkari* ("nongovernment") khadi to return to noncommercial and unsubsidized homespun production. I was told in 1988 that this program is still very small.

3. Frankel (1978: 108ff.) emphasizes Nehru's commitment to Gandhi's preindependence policy of class conciliation as helping to create the conditions that compromised Nehru's socialism. For Gandhi, however, class conciliation was a short-term experiment in the interests of achieving independence. Chandra (1985: 6–7) argues convincingly that just before independence Gandhi began to foresee the use of satyagraha as a means of protest by the poor once India was free from British rule. Given the rural populism Gandhi embraced late in life, there is good reason to believe he might himself have organized resistance to Nehru's policies of state centralization and industrialization (see Chapter 8). A more persuasive explanation for what happened in India "under" Nehru, perhaps, is Frankel's own chronicle (1978: 156–387) of the compromises Nehru made in his socialist goals, given the compelling conditions (including Vinoba's disavowal of confrontational satyagraha) he encountered in the early years of independence. As with Gandhi's battle against Muslim separatism, these conditions not only compelled, they overwhelmed.

Chapter 10

1. Indira Gandhi had succeeded Lal Bahadur Shastri, who, in turn, had succeeded Indira Gandhi's father, Jawaharlal Nehru, upon his death in 1964.

2. A subsequent split, in 1979, led to still another new Congress party under Indira Gandhi's leadership, the Congress (I), which is currently the ruling party at the national level, under Rajiv Gandhi, the prime minister and Indira Gandhi's son.

3. In a society with at least four important figures all named Gandhi — Mohandas, Indira, Sanjay, and Rajiv — what to call them in order to distinguish them becomes a problem. I follow standard practice in India and refer to Indira Gandhi as Mrs. Gandhi, but with no sexism intended.

4. J.P.'s efforts proved long-lasting. In 1980, one of his targeted villages, Akbarpur, enjoyed prosperity and strong community feeling as a result of the programs he and his fellow workers had introduced (*New York Times* 1980, December 1: 14).

5. The terms "communal" and "communalism" as used in India refer to consciousness or identity and political action based on allegiances to caste and religion, or other such status. A Hindu communal party such as the Jana Sangh I discuss later in this chapter describes itself as protecting the interests of Hindus but is often described by other parties,

especially on the left, as fascist, right-wing, and bigoted. To avoid the pejorative meaning associated with the term "communal," I have used another label, "nationalist," when referring to parties or other associations mobilizing on the basis of appeals to Hindu identity.

6. Nargolkar (1975: 9–10) disagrees with other sources and says that Communist and non-Communist student associations cooperated in the 16 March demonstrations. The important point is that by the time J.P. actively intervened, several weeks later, the two associations had split, and the hostility between them increased as J.P. took greater control.

Chapter 11

1. The following chapter analyzes present-day RSS orientation and rhetoric in detail.
2. The coalition joined the mainstay Jana Sangh, a Hindu nationalist party, with the Socialist party, the closest to J.P.'s former democratic socialist politics; the Bharatiya Lok Dal, a party representing prosperous cultivators; and the Congress (O), the remnant of the old Congress after Mrs. Gandhi's 1969 split.
3. "Other Backward Classes," because it includes middle-ranking castes, is distinguished from the designation "Backward Classes," which consists of the so-called Scheduled Castes and Tribes, or Untouchables and others at the very bottom of the caste system. The next chapter contains an extended discussion of these official designations in relation to caste and class.

Chapter 12

1. Some writers classify the trading castes as "intermediate" or even "backward" (see, for example, Vanaik 1985: 60–65), but then they have to differentiate a "higher-intermediate" category (as Vanaik [1985: 78] does) to represent the urban trading castes as against the other "intermediate" castes, the mainly rural "backward castes" in the north, recently empowered by the Green Revolution. This confusion comes about because of a failure to recognize that the urban provenance of trading castes also made them "forward" in an economic and political sense quite early, much as other, higher-ranking caste categories like Brahmans and Kayasthas were. Also, their urban location gives them very different interests from rural intermediate or "backward" castes, although there have been attempts to forge political alliances (as between the Lok Dal and the BJP parties) linking them. These alliances have generally been unsuccessful and short-lived. Bayly (1983: especially 449–54) shows a long history of relations between such merchant castes and upper castes like Brahmans.
2. An equivalent intraclass competition exists between these newly powerful "backward" castes and the old rural forward-caste/landlord class

in places like Bihar (see *India Today* 31 December 1986: 42; Brass 1985, vol. 2: 11).
3. Recent attempts by Rajiv to recapture a Gandhian identity, including the reenactment of Gandhi's 1930 Salt March, must be seen as political promotions within a tide of national consciousness based on a unitary India with a strong Hindu basis.

Chapter 13

1. I thank Bipan Chandra for instruction on Gandhi's likes and dislikes among inventions.

Glossary

ahimsa: nonviolence, nondestruction of life.

bandh: a mass procession, used as a means of nonviolent protest.

bharat: the name of an ancient king of India, now used as the official, indigenous-language name of independent India, as, for example, on postage stamps. As used by Hindu nationalists, the term or its adjectival form, *"bharatiya,"* refers to an India whose essential character derives from Hindu tradition.

bhoodan: meaning "gift of land," the basis of Vinoba Bhave's postindependence program of voluntary land reform through such gifts by landowners to the landless.

brachmacharya: a vow of celibacy, which Gandhi took in 1906 and which he considered a necessary personal discipline undergirding his truthful service to society.

charkha: spinning wheel, an important symbol of the Gandhian *khadi* program, and the central motif on the flag of the Indian National Congress until independence.

dharna: a technique used by Brahmans in traditional India to force compliance. The Brahman threatened to starve himself to death at his opponent's door and thus infect the house with a pervasive spiritual pollution.

duragraha: meaning "harsh" or coercive resistance, this term was used by Vinoba Bhave to contrast with his own "mild" vision of *satyagraha.*

gherao: a form of protest currently used in India, wherein protesters surround and "mob" opponents. Although there may be no overt physical violence, the individual who is mobbed loses freedom of movement and may be denied food, water, etc.

gramdan: meaning "gift of the village," a voluntary gift of the major portion of a village's lands to the landless as part of Vinoba Bhave's postindependence *bhoodan* program (q.v.). *Sulabh gramdan* was a "simplified" form of voluntary land reform, which in effect allowed landlords to continue to control lands they had pledged to the landless.

289

Harijan: meaning "people of God [Hari]," the term Gandhi used to refer to Untouchable castes. Untouchables are now officially referred to as Scheduled Castes. Politicized Untouchables often used the term "Dalit" in self-reference.

hartal: sometimes translated as "strike," a term referring mainly to a technique of large-scale political protest developed in the Indian nationalist movement. Employees may stay away from their jobs, but shops and other businesses, as well as municipal services such as transport, shut down or are shut down as a form of protest.

jati: the term used to refer to the highly localized and differentiated caste system, as it formerly existed in India. It contrasts with the term *varna,* which refers to the four so-called "castes" listed in Indian scriptures.

khadi: homespun thread, which could be handwoven into cloth. It became a major aspect of Gandhi's program against the dehumanization of massive industrialization and factory labor.

kisan: cultivator.

Other Backward Class (OBCs): an official designation in many Indian states for castes that are above Untouchable but still disadvantaged. Many of the castes constituting this category consist of rural cultivators, made affluent by the Green Revolution over the past twenty years.

panchayat: a council of elders or other influential persons that many Indian nationalists believed governed Indian villages consensually and in the common interest before British colonialism corrupted the system.

panchayat raj: the Gandhians' plan to reintroduce or reinvigorate what they took as the ancient pattern of indigenous village self-government.

panchayati raj: the program of local self-government introduced by Indian states during the Nehru era. Unlike the Gandhian vision of *panchayat raj,* which viewed the village as the center of India's postindependence governance, the government program took village self-government as the lowest level of state administration.

ramrajya: a term meaning "Ram's rule," by which Gandhi hopefully foresaw a morally ordered future society in which a consensual and incorporative society based on villages would have come to replace contemporary materialistic, conflict-ridden society ruled over by an oppressive state. The reference to the Hindu god Ram highlights the divine or spiritual nature of the future society; it was not meant in a sectarian way.

sampurna kranti: "total revolution," a phrase used by Jayaprakash Narayan in the mid-1970s to enlist Indians into a new and continuous nonviolent social revolution.

sarsanghchalak: the head of the Rastriya Swayamsevak Sangh, a Hindu nationalist association.

sarvodaya: often taken as meaning "welfare for all." Gandhi used this term to translate Ruskin's message in *Unto This Last.* Gandhians have used the term to sum up their hopes for a future India that is spiritually revolutionized, moral, humane, and therefore superior to Western socialism and capitalism.

satyagraha: Gandhi's method of civil disobedience based on nonviolence. Sometimes translated as "truth force" or "soul force," satyagraha depends on a moral commitment to nonviolence and a disciplined resistance to injustice. A *satyagrahi* is someone who has made a spiritual commitment to such a nonviolent resistance.

shakhas: meaning "branches." The term refers to the community-level cells of the Rastriya Swayamsevak Sangh, a Hindu nationalist association.

swadeshi: meaning "indigenous," a term that came to symbolize the refusal of Indian nationalists to buy foreign goods, especially British-made cloth (also see *khadi*).

swaraj or *swarajya:* meaning "self-rule." The term represented the demands of Indian nationalists for separation from Britain. In Gandhi's usage, swaraj also meant a personal discipline or self-rule that would give nationalists the personal strength to resist the British nonviolently.

zamindar: a landowner in India. After independence many Indian states started extensive programs of land reform, called *zamindari* abolition programs, to remove the very large, often absentee landlords.

Note on Names

Before the British conquest, the use of surnames in India was not common. Today, most last names used by Indians are not surnames, in the sense of family names, as is the common practice in the West. Some Indian last names refer to sectarian community, as in the "Singh" commonly appended to the given names of Sikhs. Others are caste denominators, such as "Gandhi," "Chatterjee," "Mukherjee," or "Upadhyaya." Still others refer to titles or positions formerly held by a family or an individual ancestor, or they make reference to a region from which the family or caste originally came.

Like so much else in India today, public appellation is an unruly amalgam of Western and indigenous practices. Given names are much more commonly used as identifications than in the West, as, for example, *Jayaprakash* for Jayaprakash Narayan, *Vinoba* for Vinoba Bhave, *Deendayal* for Deendayal Upadhyaya, or *Bankimchandra* for Bankimchandra Chatterjee. Last names are also used, however, especially when the individual has an international reputation and is known globally by the last name: Mohandas *Gandhi* is the best instance. When last names are used, an honorific suffix, *-ji*, is often appended, as in *Gandhiji*. Very commonly, the issue of which name to use is finessed by employing a nickname or title associated with the person, which sometimes can be used independently but more commonly occurs with the person's last name. Some examples are *Mahatma* ("great soul") Gandhi, *J.P.* (for Jayaprakash Narayan), *Mrs. Gandhi* (for Indira Gandhi — in this case, the English gender appellation became almost a personal designation), *Doctorji* for Dr. Hedgewar, and *Punditji* (learned Brahman) for Jawarharlal Nehru.

My practice has been to follow conventional usage in India in reference to each individual, even though this obviates any overall consistency. In citation of individuals as authors, however, I make use of last names, which is also standard practice in India today.

Citations

Abraham, A. S. 1981. "BJP's Gandhian Socialism: Formula for Ideological Amorphousness." *Times of India* 2 January: 8.
———. 1983. "BJP's Declining Fortunes: Internal War of Attrition." *Times of India* 22 July: 8.
———. 1985. "Anti-Reservation Protest: Growing Clout of Backward Classes." *Times of India* 1 March: 8.
Ackermann, Robert John. 1985. *Data, Instruments, and Theory*. Princeton: Princeton University Press.
Advani, L. K. 1979. "In Defense of the RSS." *Illustrated Weekly of India* 100, no. 27 (7 October): 8–11.
All-India Panchayat Parishad. 1964. *Seminar on Fundamental Problems of Panchayati Raj*. New Delhi: All-India Panchayat Parishad.
Ambedkar, B. R. 1945. *What Congress and Gandhi Have Done to the Untouchables*. Bombay: Thacker and Co.
Amin, Shahid. 1984. "Gandhi as Mahatma: Gorakhpur District, Eastern UP 1921–2." In *Subaltern Studies III*, edited by Ranajit Guha, 1–61. Delhi: Oxford University Press.
Anderson, Walter K., and Shridhar D. Damle. 1987. *The Brotherhood in Saffron*. Boulder, Colo., and London: Westview Press.
Arnold, David. 1977. *The Congress in Tamilnad*. Australian National University Monographs on South Asia, no. 1. New Delhi: Manohar.
Arora, V. K. 1984. *Rammanohar Lohia and Socialism in India*. New Delhi: Deep and Deep Publications.
Asad, Talal. 1979. "Anthropology and the Analysis of Ideology." *Man* n.s. 14: 607–27.
———. 1983. "Anthropological Conceptions of Religion: Reflections on Geertz." *Man* 18: 237–59.
———. 1986. "The Concept of Cultural Translation in British Social Anthropology." In *Writing Culture: The Poetics and Politics of Ethnography*, edited by James Clifford and George E. Marcus, 141–64. Berkeley and Los Angeles: University of California Press.

Bailey, F. G. 1969. *Stratagems and Spoils*. New York: Schocken Books.

Banerjee, Nitya Narayan. n.d. *Vedic Socialism*. New Delhi: Hindutva.

Banerjee, Partha S. 1984. "Cult of Terror." *Secular Democracy* 6: 14–18.

Bardhan, Pranab. 1984. *The Political Economy of Development in India*. Oxford: Basil Blackwell.

Barik, Radhakanta. 1977. *Politics of the J.P. Movement*. New Delhi: Radiant.

Barth, Fredrik. 1966. *Models of Social Organization*. Royal Anthropological Institute Occasional Paper, no. 23. Glasgow: The University Press.

Bates, Crispin. 1981. "The Nature of Social Change in Rural Gujarat: The Kheda District, 1818–1918." *Modern Asian Studies* 15: 771–821.

Baxi, Upendra. 1985. "Reflections on Reservation Crisis in Gujarat." *Mainstream* 23, nos. 41, 42, 43 (8, 15, 22 June): 15–22, 20–25, 20–24.

Bayly, C. A. 1983. *Rulers, Townsmen, and Bazaars*. Cambridge: Cambridge University Press.

Bean, Susan. 1989. "Gandhi and Khadi: The Fabric of Indian Independence." In *Cloth in Human Experience*, edited by Annette Weiner and Jane Schneider. Washington: Smithsonian Institution Press.

Bearce, George D. 1961. *British Attitudes Towards India, 1784–1858*. London: Oxford University Press.

Benedict, Ruth. 1948 [1934]. *Patterns of Culture*. New York: Mentor.

Besant, Annie. 1904. *Hindu Ideals for the Use of Hindu Students in the Schools of India*. Benares and London: Theosophical Publishing Society.

———. 1913. "India's Mission Among Nations." Article contributed to the *National Educator* n.d. Reprinted in *India*, vol. 4 of *Essays and Addresses*. London: Theosophical Publishing Society.

———. 1917. *For India's Uplift: A Collection of Speeches and Writing on Indian Questions*. 2d ed. Madras: G. A. Nateson and Co.

———. 1919. *In Defense of Hinduism*. 2d ed. Adyar, Madras: Theosophical Publishing House.

———. 1925. *The Kamala Lectures: Indian Ideals in Education, Philosophy and Religion, and Art*. Calcutta: Calcutta University Press.

———. 1966. "Hinduism." In *Seven Great Religions*. Adyar, Madras: Theosophical Publishing House.

Beteille, Andre. 1965. *Caste, Class, and Power*. Berkeley and Los Angeles: University of California Press.

———. 1988. "Individual, Person and Self as Subjects for Sociology." Typescript for Conference on the Concept of the Person, Santa Barbara, Calif.

Bharatiya Jana Sangh. 1973. *Party Documents*. 5 vols. New Delhi: Bharatiya Jana Sangh.

Bhargava, B. S., C. R. Bada, and V. N. Torgal. 1982. *Panchayati Raj System*. New Delhi: Jackson.

Bhaskar, Roy. 1979. *The Possibility of Naturalism*. Atlantic Highlands, N.J.: Humanities Press.

Bhatt, A. S. 1982. "Is the Gandhi Peace Foundation a Victim of Vendetta?" *Caravan*, no. 716 (2 March): 14–17.

Bhattacharya, Buddhadeva. 1984. "Vinoba Bhave — An Ideologue of Sarvodaya: A Marxist Appraisal." In *Vinoba: The Spiritual Revolutionary*, edited by R. R. Diwakar and Mahendra Agrawal, 133–50. New Delhi: Gandhi Peace Foundation.

Bherwani, Asandas. 1979. "The Highlights of Gram Swaraj Sammelan," *Janata* 34, no. 4 (25 February): 4.

Blair, Harry. 1980. "Rising Kulaks and Backward Classes in Bihar: Social Change in the Late 1970s." *Economic and Political Weekly* 15, no. 2 (12 January): 64–74.

———. 1984. "Structural Change, the Agricultural Sector, and Politics in Bihar." In *State Politics in Contemporary India: Crisis or Continuity?*, edited by John R. Wood, 197–228. Boulder, Colo., and London: Westview Press.

Bloch, Marc. 1953. *The Historian's Craft*. Translated by Peter Pulmain. New York: Alfred A. Knopf.

Bondurant, Joan V. 1965. *Conquest of Violence: The Gandhian Philosophy of Conflict*. Rev. ed. Berkeley and Los Angeles: University of California Press.

Bose, Nirmal Kumar. 1953. *My Days with Gandhi*. Calcutta: Nishana.

Bourdieu, Pierre. 1977. *Outline of a Theory of Practice*. Translated by Richard Nice. Cambridge: Cambridge University Press.

Brannigan, Augustine. 1981. *The Social Basis of Scientific Discoveries*. Cambridge: Cambridge University Press.

Brass, Paul. 1983. *Caste, Faction and Party in Indian Politics*. Vol. 1, *Faction and Party*. Delhi: Chanakya Publications.

———. 1985. *Caste, Faction and Party*. Vol. 2, *Election Studies*. Delhi: Chanakya Publications.

Breman, Jan. 1985. *Of Peasants, Migrants and Paupers*. Delhi: Oxford University Press.

Broomfield, J. H. 1968. *Elite Conflict in a Plural Society: Twentieth-Century Bengal*. Berkeley and Los Angeles: University of California Press.

Brown, Judith M. 1972. *Gandhi's Rise to Power: Indian Politics 1915–1922*. Cambridge: Cambridge University Press.

Burman, Debajyoti. 1986. "Sister Nivedita and Indian Revolution." In *Nivedita Commemoration Volume*, edited by Amiya Kumar Majumdar, 195–204. Calcutta: Vivekananda Janmotsava Samiti.

Byres, Terrance J. 1988. "Charan Singh 1902–87: An Assessment." *Journal of Peasant Studies* 15: 139–89.

The Call. 1979. "Kulak Power." January: 5–7.

Campbell, Bruce F. 1980. *Ancient Wisdom Revived: A History of the Theosophical Movement*. Berkeley and Los Angeles: University of California Press.

Campbell, Donald T. 1986. "Science's Social System of Validity-Enhancing Collective Belief Change and the Problem of the Social Sciences." In *Metatheory in Social Science*, edited by Donald W. Fiske and Richard A. Shweder, 108–35. Chicago: University of Chicago Press.

Carpenter, Edward. 1921 [1889]. *Civilization, Its Causes and Cure.* New York: Scribner's Sons.

———. 1910. *From Adam's Peak to Elephanta.* London: Swan Sonnenschein.

———. 1914. *Intermediate Types Among Primitive Folk: A Study in Social Evolution.* London: G. Allen and Co.

Cashman, Richard I. 1975. *The Myth of the Lokamanya.* Berkeley and Los Angeles: University of California Press.

Chandra, Bipan. 1969. "Historians of Modern India and Communalism." In *Communalism and the Writing of Indian History,* edited by Romila Thapar, Harbans Mukhia, and Bipan Chandra, 36–57. Delhi: People's Publishing House.

———. 1984. *Communalism in Modern India.* New Delhi: Vikas.

———. 1985. *The Long-Term Dynamics of the Indian National Congress.* Presidential address, presented at the 46th session of the Indian History Congress, 27–29 December, Amristar.

Charlesworth, Neil. 1982. *British Rule and the Indian Economy 1800–1914.* London: Macmillan.

Chatterjee, Partha. 1984. "Gandhi and the Critique of Civil Society." In *Subaltern Studies III,* edited by Ranajit Guha, 153–95. Delhi: Oxford University Press.

———. 1986a. *Nationalist Thought and the Colonial World: A Derivative Discourse?* London: Zed.

———. 1986b. "Culture and Power in the Thought of Bankimchandra." In *Political Thought in Modern India,* edited by Thomas Pantham and Kenneth L. Deutsch, 67–91. New Delhi, Beverly Hills, and London: Sage.

Chaudhuri, Nirad. 1951. *The Autobiography of an Unknown Indian.* New York: Macmillan.

Chaudhury, D. S. 1981. *Emerging Rural Leadership in an Indian State.* Delhi and Rohtak: Mantan.

Chitta Ranjan, C. N. 1974. "Gandhi and 'Gandhian' J.P." *Mainstream* 13, no. 5 (5 October): 10–12.

———. 1981. "The Revivalist Menace." *Mainstream* 20, no. 8 (24 October): 1–3.

———. 1982. "BJP: Groping in the Dark." *Mainstream* 22, no. 11 (4 September): 1–3.

Christy, Arthur. 1932. *The Orient in American Transcendentalism.* New York: Columbia University Press.

Church, Roderick. 1984. "Conclusion: The Pattern of State Politics in Indira Gandhi's India." In *State Politics in Contemporary India,* edited by John R. Wood, 229–50. Boulder, Colo., and London: Westview Press.

Cleghorn, B. 1977. "Leadership of the All-India Mahasabha 1920–39." In *Leadership in South Asia,* edited by B. N. Pandey, 395–425. New Delhi: Vikas Publishing House.

Clifford, James. 1983. "On Ethnographic Authority." *Representations* 1: 118–46.

———. 1986. "Introduction." In *Writing Culture: The Poetics and Politics of Ethnography*, edited by James Clifford and George E. Marcus, 1–26. Berkeley and Los Angeles: University of California Press.

———. 1986. "On Ethnographic Allegory." In *Writing Culture: The Poetics and Politics of Ethnography*, edited by James Clifford and George E. Marcus, 98–121. Berkeley and Los Angeles: University of California Press.

Cohen, Abner. 1974. *Two-Dimensional Man*. Berkeley and Los Angeles: University of California Press.

Cohn, Bernard. 1968. "Notes on the History of the Study of Indian Society and Culture." In *Structure and Change in Indian Society*, edited by Milton Singer and Bernard Cohn, 3–28. Chicago: Aldine.

———. 1989. "Cloth, Clothes, and Colonialism: India in the 19th Century." In *Cloth in Human Experience*, edited by Annette Weiner and Jane Schneider. Washington: Smithsonian Institution Press.

Collins, H. M. 1981. "The Core-Set in Modern Science." *History of Science* 19: 6–19.

———. 1982. "Tacit Knowledge and Scientific Networks." In *Science in Context*, edited by Barry Barnes and David Edge, 44–64. Cambridge, Mass.: MIT Press.

Contursi, Janet. 1987. Personal communication.

Cooter, Roger. 1984. *The Cultural Meaning of Popular Science*. Cambridge: Cambridge University Press.

Crapanzano, Vincent. 1986. "Hermes' Dilemma: The Making of Subversion in Ethnographic Description." In *Writing Culture: The Poetics and Politics of Ethnography*, edited by James Clifford and George E. Marcus, 51–76. Berkeley and Los Angeles: University of California Press.

Dagli, Vadilal, ed. 1976. *Khadi and Village Industries in the Indian Economy*. Bombay: Commerce Publications.

Dalton, Dennis. 1986. "The Ideology of Sarvodaya: Concepts of Politics and Power in Indian Political Thought." In *Political Thought in Modern India*, edited by Thomas Pantham and Kenneth L. Deutsch, 275–96. New Delhi, Beverly Hills, and London: Sage.

Dar, S. L. and S. Somaskandan. 1966. *History of the Banaras Hindu University*. Vol. 1. Varanasi: Banaras Hindu University Press.

Das, Amitananda. 1979. *Foundations of Gandhian Economics*. Bombay: Allied.

Das, Arvind Narayan. 1974. "Misleading Quiet." *Economic and Political Weekly* 9, no. 31 (3 August): 1223–24.

———. 1974a. "Revolt in Slow Motion." *Economic and Political Weekly* 9, no. 50 (14 December): 2049–51.

———. 1979. *Does Bihar Show the Way?* Calcutta: Research India Publications.

Dasgupta, Santwana. 1986. "The Sociological Views of Sister Nivedita." In *Nivedita Commemoration Volume*, edited by Amiya Kumar Majumdar, 102–24. Calcutta: Vivekananda Janmotsava Samiti.

Deshmukh, Nana. 1979. *RSS, Victim of Slander*. New Delhi: Vision Books.

Deshpande, Anjali. 1981. "Hindu Manch: Challenge to Secularism." *Mainstream* 20, no. 8 (24 October): 33–34.

Devadoss, T. S. 1974. *Sarvodaya and the Problem of Political Sovereignty.* Madras: University of Madras.

Devanesen, Chandran D. S. 1969. *The Making of the Mahatma.* New Delhi: Orient Longman.

Devdutt. 1981. "The BJP and Gandhian Socialism: A Case of Ideology-transplant." *Gandhi Marg* 3: 200–13.

———. 1984. "Vinoba and the Gandhian Tradition." In *Vinoba: The Spirtual Revolutionary,* edited by R. R. Diwakar and Mahendra Agrawal, 166–81. New Delhi: Gandhi Peace Foundation.

Diamond, Stanley. 1964. "What History Is." In *Process and Pattern in Culture,* edited by Robert A. Manners, 29–46. Chicago: Aldine.

Dirks, Nicholas. 1987. *The Hollow Crown.* Cambridge: Cambridge University Press.

Dixit, Prabha. 1986. "The Ideology of Hindu Nationalism." In *Political Thought in Modern India,* edited by Thomas Pantham and Kenneth L. Deutsch, 122–41. New Delhi, Beverly Hills, and London: Sage.

Duff, Alexander. 1840. *India and India Missions.* 2d. ed. Edinburgh: John Johnstone.

Dumont, Louis. 1970. *Religion/Politics and History in India.* Paris and The Hague: Mouton Publishers.

Durkheim, Emile. 1938 [1895]. *Rules of Sociological Method.* Chicago: University of Chicago Press.

Dutt, R. C. 1981. *Socialism of Jawaharlal Nehru.* New Delhi: Abhinav Publications.

Eastern Economist. 1978. "Farmers on Fire." Vol. 70, no. 16 (21 April): 775–76.

Economic and Political Weekly. 1978. "Farmers' Agitation." Vol. 13, no. 17 (29 April): 717–18.

———. 1984. "Editorial: Unlearnt Lessons of 1970." Vol. 18, no. 20–21 (19–26 May): 826–28.

Elkana, Yehuda. 1981. "A Programmatic Attempt at an Anthropology of Knowledge." In *Sciences and Cultures,* edited by Everett Mendelsohn and Yehuda Elkana, 1–76. Dordrecht: D. Reidel.

Erikson, Erik H. 1969. *Gandhi's Truth.* New York: W. W. Norton.

Evans-Pritchard, E. E. 1940. *The Nuer.* Oxford: Clarendon Press.

Fera, Ivan. 1985. "A City Aflame." *Illustrated Weekly of India* 106, no. 1 (12 May): 14–15.

Fischer, Louis. 1950. *The Life of Mahatma Gandhi.* New York: Harper and Row.

Fisher, Margaret W., and Joan V. Bondurant. 1956. *Indian Approaches to a Socialist Society.* Indian Press Digests, Monograph Series, no. 2. University of California, Berkeley.

Fox, Richard G. 1967. "Resiliency and Change in the Indian Caste System: The Umar of U. P." *The Journal of Asian Studies* 26: 575–88.

————. 1970. "Avatars of Indian Research." *Comparative Studies in Society and History* 12: 59–72.

————. 1984. "British Colonialism and Punjabi Labor." In *Labor in the Capitalist World Economy*, edited by Charles Bergquist, 107–34. Beverly Hills: Sage.

————. 1984a. "Urban Class and Communal Consciousness in Colonial Punjab: The Genesis of India's Intermediate Regime." *Modern Asian Studies* 18: 459–89.

————. 1985. *Lions of the Punjab: Culture in the Making.* Berkeley and Los Angeles: University of California Press.

Foxe, Barbara. 1975. *Long Journey Home: A Biography of Margaret Noble (Nivedita).* London: Rider.

Frank, Robert G., Jr. 1980. *Harvey and the Oxford Physiologists.* Berkeley and Los Angeles: University of California Press.

Frankel, Francine. 1978. *India's Political Economy, 1947–1977.* Princeton: Princeton University Press.

French, Harold W. 1974. *The Swan's Wide Waters.* Port Washington, N.Y.: Kennikat.

Galanter, Marc. 1984. *Competing Equalities: Law and the Backward Classes in India.* Delhi: Oxford University Press.

Gandhi, Mahatma [Mohandas Karamchand]. 1984. *All Men Are Brothers.* Compiled and edited by Krishna Kripalani. New York: Continuum.

Gandhi, Mohandas Karamchand. 1938. [1909]. *Hind Swaraj or Indian Home Rule.* Ahmedabad: Navajivan Publishing House.

————. 1955. *Ashram Observances in Action.* Translated by Valji Govindji Desai. Ahmedabad: Navajivan Publishing House.

————. 1957 [1929]. *An Autobiography: The Story of My Experiments with Truth.* Translated by Mahadev Desai. Boston: Beacon Press.

————. 1958–83. *Collected Works of Mahatma Gandhi.* 89 vols. Delhi: Publications Division, Ministry of Information and Broadcasting, Government of India.

————. 1965. *My Picture of Free India.* Compiled and edited by Anand T. Hingorani. Bombay: Bharatiya Vidya Bhavan.

————. 1972 [1928]. *Satyagraha in South Africa.* Translated by V. G. Desai. Ahmedabad: Navajivan Publishing House.

Gandhi, P. C. 1978. "Job Reservations in Bihar." *Times of India* 20 April: 6.

Gandhi Peace Foundation, Gandhi Smarak Nidhi, Sarva Seva Sangh, and AVARD [Association of Voluntary Agencies for Rural Development]. [c. February 1986]. *The Witch Hunt.* Delhi: Roopak.

————. [c. August 1986]. *The Witch Hunt Continues.* Delhi: Paragon.

Gandhi Smarak Nidhi. 1976. *In Memory of Mahatma Gandhi: 27 Years of Gandhi Smarak Nidhi.* New Delhi: Gandhi Smarak Nidhi.

Geertz, Clifford. 1983. " 'From the Native's Point of View': On the Nature of Anthropological Understanding." In *Local Knowledge*, 55–70. New York: Basic Books.

————. 1985. "Waddling In." *Times Literary Supplement* 7 June: 623–24.

Ghose, Aurobindo. 1972. *Bande Mataram: Early Political Writings I. Vol. 1 of Sri Aurobindo Birth Centenary Library.* Pondicherry: Sri Aurobindo Ashram.

Giddens, Anthony. 1984. *The Constitution of Society.* Berkeley and Los Angeles: University of California Press.

Gill, Sucha Singh, and K. C. Singhal. 1984. "Punjab Farmers' Agitation." *Economic and Political Weekly* 19, no. 40 (6 October): 1728–32.

Godbole, L. N. 1981. "Beware of BJP." *Organiser* 32, no. 37 (8 February): 7.

Golwalkar, M. S. 1966. *Bunch of Thoughts.* Bangalore: Vikrama Prakashan Chamarajpet.

————. 1974 [1949]. *Spot Lights.* Bangalore: Sahitya Sindu.

Gould, Stephen Jay. 1980. *Hen's Teeth and Horse's Toes.* New York and London: W. W. Norton.

Gouldner, Alvin. 1980. *The Two Marxisms.* New York: The Seabury Press.

Government of India. 1951. *First Five-Year Plan.* New Delhi: Manager of Publications.

————. 1956. *Second Five-Year Plan.* New Delhi: India Planning Commission.

————. 1961. *Third Five-Year Plan.* New Delhi: India Planning Commission.

————. 1969. *Fourth Five-Year Plan.* New Delhi: India Planning Commission.

————. 1981. *Lok Sabha Debates, Sixth Session.* Vol. 18, no. 10 (28 August).

————. 1984. *Lok Sabha Debates, Seventh Session.* Vol. 49, no. 10 (3 August).

————. Khadi and Village Industries Commission. 1967. *Khadi and Village Industries: A New Orientation.* Publication place missing [Khadi and Village Industries Commission].

————. Khadi and Village Industries Commission. 1968. *Report.* Publication place missing [Khadi and Village Industries Commission].

————. Khadi and Village Industries Commission. 1980. *Annual Report 1978/79.* Publication place missing [Khadi and Village Industries Commission].

————. Khadi and Village Industries Commission. 1981. *Annual Report 1979/1980.* Publication place missing [Khadi and Village Industries Commission].

————. Khadi and Village Industries Commission. 1982. *Annual Report 1980/81.* Publication place missing [Khadi and Village Industries' Commission].

————. Ministry of Agriculture and Irrigation. 1978. *Report of the Committee on Panchayati Raj Institutions.* New Delhi.

Green, Martin. 1983. *Tolstoy and Gandhi: Men of Peace.* New York: Basic Books.

Greenblatt, Stephen. 1986. "Fiction and Friction." In *Reconstructing Individualism,* edited by Thomas C. Heller, Morton Sosna, and David E. Wellbery, 30–52. Stanford: Stanford University Press.

Gulati, Hans Raj. 1974. "Jayaprakash and CPI." *Janata* 29, no. 36 (20 October): 5–6.

Gurjar, Rajan. 1985. "Elitist Agitation." In *Dynamics of Reservation Policy*, edited by Haroobhai Mehta and Hasmukh Patel, 153–63. New Delhi: Patriot Publishers.

Gusfield, Joseph. 1971. "Economic Development as a Modern Utopia." In *Aware of Utopia*, edited by David W. Plath, 75–85. Urbana: University of Illinois Press.

Hardiman, David. 1981. *Peasant Nationalists of Gujarat, Kheda District 1917–1934*. Delhi: Oxford University Press.

Hay, Stephen N. 1970. *Asian Ideas of East and West: Tagore and His Critics in Japan, China, and India*. Cambridge: Harvard University Press.

———. 1978. "Jaina Goals and Discipline in Gandhi's Pursuit of Swaraj." In *Rule, Protest, Identity: Aspects of Modern South Asia*, edited by Peter Robb and David Taylor, 120–31. London: Curzon Press.

———. 1988. "Jain Influences on Gandhi's Early Thought." Typescript.

Henningham, Stephen. 1976. "The Social Setting of the Champaran Satyagraha: The Challenge to an Alien Elite." *Indian Economic and Social History Review* 13:59–73.

Hindustan Times. 1983. "Boycott Commission." 31 July: 8.

———. 1986. "Bureaucratic Red Tape." 4 August: 8.

———. 1987. "Panel Plea to Take Over Gandhi Museum." 4 February: 4.

Hunt, James D. 1978. *Gandhi in London*. New Delhi: Promilla.

Illustrated Weekly of India. 1980. "Should India Be a Hindu State?" Vol. 101, no. 35 (31 August): 20–23.

India Today. 1978. "Caste Conflict." 15 April: 15–16.

———. 1981. "Kisan Rally: A Show of Strength." 15 April: 42–43.

———. 1985. "A Historic Mandate." 15 January: 16–29.

———. 1985. "Out in the Wilderness." 31 January: 32–39.

———. 1986. "Veering Right." 31 March: 19.

———. 1986. "Fighting Back." 15 April: 14–15.

———. 1986. "Militant Revivalism." 31 May: 30–39.

———. 1986. "Militancy on the Move." 15 October: 32–36.

———. 1986. "A Wounded City." 30 November: 77–79.

———. 1986. "Area of Darkness." 31 December: 40–43.

———. 1987 "Danger Signals." 15 June: 17, 19.

———. 1987. "A Pagan Sacrifice." 15 October: 58–60.

———. 1987. "Militant Defiance." 31 October: 18–20.

Indian Sociologist. London [1905–9] and Paris [1909–14, 1920–22].

Irschick, Eugene F. 1986. "Gandhian Non-violent Protest: Rituals of Avoidance or Rituals of Confrontation?" *Economic and Political Weekly* 21, no. 29 (19 July): 1276–85.

Isaac, Jeffrey C. 1987. *Power and Marxist Theory: A Realist Approach*. Ithaca and London: Cornell University Press.

Iyer, Raghavan, ed. 1986. *The Moral and Political Writings of Mahatma Gandhi*. Vol. 1, *Civilization, Politics, and Religion*. Oxford: Clarendon Press.

Jagannatham, Chundi. 1979. "RSS, Janata Party and the Nation." *Janata* 34, no. 15 (20 May): 6–9.

James, William. 1927. *The Will To Believe*. New York: Longmans, Green.

Janata. 1974. "CPI Views J.P.'s Struggle As Right Reaction's Conspiracy." Vol. 29, no. 28 (15 August): 42.

———. 1975. "Socio-Economic Programme: Draft for Discussion." Vol. 30, no. 14 (May Day Number): 23–30.

———. 1975. "The J.P. Movement as Government Sees It." Vol. 30, no. 30 (28 September): 7–11.

———. 1976. "Emergence of An Alternative: Editorial." Vol. 31, no. 4 (30 May): 1–12.

———. 1979. "RSS and Janata Party." Vol. 34, no. 10 (8 April): 4.

———. 1979. "JP on RSS." Vol. 34, no. 14 (13 May): 2.

Jarvie, I. C. 1974. *The Revolution in Anthropology*. Chicago: Henry Regnery.

Jeffrey, Robin. 1986. *What's Happening to India?* New York: Holmes and Meier.

Jha, Prem Shankar. 1978. "Bihar's Dangerous Venture: Editorial." *Times of India* 30 March: 6.

———. 1980. *India: A Political Economy of Stagnation*. Bombay: Oxford University Press.

Johnson, David L. 1981. "Religious Change, National Goals and the Janata Party." In *Religion in Modern India*, edited by Robert D. Baird, 481–97. New Delhi: Manohar.

Jones, Kenneth W. 1976. *Arya Dharm: Hindu Consciousness in 19th-Century Punjab*. Berkeley and Los Angeles: University of California Press.

Joshi, P. C. 1979. "The New Class in the Countryside." *Mainstream* 17, no. 51 (18 August): 9–10.

Kahn, Joel. 1980. *Minangkabau Social Formations: Indonesian Peasants and the World Economy*. Cambridge: Cambridge University Press.

Kala, S. C. 1975. "Slow Start and Many Pitfalls: J.P.'s Movement in U.P." *Times of India* 8 January: 4.

Kalecki, Michael. 1972. *Selected Essays on the Economic Growth of the Socialist and the Mixed Economy*. Cambridge: Cambridge University Press.

Kantowsky, Detlef. 1980. *Sarvodaya, the Other Development*. New Delhi: Vikas.

Khanolkar, S. S. 1980. "RSS and Hindu Mahasabha." *Mainstream* 18, no. 21 (19 January): 13–14.

Kihlberg, Mats. 1976. *The Panchayati Raj of India: Debate in a Developing Country*. New Delhi: Young Asia.

King, Martin Luther. 1958. *Stride Toward Freedom*. New York: Harper.

Kopf, David. 1969. *British Orientalism and the Bengal Renaissance*. Berkeley and Los Angeles: University of California Press.

———. 1979. *The Brahmo Samaj and the Shaping of the Modern Indian Mind*. Princeton: Princeton University Press.

Krishnan, N. K. 1974. "Undertones of Fascism." *Link* 16, no. 45 (16 June): 11–12.

Kroeber, A. L. 1952. "The Superorganic." In *The Nature of Culture*, 22–51. Chicago: University of Chicago Press.

Kuhn, Thomas. 1970. *The Structure of Scientific Revolutions*. 2d ed. Chicago: University of Chicago Press.

Kumar, Ravinder. 1968. *Western India in the Nineteenth Century*. London: Routledge and Kegan Paul.

Langham, Ian. 1981. *The Building of British Social Anthropology*. Dordrecht: D. Reidel.

Lannoy, Richard. 1971. *The Speaking Tree*. London: Oxford University Press.

Larouie, Abdallah. 1976. *The Crisis of the Arab Intellectual: Traditionalism or Historicism?* Translated by Diarmid Cammell. Berkeley: University of California Press.

Latour, Bruno, and Steve Woolgar. 1979. *Laboratory Life: The Social Construction of Scientific Facts*. Beverly Hills and London: Sage.

Link. 1975. "Breaking Up Conspiratorial Forces." Vol. 17, no. 48 (13 July): 10–17.

———. 1981. "Appropriating the Gandhian Trademark." Vol. 23, no. 45 (21 June): 16–18.

Mackenzie, Norman, and Jeanne Mackenzie. 1977. *The Fabians*. New York: Simon and Schuster.

Mainstream. 1974. "Editorial: Whom Does He Serve?" Vol. 12, no. 26 (23 February): 4–6.

———. 1975. "J.P.'s Identity Card: Editorial." Vol. 13, no. 27 (8 March): 4–7.

———. 1975. "Jana Sangh: Old Wine in New Bottle." Vol. 13, no. 28 (15 March): 6.

———. 1981. "BJP: Quest for Respectability." Vol. 19, no. 18 (3 January): 3–4.

Majumdar, Biman Behari. 1986. "Social and Political Ideas of Sister Nivedita." In *Nivedita Commemoration Volume*, edited by Amiya Kumar Majumdar, 52–66. Calcutta: Vivekananda Janmotsava Samiti.

Majumdar, Modhumita. 1986. "Kudal Commission." *Hindustan Times* 30 July: 9.

Malinowski, Bronislaw. 1939. "The Group and the Individual in Functional Analysis." *The American Journal of Sociology* 44: 938–64.

———. 1944. *A Scientific Theory of Culture*. Chapel Hill: University of North Carolina Press.

Mannheim, Karl. [1936]. *Ideology and Utopia*. Translated by Louis Wirth and Edward Shils. New York and London: Harcourt Brace Jovanovich.

Manthan. 1982. Special issue on *Quest for Equality: Reservation-Policy*. Vol. 4: 5–9.

———. 1984. "The All-India Workshop on 'Development and Grassroot Experiment.'" Vol. 6: 10–103.

———. 1986. "Editorial, Wanted: A Quiet Moral Revolution." Vol. 8: 3–8.

———. 1987. "On Strengthening the Movement for Constructive Work in India." Report on a workshop held in New Delhi 1–3 March 1985. Vol. 8: 1–100.

Marcovits, Claude. 1985. *Indian Business and Nationalist Politics 1931–1939*. Cambridge: Cambridge University Press.

Marcus, George E., and Dick Cushman. 1982. "Ethnographies as Texts." *Annual Review of Anthropology* 11: 25–69.

Marcus, George E., and Michael M. J. Fischer. 1986. *Anthropology as Cultural Critique*. Berkeley and Los Angeles: University of California Press.

Marx, Karl. 1967 [1867]. *Capital*. Edited and translated by Samuel Moore and Edward Aveling. New York: International Publishers.

Mathur, Girish. 1981. "A Republic in Rural Revolt." *Illustrated Weekly of India* 102, no. 3 (18 January): 8–13.

Mathur, J. S. n.d. *Industrial Civilisation and Gandhian Economics*. Allahabad: Pustakayan.

Mathur, M. V., and Iqbal Narain, eds. 1969. *Seminar on Panchayati Raj, Planning and Democracy, Jaipur, 1964*. Bombay: Asia.

Mayer, P. B. 1984. "Congress (I), Emergency (I): Interpreting Indira Gandhi's India." *The Journal of Commonwealth and Comparative Politics* 22: 129–50.

Mazzini, Giuseppe. 1907. *The Duties of Man and Other Essays*. London: J. M. Dent.

Mead, Margaret. 1931 [1928]. "The Role of the Individual in Samoan Culture." In *Source Book in Anthropology*, edited by A. L. Kroeber and T. T. Waterman, 542–62. New York: Harcourt, Brace.

———. 1953 [1930]. *Growing Up in New Guinea*. New York: Mentor.

———. 1962. *Coming of Age in Samoa*. New York: Mentor.

Mehta, Balwantray. 1969. "Reflections from the Chair." In *Seminar on Panchayati Raj, Planning and Democracy, Jaipur, 1964*, edited by M. V. Mathur and Iqbal Narain, 78–93. Bombay: Asia.

Mehta, Vaikunth L. 1964. *Decentralised Economic Development*. Bombay: Khadi and Village Industries Commission.

Mintz, Sidney. 1977. "The So-Called World System: Local Initiative and Local Response." *Dialectical Anthropology* 2: 253–70.

Mishra, Dina Nath. 1980. *RSS: Myth and Reality*. Ghaziabad: Vikas.

Mishra, Girish. 1974. "The Company J.P. Keeps." *New Age* 22, no. 47 (24 November): 8–9.

Mishra, R. N. 1972. *Bhoodan Movement in India*. New Delhi: S. Chand.

Mitra, Ashok. 1977. *Terms of Trade and Class Relations*. London: Frank Cass.

Mohan, Braj. 1979. "The Kisan Movement." *Illustrated Weekly of India* 100, no. 4 (28 January): 26–29.

Mohen, Surendra. 1974. "People's Struggle Without Precedent." *Janata* 29, no. 28 (15 August): 21–23.

Mohiddin, Ahmed. 1981. *African Socialism in Two Countries*. Totowa, N. J.: Barnes and Noble.

Morgan, Arthur E. 1944. *Edward Bellamy*. New York: Columbia University Press.

Mukherjee, Aditya. 1986. "The Indian Capitalist Class: Aspects of Its Economic, Political, and Ideological Development in the Colonial Period 1930–1947." In *Situating Indian History,* edited by Sabyasachi Bhattacharya and Romila Thapar, 240–87. New Delhi: Oxford University Press.

Müller, Max. 1883. *India: What Can It Teach Us?* New York: Funk and Wagnalls.

Munslow, Barry. 1986. "Introduction." In *Africa: Problems in the Transition to Socialism,* edited by Barry Munslow, 1–39. London: Zed Books.

Nandy, Ashis. 1980. *At the Edge of Psychology.* Delhi: Oxford University Press.

———. 1983. *The Intimate Enemy: Loss and Recovery of Self Under Colonialism.* Delhi: Oxford University Press.

Narain, Iqbal. 1969. "The Emerging Concept." In *Seminar on Panchayati Raj, Planning and Democracy, Jaipur, 1964,* edited by M. V. Mathur and Iqbal Narain, 19–34. Bombay: Asia.

Narayan, Jayaprakash. 1974. "JP On His Bihar Movement." *Janata* 29, no. 24 (21 July): 3–4.

———. 1975. "Jayaprakash Narayan Replies." *Illustrated Weekly of India* 96, no. 17 (27 April): 5.

———. 1977. *Prison Diary 1975.* Bombay: Popular Prakashan.

———. 1978. *Towards Total Revolution,* edited by Brahamanand. 4 vols. Bombay: Popular Prakashan.

———. 1979. *May You Fulfill My Dream.* Translation of Hindi speech given at RSS camp in Patna, 3 November 1977. Bangalore: Jagarana Prakashana.

———. 1980. *A Revolutionary's Quest: Selected Writings of Jayaprakash Narayan,* edited by Bimal Prasad. Delhi: Oxford University Press.

Nargolkar, Vasant. 1974. "Satyagraha and Sarvoydaya." *Janata* 29, no. 28: 9–10.

———. 1975. *JP's Crusade for Revolution.* New Delhi: S. Chand.

———. 1978. "Gandhi, Lohia, and Deendayal." In *Gandhi, Lohia, and Deendayal,* edited by P. Parameswaran, 1–23. New Delhi: Deendayal Research Institute.

New Age. 1975. "JP's Movement Strengthens Semi-feudal Bondage." Vol. 23, no. 17 (27 April): 5.

New York Times. 1974. "5 Dead in Student Riots in Indian State Capital." 19 March: 6.

———. 1974. "10 Indians are Slain at Bihar Protests; 22 Dead in 3 Days." 20 March: 9.

———. 1974. "Quiet Voice of the Past Stirs India." 4 November: 6.

———. 1974. "Tear Gas Quells Protest in Bihar." 5 November: 5.

———. 1974. "Indian Parliament Holds a Stormy Debate on Food and Narayan." 12 November: 17.

———. 1975. "Leaders of India Irate at Killing." 5 January: 8.

———. 1975. "Foes Intensify Drive Against Mrs. Gandhi." 18 February: 3.

———. 1975. "Ousted Aide Sees India in Jeopardy." 6 March: 11.

———. 1975. "Hero of India's Independence." 7 March: 2.

———. 1975. "100,000 March Through New Delhi in Anti-Government Protest." 7 March: 2.

———. 1975. "Mrs. Gandhi Asks Support As Rivals Demand She Quit." 14 June: 1.

———. 1975. "Mrs. Gandhi's Foes Open National Drive to Oust Her." 15 June: 3.

———. 1975. "Many Opponents of Mrs. Gandhi Arrested in India." 26 June: 1.

———. 1975. "Many in India Doubt Charges of Plot." 28 June: 8.

———. 1975. "One Man's Call to India's Opposition: Why It Led to Crackdown." 2 July: 8.

———. 1977. "New India Bloc Picks Desai To Be Premier." 24 March: 1.

———. 1980. "A Village in India Prospers Because of Reformer's Zeal." 1 December: 14.

———. 1986. "Police in India Fire on Rioters." 15 July: sect. 1, 8.

———. 1986. "4 Die as Hindus and Indian Police Clash." 27 July: sect. 1, 3.

Nivedita, Sister [Margaret Noble]. 1968. *The Complete Works of Sister Nivedita*. Calcutta: Ramakrishna Sarada Mission.

Oomen, T. K. 1972. *Charisma, Stability, and Change*. New Delhi: Thomson.

Organiser. 1974. "How JP had his way in spite of Vinobaji's dilatory tactics." 27 July: 3.

———. 1974. "J.P. has become the symbol of people's revolt, says Atalji." 17 August: 3.

———. 1974. "Chhatra Shakti." 16 November: 3.

———. 1975. "Of 'Targets' and 'Rehearsals': Editorial." 18 January: 3.

———. 1975. "When JP Visited Bardoli." 8 February: 7.

———. 1975. "JP Condemns Motivated Move to Ban the RSS." 22 February: 3.

———. 1975. "Balasaheb asks PM to Shed Bias Against RSS." 8 March: 7.

———. 1975. "Right to Disobey and Right to Revolt." 8 March: 4.

———. 1981. "BJP Has Arrived." 11 January: 2.

———. 1981. "Gandhi and BJP: Two Emanations of the Same Spirit." 25 October: 15.

———. 1985. "BJP Has Retained Its Base." 27 January: 1.

Ortner, Sherry. 1984. "Theory in Anthropology Since the Sixties." *Comparative Studies in Society and History* 26: 126–66.

———. n.d. "Patterns of History: Cultural Scenarios in the Foundings of Sherpa Religious Institutions." Typescript, to appear in *Symbolism Through Time*, edited by E. Ohnuki-Tierney.

Ostergaard, Geoffrey. 1984. "Vinoba's 'Gradualist' Versus Western 'Immediatist' Anarchism." In *Vinoba: The Spiritual Revolutionary*, edited by R. R. Diwakar and Mahendra Agrawal, 75–96. New Delhi: Gandhi Peace Foundation.

————. 1985. *Nonviolent Revolution in India*. New Delhi: Gandhi Peace Foundation.

Ostergaard, Geoffrey N., and Melville Currell. 1971. *The Gentle Anarchists*. Oxford: Clarendon.

Overing, Joanna. 1985. "Introduction." In *Reason and Morality*, edited by Joanna Overing, 1–28. London and New York: Tavistock Publications.

Pantham, Thomas. 1986. "Introduction: For the Study of Modern Indian Political Thought." In *Political Thought in Modern India*, edited by Thomas Pantham and Kenneth L. Deutsch, 9–16. New Delhi and Beverly Hills: Sage.

Paranjape, H. K. 1964. *Jawaharlal Nehru and the Planning Commission*. New Delhi: Institute of Public Administration.

Prasad, Negeshwar. 1984. "Vinoba's Consensual Revolution: A Critical Appreciation." In *Vinoba: The Spiritual Revolutionary*, edited by R. R. Diwakar and Mahendra Agrawal, 97–112. New Delhi: Gandhi Peace Foundation.

Pratt, Mary Louise. 1986. "Fieldwork in Common Places." In *Writing Culture: The Poetics and Politics of Ethnography*, edited by James Clifford and George E. Marcus, 27–50. Berkeley and Los Angeles: University of California Press.

Pulparampil, J. 1975. "Revolution J.P. Style." *Social Action* 25, no. 2 (April–June): 178–82.

Rabinow, Paul. 1986. "Representations Are Social Facts: Modernity and Post-Modernity in Anthropology." In *Writing Culture: The Poetics and Politics of Ethnography*, edited by James Clifford and George E. Marcus, 234–61. Berkeley and Los Angeles: University of California Press.

Radin, Paul. 1933. *The Method and Theory of Ethnology*. New York and London: McGraw-Hill.

Raghava Rao, D. V. 1980. *Panchayats and Rural Development*. New Delhi: Ashish.

Raghavan, T. C. A. 1983. "Origins and Development of Hindu Mahasabha Ideology: The Call of V. D. Savarkar and Bhai Parmanand." *Economic and Political Weekly* 18, no. 15 (9 April): 595–600.

Raj, K. N. 1973. "The Politics and Economics of 'Intermediate Regimes.' " *Economic and Political Weekly* 8, no. 27 (7 July): 1189–98.

Raje, Sudhakar, ed. 1978. *Destination*. New Delhi: Deendayal Research Institute.

Ram Reddy, G. 1974. *Panchayat Raj and Rural Development in Andhra Pradesh, India*. Ithaca: Cornell University Press.

Ramachandran, G. 1974. "Jayaprakash Narayan's New Role." *Gandhi Marg* 18: 139–42.

Rao, V. K. R. V. 1979. "Sarvodaya, Trusteeship, and Gandhian Socialism." In *Gandhi in Today's India*, edited by B. C. Das and G. P. Misra, 167–80. New Delhi: Ashish Publishing House.

————. 1982. *Indian Socialism Retrospect and Prospect*. New Delhi: Concept.

Redfield, Robert. 1957. *The Primitive World and Its Transformation*. Ithaca: Great Seal Books.

Raymond, Lizelle. 1953. *The Dedicated: A Biography of Nivedita*. New York: John Day.

Richards, John. n.d. "Wallerstein and South Asia." Typescript.

Ricoeur, Paul. 1965. *History and Truth*. Translated by Charles A. Kelbley. Evanston: Northwestern University Press.

————. 1986. *Lectures on Ideology and Utopia*. Edited by George H. Taylor. New York: Columbia University Press.

Risley, Sir Herbert Hope. 1915. *The People of India*. London: W. Thacker and Company.

Rosaldo, Renato, 1986. "From the Door of His Tent: the Fieldworker and the Inquisitor." In *Writing Culture: The Poetics and Politics of Ethnography*, edited by James Clifford and George E. Marcus, 77–97. Berkeley and Los Angeles: University of California Press.

Roseberry, William. 1982. "Balinese Cockfights and the Seduction of Anthropology." *Social Research* 49: 1013–28.

Rothermund, Indira. 1984. "Vinoba: 'The Reluctant Leader.' " In *Vinoba: The Spiritual Revolutionary*, edited by R. R. Diwakar and Mahendra Agrawal, 113–21. New Delhi: Gandhi Peace Foundation.

Routh, Jane. 1977. "A Reputation Made: Lucien Goldmann." In *The Sociology of Literature: Theoretical Approaches*, edited by Jane Routh and Janet Wolff, 150–62. Sociological Review Monograph 25, University of Keele, U.K.

Roy, Ajit. 1981. "Farmers' Agitations: Tailing Behind Rural Rich." *Economic and Political Weekly* 16, no. 8 (21 February): 154–55.

Rudolph, Lloyd I., and Suzanne Hoeber Rudolph. 1967. *The Modernity of Tradition: Political Development in India*. Chicago: University of Chicago Press.

Rudwick, Martin J. S. 1985. *The Great Devonian Controversy*. Chicago and London: University of Chicago Press.

Ruskin, John. 1967. *Unto This Last*. Edited by Lloyd J. Hubenka. Lincoln and London: University of Nebraska Press.

Sachs, Karen. 1979. "Causality and Change on the Upper Nile." *American Ethnologist* 6: 437–48.

Sahlins, Marshall. 1976. *Culture and Practical Reason*. Chicago: University of Chicago Press.

————. 1981. *Historical Metaphors and Mythical Realities: Structure in the Early History of the Sandwich Islands Kingdom*. Ann Arbor: University of Michigan Press.

————. 1985. *Islands of History*. Chicago and London: University of Chicago Press.

Said, Edward. 1978. *Orientalism*. New York: Vintage Books.

Sampuranand. 1961. *Indian Socialism*. New York: Asia.

Sanghavi, N. H. 1977. "The Future of the R.S.S." *Janata* 32, no. 43: 10.

Sarkar, Sumit. 1973. *The Swadeshi Movement in Bengal, 1903–1908*. New Delhi: People's Publishing House.

———. 1976. "Logic of Gandhian Nationalism: Civil Disobedience and the Gandhi-Irwin Pact 1930–1931." *Indian Historical Review* 3: 114–46.

———. 1983. *"Popular" Movements and "Middle Class" Leadership in Late Colonial India: Perspectives and Problems of a "History from Below."* Calcutta and New Delhi: K. P. Bagchi.

Sayed, Ashraf. 1986. "Calling Out Army Overdue in Gujarat." *Times of India* 15 July: 5.

Scarfe, Allan, and Wendy Scarfe. 1975. *J.P.: His Biography*. New Delhi: Orient Longman.

Schwab, Raymond. 1984. *The Oriental Renaissance: Europe's Rediscovery of India and the East 1680–1880*. Translated by Gene Patterson-Black and Victor Reinking. New York: Columbia University Press.

Seal, Anil. 1970. *The Emergence of Indian Nationalism: Competition and Collaboration in the Later Nineteenth Century*. Cambridge: Cambridge University Press.

Secretary of State for India, United Kingdom. 1907. *Report and Minutes of Evidence of the Committee Appointed by the Secretary of State for India to Inquire into the Position of Indian Students in the United Kingdom*. London: Eyre and Spottiswoode.

Secular Democracy. 1982. "Fraud in Gandhi's Name?" No. 15: 23–30.

Senghor, Leopold Sedar. 1968. *On African Socialism*. Translated by Mercer Cook. New York: Frederick A. Praeger.

Seshadri, H. V. 1984. *Hindu Renaissance Under Way*. Bangalore: Jagarana Prakashana.

Sethi, J. D. 1975. "Jayaprakash Narayan and His Revolution." *Gandhi Marg* 19: 77–91.

———. 1979. *Gandhi Today*. 2d ed. Sahibabad: Vikas.

Shah, Kanti. 1979. *Vinoba: Life and Mission*. Varanasi: Sarva-Seva-Sangh-Prakashan.

Shakir, Moin, and Vanana Sonalkar. 1981. "Farmer's Agitation and Left." *Mainstream* 19, no. 23 (28 February): 11–13.

Shapin, Steven. 1979. "The Politics of Observation: Cerebral Anatomy and Social Interests in the Edinburgh Phrenology Debates." In *On the Margins of Science: The Social Construction of Rejected Knowledge*, edited by Roy Wallis, 139–78. Sociological Review Monograph 27, University of Keele, U. K.

———. 1982. "History of Science and Its Sociological Reconstructions." *History of Science* 20: 157–211.

Shapin, Steven, and Simon Schaffer. 1985. *Leviathan and the Air Pump*. Princeton: Princeton University Press.

Sharad, Onkar. 1972. *Lohia*. Delhi: UBS Publishers' Distributors.

Sharma, Narendra. 1981. "BJP's New Look." *Mainstream* 19, no. 19 (10 January): 5–6.

Sharp, Gene. 1979. *Gandhi as a Political Strategist.* Boston: Porter Sargent.

Shi, David E. 1985. *The Simple Life: Plain Living and High Thinking in American Culture.* New York and London: Oxford University Press.

Shiviah, M., K. V. Narayana Rao, L. S. N. Murty, and G. Mallikarjuniah. 1976. *Panchayati Raj: An Analytic Survey.* Rajendranagar, Hyderabad: National Institute of Community Development.

Singh, Jitendra. 1974. "Bihar Agitation: New Phase: Very Few Samitis Yet." *Times of India* 9 August: 4.

Singh, K. N. 1982. "The Bharatiya Janata Party." In *Political Socialization and Recruitment in the National Political Parties at the Muzaffarpur District Level,* edited by D. N. Mallik, N. K. P. Sinha, A. Sharma, R. Pandey, M. R. Kazimi, K. N. Singh, C. S. P. Thakur, and M. M. Sharma, 65–78. Muzaffarpur: University of Bihar Department of Political Science.

Singh, Karan. 1983. "Hindu Renaissance." *Seminar* 284 (April): 14–18.

———. 1984. "The Great Hindu Renaissance." *Illustrated Weekly of India* 105, no. 2 (8 January): 24–27.

Singh, Khuswant. 1975. "A New Wave from the Old India." *New York Times* 30 March: sect. 6, 15.

———. 1975. "'Total Revolution.'" *Illustrated Weekly of India* 96, no. 14: 6–15.

Singh, N. K. 1975. "JP and Jan Sangh." *Economic and Political Weekly* 10, no. 17 (26 April): 691–92.

Singh, Yogendra. 1969. *The Panchayati Raj of India.* New Delhi: Young Asia.

Sinha, Indradeep. 1974. "JP Unleashes Civil War Among Students." *New Age* 22, no. 31 (4 August): 8.

Sinha, Tarakeshwan. 1974. "Questions — JP Must Answer." *Mainstream* 13, no. 15 (14 December): 9–10.

Spodek, Howard. 1971. "On the Origins of Gandhi's Political Methodology: The Heritage of Kathiawad and Gujarat." *Journal of Asian Studies* 30: 361–72.

Srinivas, M. N. 1962. *Caste in Modern India.* Bombay: Asia.

Stokes, Eric. 1959. *The English Utilitarians and India.* Oxford: Oxford University Press.

Swan, Maureen. 1985. *Gandhi: The South African Experience.* Johannesburg: Ravan Press.

Tahmankar, D. V. 1956. *Lokamanya Tilak.* London: John Murray.

Tandon, Vishwanath. 1965. *The Social and Political Philosophy of Sarvodaya After Gandhiji.* Varanasi: Sarva Seva Sangh Prakashan.

———. 1984. "The Bhoodan-Gramdan Movement 1951–74 — A Review." In *Vinoba: The Spiritual Revolutionary,* edited by R. R. Diwakar and Mahendra Agrawal, 58–66. New Delhi: Gandhi Peace Foundation.

Tarde, Gabriel de. 1969. *On Communication and Social Influence; Selected Papers,* edited by Terry N. Clark. Chicago: University of Chicago Press.

Tayal, Maureen. 1978. "Indian Indentured Labour in Natal, 1890–1911." *Indian Economic and Social History Review* 14: 519–47.

Terdiman, Richard. 1985. *Discourse/Counter-Discourse: The Theory and Prac-*

tice of Symbolic Resistance in Nineteenth-Century France. Ithaca and London: Cornell University Press.

Thoreau, Henry David. 1968. *The Variorum Walden and the Variorum Civil Disobedience*. Annotated by Walter Harding. New York: Pocket Books.

Tilak, Bal Gangadhar. n.d. *His Writings and Speeches*. Madras: Ganesh and Co.

Times of India. 1974. "JP Charisma Works in Ballia." 10 December: 2.

———. 1975. "Seva Sangh 'Frozen' Till December." 15 March: 2.

———. 1975. "Split in SSS: Editorial." 15 March: 4.

———. 1975. "Approver Denies CBI Promised Pardon." 5 July: 5.

———. 1975. "Human Skulls Found in Anand Marg Offices." 6 July: 1.

———. 1978. "JP, Kripalani Unhurt at Patna Meeting." 13 March: 1.

———. 1978. "Stop to Critics: Editorial." 23 March: 6.

———. 1978. "Three Killed in Violent Clashes in Bihar Town." 1 April: 1.

———. 1978. "Violence Again Rocks Bihar on Job Quota." 7 April: 1.

———. 1978. "Bihar Job Quota Plan Runs into Trouble." 2 November: 1.

———. 1980. "Bharatiya Janata Party Born Out of Third Split." 7 April: 1.

———. 1980. "Nasik Farmers Court Mass Arrest." 18 November: 1.

———. 1980. "BJP for Economic Decentralisation." 25 December: 9.

———. 1981. "Take Over of Capital by Kisans." 17 February: 1.

———. 1981. "Soviet Action in Kabul Threat to India: BJP." 14 April: 1.

———. 1981. "Vajpayee for Review of Reservation Policy." 15 April: 1.

———. 1981. "BJP Against Class and Caste War." 26 April: 5.

———. 1985. "Editorial: A Cynical Ploy." 17 January: 8.

———. 1985. "BJP Abandons Gandhian Socialism." 10 October: 1.

———. 1985. "BJP's Volte-face on Gandhian Socialism." 13 October: 7.

———. 1985. "Vajpayee Denies Ideological Rift." 14 October: 1.

———. 1986. "Thousands of BJP Men Court Arrest." 17 June: 3.

———. 1986. Photograph of RSS peace marchers. 1 December: 1.

———. 1986. "Mobs Burn Houses, Shops in Delhi." 3 December: 1.

Tolstoy, Leo. [1908]. *Letter to a Hindu*. Classics of Nonviolence No. 3. London: Peace Pledge Union.

Tomlinson, B. R. 1979. *The Political Economy of the Raj 1914–1947*. Cambridge: Cambridge University Press.

Trevaskis, Hugh Kennedy. 1932. *The Punjab of Today*. 2 vols. Lahore: Civil and Military Gazette Press.

Tyler, Stephen A. 1986. "Post-Modern Ethnography: From Document of the Occult to Occult Document." In *Writing Culture: The Poetics and Politics of Ethnography*, edited by James Clifford and George E. Marcus, 122–40. Berkeley and Los Angeles: University of California Press.

Unnithan, T. K. N. 1969. "Panchayati Raj and the Gandhian Ideal." In *Seminar on Panchayati Raj, Planning and Democracy, Jaipur, 1964*, edited by M. V. Mathur and Iqbal Narain, 42–49. Bombay: Asia.

Upadhyaya, Deendayal. 1968. *Political Diary*. Bombay: Jaico.

————. 1974. *The Integral Approach*. New Delhi: Deendayal Research Institute.

Upadhyaya, Deendayal, Sri Guruji, and D. B. Thengdi. 1979. *The Integral Approach*. New Delhi: Deendayal Research Institute.

Vaid, Minnie. 1985. "Gujarat Is Going the Way of Assam." *Illustrated Weekly of India* 106, no. 8 (30 June): 36–37.

Vajpayee, Atal Behari. 1974. "JP Has Become the Symbol of People's Revolt, Says Atalji." *Organiser* 17 August: 3.

Vanaik, Achin. 1985. "The Rajiv Congress in Search of Stability." *New Left Review* 154: 55–82.

Van Der Veer, Peter. 1987. " 'God Must Be Liberated!' A Hindu Liberation Movement in Ayodhya." *Modern Asian Studies* 21: 283–301.

Wallerstein, Immanuel. 1974. *The Modern World-System*. New York: Academic Press.

Washbrook, David. 1976. *The Emergence of Provincial Politics: The Madras Presidency, 1870–1920*. Cambridge: Cambridge University Press.

Watson, Graham. 1987. "Make Me Reflexive — But Not Yet: Strategies for Managing Essential Reflexivity in Ethnographic Discourse." *Journal of Anthropological Research* 43: 29–41.

Weisman, Steven R. 1986. "Hindu Revivalism Makes for Moslem Anxiety." *New York Times* 2 March: sect. 4, 3.

————. 1986. "No End in Sight to Sikh-Hindu Strife." *New York Times* 3 August: sect. 1, 3.

White, Leslie. 1949. *The Science of Culture*. New York: Farrar, Straus, and Cudahy.

Whitman, Walt. 1926. *Leaves of Grass*. Edited by Emory Holloway. Garden City, N.Y.: Doubleday.

Williams, Raymond. 1961. *The Long Revolution*. New York: Columbia University Press.

————. 1971. "Literature and Sociology: In Memory of Lucien Goldmann." *New Left Review* 67: 3–18.

————. 1977. *Marxism and Literature*. London: Oxford University Press.

Wolf, Eric R. 1974. "American Anthropologists and American Society." In *Reinventing Anthropology*, edited by Dell Hymes, 251–63. New York: Vintage.

————. 1982. *Europe and the People Without History*. Berkeley and Los Angeles: University of California Press.

Wolpert, Stanley A. 1961. *Tilak and Gokhale: Revolution and Reform in the Making of Modern India*. Berkeley and Los Angeles: University of California Press.

————. 1984. *Jinnah of Pakistan*. New York and Oxford: Oxford University Press.

Wood, John R. 1975. "Extra-Parliamentary Opposition in India: An Analysis of Populist Agitations in Gujarat and Bihar." *Pacific Affairs* 48: 313–34.

————. 1984. "Congress Restored? The 'KHAM' Strategy and Congress (I) Recruitment in Gujarat." In *State Politics in Contemporary India*, edited by John R. Wood, 203–31. Boulder, Colo., and London: Westview Press.

Yagnik, Achyut, and Harshad Desai. 1985. "The Wages of Populism." *Illustrated Weekly of India* 106, no. 8 (30 June): 38–39.

Yajnik, Indulal. 1950 [1934]. *Shyamji Krishnavarma: Life and Times of an Indian Revolutionary*. Bombay: Lakshmi.

Yeager, Roger. 1982. *Tanzania: An African Experiment*. Boulder, Colo.: Westview Press.

Young, Crawford. 1982. *Ideology and Development in Africa*. New Haven and London: Yale University Press.

Index

315